Also by Linda Dowling

Red Dust Series
Splintered Heart

A Red Dust Novel

SINISTER INTENT

INGRAM. | Lightning Source

Cover design by Chris Hildenbrand
Cover images by Dreamstime.com and Getty Images.com
Typeset in Estrangelo Edessa 18/36 pt and Goudy Old Style 9/12pt
Printed and bound in Australia by IngramSpark
Prepared for publication by Dr Juliette Lachemeier @ The Erudite Pen: theeruditepen.com

A catalogue record for this book is available from the National Library of Australia

Sinister Intent: A Red Dust Novel/ Linda Dowling. — 1st ed.
ISBN 978-06487148-2-8

'We are the captain of our soul. Keep your face to the sun and you will never see the shadows.'

For the girls of Parramatta, Hay, Minda and Cootamundra – all those children whose innocence was stolen.

For our Aboriginal people who believe we are all visitors to this time, this place. We are just passing through. Our purpose here is to observe, to learn, to grow, to love . . . and then we return home.

Author's Note

This is a work of fiction set in Australia around the 1970s. The attitudes towards Indigenous people were different back then compared to the codes of conduct and morals of today, and particularly our more recent anti-discrimination laws. The Indigenous peoples of Australia had lived in Australia for at least 65,000+ years before the arrival of British settlers in 1788. They were dispossessed from their land in 1788 by Britain, which claimed eastern Australia as its own on the basis of the now discredited doctrine of *terra nullius*. Initially, Indigenous Australians were in most states deprived of the rights of full citizenship of the new nation on grounds of their race, and restrictive immigration laws were introduced, giving preference to white European immigrants into Australia.

Discriminatory laws against Indigenous people and multi-ethnic immigration were dismantled in the early decades of the postwar period. A 1967 Referendum regarding Aboriginal rights was carried with over 90% approval by the electorate. Legal reforms from the 1970s won by Aboriginal and Torres Strait Islander people have re-established Aboriginal land rights under Australian law, 200 years after the arrival of the First Fleet.

Parramatta Girls Home has also been known as Parramatta Industrial School for Girls, Girls Training School Parramatta and Girls Training Home. First built by convicts in 1841, Parramatta Training School was a brutal and cruel institution for the incarceration of young women for more than 125 years.

These were not schools as we know them but prisons where harsh and oppressive conditions were concealed under the guise of child welfare philosophies to justify their creation. In 1946, Parramatta Training School for Girls was re-established for the reception, detention, maintenance, discipline, education and training of young women. It then became known as Parramatta Girls Home, but the name belied its function: it was no home. In reality, it was a prison where young girls were stripped of their dignity and liberties and were punished frequently with physical force and threatened with imprisonment.

The Forgotten Australians are the survivors of neglectful and often cruel institutional care in Australia between 1930 and 1970. Roughly 500,000 children who were put into orphanages or so-called homes and institutions suffered at the hands of callous institutional staff. These children suffered deep and lasting feelings of abandonment and many were physically and psychologically scarred.

Although this novel does make reference to the Parramatta Girls Home, this is for fictional purposes only, and the content and characters do not depict any person, either living or dead, who was connected with the institution.

CONTENTS

PART ONE

JUSTICE

ONE

ROAD TO JUSTICE

The shearing season had long ended and a stillness had settled over Woori. Lisa O'Connor breathed the country air in deeply as her eyes roamed over the red dust of the outback landscape. Woori, her aunt and uncle's sheep station and homestead, had been her home for three years now. She never tired of looking at its majestic plains and variety of wildlife. Today, however, the serenity of the scenery before her contrasted harshly with the knot of anxiety she felt in the pit of her stomach.

With each passing day, as the month of November drew closer, her apprehension mounted. How was she ever going to survive this investigation? It would bring back so many horrible memories, not to mention the demons she fought daily to keep from entering her consciousness. Talking to strangers about her ordeals was going to be dreadful. It would be even more difficult without Billy. The months had been long and lonely since he left to go Walkabout, and her heart ached for him.

It was mid-morning when Lisa eventually came inside. Aunt Zena raised her eyebrows and looked at her as she walked into the kitchen and slumped into a chair at the table. Sensing Lisa's unrest, she said gently, 'The police arrive next month, Lisa. It's the fifth of November, remember?'

Lisa's mouth suddenly went dry. She inhaled deeply in attempt to calm her nerves and steady her voice. 'No, Aunty, I haven't forgotten. How could I? This investigation, strange people, reliving everything again is something I've not stopped thinking about. I feel anxious all day, in the pit of my stomach. There's this constant churning, even when I go to sleep. I really have to push it out of my head, and then my heart starts thumping. Sometimes I feel like I'm spinning out of control, and I am so nervous having to tell the police about the things Lenny did to me when I was younger . . . and what Superintendent Ash did at the Girls Home. What if the police look at me like I'm dirty, or like I'm damaged goods or . . . or that I led them on, like . . . like it was all my fault! My own mother calls me a liar; maybe they'll think that too!' She looked beseechingly at her aunt as she fought to control her rising panic.

Aunt Zena laid a comforting arm around Lisa's shoulders. 'Please stop thinking like this, sweetheart. Why do you project this continual shame on yourself? Don't blame yourself! There is no way a girl your age could have made these things up. Alan and I will be right here with you every step of the way, and just remember, there is a female constable coming along with the two detectives. She will basically be a support person for you. Andrew Collette said she will help to reduce the interview tension and provide reassurance to you, especially to decrease any tendency for self-blame, and you do have that tendency Lisa.'

Lisa began to fidget, hoping Zena didn't notice her kicking her feet back and forth under the table. Her aunt knew Lisa was agitated, and that lately there had been a pervading sense of powerlessness surrounding her. She didn't want to worry her aunt even more, but the thought of revealing her painful past to police officials was filling her with dread.

'What if they don't believe me?' Lisa's voice pitched higher, her breathing becoming more rapid. 'I know I've told the truth. These things did happen and . . . and they just have to believe me! Why would I make it up?' Her face twisted in anguish, and her fists were clenched on the table. She began to crack her knuckles, which were now turning white.

'Take a couple of deep breaths, Lisa, please. This is only the beginning. We have a lot to get through and the detectives will cover everything with you. They have to, in order to get these men prosecuted. They will gather and probe for information. That's what they do. It's their job. You can trust them. And besides, Detective Collette has already told us they have more information on both Lenny and the superintendent. There's no reason for them to doubt you. You must remain positive.'

Lisa's face flushed with colour. She suddenly jumped up, the chair falling backwards, fire flashing though her spirit once more. 'They have to get those bastards. If they don't, I will. I will find a way to make them pay for what they did to me, and all the other girls!' She stormed out the house, the door banging loudly.

Lisa ran to the ute. A billow of red dust followed her as she started it up and raced wildly down the road, heading to the far paddocks.

The lanky figure in the distance was unmistakable. Her Uncle Alan was bent over, fencing. He looked up as Lisa approached in the ute. She dried her eyes so he didn't notice she'd been crying.

When Lisa pulled up, he took a puff on his cigarette and drawled, 'In a bit of a hurry kid?' She smiled. He always had a calming effect on her. 'Too early for tears as well. What's up?'

Lisa attempted to conceal her uneasiness. 'I'm just getting really anxious about the police coming, Alan, and telling them all that stuff, the personal stuff that went on. I don't want them to think I'm lying or I've made this up.'

'Only you can tell the police what happened, Lisa . . . you know that. I'd gladly swap places with you but I can't. No-one can. You lived this horror, now it's up to you. Finish the job. Make sure those mongrels get what they deserve.'

Lisa relented. 'Yes I know, but . . . but I feel so much hatred and so many other feelings. I just want to yell and scream or punch something. Why did it happen to me?' Her chin rested on her arms as she watched Alan repair the fences out the window of the ute.

Alan straightened up and hesitated before restarting the conversation. 'Lisa, why does anything happen to anyone? It just does. Do you ever tell yourself you're safe, kid?'

Lisa shrugged. 'Huh? Not really. Why?' She swallowed hard and wondered what his next comment would be. Alan always seemed to have a logical answer for most things.

'Because you are, Lisa . . . here with me and Zena, safe as a house, as they say, and protected. Nothing will harm you here. So, you have to keep telling yourself that while you tell the coppers what went on. Hard, yep, for sure; it certainly doesn't conjure up a warm, fuzzy feeling. And maybe when you provide all the information, you'll be off your rocker slightly but there will also be a huge sense of relief. Anyway, just remember how those dickheads are feeling right now. They would be shit scared, terrified. Quaking in their boots.' He gave Lisa a wry smile. 'They're the ones who are probably thinking of running away. Probably on their bikes now and peddling bloody hard. Like a rabbit caught in the spotlight.'

Lisa mulled this over. 'I never thought of it like that.'

'Trust me, the coppers would have told those bastards what they're investigating. They know they've done it. Guilty as. So you're in the driver's seat. Have courage, Lisa. You'll need to have more courage than you ever had before. But you've got that in spades. I doubt your courage will desert you now.' Alan smiled at her encouragingly.

Lisa felt her spirits lift once more. 'Thanks, Alan. You have a way of putting things that sort of makes me see sense.' Alan seemed to have answers for everything. He always made her feel good and put things into perspective. Lisa tilted her head to the side and pensively looked across the vast paddocks. *If only I didn't have to face what was coming. If only there was another way for this to be handled.*

'Best wipe your face some more and we'll head home for a cuppa. I'm done here,' said Alan, hopping onto the motorbike.

'I can't wait for the next shearing season, Alan,' Lisa said, her voice sounding melancholy.

'Missing Billy? . . . Oh, yes, and of course the rest of the crew?' asked Alan, with a wink.

'Yes! I didn't realise how much I would. The place seems so quiet and empty without everyone.' *Especially Billy.* Her heart leaped at the thought of him.

'They'll be back, kid, next season. Never know for sure who will turn up, but you have to concentrate on what's coming. The coppers, the charges unfolding, court, all that. Come on, let's head back. See you at home, chin up now.'

Lisa, feeling calmer, drove back to the house far slower than when she left.

Zena quickly came to the back door. Alan took off his hat and kissed her cheek while Lisa parked the ute in the shade. She knew her aunt was worried about how she was going to cope with the official investigation, and that she didn't want her healing to go backwards.

Lisa came up the back stairs. She was sheepish as she sat down. 'Sorry, Aunty. I'm just so scared and angry at the same time. I want to get through this but I'm so worried that I won't be believed. That I'll go through all their invasive questions and for what?'

Zena gave her a hug. 'Don't be sorry, darling girl. Anger is a good thing when it's channelled the right way. And being scared is okay too. But deep down inside you must know that they have a lot of evidence to go on. I agree with what Alan just said while you were parking the ute. Your anger and resilience will help give you the courage to work with the detectives and put these men away for good. Even though it might feel paralysing to relive all that trauma, your anger will see you through. And these men know they're guilty, so they must be really panicked right about now, just like Alan said.'

Lisa looked at Alan. 'Rabbits in a spotlight,' she murmured as a faint smile crept across her face.

'That's it, kid. Keep that thought.' His eyes were kind as she looked at him.

'Am I missing out on something here?' Zena asked.

'Nope. I let Lisa know what happens when you throw a spotlight onto an animal in the dark. They sit there stunned because they're so frightened or surprised that they cannot move. Our friends Lenny and Superintendent Ash will be the same when the boys in blue come knocking. How I'd like to be a fly on the wall.'

Zena laughed, breaking the tension they'd all been feeling. 'Husband of mine, you do have a way with words. But changing the subject, when are you riding out to see Binna again, Lisa?' Zena probed.

'Maybe tomorrow. Why, Aunty? I did say I'd come back as soon as I could. Binna said she wants to do a special ceremony.'

'Special? That sounds good. How wonderful of Binna. You know the effect she has on you, and you have made so much progress. Don't let anger or fear tear you down now. Stay focused. I think what we have set in place, in terms of Dr Tyler and Binna, will hold you in good stead for what's coming. The police will be here in just over three weeks' time and will stay for a few days or for however long it takes. They're in no hurry. The detective I spoke to said it often takes a few days to go through everything thoroughly as they don't want to put too much pressure on you. And I do want them to have all the facts before they leave here. You would understand that.'

Lisa nodded but felt a gnawing anxiety at the thought of the police staying in their home. Under the same roof and facing them every day.

'Are you happy to review all of your statements before the police arrive? I know it's horrible, but the more we talk about it, the more we have it out in the open, and you'll be able to recall things with greater clarity.'

'Okay,' said Lisa hesitatingly. To go over her statements and revisit the horrible abuse made her stomach churn again.

Zena tried to allay her fears. 'I have very positive feelings about Dr Tyler. Don't forget your first appointment is this Thursday in Walgett. A few sessions with her before the police arrive will provide you with more mental armour.'

Lisa hoped so, although she knew her whole life was about to be audited by three strangers.

◊

Over dinner that night, Lisa was very quiet. Zena watched her niece play with her food. Her spark had been missing since Billy left. She hoped Lisa would pull out of it with the tasks at hand and console herself with the fact that he was coming back. *But what if he doesn't?* Zena wondered. She pushed that thought to the back of her mind. Her niece had enough to deal with. Zena would remain positive that Billy would return. She suddenly had an idea that might cheer Lisa up.

'Lisa, you should come to the RSL this Saturday with us. Be good to get out of the house.'

'Sure, if you want,' responded Lisa, giving her aunt a droll look.

'Of course we want. If possible, it might take your mind off things momentarily. The worst is yet to come but at the end of it, the best will come.'

Lisa helped wash up with Zena and stacked the last few dishes.

'Let's hit the sack, Zena,' Alan said as he placed an arm around his wife's shoulders. 'It's trying times but nothing we can't get through. Get some sleep, kid,' he said as they watched Lisa head to her room.

◊

The softness of the morning light filtered through the windows. Lisa stirred. She heard the laughing call of the kookaburras while the magpies chortled. Her eyes slowly fluttered open to meet the streaks of colour that radiated into her bedroom, the bright plumes of orange and red, the darkness lifting into the sky. She never closed the curtains at night, always eager to meet the beginning of a new day. Billy would say every day is a new beginning, with new dreams. How she missed him. She rolled on her side and looked at his necklace. *What if he doesn't come back?* The loneliness stabbed at her heart like a dagger, cold and sharp.

She wandered into the kitchen where Zena was busy making chutneys. The sweet aroma filled the air.

'Morning, darling girl. It's a beautiful day, getting warmer now though as summer approaches.'

Lisa kissed her aunt as she threw some bread into the toaster.

'Good day for a ride, Aunty. I'll head out and see Binna and Ningali after my chores.' Lisa brightened at the mention of a visit to the ladies.

'Great, hun. Take these fresh vegetables I picked from the garden this morning and a jar of this sweet chutney and say hello for me. I must try and get out there soon to see them as well.'

Lisa buttered her toast. Seeing Binna and Ningali always gave her something to look forward to.

As if reading her mind, her aunt ventured, 'Billy will be back, Lisa. You never hear from them until the season starts. They do their own thing, go Walkabout and go further inland to their country. He's still going through his rite of passage and other rituals. As Alan and I have told you, they have their own laws. You must keep busy and time will soon pass. The next few weeks will be challenging, so we need to focus on this now. You are the voice for all those girls in the Home, past and present.'

Lisa knew she was right. As she thought of those girls still imprisoned in Parramatta Girls Home, her spirit steeled itself to help them.

'Yes, Aunty, you are so right . . . you and Alan always are. I want to help all those other girls. There are so many who have been in those places, all suffering some sort of punishment and humiliation. Sometimes that thought alone is unbearable.' The anger in her voice was evident.

'Keep thinking that way, Lisa,' said Zena as she bundled the vegetables and sweet chutney into a calico bag. 'For the ladies. They both have a sweet tooth. By the way, Alan is keen, as am I, to get our breeding program under way. He may try to put Noir and Khartoum together this week.'

Lisa enthused, 'That will be great. What beautiful foals those two will have together.'

'Yes, so you may like to give Alan a hand and watch what he's doing. He's looking at buying some more mares at the sales, so you'll be busy getting them settled in if he finds something he likes. Always something to do around here.'

'Sorry, Aunty. I guess I have been moping, I miss Billy. He was just so different . . . different to anyone I've ever met.'

Zena's expression softened. 'He is a lovely boy, Lisa, and Alan thinks he's been one of his best workers, but you mustn't let it get you down. He'll be back. Try and brighten up; we have a lot do to before the next season.'

Lisa washed up her plate and then hugged her aunt. Zena was always trying to cheer her up. She was so grateful for both of them in her life. God knows where she'd be now if it weren't for them. She resolved to not be such a misery guts. 'I'm off to do my chores then and I'll be better in my outlook after that.' Lisa looked at the calico bag on the table. 'I'll grab this when I saddle up.'

'Good girl. I'll see you later. Have faith and stay strong.'

As Lisa cantered along the dusty road towards her friends' humpy, she saw Binna's white hair in the distance, where she stood proudly, looking up the road. Her frail arm lifted, and she gave Lisa a small wave.

'Hey, Binna,' Lisa greeted as she pulled Neddy up near their shelter, tethering him to the closest tree. She grabbed the calico bag and came to Binna, who now sat cross legged, waving at the flies with a eucalypt branch. Ningali was nowhere to be seen.

Giving the old lady a hug, Lisa said, 'I've brought some vegetables from our garden as well as a sweet chutney Zena made.' Binna flashed her toothless grin as Lisa sat down next to her.

'How have you been, my friend?' Lisa asked gently.

'Bin good. Ningali look after me well, true and proper. How you bin now season finished up.'

'I'm okay, but it's different. So very different, Binna. I did love all the people around, and the atmosphere. It was fun. It's just us three now, and even though I love my aunt and Alan, I still miss everyone else.' Lisa picked up some red dirt and let it fall through her fingers. She knew Binna sensed that her thoughts were drifting.

'You bin missing dat boy . . . Billy. He get under your skin. Everyone like dat boy. He can touch your soul. Burnu, he dun good with him. I hear da sadness in your voice.'

'Yes, you're right as always. I miss him, Binna. I haven't heard from him. Has anyone? Do you know anyone who may have heard where he is, what he's up to?'

Binna drew lines in the dirt, circles and hills and what appeared to be a snake.

'Billy crosses from boy to man now, through da bush and da deserts. In da ranges, under da sun, da moon and da stars. He come back, but then proper good man. No boy left.'

'When? When will he be back, Binna?' Lisa asked earnestly.

'Not know for sure, but he be back when ready.'

Lisa's sadness filled the air. 'Big sorrow for you now, little one, but it get better.'

Lisa sighed as she looked at the drawings in the dirt. 'Tell me a story, Binna. I want to hear one of your special ones. They always make me feel good inside.' The old lady tapped her stick on the ground.

'I tell you about da turtle. You bin swimming in da creeks and rivers with dem turtles.' Lisa nodded, although she had never seen one.

'One day, Wayamba, da turtle-man. . . he out gathering food. He see another man's wife, Oola, and her three children digging yams. Wayamba decide he would like a wife and family so he took dem home. When Wayamba's tribe saw what he had done, dey were very angry and dey go see dis turtle-man. Dey agree Wayamba must be punished, so he was showered with da spears. Wayamba chose big shields and slung one on his back and da other one on his front. Dem spears come whizzing through da air, Wayamba drew his arms inside da shields and duck his head down between them. Da spears of his tribe, dey come down on him, and there was nowhere to run. So he dived into da creek and swim down deeper and deeper. Dat was the last time da tribe saw Wayamba; he never surfaced again. Some-time later in dat water-hole where he had dived down, da tribe saw a strange creature that had a plate fixed to its back. When dey tried to catch da creature, it drew in its head and limbs, and dey don't capture, so dey said it must be Wayamba. Dis da beginning of Wayamba, or as we now say da turtles, and dey live in da creeks and water holes.'

Binna drew a picture of a large turtle. 'Good eating, dem turtles,' she cackled.

'Great Dreamtime story, Binna, but I'm not sure I'm up to eating turtles yet. I've tried goanna but I may have to pass on the turtles! I'd feel sorry for them.' Binna just cackled again. 'Will Ningali be long?' Lisa asked her.

'Ningali down at da river. She bring back maugro.'

'What's maugro?'

'Fish.' Binna made hand movements like a fish swimming. 'Maugro taste proper good.'

'We have da special ceremony. Secret women's business. Just you and me, little one. Healing. We use da sky charms,' said Binna as she pulled out some glassy stones.

'What are sky charms?'

'Dey glass stones, dem fall from da sky. Dey connect to da sky spirits. Lookem like emu eyes. Sky charms very powerful medicine. Good for da storms in your life. Get you on da right track. Now we begin.'

Directly behind Binna was a large shell filled with herbs, na-tive tobacco and some bush cherry bark. She began to rub two sticks, her frail hands working vigorously, and a small flame ignited. She fanned the flame and the smoking began. She be-gan chanting and held Lisa's hands.

Lisa closed her eyes and breathed the sweet smell of the fire. It was like her body was floating and no longer of the earth. She felt her shoulders relax and her mind clear, while an energy moved through her body. Binna finally stopped chanting, and

Lisa opened her eyes. She breathed in the old lady's strength and wisdom. Binna moved her hand towards Lisa and placed two stones in her right hand. She began chanting again and then stopped. 'Throw da stones now. You calm your mind. Sickness not return.'

Lisa picked up the stones and threw them into the bush. Binna smiled and nodded. She looked very pleased.

'You plenty strong now. No more pain. Dem bad spirits, dey leave you now. You lay down, let your mind flow . . . open da senses. All da Spirits of the Land, dey here watching,' said Binna as she ran her wizened hand over the red dust.

Lisa curled up in a ball and lay down under the shade of the humpy. Binna sat next to her and picked up two clap sticks, moving them together and singing softly as she clicked them.

Lisa fell into a deep sleep, happy to lie on the red dirt floor, the smoke wafting around her, the sounds of the bush and Binna next to her. She murmured softly. Billy was there. His spirit had come to her. She felt him. Oh how she yearned to see him in the flesh.

Just then, Ningali entered the humpy, carrying fish. 'Da baby she bin sleeping?' Binna nodded.

Lisa opened her eyes and sat up at the sound of Ningali's voice. She stretched slowly and felt the energy and peace in her body and mind. 'Hello, Ningali,' Lisa smiled. 'What have you got there?'

Ningali held up three maugro and looked very pleased with herself. 'Me catchem maugro. Plenty big feast tonight, missy. Me makem da cook up,' she chuckled as she put the fish down.

Lisa reached over and took Binna's hands. 'Thank you, Binna. I feel at peace, and my mind is clear. You chase the bad spirits from me. I'm happy. But now I have to get going or they'll have a search party out for me,' she teased as she dusted off her jeans.

After hugging both ladies, Lisa set off, waving goodbye as she headed back to the homestead. 'Come on Neddy, I've been away for over half the day.' As Lisa rode, she thought of Billy and wished he was by her side. *Stay safe, Billy, wherever you are. I know you were with me today.* That thought filled her with some comfort as she made her way back to the Woori homestead.

After hosing down Neddy and giving him a hay bag, Lisa went inside.

'Well there you are! I was getting worried,' said Zena as she put down the newspaper.

'I fell asleep after Binna's ceremony. It was just her and me, Aunty, and she used these sky charms. It was amazing.'

'What are sky charms?' asked Zena, somewhat curious.

'Emu eyes,' Lisa giggled. 'No, they look like emu eyes. Binna said they are glass stones that have fallen from the sky. I can't describe how I feel inside, in my mind,' she exclaimed as she pointed to her head. 'How do they do this to you? How can they have this power?'

'I don't know, Lisa, but I'm so very grateful and wish I had just some of that power. Binna is well respected as a healer, you know that. You're glowing,' observed Zena. 'Well, go wash up. We're not long off dinner and an early night is needed as we're heading into Walgett tomorrow to see Dr Tyler.'

Instead of fear or apprehension crossing her face, Lisa took a deep breath. 'Yep, Aunty. I'm ready. Can you sit with me before we go to bed so we can go over our notes.'

Zena looked surprised. 'Yes, of course. I didn't want to push it, but that's a great idea before we see Dr Tyler.'

After dinner, they headed to the sitting room where the notes were filed, categorised in two piles.

'Where do you want to start, Lisa?' Zena asked encouragingly.

'Here,' she decided, pointing to home - Fairfield. 'Where it all began,' she said defiantly, the heat surging into her cheeks. Over the next two hours, Lisa would stop and then take a few breaths before reading again. Waves of nausea stopped her talking on many occasions but she quickly recovered with steely determination and turned the pages. Once she'd read through everything she'd written on both Fairfield and the Parramatta Girls Home, she turned to her aunt, her eyes shining with tears.

'I'm confident I've not left anything out. I feel prepared but still am shaking in my boots. I have so much to tell the police. I just think of the girls in all those Girls Homes, not just Parramatta. I heard the other girls talk about Hay and Minda and what they referred to as the 'Cooty' girls. Short for Cootamundra,' said Lisa.

'There's no doubt in my mind, Lisa, that the same conditions would apply there, just the same harsh discipline and punitive treatment,' sighed Zena. 'I'm just so glad they allowed the police to come to Woori. I think it was your notes that we sent them that got us over the line. I stressed you were deeply affected by the events and that having to go down to Sydney when we were meant to be attending regular psychiatric counselling would be very disruptive for your recovery. Andrew agreed and admitted there were no set protocols. It's entirely dependent on the individual, and each person is assessed on a case-by-case basis. The purpose of their interviews with you is to replicate our notes into formal typewritten statements, which will be used in evidence.

Lisa felt her anger bubble to the surface. 'And there were the girls that were raped and fell pregnant, and their babies were taken from them. I get so sad thinking about what happened to all of the girls put into these places, and of course, my friend, Julie. What happened to her body? What did they tell her mother? All those things are in my head, but worst of all, I heard girls saying the police knew all about it and everything was covered up.'

'Maybe, but who knows for sure. I would say though, a lot has been covered up over the years but that is about to all spill out. It's a matter not just for the police but also the appropriate authorities. The main thing is that you have started the process to bring justice for these girls. You are now their voice and this voice must be heard.'

Lisa yawned, the weariness now creeping into her body. 'I'm sleepy now, Aunty, but I hear what you say. Although I've never been a champion of any cause.'

'Well, you are now,' murmured Zena.

Lisa kissed her aunt goodnight. She knew she was safe, even though her heart was pounding at the thought of telling the psychiatrist tomorrow what had happened to her.

Before sleep came, Lisa picked up the quartz stones Burnu had given her when he left and kissed them, squeezing them tightly. *I hope Dr Tyler will be able to help me*, she thought as she fell into a fitful sleep.

TWO

THE PATH TO HEALING

Sleep was no friend. Lisa woke early, quickly showered and put on the navy blue shift dress she'd laid out the previous night. Sometimes Mrs Dunphy got some good clothes in at the haberdashery store in Walgett. Patent black shoes with a small heel and she was ready. The quartz stones sat neatly in her pocket.

'Good morning,' said Alan as she walked into the kitchen. 'You look lovely. All set to go?' Lisa wondered if he could sense the fear in her heart, even though she did feel much calmer after her healing with Binna yesterday.

'Err . . . yes, thank you, Alan, but I'm a bit nervous. My stomach has flutters, but then again, I know I'm prepared. Where's Aunty?'

'Getting ready, kid. She's just as nervous as you. Tossed around like a fish on a boat last night. Here, help yourself to some bacon and eggs,' Alan offered as he slid the plate across.

'I'm not that hungry, Alan. Too jittery and . . . well, you know, it's the feeling of the unknown and another stranger.'

'Yep, I can understand that, but your aunt's orders. Try to have something.'

When Zena came into the kitchen, she wore a grey suit with a white shirt. Zena cast her eye over Lisa. 'Good choice, dear. Have your breakfast and we'll get on our way. Don't forget your sandshoes for the gates and one of Alan's old shirts to throw over the dress. Helps stop the dirt getting all over your clothes.'

Alan placed a cup of tea in front of his wife with some buttered toast. He knew, instinctively, she felt the same as Lisa.

'Alright, we're done here! Time to hit the frog and toad. Don't want you to be late,' he exclaimed. As they were about to leave, Alan held Lisa's hands. 'Remember what I told you, kid. Be strong now. This lady today will be able to help you.' He kissed them both on the cheek. 'See you when you get home.'

◊

As they pulled into Walgett, Lisa felt her first rush of nerves and gritted her teeth. She remembered what Alan had said about the Freedom Riders, the crazy Sydney University students led by Charles Perkins who made a significant protest outside the Walgett RSL Club as they would not let indigenous ex-serviceman into the club. *How brave they were to do that. I must be as brave.*

The streets were wide, and it was always fascinating to people watch. There were the cow cockies in their Akubras having a yarn in the street, stock trucks, people coming and going, just the bustle of a small country town. But her favourite was the Walgett War Memorial, erected in 1922. So many names, so many lost young men. Alan always spoke so proudly of the men who lost their lives serving their country. The Aboriginal meaning for Walgett was where the two rivers met, and every time she plunged into the river after riding, she thought of this. Lisa had also wanted to do the Norman Walford walk one day, after Alan had told her his story. The track was nearly two miles long but it celebrated Norman's life as a tracker with the NSW police for many years. It was this history, the birdlife and the Namoi River that held her fascination.

'Here we are,' said Zena as the old blue Zephyr drove slowly past the shingle with the name Dr Helen Tyler. 'I'll park up the road and we'll walk back. Are you okay, Lisa?'

'I can feel my heart racing, Aunty.' Lisa nervously felt for the quartz in her pocket, 'But I'm okay.'

'That makes two of us,' Zena said softly. 'It's good to be apprehensive but I'm sure you'll really appreciate what this lady has to offer. I'm told by Michael Raby that she's an expert in her field and has handled a lot of cases similar to yours over the years. You've nothing to lose, Lisa, and only good things to learn. I think if Michael, being the superintendent of police here in Walgett, offers her name as an expert then we are well on the right track.'

'What will I learn?' asked Lisa as they reached the front door of Dr Tyler's office.

'Coping strategies for one thing, relaxation techniques, as well as therapy,' said Zena as she pushed the door open.

'Afternoon,' Zena said to the receptionist, a young red-haired woman in her early twenties with a very friendly face. Lisa glanced around. They were the only ones in the office.

'I'm Mrs Smith and this is my niece who has the appointment, Lisa O'Connor.'

'Just take a seat, Mrs Smith. Dr Tyler won't be long,' the young woman said warmly.

Zena held Lisa's hand. She was fidgeting and trembling slightly. Zena squeezed her hand reassuringly.

A door opened and a woman in her early fifties entered the waiting room. Lisa knew instantly that coming to see her was a good move. Dr Tyler wore her blonde hair in a loose chignon at the nape of her neck. A simple white linen blouse, tapered tweed skirt and flat shoes were finished off with a string of pearls. When she smiled, her blue eyes crinkled, and she exuded kindness. She was warm and engaged Lisa with her eyes.

Dr Tyler walked over to where they sat. 'I'm Dr Tyler, ladies,' she greeted with an outstretched hand. Her voice was soft but confident. Lisa wondered how many horrible stories this woman had heard over the years. The doctor shook Zena's hand first. 'Mrs Smith,' she said warmly, and then turned to Lisa. 'And you must be Miss O'Connor. Welcome. This must be a very difficult thing for you to do, to come here today.' Lisa nodded and smiled. She liked this woman.

'May I call you both by your first names?'

Lisa looked over at Zena and both could feel their tension visibly melting away.

'Yes, Dr Tyler, this is fine with both of us,' she agreed.

'Umm . . . yes, it's okay, I would like that,' chimed Lisa.

'Good! Then you can call me Helen. Please come this way.' They followed Dr Tyler into her office. It was a large, airy room with soft bluish-grey walls. Fresh flowers were on her desk, and the walls were covered with beautiful art work, a mixture of Aboriginal and Australian landscapes. A rich brown leather couch was opposite her desk, but two large floral chairs were next to a bay window that overlooked a small cottage garden. There was a peaceful feeling to the room.

'Thank you for reaching out, Lisa. Counselling for sexual abuse is about healing and teaching. There are three phases to my therapy. The early phase will focus on building trust and preparing you for the healing process. I will encourage you to tell me what has happened to you, and this may prove to be very difficult.' Lisa's throat felt tight and dry upon hearing this, but she nodded slowly, her hand still clutching Zena's.

'Sometimes, the memories are all jumbled, and the pain of these memories can be overwhelming, and sometimes, you just don't know where to start.'

Dr Tyler spoke calmly so Lisa started to relax. 'Do you feel this way, Lisa . . . with the pain and the thought of being over-whelmed?'

'Yes, I do, I don't know where to start, and I feel such hatred and anger sometimes.'

'Understandably, Lisa. This is a natural reaction, but we will deal with this emotion as we progress. Peace and contentment needs to come from within when we are facing our inner struggles. The middle phase is where the brunt of my work is done. We reprocess the trauma. In general, in these situations, I've found there is anger towards the abusers, non-protective parents, siblings and even caretakers. During your sessions with me, this is where you will release some of the feelings associated with the trauma, and the impact. From there, you can move forward.'

Lisa felt hot tears stinging her cheeks, hearing Dr Tyler's words. It was the mere phrase 'non-protective parents' that made her bottom lip tremble. Dr Tyler handed Lisa the box of tissues. 'This is where I will teach you coping strategies while educating you in terms of cognitive restructuring.'

Dr Tyler rose from her chair. 'I'll just stop for now, as that is a lot to take in.' She pressed her intercom, and the young receptionist woman appeared shortly after with a tray of water and glasses. 'Thank you, Sandra.'

Dr Tyler poured three glasses and handed one to Zena and Lisa. 'How does this sound to you so far, Lisa?'

Lisa nodded, her voice cracking with emotion. 'I understand, Dr Tyler. I'm looking forward to trusting you and working with you,' she admitted, pressing the glass of water to her lips, which felt as dry and parched as a desert.

'Zena, your thoughts or questions?'

'I am so grateful to you, Dr Tyler, oh sorry . . . Helen. This is harrowing for Lisa, particularly as the detectives from Sydney will be here in just over three weeks' time. Lisa will have to revisit everything we have documented here.' Zena handed a brown envelope to Dr Tyler.

'These are the notes we both made over the past few weeks. It may help you with Lisa's sessions. I'll give a copy of these to the detectives when they come to our property, although I did send the documents to them in Sydney for review.'

'Thank you, Zena. This will be of significant value.' Her eyes moved to Lisa.

'This will be horrific for you, Lisa, but we will work together to get through this. You were not responsible for what happened to you. When we've finished, you will feel more in control and hopefully, more able to deal with the impact the abuse has had on your life. In view of the fact the police will be arriving shortly, I want to see you twice weekly. Is that a possibility, Zena?'

'Yes, absolutely.' Zena was pleased. 'Do you know how long the treatment will last. I guess that's asking how long is a piece of string?'

Dr Tyler smiled. 'Yes, it is. Some people respond quicker than others. But in the termination phase, I'll teach Lisa empowerment and how to make her own choices and decisions. It is important at this time that she is supported.'

'My husband Alan and I are always here for Lisa.' Zena took Lisa's hand again.

Dr Tyler acknowledged this with a look of approval. 'Very good. I can see she is loved, which is so crucial. I now need you to leave Lisa with me for an hour.'

Zena nodded. 'Okay. I have a few things to do. I'll see you in an hour.'

'Perfect,' said Dr Tyler. 'We'll book a few further appointments for Lisa before you leave today. Thank you for providing me with this documented information. I'll ask Sandra to photocopy the documents as she said you needed these back for the police.'

As Zena rose to walk to the door, Lisa felt frightened. Dr Tyler seemed to sense her fear. 'It's okay, Lisa, to feel fear, but I am only here to help you and teach you techniques that you will utilise all throughout your life.'

Zena's eyes met Lisa's. 'You'll be fine, darling girl,' she whispered, closing the door behind her.

As Zena left the office and stepped out into the street, she took a deep breath and released it slowly. *A perfect start.*

When Zena came back to the office, Dr Tyler had finished her session. It was just after 2.15 p.m. Lisa's eyes were red and puffy, signalling that she had spent the last hour crying her heart out. But she also exuded a sense of peace, like a warm blanket had been pulled around her. Although Lisa looked drained, her posture appeared relaxed, as if she had released her anxiety, her distress.

Lisa brought a tissue up to her swollen eyes. Her chest was sore from sobbing but she met Zena's gaze with a welcoming smile. Her aunt was so correct in providing the documented details to Dr Tyler, who had consistently reviewed and referred to them during the interview process.

'How did you go?' asked Zena, her eyes addressing both of them.

Dr Tyler spoke. 'Lisa has amazing courage. We have a long way to go but her resilience and inner strength has been her saviour.' Dr Tyler's eyes were warm and encouraging.

'Lisa mentioned that she has spoken to an Aboriginal healer, and how she feels after her visits to this woman.'

'Yes, I am very fortunate to have these two wonderful Aboriginal women who came for a shearing season about five years ago and never left. Mother and daughter. Binna is the elder lady, a powerful healer, and she's a real character. I give them things I make, chutneys or fresh meat and vegetables, anything

I can provide, really, just to give them a hand. They have become great friends over the years. If only the white people would listen to our indigenous souls. They are the true wanderers of the earth and understand everything about flora, fauna, medicines and natural healing. They are the original custodians of the earth, and the two ladies have done wonders with Lisa.'

'Yes, I agree, Zena. We could learn a great deal from them. A wonderful 60,000-year-old culture,' acknowledged Dr Tyler.

'I'd like to see Lisa on Fridays and Saturdays, back to back sessions for the next three weeks. I know you travel a great distance to see me, but Lisa mentioned you frequently come into Walgett, so I thought this would be the best solution before the police arrive. You'll get in a further seven sessions, eight including this one. I don't usually work in Walgett on a Friday or Saturday, but due to the extent of the abuse, and the pending investigation, I will make an exception. I think Lisa needs it, and she agrees. We did go over some of the notes, and it has been reading, just horrendous.'

Dr Tyler turned to Lisa and studied her carefully. She was a beautiful young teenager growing into womanhood, but despite the love and care she was receiving, her fragility was evident. She did appear stronger mentally than some of the other girls she had seen over the years, but she knew that the trauma would never leave her, and like the others, she would have to try and learn to live with what happened to her. To some, this was an impossible task, and she knew the potential for regression.

'If you need me, just call, Lisa, and don't forget your aunt is always there for you. It's important to keep talking as we process the trauma.'

Sobs trapped in Lisa's throat. 'Thank you, Helen. It was hard at first but once I opened up, I guess I was . . . I was like a river.' Her thoughts flashed to Billy. *Be like a river, be open and flow.*

Dr Tyler smiled warmly. 'I will see you next Friday.'

◊

The drive home was quiet. Lisa felt an inner contentment yet conflict at the same time.

Zena spoke. 'You are very quiet, my dear.'

'Yes, I know. She was wonderful, Aunty. My anger and hatred bubbled to the surface on many occasions but talking to her was like . . . like this big release. There were times I was even shouting. It was exhausting talking about the really horrible sexual things they did to me. I got really angry . . . I mean, really angry, and I did swear and punch the desk, but she just listened.'

'I'm not a counsellor, Lisa, but I think what you just expressed is probably how most people would feel. I knew Dr Tyler would be empathetic and the ultimate professional. We have done the right thing.'

Lisa nodded. She looked forward to the next session. It was different discussing what she had been through with another female, a stranger, who allowed her to express her emotions without reprehension.

As they reached the house, Zena was happy to be home. She herself felt totally drained.

The sound of Alan's saxophone pierced the air. 'He must be getting in some practice,' said Zena as they came up the back stairs.

Alan put the saxophone down when he saw them. 'How did it go?' he asked as they came into the sitting room.

Lisa spoke. 'It was . . . She was amazing, and I really appreciated talking to her. It was hard, Alan, and I felt so ashamed, sort of dirty, and I wondered what her receptionist Sandra thought when I began shouting.'

'I'm sure you'd not be the first young girl to yell her head off, and you certainly won't be the last. It's all part of the process,' he said as he looked at his wife's tired face.

'But I got through it and it was like talking to Aunty . . . or a white Binna.'

'That is great news,' enthused Alan. 'So obviously you are happy to go see her again.'

'Yes. I will . . . I want to, I really want to.' Lisa put her head down. 'Umm, I'll just go change. I'm tired, but it's a different tired.'

Alan turned to Zena, who had kicked off her shoes and plonked herself onto a chair. 'And you, my darling wife, you look exhausted.'

Zena smiled as his lips softly met hers. 'Dr Tyler was very good with her. I must thank Michael Raby for giving me a good lead. I'm not sure Lisa will be that hungry after today but your roast sure smells good.'

Alan nodded. 'I put it in about an hour ago, just following your instructions.'

'Bless you. I'll get out of these clothes and be with you shortly. I'm beat.'

Over dinner they decided not to play at the Walgett RSL. Rather, for the next three weeks, they would concentrate on getting Lisa to the consultations and supporting her through the healing process. It would be a united effort to help her grow stronger over the ensuing three weeks.

◊

Each visit with Dr Tyler was distressing, and Lisa broke down many times. It was nothing Dr Tyler hadn't seen before. She wondered how the girl had survived. She had seen so many slip off the rails, commit suicide, become prostitutes and suffer depression for years. Most never got the professional help they should have received.

As they arrived for their last session, Lisa seemed much more positive. Dr Tyler noticed a new confidence developing and hoped Lisa would stay this way. She knew Lisa would need all the mental strength she could muster with the police interviews one week away. The events that lay ahead would produce the worst emotions.

As she opened the door to her office, Dr Tyler greeted them. 'Hi ladies, how was your trip in?'

'Dusty,' laughed Zena, 'but that's the outback for you.'

'Indeed, Zena,' Helen replied.

◊

'Well then, Lisa, how are you feeling?' Dr Tyler asked warmly as they both sat down. 'The police arrive next Friday, if my memory serves me correctly?'

Lisa's posture suddenly shifted. 'Yes, that's correct.' Her eyes were downcast and her lips pressed together. She did not lift her glance. The young girl sitting on her own suddenly felt lonely and frightened. It was the mention of the police.

'Always remember, Lisa, the police are just doing their job. You have done the right thing and there is no shame. These people need to be held fully accountable for the atrocities and the harm they have caused you and the other girls. After you talk to the police, you may find you relive the events. This is not uncommon. You may have flashbacks, or nightmares, and you may question your self-worth. Try and work through these feelings with what I have taught you. When you are feeling flooded by obtrusive thoughts, breathe and close your eyes, repeating that you are safe. This will help you to negate them,' said Dr Tyler.

'I feel very nervous . . . sort of like I'm about to panic, or explode, but then I remember what you said, breathe and focus. I have had a few nightmares but when I wake, I concentrate on breathing and tell myself I'm in a different place and that I choose strength. I seem to regain my sense of safety. I can see my panic symptoms aren't dangerous and writing my thoughts in a journal, as you suggested, has really helped me.'

'Wonderful.' Dr Tyler let the girl continue without interrupting her flow of speech.

'I really enjoy these breathing techniques and the muscle relaxation. They're not dissimilar to how my friends, the Aboriginal ladies, make me feel.'

Dr Tyler nodded. 'Yes, you seem to have responded very well to the Aboriginal ladies and have a great bond with them. They are very powerful, and their methodology is to cleanse the spirit.'

'Yes,' agreed Lisa. 'They have these healing ceremonies and I always feel my spirit being lifted and cleansed. They're my friends now, who I visit often, as they live not far from the homestead.'

'Yes, I must agree,' said Dr Tyler. 'The Aboriginal elders have a powerful mystique about them. I am always in awe of their spiritual ceremonies. To them, healing is seen as more than just a quick fix. It is a journey and a process that is just as spiritually based as it is physically based. I'm very pleased to hear that, Lisa.'

'Let's begin our last session then,' said Dr Tyler.

After the hour, Dr Tyler gave Lisa a card. 'This is my private number if you or your aunt want to talk to me. Do not hesitate to call me if you want to reach out.'

Lisa looked down at the little white card. 'Thank you, Helen,' she murmured as she tucked it into her pocket. Helen opened her door and walked with Lisa to reception where her aunt sat waiting.

'It went well today, Zena. Lisa and I are making progress, and she is releasing the feelings she has associated with the trauma more easily. We also spoke about the cleansing ceremonies her Aboriginal friends have performed. It is something that has always interested me.'

Zena smiled. 'Yes, as I said, I'm very lucky to have these wonderful women living on our property. Binna, the elder lady, is renowned for her healing powers. They have helped a great deal.'

'I must mention though, something that keeps popping up in our sessions,' said Dr Tyler.

'Oh, what's that, Helen?' asked Zena, concerned.

'Lisa is missing her brother, Mark. She has mentioned him a few times in our sessions. They are obviously close. Are you able to call him or speak to the mother, so they can touch base?'

'Not as easy as you think, Helen. It's like dealing with a rattlesnake, but yes, of course, we'll keep trying,' said Zena, looking at her niece.

'On the occasions I have tried to call and speak to her brother Mark, their mother, Agnes, is extremely unco-operative, and it's like hitting a brick wall. I'll call when we get home, and thanks for letting me know. I'll make this a priority.' Lisa kept her head down. The mere mention of her mother made her cringe.

'I have given Lisa my business card, which has my private phone number. Call me if you need to speak to me, no matter what the hour. I'm worried about the police interviews, which will no doubt start in a few days. My best wishes as I know it will not be easy, but the police in these matters are very compassionate.'

'Thank you so much, Helen. We both really appreciate this,' said Zena.

'Just practise your techniques, Lisa, and don't forget to stop if you feel overwhelmed.'

Lisa suddenly hugged Dr Tyler. 'Thank you . . . thank you so much.'

As they drove home, Lisa spoke about the sessions. 'Dr Tyler really is like Binna. She has a way of making me feel peace within my own body. It's like emptying my mind of all the garbage. Sometimes I think I have so much garbage stored there. Just a garbage head, I guess, but I do get a lot out of the sessions, Aunty.'

'That makes me so happy, darling girl, but please don't think the garbage will stay. . . the garbage always gets thrown out,' reassured Zena. 'I really was apprehensive as to how you would respond, but you can see Helen is gifted in her therapy approach. I can see it in you, and this will help when the interviews begin with the police.'

'I do feel stronger and I so want to make Lenny and Superintendent Ash suffer . . . suffer pain and humiliation at what they've done, and be brought to justice.' Lisa stared wistfully out the car window. 'Is it because I'm older or because I'm getting more confident that I feel so much stronger?'

'Probably a combination, but I didn't know your thoughts about Mark. Silly of me not to have given this priority as I know how close you are to him. But as you're aware, I've tried, many times, to call, but Agnes is a tough and unforgiving lady. It's like sparring with a funnel web. We'll give it another go when we get home tonight. I'll probably get my ears blasted but what's new. Let's just hope your mother lets Mark come to the phone.'

It was early evening as they came through the last gate at Woori, and they could see the lights at the homestead. It was a welcoming sight.

'Tired, hun? asked Zena.

'A little, but I feel more relieved that I've been able to express my thoughts. It does get easier in one way the more you talk about it.' As they pulled up and came inside the gates, Alan came down the back stairs.

'Heard the car. How did it go?' he asked as he opened the driver's door.

'Great, just gets better with every session, Alan,' said Zena as she stepped out of the vehicle.

'How about you, kid?' asked Alan as he rubbed the back of his neck.

Lisa met his gaze with a welcoming smile but a slight blush spread across her face as she spoke.

'I just don't know how to thank you both, and Dr Tyler. I feel as if I'm letting go, growing stronger, like this big pressure valve has been opened. I know I was angry and so mixed up from the abuse. It almost destroyed me, but I will not crumble now. I'm going to be strong and go forward.'

'Good on you, Lisa. Being strong is the only choice you have, and it will be tested. Sink or swim. Come on in now, dinner is waiting for my two girls.'

Conversation that evening covered the sessions with Dr Tyler, the arrival of the police tomorrow and their preparedness.

As they washed and dried the dishes, Zena turned to Lisa. 'Well . . . shall we give it a go? Make that call to Fairfield and see if you can chat to Mark?'

'Oh yes . . . yes please, Aunty.' Lisa's excitement was growing. She followed her aunt to the phone in the hallway and sat on the floor, watching intently as her aunt's long, slender fingers dialled the number.

'Fingers crossed, Lisa,' Zena said quietly.

◊

'Hello . . . Hello, Des. It's Zena. How have you been?' Zena heard a sharp intake of breath on the other line. Des was obviously unprepared and clearly taken aback at hearing his sister's voice. He must have recalled the previous angry conversation with Agnes and Zena.

'Oh, you know, just going along with things.' He nervously cleared his throat. 'How's Lisa?'

'She is doing extremely well, Des. She's really taken to the bush and the outback, loves the horses. She's settled in nicely. You would be so proud of her,' said Zena.

'That's good. Less bloody stress for me and Agnes. You and Alan have obviously done your job.' There was a long awkward pause as Zena mentally questioned his responses. There was a lack of sincerity.

'Des, I'm wondering if Lisa could have a chat to Mark. It's been a while, well over twelve months. Agnes must have told you I've tried on many occasions to let them talk on the phone. Lisa is missing him and obviously being as close as they were, wants to talk to her brother and give him her news.'

'Not too sure Agnes would like that. She doesn't want Lisa filling his head with any of her rubbish.'

Zena was getting exasperated but knew when to hold her tongue. 'Rubbish? Really, Des, that is nonsense. It would only be the news she has from here at Woori. I really don't know what you mean by rubbish. It would make her so happy, and I'm sure Mark would feel the same way. You can never change the fact that they are brother and sister.'

Zena continued. 'Come on, Des, you know this is the right thing to do. Please make your own decisions for God's sake!'

Zena bit her lip. She did not want to aggravate Des but he was being so unreasonable.

'Just a minute. I'll see where he is.'

Zena covered the mouthpiece and looked down at Lisa squatting on the floor. 'He's seeing where Mark is.'

Lisa clasped her hands under her chin and held her breath. There was a rustling on the phone and then Zena heard Des say gruffly, 'It's your sister, she's wanting to speak with you.'

Zena handed the phone to Lisa when she heard Mark's excited voice.

'Hello, hello, Lisa . . . it's me, Mark.'

'Oh Marco, I have so much to tell you . . . and I miss you so much and how are you and how is school and how . . . how is Cassius? So many things!' Lisa was bursting with happiness.

Zena smiled and headed back to the kitchen. She could hear the excitement in Lisa's voice and no doubt it was the same on the other end. *I have to work out a way to get him up here. That's going to be hard,* but they deserve to see each other again.

It was a good twenty minutes before she heard Lisa's voice grow quiet. Zena quickly came out to the hallway. Lisa was still on the line and turned to her aunt. She whispered, 'Dad is telling him to finish up. He just stopped talking.' Zena frowned.

Lisa was startled when she heard her father's voice suddenly come on the line. 'Dad? Oh Dad, it's me, Lisa. How are you? I was just telling Mark all the wonderful things I'm doing here now.' Her voice sounded confident but there was a touch of fear. Re-visiting old ground.

'Yeah, right, Lisa. Mark can't speak anymore. I have to go now too.'

Zena extended her hand and was making signs to Lisa that she wanted the phone.

'Umm . . . okay. Aunty wants to say something.' Lisa quickly handed the phone to Zena.

'Des, it's me. Thank you for allowing the conversation. I'm sure that it's made both of them happy. There is no harm, surely you can see that. Mark is welcome to come up at any time and we'd be happy to pay for the flight.' Silence.

'Des . . . Des are you there, I know you are. Please speak to me.' Zena's annoyance was building.

'Right now, that's not a good idea.' His voice suddenly had more authority.

'Agnes was deeply upset the last time you two spoke, and she has taken a long time to get over the stress of what Lisa did in the supermarket, embarrassing us. Gave all the neighbours good gossip. My wife's nerves were and remain shattered. She doesn't like it when you call, and that counts for Lisa as well. We need no further discussions, so please don't bother us again. Goodbye, Zena.' The line went dead. No doubt Agnes was in his ear while Mark was chatting to Lisa. The bitch, damn bitch, always silently beavering away in the background!

Zena clenched her jaw. *Agnes's stress. What about his own daughter!* Lisa and Zena stared at each other in the hallway. 'It went better than I thought, Lisa. At least we got through,' said Zena, trying to sound cheerful, but Lisa had seen her annoyance and frustration.

'It was great to talk to my brother, Aunty. I so miss him. I hope he can get here sometime soon. He said he loved me and missed me.'

'I'm sure he does, Lisa, and we can continue working on communication with them and, of course, trying to get your brother up here for a visit. It's not out of the question, and you heard what I said. We are happy to pay for his flight up here.' *That's if the bitch Agnes will let him go.*

'At least we've touched base. I think it's time for bed for all of us. Big day tomorrow with the boys and girls in blue here. Come on, let's get some sleep.'

Alan rose as they entered the room. 'Good or bad?'

'Both,' said Zena. 'Good in that we finally got the two to chat together but bad as it may be a task to get the boy up here. Agnes is like a dog with a bone. Just not letting go. Let's see what tomorrow brings.'

THREE

THE BOYS AND GIRLS IN BLUE

It was just after midday as Lisa finished her School of the Air lesson when heard her aunt called out.

'Lisa . . . Lisa, the police have arrived.' When she came out into the kitchen, two male detectives were chatting to her aunt, and a young female in police uniform was coming up the back stairs, carrying equipment.

'Come, Lisa,' invited Zena as she extended her arm. 'This is Detective Andrew Collette and Detective Jim Adler.' They smiled at her warmly.

'Gentlemen, this is my niece, Lisa O'Connor.' Lisa moved forward and shook their hands apprehensively. Zena opened the back door and the young woman in uniform stepped in. 'Hello, I'm Constable Lynette Harrison. Where can I put this down, Mrs Smith.'

'Please, call me Zena, and just on this table for now is fine.' The young constable dusted her hands and then Zena introduced Lisa to her. Lisa guessed she was in her early thirties, but she had a youthfulness about her and open, honest clear blue eyes. Her blonde hair was pulled back and she wore no make-up. Her skin was like porcelain, a face that had never seen the sun.

'Hi, Lisa, please call me Lynette. Constable Harrison is such a mouthful.' Lisa smiled. She liked her. There was a warmth to her voice.

'Ditto for us too ladies,' chimed Detective Collette. He pointed to his partner. 'He's Jim and I'm Andrew.'

Jim was short and portly with a cherubic face. A fat bloke as Alan would say. Andrew was tall and lanky with soft brown eyes. Both had a comfortableness about them, and they chatted easily.

'I'll show you to your rooms, and let me know what you'd like to do, or where to start or . . . well, you know, we're now in your hands. Just this way,' said Zena.

Lisa followed the men with her eyes. Lynette came over to Lisa as her eyes widened with apprehension. 'It'll be okay,' she comforted, touching Lisa's shoulder lightly. 'I'll see you in a bit.' Then she walked down the hallway as well.

'Let me know if you need anything,' Zena said as she opened the doors to their bedrooms. 'Men on the left, and Lynette, you're over here on the right.'

'Oh what beautiful rooms. We really did not expect this,' exclaimed Lynette.

'No, please, make yourselves comfortable and pop out when you're settled in. It would have been a real chore heading back into town and then out here day after day. You saw how many gates Woori has. I think you'll get more done here, and it will probably be more relaxing – if that is even possible in this type of situation. But you know what I'm trying to say.' Zena left them to unpack and settle in.

After about fifteen minutes, both men came into the kitchen, followed by Lynette shortly after. 'We thought we might start the interviews tomorrow, Lisa, if that's okay with you.'

'Er, yes that's fine, I guess.' She looked at her aunt for confirmation.

'I think that's a great idea. We can perhaps have a quiet beer this afternoon when my husband makes an appearance. It's usually about 4.00 p.m. when he wanders in.'

'I won't say no to a cold beer,' said Jim. 'It's a bit dry and dusty out here. Got so much red dust over me already. White shirts don't stay white, especially opening all those gates!'

Zena laughed. 'No they certainly don't, Jim, but you get used to it.'

'We received the documentation you ladies put together. It was very detailed. Probably helped the powers that be give us the green light to actually do the interviews out here. But I did make the point that Lisa had suffered terrible sexual assaults and was seeing a psychiatrist up here regularly,' said Andrew. 'That must have been very, very difficult.'

'Yes it was, Andrew, but we wanted to write as much as we could for you,' affirmed Zena.

Andrew looked at his watch. 'Right then, that gives us a couple of hours. We want to discuss it jointly before we proceed.'

'Perfect,' said Zena. 'I know you've brought the documentation I sent you, but I've left the two sets of documents and notes we made in the sitting room, which are clearly marked. I don't know if you want to use those. The coffee table is where you can set up your equipment as well.'

'Great,' announced Lynette as she scooped up the equipment.

'Follow me, it's just down this way.'

'What a lovely room, Mrs Smith,' marvelled Lynette as they entered the sitting room. 'It makes you feel comfortable, very relaxed. I think it's those big windows looking out across the plains.'

'Yes, always a favourite room, it has a very soft feel. We love the big windows too. It feels as if the outdoors is right here. It is very peaceful in here – a lot of people say the same when they come in here. We actually made our notes in this room for that very reason.'

Zena rubbed her hands together. 'Look, I know you'll understand when I say this, but Lisa is terribly nervous, as you've probably noticed. She seems to think she'll be carted off for speaking up. She's been more quiet of late, probably due to your arrival. But as you know, we've had a few sessions with a wonderful female psychiatrist who comes to Walgett. This has helped a great deal. Anyway, I'll leave you to it, but the documentation as you are aware, says it all. The abuse was very horrific, in both homes.'

'We have seen a lot of these cases, Zena, and it's what our unit specialises in with the New South Wales police. We hope we can make your niece feel at ease talking to us,' said Lynette.

Zena nodded. 'I'll go and see how she's feeling. Please make yourselves at home.'

Lisa was not in the kitchen nor in her bedroom. Her aunt went outside and called her name.

'In here, in the Tack Room.' Lisa sat polishing her saddle, while the cats lazed nearby, purring.

'How are you feeling?' asked Zena.

Lisa drew a deep breath. 'I'm ready but I don't know where to start or whether they'll believe me. I keep hearing what the girls said, that the coppers all knew what was going on at Parramatta.'

Zena sighed. 'For now, let's concentrate on the task at hand. That is, providing the information and confirming what we've written. It'll be like with Dr Tyler. They're looking at their notes now, as well as the ones we provided. They'll know in advance what they'll be asking of you. They'll start the question process, which will be diligent and thorough. The detectives can't leave anything to doubt. Just answer them and provide comment as you did with Dr Tyler. I know it will be a horrible process, but as I said if we don't speak up now, these people get away with what they've probably been doing for years. It is unfortunate that very few people believe that priests, superintendents of institutions, relatives, friends, and even fathers are capable of sexual abuse, misuse of power and other forms of mistreatment. The general level of trust within our community really adds to the tendency not to believe the complainants.'

Lisa's look suddenly turned ferocious. 'They are not getting away with anything! My notes are accurate and truthful and everything I said, occurred. I didn't lead anyone on. I never wanted any of this to happen to me. I am the victim here!' she raged.

'Yes, Lisa, that is what we need to remember. Come in when you're done.' Zena hugged her niece before she headed for the house.

'Yes Aunty. I won't be long. I just want to gather my thoughts,' said Lisa.

It was about 4.30 p.m. when Alan pulled up alongside the Tack Room on his motorbike. Lisa popped her head out.

'Hey, kiddo, what are you up to? What are you doing in here . . . hiding with the cats?' he said as he swung his long legs over the bike.

'Polishing my saddle, then I thought I'd polish all of them. I just wanted to keep busy.'

'I see the coppers are here,' Alan added as he lit up a cigarette.

Lisa nodded, 'Yes, they're all inside.'

'Are you done, kid? You can't stay here forever.'

'I guess so,' murmured Lisa as she put her polishing cloths to one side.

'Rabbits in a spotlight,' he whispered. Lisa nodded.

They headed inside, Alan's arm around Lisa's shoulder.

'Ah, there you are. This is my husband, Alan,' introduced Zena as they all shook hands.

'Welcome to Woori. This is a very difficult time for Lisa, and I'm sure my wife would have explained this to you. I want you to catch these bastards,' exclaimed Alan.

Detective Collette smiled. Alan was nothing if not straight up. 'That's the plan, Alan. I have two daughters myself. The abuse Lisa has suffered is appalling, and probably up there as amongst the worst cases. We will take formal statements tomorrow. Lynette will sit with us as a support person for Lisa. However, we will do the interviewing. It will all be officially documented.'

Lisa looked down, which was not unnoticed by Lynette. She knew it would be the girl's worst nightmare to go over the information she had provided to strangers. It was never an easy process, and she always felt sorry for the girls. To recall and go through everything again was almost as humiliating as the abuse.

Alan looked at his watch. 'Time for a quiet beer, gentlemen.'

'Sounds good,' said Jim.

Alan grabbed three long, cold glasses and a few cans of Tooheys.

'Lynette, what would you like?' asked Zena. 'I usually have a gin and tonic. Lisa has the tonic water with a twist of lemon.'

'Well, that makes two of us,' smiled Lynette. 'I'll have the same as Lisa.'

Lynette sat down on one of the big lounges on the verandah and patted the seat next to her. 'Come tell me about life on the land, Lisa,' she said as her aunt disappeared to make the drinks.

It was a casual conversation as they all sat on the verandah, watching the changing vista of the sun and the animals arriving at the bore.

'Lovely spot,' marvelled Jim. 'Not sure I could live out here though. So isolated.'

'Do you like the outback, Lisa?' asked Lynette.

'Yes, very much so,' she replied shyly.

'What do you like the most?' She was trying to relax her, get a conversation flowing and establish trust.

'Everything. The vastness of the land, the changing colours, the remoteness, the horses, the Aboriginal culture, all of it. I never want to leave. It's in my soul now. People say the climate here is similar to Texas and Mexico . . . Umm, I've never been there, but if those places are as nice as Woori, then I'll like them too.'

Zena arrived with a tray of drinks, and they all chatted for the next hour. The conversation over dinner was casual, and it felt good to have different company at Woori. Lynette easily engaged Lisa, and Zena felt confident that a bond would be established just by having the detectives in their home rather than at a police station.

'I'm getting sleepy, Aunty. May I be excused?' asked Lisa.

'Yes, of course, darling.'

'Goodnight everyone,' said Lisa as she kissed her aunt goodnight. Lying in bed, she was not as nervous as when the detectives had first arrived. It was easy to talk to them, particularly Lynette, although Lisa still had fear gnawing at the pit of her stomach.

Sleep was late in coming but in her dreams, Billy was riding Jed, galloping towards her. He was happy. He was coming for her, giving her guidance and strength. *Please let me be strong for tomorrow.*

◊

As the morning broke through her curtains, Lisa could hear voices in the kitchen. The police were up early. She stared out her bedroom window as the colours of the day changed with the rising sun. But as beautiful as the morning was, as the rays stretched across her room, she knew the day would be horrible. *I'm living this nightmare again.*

'Morning Lisa, the detectives are waiting for you,' Zena said as she poured a cup of tea. She hoped that a bond would be established just by having the detectives and the young female constable in their home.

'I'll take the tea with me, Aunty, but I have no stomach for food.'

Zena nodded. 'Ready then, sweetheart?'

'Yes, Aunty. Ready.' Although her voice was soft and raspy in reply.

They both walked to the sitting room, and the detectives stood up as Lisa appeared at the door.

'Come and sit here, Lisa, next to me,' offered Lynette. Lisa felt the quartz stones in her pocket as she entered the sitting room.

There was a typewriter and reams of paper next to her handwritten statements, which were strewn all over the coffee table. There were another two piles that had been ear-marked, and some sections were in paper clips. Paragraphs were highlighted, some sections underlined. Red and blue writing covered the documents. These were the detectives' copies, and they had obviously scrutinised every word, every detail. Lisa shuddered. Her past life, written on paper, sat on the coffee table for everyone to read.

Detective Collette spoke. His voice was now more formal. 'We want you to be as comfortable as possible, Lisa. Please ask us to stop if at any time you need to. You are safe, and we thank you for being here and having the courage to come forward. The purpose of our interview is to gather as much information as possible about what has happened. It's important that you don't leave anything out, no matter how trivial you think it might be. Some things will be extremely difficult to talk about, and you might have difficulty recalling other moments, and then of course, there is the pain of going through all of this again. Sometimes we need to ask hard questions. They will be brutal. Just remember it's okay if you say "I don't know" or you would like to stop.'

Lisa nodded. Her aunt said they would be diligent and thorough, but the detectives also displayed empathy. Her aunt brought in four tall glasses and a jug of water.

'I'm just outside,' said Zena, clenching her jaw. She knew what the girl had to face. 'Come get me if you need me.' Lisa smiled at her aunt, but what she really felt was pure fright.

Lynette touched her hand lightly. 'We'll go at your own pace, Lisa. Jim will be typing. You can see all that carbon paper on his desk and blank paper, so we have to make six copies.' Don't be frightened and tell me when you want to stop. We're here to listen. You need to give us a full account of what happened.'

Lisa felt her muscles clench subconsciously. She was bracing herself against the pain that was hurtling towards her.

'I do understand this process. I know you need to ask me everything and I will try to provide everything, but I just want things to happen quickly. I think of the girls left in the Girls Home, and all the other Homes, their treatment, what the people in authority get them to do, scrub floors with toothbrushes, peeling bag after bag of potatoes, getting sent to the dungeon, all this humiliating stuff, and it wasn't just sex things but also the general day-to-day things. It was just so horrible,' whimpered Lisa.

'Yes, Lisa, we believe this to be the case. We will try to move quickly, but we cannot move that quickly that we will jeopardise facts and details,' said Lynette sincerely.

'Ready to go when you are, Lisa,' announced Detective Collette as Jim began to type. He began with a stream of questions, to which Lisa answered without faltering or hesitation. They covered the questions they needed to ask about both the home (Fairfield) and the Parramatta Girls Home. It took well over three hours.

'I think we can take a break here, guys,' ventured Lynette. Lisa was grateful, she was feeling woozy and wanted fresh air.

'You've done so well, Lisa,' advised Lynette. 'These are unspeakable horrors. Do you want to continue with anymore today?'

'Yes, I do,' said Lisa. They wandered out on to the verandah.

'We can have a good break and come back to it when you are ready, Lisa,' said Detective Adler. Her aunt had placed cookies and a large pot of tea on the coffee table.

'Very good, thank you so much, Zena,' said Lynette as they all sat down.

'You have been amazing, Lisa. Most would have run away at the thought of this interview process. Courage such as yours is what brings these people to justice.'

Lisa wiped her eyes and choked back the tears. 'It's okay to cry. No-one is judging you. You have had all of your innocence removed by indecent people in power,' asserted Lynette.

Lisa took a deep breath and gazed solemnly across the plains. Lynette poured her a cup of tea, but she waved her hand at the cookies. Her stomach was churning, and the feeling of fleeing the room or running to safety pervaded her.

Detective Collette looked at his watch. 'We'll head back in now.'

After Lisa and Lynnette got comfortable in the sitting room again, Lynette asked, 'Are you ready?'

'Yes, I am,' said Lisa softly.

They continued for a further two hours. Lisa described the family home at Fairfield and Lenny's advances in detail, responding to all questions posed, answering them with clarity. Tears streamed down her face and her body was tense, but she felt the quartz crystals in her pocket and practised her breathing. At times she closed her eyes and paused, but then found strength to resume. *Be like a river.*

'Let's just take a breather, Lisa, before we move to the Girls Home. Are you okay with answering more questions?'

'Yes.' Her voice was shaky. 'Yes, I want to continue.'

Lisa described in detail the horrendous conditions at the Girls Home, the beatings, the dungeon, the raping and what Superintendent Ash had done to her. Visions of the Girls Home flashed in her mind, and the smell of the dungeon filled her nostrils. Damp and cold. Faeces, urine, semen.

Lisa broke down when describing the death of her friend Julie, lying on the laundry floor, the blood seeping from her head. Unfocused words fell from her lips, but then she felt the bile rise in her throat when she saw the images of the two men who abused her. She wanted to scream but her voice was little more than a whisper. As Lisa continued, Lynette knew that the superintendent had been extraordinarily cruel, bordering on sadism. When finally the questions stopped, Lisa was emotionally exhausted, and a bone-weary fatigue crept over her body.

'Thank you, Lisa. Words truly fail me what you have been subjected to, as well as all those other young girls. But just one more thing,' said Andrew. Lisa looked at him with blank eyes.

'Are you able to describe to me how you felt at that Girls Home and the general conditions suffered by all the girls? I'm looking for an overall description. Are you up to doing that?'

Lisa nodded and exhaled deeply. 'It was so bleak and run down, and it didn't matter what offence you committed, we were all punished for every minor thing. Everyone felt so powerless, and sometimes through the day, you could hear this pitiful screaming. It was scary as some of the older girls who had committed serious crimes preyed on the vulnerable, the younger ones. I remember one girl carrying around a brick for protection. But you were frequently slapped and caned for even humming in the laundry, and sometimes made to stand for two hours with your arms behind your back. It was humiliating to show your bloodstained underwear to a staff member so our periods could be monitored. There were no doors on the showers or toilets. We had no privacy. Some girls arrived pregnant and some fell pregnant while there because they were raped. Those girls were taken away. I don't know what happened to them. I was always so tired as sleeping was impossible. I was terrified. If you were caught sleeping facing the wall, you would be dragged out of bed and taken to scrub the concrete walkways or floors. And everyone was hungry . . . so hungry, and weevils filled some of the foods. I heard that one girl was taken to the dungeon for isolation as she had plucked her eyebrows. Julie, my friend who was killed, said it took her twelve hours of scrubbing floors on her hands and knees with a toothbrush.'

'Did you have to do that, Lisa?' asked Andrew.

'No, I spent more time in isolation, down in the dungeon. I don't know if that was worse. But I know some girls had their teeth forcibly removed as punishment. The girls who spent time in isolation cells . . . that's where they were sexually and physically abused by staff . . . and they drugged us before they did the physical examinations.'

Lynette couldn't keep the horror from showing on her face as she looked across at Andrew and Jim. 'I think I have enough information for now, Lisa. We should stop here,' said Andrew. Lisa was numb by now and leaned back into the big lounge, the horrible smells and visions confronting her again.

Lisa looked at Lynette, an inferno building inside. 'I don't just want you to get them for me; I want you to get them for everybody still in there or who have gotten out of there . . . alive. For what is probably still going on in there now, the raping of the girls, the torturing of the girls . . . the punishment and all those girls raped who fell pregnant, their babies taken!' Lisa's voice was bitter and her eyes flashed with anger.

'We understand, Lisa,' said Lynette compassionately. 'Lisa, we are just going to duck out for a moment. Are you okay to stay here? We won't be long. I just need to confer privately with my colleagues.'

Lisa nodded as she watched the door softly close.

Lisa closed her eyes and rested her head, weary in body and spirit. She shook her head and opened her eyes, concentrating on her breathing.

◊

As they stood in Andrew's room, it was Lynette who spoke first. 'God that was harrowing. Truly, it is a wonder she's not mad or has tried to commit suicide. Lisa really has an unbreakable spirit. I am sure if her aunt had not stepped in, we may have found her on the streets of Kings Cross, prostituting herself, or floating in a river. We have got to get these guys,' emphasised Lynette.

Andrew, Jim and Lynette returned to the sitting room, and Lisa looked at them warily. For a moment her heart beat overtime. *Please, no more questions.*

It was Detective Collette who spoke. 'Lisa, thank you for providing these statements. The depth and detail will really assist us in the prosecution process. You have been unflinching and fearless in your responses. We believe you. This is powerful evidence.' Lisa nodded ruefully, but also felt a huge weight lift from her heart. This was what she had needed to hear.

Lisa was glad they had stopped the interview. She could take no more. Even though her voice was shaky, there was still a strength to it.

'I needed to provide this information to stop those monsters and stop the other girls being hurt, Andrew. I am sure if you went there and spoke to the other girls, a lot of similar information would be provided. You have to get to that Girls Home and quickly, please, I am begging you,' implored Lisa.

'We will get to that, Lisa, as soon as we get back to Sydney. We promise,' reassured Jim. 'But for now, we just need your evidence. When we get back to Sydney, a visit to the Girls Home will be a priority. We want to give this evidence and your statements to the prosecutor, and discuss what we can do quickly to assist the other girls.'

Lisa felt relieved but her mind momentarily went back to Julie and the horrific vision from the laundry. She felt the tears welling. If only she could have saved her friend.

'Come, Lisa, let's stretch our legs.' Lynette opened the door to the sitting room and called out to Zena.

Zena came from her bedroom and walked towards them. Lisa sat in a slumped position, and her eyes were puffy from crying.

'How is it going, Lynette?' Zena's face clouded with sadness at the sight of her niece. She glanced at Detective Collette.

'Lisa has clarified everything you have written down and more. It has been a very harrowing experience for her to go all over this again, but we needed to have concrete evidence to present to the prosecutor. Superintendent Ash and Lenny Wilkinson are the alleged offenders. We will review Lisa's statements tomorrow so everything is water-tight. No doubt they will both deny all allegations but with your information, we can hopefully press charges.'

'I see,' Zena said as she came to sit with Lisa.

'This is why it is so important we get as much detail as possible to present to the prosecutor, stating we have a strong case. The matter is then referred to the Department of Public Prosecutions, who will take carriage of the matter. In some cases they refer it back to the police to be dealt with in the local court,' added Lynette.

'When do you think that will happen?' asked Zena.

'With the information you have provided, the detail, the accuracy, I believe we have a good case for prosecution. The prosecution needs to prove that the act was not consensual,' said Lynette.

'Oh dear God, how can anyone believe that it could be consensual. A thirteen-year-old virgin!' exploded Zena.

'I understand how you feel, Zena. It doesn't seem right, but with the statements and information you have provided, we are all satisfied an offence has been committed both in the family home and at the institution. So, basically, when we finish here, we speak to the prosecutor and then go and see the offenders, bring them down to the station and interview them about the allegations,' said Lynette.

'What happens then?' asked Zena.

'Well, they have a right to silence and to obtain legal assistance. I suspect they will deny everything, most do. If they are charged, the police place them in a remand jail until a court date is affixed. At that time, they appear in court and can apply for bail. Often it is refused due to the seriousness of the offences. Most rape cases get refused bail by the police. We are hoping this will occur in Lisa's case,' explained Lynette.

'Does Lisa have to appear in court?' asked Zena.

'She may do, if they deny the allegations. If they confess and both parties admit guilt then the matter will still need to proceed to the district court. In that case, Lisa would not need to appear. It is then they are sentenced.'

Lisa was vehement. 'I don't want to ever see them again. I never want to be near them,' she spat.

Andrew spoke. 'Once they hear the allegations read out to them, they would be foolish not to admit guilt. But always expect the unexpected. Sometimes they just break down, like it's an emotional relief for them to admit guilt.'

'It's enough for today, Lisa,' said Lynette. 'I will confer with my colleagues. They may have more questions.'

'It's just before 3.00 p.m.,' said Zena, looking at her watch. 'You must all be hungry. I have a plate of sandwiches out in the kitchen.'

Lisa looked totally drained, her gaze fixed on the wide open spaces and the sun shimmering across the plains.

'Do you need to rest, Lisa?' asked Zena.

'Yes, I have had enough, Aunty.'

'Let's go to your bedroom then. Please excuse us,' she said as they left the sitting room.

◊

'The things that have occurred are heinous and only her strength and resilience has pulled her through. Grab some sandwiches and let's head back to the sitting room and go over what we have. We need to nail these bastards,' said Andrew as Zena and Lisa retreated down the hallway.

Zena came out to find the kitchen empty. She made a cup of tea and took a plate of sandwiches into Lisa.

'I know you probably don't feel like eating, but I'll leave these here. Do you want to talk about anything?'

Lisa shook her head. 'I feel very tired but I also have a sense of personal fulfilment. I have done the right thing. I've managed to get through this, even though all the memories flooded back. I could even smell the dungeon, Aunty, feel his horrible disgusting hands on me . . . the stink of him.' Lisa shuddered and pulled her knees up to her chest in a protective manner.

'My darling girl, I wish I could take all your hurt away but this is the only path to resolution and to catch these men. I'll leave you to rest. It may be a good idea to shut your eyes.' Zena stroked her hair softly. 'Things will get better, my dear, they always do.'

When Zena left the room, Lisa took out the quartz stones and placed them on the table next to her bed. *Spirits protect me. I wish I could ride out and see Binna. Please let this be over with soon.* She began to practise her breathing techniques, relaxing the tension in her body. I am safe. I am here. Her breathing slowed down, and she quickly fell asleep.

It was early evening when she woke. The tea had gone cold, but the sandwiches remained intact. There was much chatter outside. Alan must have joined Zena and the detectives with a cold beer. The rest had done Lisa good, lifting her exhaustion. Lisa stared blankly at the ceiling, her thoughts swirling with images of the Girls Home and her brother-in-law. She shook her head and tried to clear their faces from her mind. She wanted to crawl inside her own body. Fear suddenly clutched at her heart. *What if the bastards get away with it?*

Lisa got up and splashed cool water over her face. She stared at her wet-faced reflection in the mirror. *I'm not a little girl anymore and I am not a plaything. I want justice!* She ran a brush through her hair and then followed the noise out on to the verandah.

'Come join us, sweetheart.' Zena rose and came to her side. 'We are just watching your favourite part of the day.'

'Told the coppers here, once they see a few of these sunsets, they won't want to go back to Sydney,' said Alan, barking out a laugh. The conversation was light as Alan explained the animals that came to the bore.

'Not much chance of that, Alan,' scoffed Jim as he grabbed another can of Tooheys.

Lisa sat down with her aunt and rested her head on her shoulder. Zena held her hand tightly. It was clear the interviews were taking their toll on her, mentally and physically.

'I must admit, it is very different to taking statements in the station in Sydney,' said Andrew.

'Dinner will be ready in thirty minutes. Does anyone need to freshen up?' asked Zena.

'Great idea, I need to, if you will excuse me,' said Lynette, who went inside. She was quickly followed by Andrew and Jim. Lisa sat alone on the verandah with Zena and Alan.

'Do you feel like dinner, hun?'

'Not really,' said Lisa, looking at her aunt unsteadily. 'I just don't think I can eat anything at the moment.'

'Understandable,' ventured Alan.

'Well, go shower and I'll bring you in a small plate of something. See how you go with it.'

'Thanks, Aunty. A warm shower does sound good.' When she moved, Lisa's limbs felt heavy. It was like her own body couldn't bear its weight.

'I'll be in shortly, Lisa,' said Zena as she watched her niece with a furrowed brow.

◇

'It's taken its toll, that's for sure,' murmured Alan to his wife as soon as Lisa was out of earshot. 'And there's another day to go.'

'I think I'll call Dr Tyler. Hearing her voice may give Lisa some more encouragement. I'll call her tonight and see if she's available early tomorrow.'

Zena left Alan and quickly moved to the phone in the hallway.

Zena hoped she would be there – her gut feeling told her Lisa needed help. The phone rang a few times and then, finally, that soothing voice spoke in greeting.

'Dr Tyler . . . Helen, hello, it's Zena Smith.'

'Hello, Zena, how are you and Lisa doing? I hope things are going smoothly.'

'Yes and no. Lisa has been very brave, but it's like she's now retreating, shutting down. The detectives will take more information tomorrow. I wondered if you thought it would be a good idea to speak to her on the phone so she could be reassured by your voice.'

'Yes, of course. I'm sorry to hear this news but it is not unusual. She would be reliving the trauma, and it is now fresh in her mind. Where is Lisa now?'

'She's gone to take a shower. I said I'd bring some dinner to her room.'

'Okay, leave her to process things in her mind. Stay and talk to her when you take something in and encourage the breathing and muscle relaxation techniques. I'll call tomorrow morning around 9.00 a.m. before they start the interview again. Is that alright with you?'

'That would be most kind of you, Helen. I'll let Lisa know.' The relief flooded into Zena's mind as she put the phone down.

Zena put her hand to her chest and leaned against the wall. *I am so grateful Dr Tyler. I so wish this nightmare would end.*

When Zena opened Lisa's bedroom door slowly, Lisa was curled up in a ball on her bed.

'Oh, Lisa.' Zena quickly came to her side, seeing clearly her niece's distress. Lisa's breathing was erratic, and the grinding of her teeth was audible. Zena sat on the side of the bed and held her hand. 'You are safe, sweetheart; you are here with us and you have done amazingly well. I just spoke to Helen, who said to practise your breathing and your relaxation techniques. She's going to call in the morning to speak to you.'

Lisa relaxed a little under Zena's hands. 'My mind feels like a rudderless boat in the middle of a choppy ocean. I fear I will sink. I'll drown with no-one there to save me.' Her voice was barely a whisper.

'No you won't, my darling girl. I will not let anything happen to you. You must know that. Do you think you are up to more questions tomorrow? I'm not sure that you are . . . but only you can tell me if you want to stop.'

The words seemed to bubble up from nowhere and Lisa practically yelled. 'No, don't stop! I want to get it over with, Aunty. I so want it over. I want them to pay for what they have done. They must pay!' Lisa sobbed uncontrollably.

'Calm your thoughts down. Focus on breathing,' said Zena soothingly.

'I'm sorry, Aunty.'

'Nothing to be sorry for; you have done nothing wrong. We knew this would be hard, impossibly hard, but we are nearly there. Breathe and relax. I'll come back shortly.' Zena pulled the covers around her niece. 'Rest now. Alan and I are just outside.'

When Zena came out into the kitchen, Alan had taken over the cooking. 'Not good?' he asked as he looked at his wife.

'No, almost like an anxiety or a panic attack but she wants to continue tomorrow. She wants to finish it. Dr Tyler is calling at 9.00 a.m. tomorrow, and I hope this will give her a mental boost. Thanks for saving the roast.' She touched Alan's face lightly.

'Do you want me to have a talk to her?' asked Alan.

'If you want to, Alan. She's just so exhausted from rehashing the trauma. Didn't eat the sandwiches I left her at lunch time and wants no dinner.'

The door was ajar when Alan poked his head around. Lisa lay on her side facing the door.

'Hey, kid, feel like talking to this silly old goat?' Alan asked with his usual grin.

Lisa smiled.

'I gather that's a yes. Phew, I thought you might throw something at me.'

Alan sat on the side of her bed, taking her hand gently. 'How is my girl doing?'

Her lips trembled as Alan brushed the hair from her eyes. 'Nearly there. You know, when you feel you are at the end of your rope, tie a knot and hang on. Just remember you have nothing to be ashamed of. In fact, your aunt and I are so proud of you.' Alan's words were soft and he spoke to her gently.

Lisa gave a short laugh but her eyes were moist.

'That's my girl. So tomorrow, we finish the job. Rabbits in the spotlight.'

'Rabbits in the spotlight,' she repeated.

'We are both right here if you need us.' He kissed her cheek lightly.

'Thank you, Alan. I love you both so much,' Lisa said hoarsely.

'Ditto, kid.' Alan rose and headed back to the kitchen.

'Did she speak?' asked Zena worriedly. The police were seated at the table.

'There is no stopping her,' Alan said looking at Andrew. 'Sure it's taken its toll on her to relive all that shit she has gone through, but she wants to keep going.'

'Lisa has made our job much easier with the details and statements that were provided,' said Lynette. 'And it will also assist all those other girls who have been abused. We have a lot of work to do when we get back to Sydney.'

'Yes, I thought documenting everything that occurred was practical, just in case Lisa did forget anything. Although how could anyone forget the atrocities that have occurred. But writing is very therapeutic,' said Zena.

'Exactly,' agreed Lynette.

'Alan, please carve, and everybody just help yourself. I'll take this plate into her. I know she said she wasn't hungry, but the smell may arouse her.' Zena also grabbed a freshly made cup of tea and headed back to Lisa's room.

She was showering when Zena entered the room. 'Hi, hun. I've left some dinner here for you and a cup of tea. Try and eat something. I'll be back shortly.'

'Thanks, Aunty.'

When Zena returned, Lisa was fast asleep and the plate empty. *Thank you. Thank you.* Zena clasped her hands together and breathed a sigh of relief. As she lifted the empty plate, she noticed the little quartz stones in Lisa's hand, and then closed the door softly.

◊

When Lisa woke just before dawn, there was a strong feeling of a spirit in her room. 'I know someone is here with me,' she whispered. *Is it you, Billy?* It felt like a powerful being. She listened to her breathing. In and out, letting the sensation of lightness take over her body. *I am moving like a river, flowing and bending, winding through the landscape, widening and deepening. I shall flow freely. Binna is chanting, and the smell of the herbs from the fire filled the room. I have to be strong. My mind is in a storm but I will survive.*

Lisa dressed and came out into the kitchen where the three detectives as well as her aunt and Alan were all talking.

'Morning, Lisa,' said Alan. She came to her aunt and hugged her.

'Good morning, everyone,' greeted Lisa.

Lynette smiled at the girl. Lisa did look like she had slept, but her eyes told her she was still traumatised. She had seen those empty and haunted eyes many times before. The spark was not back yet, and Lisa had another harrowing day ahead of her.

'Helen will be calling at 9.00 a.m. this morning, so allow for that before you proceed to the sitting room, Lisa.'

'Thanks, Aunty. I haven't forgotten.' She sipped a cup of tea.

'We're done here,' said Andrew, rising from the table. 'We'll start our prep work and the things we need to ask Lisa to clarify.' He looked at his watch. 'Shall we say around 10.00 a.m., Lisa, in the sitting room?'

'That should be okay . . . I think,' she mumbled, glancing at her aunt.

Zena nodded. 'If there's a problem, I'll let you know.'

The phone ringing stopped the conversation. Lisa raced down the hallway and picked up the receiver.

'Hello, Lisa speaking.' She wanted to hear Helen's voice badly.

'Morning, Lisa. It's Helen. I heard you're battling the demons and that the days have been awful, so I thought I would touch base. Can you talk for about forty-five minutes?'

'Yes,' agreed Lisa, sitting on the small stool next to the phone.

'Very good. We will go over what we discussed at my rooms and focus on the positives. You are safe and people love you and will protect you. Breathe deeply for me, and I will begin.'

Lisa closed her eyes and concentrated on Helen's soothing voice. Helen asked questions and explained about reactions to questions and how to stay focused. Inwardly, Lisa began to feel a sense of calm.

The time passed quickly. 'Okay, I hope I've helped. You're navigating real challenges in life. Locate yourself in the present, Lisa, and confirm your physical safety. You are discussing what has happened to you, but you must remember, you are not in that place anymore. I will see you next Thursday.'

Lisa pondered that momentarily. 'Yes Helen, I know . . . and yes, I am safe and loved. I really know that. See you next week.'

She went to the kitchen where her aunt was waiting for her.

'Boy, I really needed that Aunty.' Lisa placed a glass under the tap, bringing the water to her parched lips. 'Helen makes me see things better . . . unscrambles me, just like Binna,' confided Lisa as she gulped the water thirstily.

'You best go then. It's just on 10.00 a.m., Lisa. The detectives will be waiting for you. It's almost over,' said Zena.

Lisa wiped her lips with the back of her hand and took a deep, slow breath. 'I'm ready.' She walked to the sitting room.

'Are you ready to proceed, Lisa?' asked Andrew.

'Yes, I am.' Lisa was asked more questions regarding her brother-in-law. She never hesitated and could clearly remember the day of the assaults, the time and the circumstances surrounding the sexual assaults. They spoke for another three hours. It was gruelling, and the distress was clearly visible on Lisa's face.

'I think we have enough information for now. The interview is terminating,' said Andrew. Lisa's eyes were downcast. *I have so had enough. I want to scream.*

'You've done so well, Lisa,' added Lynette, who noticed Lisa clenching and unclenching her hands. The inner turmoil felt like assaults to her mind and body.

'My mother called me a liar about those assaults.' Lisa's voice was tinged with anger, catching the detectives by surprise.

'It's too graphic, Lisa, and a lot of information no minor would have, or would even know. So again, we will build a case and present it to the prosecutor,' explained Andrew.

Lynette looked over at Lisa. 'Do you want to add any more?' she asked as she reached out and touched her hand.

'No,' Lisa said softly.

Jim began to pack up the reams of documents and placed them and the typewriter into a large carton. 'This is all we need.

Lisa,' stated Andrew. Once we get to Sydney, things will move quickly. We will let you and your aunt know what transpires. Can you let Zena know we have finished and we'll be out once we pack up our gear.'

Lisa nodded and headed off to find her aunt.

It was early afternoon when the detectives moved with their bags and equipment to the back door.

'We'll be off now then,' said Andrew as Zena came into the room. 'Lisa has been extraordinary and there is no doubt, in our minds, that she has been totally factual. Thank you for your hospitality. It certainly made our job easier staying here. But right now, we want to get this information processed as quickly as possible. There is also the matter of contacting the Department of Child Authorities. They will be all over that institution like a rash, but we want to get there first.'

'Thank you, Andrew. We . . . Alan and I, are most grateful for the way you handled this, and for your sensitivity,' said Zena as she handed them a brown paper bag. 'It's not much, but they say my fruit cake is pretty good. Keep the Thermos. You may appreciate a cuppa on the way home. I'll collect those when we no doubt have to come to Sydney.'

Alan shook their hands and conveyed his thanks. 'If you blokes are in the area, just drop in, always a cold can of beer in the fridge.'

Lisa gazed at the strangers who had become friends over the past few days.

'Take care of yourself, Lisa. We will be in touch.' Andrew lightly touched her shoulder.

They followed the detectives to their car. 'Be careful on the roads. Lots of roos and pigs and the odd curious emu,' cautioned Alan.

As Andrew started up his car, Alan leaned into the driver's window. 'Get the bastards,' were his final comments as he watched them head out onto the road.

Lisa murmured, 'I hope they get to the Girls Home quickly. I think about all the girls there now and that place . . . the dungeon.'

'I have no doubt they will,' reassured Zena.

The light of the day was slowly fading. The glowing sun was beginning to fade as the blackness descended over the plains. Lisa sat alone on the verandah and gazed at the sunset in its various hues of pink and red, until the big orange ball went down and down. She thought of Goobang and Billy. He was near but far.

'Hey, in your favourite spot?' asked Zena as she sat next to Lisa.

'The pink galahs filled the sky, such a beautiful sight. It's a simple thing, but the blackness that can be in your mind is always eased by Mother Nature,' said Lisa solemnly.

'I agree, but for now, this part of the job has been done. We still have a ways to go. Prosecution, court appearances.'

'I figured that.' Lisa's voice resonated with sadness and despair.

'Alan I will both be there in that court room. But you heard what the police said, when they present the allegations and your statements, those bastards may confess. Let's hope so, as then there will be no court appearance for you. I shudder to think what the barristers can and would do. We will face this when the time comes, Lisa. For now, the police will keep us informed, and I for one can hardly wait for their news.'

As they sat down for dinner, the air felt less tense and it was good to have the house to themselves once again.

'You did good, Lisa. As I said, we are so very proud of you,' said Alan.

'Thanks, Alan, but I am so glad they're gone. I was angry towards the end. Angry at those monsters. Just reliving everything again, I felt so sick . . . but I am glad I got through it. It's hard to see your experiences and your life scattered across a coffee table.'

'New day tomorrow, Lisa,' said Alan. 'We're all glad that this is over for now.'

As Zena passed by her door just after 11.00 p.m., the girl was sleeping soundly, the quartz stones again in her hand.

FOUR

MISSING BRIDLE

Lisa stirred as the dawn broke. She could feel that same spirit of total tranquillity around her replacing the anxiety of the past few days. The air shimmered. Her breathing was even and barely audible. She smiled as she took in the rapture of the birds, fluttering and screeching to meet the day. *At this time in the morning, I have the whole world to myself. It's like the earth is sleeping, with only its wildlife stirring.*

She heard a door close. It must be Alan. He was always the first one up. Lisa suddenly wanted to join him, tumbling quickly out of bed. *A brand new day with no police and no questions.*

When she made her way into the kitchen, Alan grinned at her. 'What a nice surprise, you're up early. Have a seat, kid. Breakfast is on me. What will it be?'

'Cocky's Joy,' she replied.

'Whoa, Cocky's Joy, now that's getting serious. I think I'll join you on that one.' Alan threw two chunky pieces of bread into the toaster. The aroma filled the kitchen. He lathered the toast with butter and golden syrup. They smiled affectionately at each other as they ate.

'Be interesting to see if Cookie arrives this year. We're nearly out of this wonderful golden syrup of his. He always makes me Cocky's Joy when he's here. May be hard though, without Harry.' Lisa nodded, her mouth full of the sweet bread.

Zena came into the kitchen. 'Morning, sweetheart, being entertained by Alan, I see,' she smiled as she poured herself a cup of tea. 'Don't forget we have a visit with Helen tomorrow.'

'Yes, I remember. I'm looking forward to it,' said Lisa.

'What's the day looking like, Alan? asked Zena.

'Hmm. I'm going to take Neddy out of the yards at the back of the Tack Room and bring Noir in. She may be ready for a service from Khartoum. Not sure, but I want to take things steady with her. Are you still interested in helping me, Lisa?'

'Yep, sure. I think their foals will be beautiful if that eventuates.'

'Okay, then, let's get started.' Lisa followed Alan down the back stairs. Zena watched as she sipped her tea. It was a different atmosphere that morning.

Alan took off on his motorbike towards Noir, who was in a paddock with the old gelding, Tidgy. He rode Noir bare back up to the home yard near the Tack Room and slipped off her back where Lisa stood waiting.

'Noir looks good, Alan. She's such a beautiful mare.'

'She sure is, Lisa.' Noir fidgeted. 'Not sure our girl is ready, but she does need a good curry comb through her mane and tail. Lots of burrs,' he added as he went inside to get the combs.

'Hey, kid, why is your saddle upside down and in the corner? It's not good for the pommel.'

'Corner, what corner?' Lisa asked curiously, coming in to see what he was talking about. 'I left it on the saddle mount like I always do after cleaning it . . . why . . . where is it?'

As she looked around, she could see the saddle was in a far corner on its pommel. *That's odd. I didn't put it there.*

'I didn't put it there, Alan. I'd never do that. I know to keep my tack in good order. Where's my bridle? I hung it up and now it's not there!' Lisa started turning things over, with the cats scattering. 'It's not here, Alan. I swear I hung the bridle up above the saddle mount.'

'Well, that is odd, you sure you didn't . . . maybe a bit upset . . . you know, after the coppers?'

'No,' her voice was firm. 'I put the saddle on the mount and I hung the bridle above it. Now the bridle has disappeared and the saddle is thrown in the corner. That's just not me!'

Alan knew he had to change the subject as Lisa was getting agitated, but it was odd, the position of the saddle and the bridle missing. He remembered telling Lisa many moons ago the importance of keeping saddles, bridles and anything they use for riding to be returned clean and in their right place. But the saddle had been thrown in the corner, like it was suddenly dropped. Maintenance of the gear was paramount. Until now, her routine in this regard had been faultless. Something wasn't right.

Alan scratched his chin as they moved outside. 'Ghosts then, Lisa. You've been conjuring up those spirits,' he chuckled as he picked up the curry comb and continued to remove the burrs in Noir's mane and tail. 'Don't worry your head, kid, they'll turn up somewhere. I'll run it by Zena; she may have moved them or something.' Lisa wasn't so sure.

'This little girl will throw some great foals,' said Alan, changing the subject. 'But somehow I think she is way too fidgety, so maybe another twelve months will settle her. Don't want her rejecting the foal, or any other problems by an early service. Have to look after our girls.'

Lisa nodded and thought about what he had just said. A man so considerate of a horse and not wanting to cause harm. She compared that to the physical abuse and harm men had done to her.

She remembered what Lynette had said to her on one occasion. Some men genuinely convinced themselves that their heinous actions towards young girls were loving and welcomed. Lisa snorted. *I want revenge. I want to be a fly on the wall when the sick bastards sit opposite the police.*

FIVE

THE BOY NEXT DOOR

Lisa felt brighter than ever when she finished up her next appointment Helen. They had a longer session as it was the first appointment after the police visit. They both walked out to reception where Zena was waiting.

'Zena, lovely to see you. We covered a lot of ground today. We discussed how the abused child can be integrated with the adult self so they can work together as a unified whole, rather than being split and working against each other. I'm happy with Lisa's progress, although the police interviews did rehash everything.'

'Yes, it was exhausting, and I thank you for calling the house the other day. Lisa really needed it,' said Zena.

Lisa nodded. 'I'm grateful too, Helen. I was really getting out of sorts.'

'It's what I'm here for, Lisa. I'll see you ladies next week then. As usual, any problems, please don't hesitate to call me.'

On the way home, Zena thought it was a good time to broach the subject of guardianship.

'Lisa, I didn't want to bother you with this as it was an extra thing you would have had to think about, and I didn't want to add this issue to the investigation.'

A puzzled look spread across Lisa's face. 'What is it?'

'When you came to Woori from the Girls Home, Alan and I took responsibility for you. So we became your legal guardians. You mother agreed to this as she said she did not want you back. I know that hurts, but that is the way she wanted it. I'm sorry your own father was in agreement. But we want to go to another level in terms of your care.'

Lisa froze. 'Are you sending me away?'

'Heavens, no. We have told you so many times, you are never leaving unless you want to. We would never send you away. But we both think that we could start an adoptive process. That is, you would be our child legally.'

Lisa squealed. 'Oh Aunty, it would be all I could wish for. That day you came to the Home, I wished it then. I would love to be your daughter!' Lisa felt a mixture of emotions. Shock, excitement, and a feeling of really leaving the past behind.

'I will have to contact Agnes and Des again and tell them of our decision, and of course they have to provide a written agreement. That's going to be tough. I can hear Agnes now. But it basically means they give up all rights to you. I hope they agree. It's called a kinship adoption. I will then ask my solicitor to proceed with all the necessary arrangements. The matter will be filed in our local court. There are a few hoops though. We have to prove that we have a long-standing relationship with you and are capable of substituting for your parents and that it is in your best interests . . . and that it would be detrimental to be left with your parents. That's not hard to prove,' Zena scoffed.

'The woman from the Department of Child Authorities, Jane Fothergill, will also touch base with us this week, so I'll let her know I have discussed this with you. My solicitor will also speak to her and the department, advising them formally in writing of our intention. You can see why I have held off. Just too much for you when you were already under the pump.'

Lisa nodded. 'But it is really something to look forward to, Aunty. It makes me so very happy.' Zena reached over and squeezed her hand. 'It makes us happy too, Lisa.'

'Have you made up your mind about coming to the RSL this Saturday? We thought we may do a few weekends in there. John the Publican called and said people were asking when we may be back. I put things on hold for the investigation and also just to let things settle a bit.' Zena hoped she would say yes.

'I think that would be a great idea. I'd like to hear you both play again. At sixteen, I'm still underage though, Aunty.'

'Yes, I know, but John won't mind you sitting at our table.' Zena was delighted. 'Do us good to get out of the house for a bit of fun and enjoyment. I know we get out when we see Helen, but that's different. Her visits are certainly not entertainment.'

When Saturday morning arrived, Zena was clearly excited. She did love to sing and entertain. Alan loaded the Zephyr as Zena carried out their clothes in zippered bags.

'Right, all set?' asked Alan.

'Yep, all good to go,' replied Zena as they wound up the windows and took off.

Lisa never tired of the ride into town. The late afternoon sun always had a magical feel with the different colours sweeping across the wide plains, outlining the vastness of the outback and the sense of unbridled freedom. She was actually looking forward to the night.

'While we're all here, Zena, did you happen to move Lisa's saddle, the one we got for her sixteenth birthday, or for that matter, her bridle,' queried Alan.

'No, why do you ask? I haven't been in the Tack Room for quite some time,' mused Zena.

'Funny . . . well, not really that funny. Lisa's saddle was sort of dumped onto the floor and her bridle is missing,' revealed Alan.

'Missing! What do you mean by missing?' Zena asked.

'The bridle is gone – that's what I mean by missing.'

'Well, where would it be, who would have it?' persisted Zena.

'Buggered if I know, luv, that's why I'm asking you.'

'Yes, Aunty,' Lisa interjected. 'I know I put my saddle onto a mount and hung the bridle above it. I always do!'

Zena looked at Alan, uncertainty in her eyes, and he reached for her hand. 'Look, we're nearly at Walgett, let's not worry. We'll have a good look around tomorrow. Has to be somewhere, things just can't disappear.'

Alan pulled up not far from the RSL. It was close to 5.30 p.m. Some Aboriginal children played in the dirt, the exact spot Lisa had first met Billy. Her thoughts turned to him and the movie they watched together. Sadness swept over her. She so longed for him to be near her. *Billy where are you? No-one seems to have heard anything of you. I must ride out next week and see if Binna or Ningali have heard anything.*

When they stepped inside, she caught sight of the same grumpy barmaid. Nothing had changed here. *I wonder if she'll have a go at me about my age again.*

After setting up, they used the little room to freshen up, and Lisa changed into her white lace dress.

'Oh dear, that's looking a bit tight,' observed Zena. 'You seem to be filling out, Lisa. We may have to go shopping. That must be uncomfortable. Maybe a trip down to Sydney is in order. It's been a while since I was down there. I'll speak to Mrs Dunphy as she often goes to Sydney to order stock.'

Lisa felt excited about the prospect of a trip to Sydney and raced over to hug her aunt. 'I would love to go shopping with you, Aunty,' squealed Lisa.

'Ditto, darling girl, but for now Mrs Dunphy will have to do.'

Arm in arm, they headed out to join the people who were now flowing into the RSL. News had spread there was going to be a dance tonight. Lisa drew many admiring stares. She was taller, her jet black hair was now down past her shoulders and her skin the colour of warm honey.

John the Publican couldn't stop talking about their local beauty queen. A few people came up to say hello to the Smith family and introductions continued through the night.

'Are you okay with a bit of attention, Lisa? People are curious creatures, and I can see why they're staring. You do look great, kid,' said Alan proudly.

'I'm not used to it, and it does feel strange, but it's also kind of flattering in a way,' Lisa said shyly.

The older Lisa got the more she looked like her aunt. She was a striking-looking young girl. 'I think there are a few eligible bachelors here tonight, Zena. Their parents will probably try to get first dibs for their sons. People always want to match-make, especially the women – they can't help themselves,' said Alan, winking.

'Lisa, could you order three lemon squashes and ask for it to be put on our bill, please,' asked Zena.

Zena turned to Alan after Lisa was out of earshot. 'I just hope she doesn't get uncomfortable with the attention, particularly attention from boys. The police have just left this week, and reliving her experiences was such an ordeal for her. Not sure she's ready, Alan, and my mind tells me anything in this area would need to be extremely slow. With Billy, it was progressive, and she totally trusted him,' said Zena. 'But getting her out and about and meeting new people is not a bad thing.'

'No, not at all, and I think tonight we all needed it,' acknowledged Alan.

Lisa watched while they played their first set. People really enjoyed her aunt and uncle's selection of music, and the dance floor was full.

John the Publican was happy as the bar was busy. As they all returned to their table for the first break, David and Kate Walker came into the RSL with their son Mitch.

'Oh look, Lisa, there's Dave and Kate Walker. My goodness, their boy Mitchell has grown into a handsome young man. He must be close to nineteen now. He attended Hawkesbury College near Richmond and got his Diploma in Agriculture. Mitch was the youngest student to be accepted into the Ag program. He's a smart young fellow, and skipped a year at school. He also graduated from the program early, probably because he's worked on the land since he was a young'un and is so dedicated to farming. After he got his diploma, he took off for the UK and worked on some farms over there. Been gone for the past six months. They've just returned from a holiday through Europe with him.'

'How do you know them, Aunty?' Lisa asked.

'They have the property next door to us. Their place makes ours look small. The Walkers are three generations of sheep farmers. They are a delightful couple. That is their only son, Mitch. Kate absolutely dotes on him, which isn't really a good thing, but she nearly lost him at birth. A very difficult pregnancy.'

'Why is that not a good thing? I wish someone had doted on me.' Lisa was puzzled.

'You had the other extreme, Lisa. Too extreme. But when you get everything you want, and I mean everything, you are never really challenged. Life is all about challenges, and Mitch

72

has had everything laid out before him. His parents are quite wealthy, and the boy has never wanted for anything. What Mitch wants, Mitch gets, but I don't say that in a bad way. It's just the way it is.'

Alan waved and walked over to where the Walkers were sitting. 'Dave,' greeted Alan as he vigorously shook his hand. 'Kate,' he smiled, and kissed her on the cheek. 'Great to see you are all back, safe and sound. Mitchell, you sure have grown.'

'Yep, just over six foot,' said Mitch quite proudly. 'I like being tall, you can see everything,' he laughed.

'Zena is over there with our niece, Lisa.' Why don't you join us,' suggested Alan.

'That would be lovely,' said Kate as she walked with Alan to their table by the small stage.

'Lovely to see you all,' exclaimed Zena as she hugged Kate. 'This is my niece, Lisa. She's staying with us.'

'Must be nice to have some female company, Zena,' winked Kate. 'I seem to be surrounded by men at Woodside.'

'Pleasure to meet you, Lisa,' said Dave, as he extended his hand. 'We're on the property next door. Oh, this is my son Mitchell, but he goes by Mitch.'

Lisa looked over at him. He seemed to go on forever. 'You're very tall,' she blurted.

'Yes, like I just said to Alan, just over six foot,' he grinned. He had already noticed Lisa from across the room. She was the most beautiful girl he had seen in a while, even with all his travels.

'You look Spanish to me,' he admitted to Lisa.

'Spanish?'

'Yes, you are so dark, and your skin is such a beautiful colour – like the Spanish girls I saw in Europe.'

Lisa blushed. She didn't know what to say so fidgeted with her hands in her lap. He made her nervous.

'So how have things been, Alan?' asked Dave.

'Pretty good with the sheep industry, and also the wheat. The grain solo, which was erected at Burren Junction in 1963, can now take 500,000 tonnes, and the Walgett Wheatgrowers Association is getting new members constantly. A good time for agriculture. The chillers that opened in 1964 for trade in kangaroo meat is also doing well. The local shooters have got a job on their hands, and the park's people control the culling on our properties. Saves us going out and doing it. The shearing season was also very good this year at Woori. Fat sheep, great wool but we unfortunately we had an old shearer, Harry, pass on while he was on the property. A good bloke. Sorry business, as the Aboriginals say.'

'Awful news, Alan. Sorry to hear that,' said Dave. No-one liked a death on their property.

Zena changed the mood. 'Are you passing through or staying for our wonderful entertainment.'

'Staying. I just invited them to our table, Zena,' said Alan. 'I'll just grab a few more chairs.'

'How old is Mitch now?' asked Zena, turning to Kate.

'Turns nineteen in a couple of months. We'll let you know the date of his party. We'd love to have you come and help celebrate.'

'Sounds wonderful, Kate, count us in.'

After a couple more sets of music and dancing, the night came to a close, and Mitch helped Alan carry his equipment and bags to the Zephyr.

He looked up when he saw the Aboriginal children still playing. 'Stupid boongs,' he grunted. 'They should be off the street.'

Lisa frowned. 'What did you say?'

'Those kids,' Mitch said pointing. 'The boongs, they shouldn't be out here.'

'They're not boongs!' Her voice rose with indignation. 'They are Aboriginal people.' Mitch was taken aback. Her face said it all. Her eyes were glowing and fierce.

Lisa slid into the back seat. The night was haunted by memories of Billy. She recalled vividly the fun they had the night at the movies but how racism had reared its ugly head. She had hated the way he'd been treated.

'Goodnight, Mitch,' Alan said as he closed the car door. The young man stared after them as the car drove away. He'd obviously hit a bit of a raw nerve there with Lisa after his comments about the boongs.

Zena drove home, and Alan had been relegated gate duty, much to Lisa's relief. She was still stewing over Mitch's racist comments about the Aboriginal people.

'Hey, kid. Zena mentioned the kinship adoption process. Makes me a happy man,' said Alan.

'No-one is happier than me, Alan. I never want to leave here. The sense of freedom the outback gives me, I'm addicted to it, and just being with you guys, I'll have to be dragged out of here.'

'You sound like me, Lisa.' Alan was chuffed. 'There is an old bush quote that I love, which says it all. Old fashioned but my father kept it and would always read it out.'

'What is it? Can you say it now?' Lisa asked.

'Sure, I'm no thespian but here goes – "But the bush hath moods and changes, as the seasons rise and fall and the men who know the bush-land are loyal through it all".'

Zena smiled. 'It's a lovely quote, Alan, and proper true as our Aboriginal friends would say. You really have to tolerate everything out here, particularly drought.'

'And flies and heat,' laughed Alan.

'Anyway, not sure how long this kinship adoption process will take, but you are like our own now anyway, Lisa. We both love having you here. You're the daughter I never had. Just need to make it legal,' said Zena.

Zena's voice was soft and sincere. Lisa loved them both so much.

'What did you think of the Walker family, Lisa? They've been friends of ours for a long time. Very good at breeding sheep, and their property is huge. Travel and working overseas has been a great experience for Mitch,' said Zena.

'They seem nice people, Aunty. You were right. It was good to get out and meet new people. It wasn't that hard to talk to Mitch . . . he's very confident. But I don't like the Aboriginal kids being called boongs. I did fire back at him when he said that.'

'It's like slang, Lisa,' said Alan. 'I'm sure he didn't mean it to sound malicious. And Mitch is well-travelled, so he would be very confident.'

'And just in case you didn't notice, he's quite easy on the eye, which was not unnoticed by a few of the girls there tonight,' added Zena. 'I know you still think of Billy, and time will pass quickly, so the next season will be here before you know it. But there is nothing stopping you from getting out and about and doing new things and meeting new people.'

Zena looked at her niece in the rear vision mirror. Lisa's thoughts were elsewhere. 'I agree with Alan . . . it was probably just the usual slang people use, Lisa, as certainly, there is no room for racism at all in our house. You know that. Billy is always welcome, and Binna and Ningali are good friends of ours. We have never drawn a line between black or white.'

'Sure, Aunty. I actually may ride out and see the ladies tomorrow. Do you want me to take anything?'

'I have a few things you can take, so let me know when you're going. I somehow think a lot will happen next week, mainly some sort of a response from the police statements. I'm sure we will hear something. The detectives said they would act quickly on a visit to Lenny and Superintendent Ash once they spoke to the prosecutor and produced your evidence.'

Lisa drew a sharp intake of breath. It would all be on her in no time. Fear crept into her body once more. 'I hope so, Aunty. I want to know what's happening to them.'

'No need to worry, Lisa. We all want to get on with the process. I'll also call my solicitor about the kinship adoption. But I have to make the dreaded call to Agnes and Des first before they get any legal notification. Can you imagine if Agnes got notice in the mail of my intention. She would spontaneously combust!'

Lisa started to giggle, and Alan joined in. 'Don't laugh, you two,' said Zena. 'It's always me that bears the brunt of her anger, but I have to call . . . there's no way out as they need to provide a written agreement even before we can proceed in that direction. Then there is Jane Fothergill from the Child Authorities with her follow-up call. No doubt Jane would have heard from the detectives, so things at Woori will be somewhat hectic, I'm thinking.'

Lisa wanted all of it behind her and thought constantly about the possibility of going to court. She did not want to face either of the men and felt sick to the stomach at the thought. All she wanted to do was be with Billy and to feel how she did last season.

The final gate was closed as they headed to the homestead. It was just after midnight. 'By the way, Zena, I want to have a good look around tomorrow for that bridle. Just remind me. It has to be somewhere,' said Alan.

When Lisa closed her eyes that night, her thoughts turned to Billy. *I want to hear your stories. I want to hear your laugh. I miss you, Billy. Goodnight, wherever you are.*

SIX

JUSTICE WILL PREVAIL

'What do you want me to take when I ride out to see Binna and Ningali?' Lisa asked Zena as she moved over to a kitchen bench.

'These jewels,' she said, holding up three glass jars. Plums, apples and pears. They have a sweet tooth those two, so this will be a real treat for them.' Zena placed them into the usual calico sack.

'I'll get going shortly to do my chores and be back about lunch time. I'll grab the sack then.'

'I have to help Alan with tagging the new lamb's ears, so see you when you get back,' said Zena as she kissed the top of Lisa's head.

Lisa saddled up Neddy. She looked forward to sitting with the two Aboriginal women. As she travelled along the road, she felt she was finally living in a place she loved. It was the land and everything about it. She watched as the pink galahs flooded the blue sky. *Unless you're connected to the land, you're not connected to yourself*, she thought.

She smiled and remembered the Dorothea McKellar poem she once learned at school. She recited loudly, revelling in the solitude as she cantered along the dusty road. 'I love a sunburnt country, a land of sweeping plains, of rugged mountain ranges and droughts and flooding plains. I love her far horizons and her jewel sea. Her beauty and her terror, the wide brown land for me.' Lisa had never thought she would one day be living that dream.

'Says it all doesn't it, Neddy. This landscape has claimed me.' In the distance, hazy smoke travelled lazily up to the sky. She spurred Neddy on but suddenly swerved quickly to the right, jerking the horse hard as the object on the road suddenly moved. An echidna!

Lisa waved and cantered quickly to the bloodwood tree next to Binna's camp. After tethering Neddy, she took the bag of fruits and headed to the humpy.

'Morning, ladies. It's so lovely to see you. I've missed you both.' Lisa felt that same rush of happiness whenever she was in their presence.

'Here, you sit,' said Ningali, patting the ground. 'You look like you going another way, you suddenly pull out. We think you change your mind mebbe.'

Lisa laughed. 'Oh no, I was focused on your fire and then this little thing on the road sort of spooked Neddy, and when I looked down, it was an echidna. I didn't want to squash it or hurt it with Neddy's hooves, so I swung hard to the right.'

'Ahhh, little one, soft heart,' said Binna.

'This is from Aunty.' Lisa pulled out the jars of fruit.

'Good grub, Binna. She bring da fruits,' said Ningali excitedly. 'Tell Aunty, she make us both very happy.' They both giggled like small children holding up the jars.

'We eat echidna,' said Ningali happily.

Lisa pulled a face. 'I don't think I could. They're so cute.'

'Binna know a story about the echidna,' said Ningali as she drew the strange creature in the dirt with the spikes.

'Tell me, I want to know too,' smiled Lisa.

Binna began the story. 'Echidna and long-necked turtle, dey was friends who lived near a billabong, and dey share da food, but one day dey run out. Echidna had a baby and she take da baby to da turtle to look after. She go to look for food but long time passed and da turtle, he get very hungry so he ate da baby. When echidna come back, she say where my baby? I have food for you. Turtle look bad and say I ate da baby because I so hungry. Echidna said, "Stay here turtle, I get some stones," but turtle did not want to wait, so he go and get spear grass. Echidna she threw da stones at da turtle and dey stick to her back. Da turtle threw spear grass at echidna and the spear grass dey stick to her back. Dey fight all day. So da stones, dey form a hard shell on da turtle's back, and da grass spears, dey form the spines on the echidna. Turtle say she never want to see echidna again, and go to live in da billabong. Echidna say, I never want to see you again, I go to live in da outback, big country. So dey live in separate places now.'

Lisa laughed. 'What a funny story, Binna. The echidnas are one of my favourites; really, they are just so cute. I couldn't eat them, even if I was starving to death!' Her eyes sparkled and Binna could feel her energy. 'You feel dem good spirits, Lisa.'

'Yes I do, Binna. The bad spirits are going, well . . . I hope. But the road ahead is going to be tough in lots of ways. Anyway, do you have any news for me, ladies?'

Ningali knew what she meant. Lisa always asked this question, hoping there would be news about Billy. Binna slowly nodded as she looked into the distance.

'We heard somethin',' said Ningali as her long legs picked their way around the fire like a flamingo in water looking for food.

Lisa's eyes flew open. 'Oh, tell me, tell me, what have you heard? Please, please, Ningali!'

'Me down at river catching maugro and a few young black fellas dey ride by. We sit and talk. Heading north for work. Said joining Billy and Burnu on a big station, called Angus Downs. Plenty of work until next season up dat way. Had some trouble there too. Plenty big trouble. Dem boys said there had been fightin' and another boy he lose his eye in da fight. He drew da knife.'

'Oh, God no!' Lisa's face crumpled. Just the mention of his name and the fact that she had heard some news made her heart race. 'What boy lost his eye, Ningali? Who was fighting? Did they say what boy . . . who drew the knife?'

'Jimmy. Name Jimmy. He runned off after da fight but he was wanting to get Billy real bad. Jimmy drew da knife.'

'This is horrible news. Billy had trouble here last season with Jimmy. I never liked him. He scared me, always prowling about . . . like a cat stalking something.'

Lisa looked at the two women. 'I so miss Billy.'

Binna spoke. 'I hear dat in your voice. Billy protected by da spirits. Him belong in your heart. Make you sing like da birds. He be alright, missus. Come back when ready.'

Lisa felt her face burn with embarrassment. Ningali giggled. 'Billy good boy . . . yeah, he come back. You see.'

'I hope so, Ningali. Well, I had best be off,' said Lisa. She hugged her two friends fiercely then she made her way down to Neddy.

Ningali watched Lisa ride away, swatting flies with a piece of eucalypt tree. She glanced at Binna who sat eating a peach from the bottle, her fingers dripping with juice.

'Dat boy Billy . . . he come back for sure. Their spirits, dey connected,' said Binna as her long bony fingers dipped into the jar.

◇

Lisa felt exuberant all the way back to the farm despite the news about Jimmy.

Billy. He was working and he was coming back. She hurriedly hosed Neddy down, packed her saddle away and raced up the back steps. Zena was talking on the phone as she came inside.

'Very good, Andrew, thank you for calling. Yes, I'll let Lisa know.' Zena put down the phone and turned to Lisa, who stood in the hallway.

'What's up?' asked Lisa.

'That was Detective Collette. Andrew.'

'So I gathered,' said Lisa, the muscles in her back becoming tense. *What, Aunty? Please God let this be good news.*

'Let's sit,' said Zena as she pulled the chair out for Lisa. 'Detective Collette and Detective Adler went out to see Superintendent Ash. The prosecutor, after reading your statements, wanted to formally charge him. He was satisfied that the brief of evidence supplied by the detectives contained enough evidence to obtain a Prima facie, which basically means the statements were accepted as correct until proved otherwise. But the prosecutor believed without doubt that offences had been committed.'

Lisa blew a sigh of relief. Her hands trembled as she began to fidget. 'Well . . . what happened?'

'Superintendent Ash was not expecting them, so of course it was a big surprise. A very big surprise.' Zena gave a hint of a smile.

'Oh!' Lisa exclaimed and slapped her thighs. 'I so wish I had been there to see his rotten face . . . to see him in the spotlight. The spotlight . . . like a rabbit . . . ha ha ha.' Lisa jumped to her feet. 'Wait till I tell Alan! Please, Aunty, go on!' The vision raced through Lisa's mind of the super being confronted by the police in his dirty, musty office with his stupid so-important name plaque.

Zena continued. 'They said that they were carrying out a formal investigation based on your complaint of sexual assault on numerous occasions. They asked him to come down to the station with them. He vehemently denied everything and apparently became quite hostile. He said you were uncontrollable in the Home, and the discipline administered was to keep you under control, and that you were a danger to yourself and others, continually causing problems.'

Lisa's face turned red with rage. 'Danger! Danger! What a bloody liar! He's lying. He's a lying bastard. I hope they did not believe that!' She was now shaking and felt nothing but hatred as she paced the floor.

'Take a deep breath, Lisa. Calm yourself, if that's possible. It gets better,' soothed Zena.

'Huh? Better, what do you mean?' the words came tumbling out of Lisa's mouth.

'The superintendent then called you all the names under the sun and seemingly lost control, stating he was surrounded by lesbian bitches and all the girls were sluts who needed to be disciplined. When Detective Collette said they wanted to take him down to the station, he became violent, striking out at them with a baton and then tried to run for the door. He even pressed the buzzer for assistance, in his panic, just prior to trying to escape, and a portly woman came in and was knocked over in the scuffle.'

Lisa started to laugh. 'It was Eve. Oh, I wish I had been there. Rabbit in a spotlight with his long crooked nose.'

'He put up quite a fight. As I said, he even tried to strike Andrew with a baton.'

Lisa suddenly stood still, and her hands covered her face in anguish. She shook her head from side to side. 'The baton, Aunty. I so remember his baton.' Her hands slowly came away from her face and became fists at her side.

'Are you okay, sweetheart? Maybe this is too much for you.'

'No, no, sorry, Aunty. I just remember the baton, and it all came rushing back to me, this day down in the dungeon. I can feel the baton . . . feel what he did to me. Sorry, I want you to continue.' Lisa sat once again, hanging on every word that spilled from her aunt's lips.

'Well, they had to handcuff him and put him in the back seat of the police vehicle.'

'What happened next?' Lisa was on the edge of her seat.

'At the station, he was introduced to the custody sergeant, where his rights were explained to him. Andrew said he would also be formally charged for assaulting the police. He was then taken to an interview room, and the detectives asked him if he wanted to proceed. They could only hold him for six hours but Andrew obtained a warrant from the court for a further six hours,' said Zena.

'He would have hated that, all the loss of power,' smiled Lisa.

'Yes, I would agree, Lisa. So, the custody sergeant refused bail due to the serious nature of the charges, and he was to appear before the next available local court, near the police station. After reading him his rights, our friend Ash called his lawyer, who arrived an hour later. Ash said he declined to be interviewed unless in the presence of his lawyer. So, after some discussions, they finally agreed to proceed, and the police began their record of interview. The police provided the statements regarding your allegations. Apparently he looked quite shocked and was in a state of confusion. He denied the offences, bail was refused and the matter was put to the local court. He was then taken to the remand centre.'

'Yes, yes, yes! Into the dungeon, you go!' yelled Lisa, leaping from her chair. 'Hooray!' she shouted, dancing around the kitchen. It was an overwhelming sense of relief and pure elation.

'While he was detained and the matter adjourned, Jim Adler set up office at the Girls Home with two other female police officers and began interviewing all the girls and taking statements. So, further charges were laid against Ash, including his assault on the two detectives, and he just broke down, pleading guilty, babbling like a baby. The final date for the hearing is up to the district court, so by confessing, you will not have to appear, Lisa.'

'Oh, Aunty.' Tears began to stream down Lisa's face. Zena went to her side and they held each other. Sobs racked her body until she finally lifted her head.

'Here, take this tissue, it's clean.' Zena pulled one out of her pocket. 'I didn't mean to upset you with this news.'

'No . . . they are tears of joy, tears of relief. I have so many mixed feelings . . . that they believed me, that Superintendent Ash was arrested and that something is actually being done!'

'I had no doubts, Lisa. It is good news. Let's see him worm his way out. It will be like a flood gate opening, all those girls and their statements. But it also saddens me as it was a situation for you and all those other girls that should never have occurred. Never!'

Lisa suddenly cocked her eyebrow. 'What about Lenny?'

'Amusing chap . . . now that he has been cornered. The officers went out to see him on the weekend, and Janine answered the door. He wasn't home. She said she didn't know where he had gone as she had been out shopping, and he wasn't home when she got back. They left their business cards and asked her to let Lenny know they had called. Lenny was to call them when he got home. So, of course Janine asked what it was all about. Andrew said they just wanted to ask Lenny a few questions. Well, that got her stirred up, didn't it. She apparently went straight on the defensive, saying is this about Lisa, the little liar and so forth. I would say Agnes told her the whole story and what you had said. I can see Janine now, Lisa, like a rooster with spurs.'

'What happened then?' Lisa asked nervously.

'No-one knows, but Lenny has not been seen since. Shot through. I would say Janine told him when he got home that the police had been there wanting to see him. Anyway, there is an APB out on him with photos being distributed.'

'What's an APB?' queried Lisa.

'It's an All-Points Bulletin used by the police. It contains information about a wanted suspect who is to be arrested or a person of interest for whom the police are seeking. It doesn't look good that he's missing now, does it?' Makes him look as guilty as sin, but we already know that. He is on the run. Coward. I hope he is consumed by absolute fear and terror.'

'Me too, Aunty. The worst fear he could ever imagine.'

It was close to 4.00 p.m. when the phone rang.

'Hello,' said Zena. 'Oh, hello Agnes, good afternoon. I was—' Zena's voice was cut off.

The tone on the other end was venomous. 'Shut up . . . you stupid, stupid fucking bitch. You and that daughter of mine have caused absolute havoc. Fucking havoc. I have just got off the phone to Janine who, as we speak, is hysterical. Do you hear me, she is hysterical! The police have been around there to her home. Lisa has made all those awful accusations about Lenny and now they are wanting to speak to him. He's done nothing wrong. You are going to ruin their marriage. The pair of you deserve each other. She is no daughter of mine. Keep her. Keep that fucking little bitch! I never want to see her again. She has been nothing but trouble. No wonder they build Homes for these girls, uncontrollable. They should lock them all up and throw the keys away. Some girls are just born trouble. And . . . And don't bloody well ring here ever . . . expecting to speak to *my* husband Des or *my* son Mark. My husband is disgusted with you as well. Do you hear me, don't ring here ever again!' Her voice was shrill and the air was punctuated with hatred.

The phone was slammed down.

Zena placed the receiver down and stared at the wall opposite her, shaking her head.

Lisa just stared at her aunt open-mouthed, all blood drained from her face. 'No guesses as to who that was,' said Zena.

'I feel bad, Aunty, that you get these calls from her, that you have to make calls to her on my behalf. You are getting battered. I know that feeling,' said Lisa sadly. 'I don't know what I can do to help you . . . maybe I should take all the calls.'

'Don't be silly, Lisa. Goodness, that woman, and that's a term I use loosely, she sure can deliver. I feel like a good stiff drink. Couldn't get a word in, it was just an absolute torrent of hate-spewing, vile negativity,' said Zena.

'I'm sorry, Aunty. This is all my fault. I don't want them to hurt you and then we have to go to court and then—'

Zena held up her hand to Lisa. 'Stop thinking that way. Agnes was being Agnes. Nothing new, although I do feel like telling her sometimes to get on her broom.' Lisa giggled, the colour returning to her face.

'You have to believe in yourself despite what Agnes or anybody thinks. I can only say the toughest times will only make you stronger. Let her rant and rave. The only one I am thinking about is your brother, keeping in contact, but there will be a way around that too. In any event, I will have to call again, despite what she said. I hope Des picks up when I call about your adoption. Who knows what he's thinking now. One thing is for sure, Agnes would be lifting the roof off with her venom. Put your crash helmet on, Des.'

Lisa put two glasses of water under the tap and handed one to Zena as they sat at the kitchen table. 'Anyway, I'm sure we'll find out more tomorrow. I'd say Jim Adler and his team will have a briefcase full of statements from those poor souls in that

Girls Home. But the good thing about that is the further evidence they will gather against Superintendent Ash. It's all unravelling now, Lisa, which is a good thing. How are you feeling, hun?'

'First and foremost, relief. That something is being done for all the girls before me that suffered the same treatment, the girls in there now, and my friend Julie. That vision of her lying on the laundry floor is hard to erase, Aunty.' Lisa closed her eyes. She could see it so clearly.

Opening her eyes, Lisa asked, 'What can I do or what do we need to do now?'

'Well, I will try again speaking to Agnes. I have to as I need that written agreement. It's an endless battle, Lisa, but I know her well. Her reactions and defensive verbiage do little to deter me. It's never been any different. I'll give it a few more days. She was well and truly rattled on the phone. Red to the gills and puffing like an old steam train. Even referred to Des as *her* husband! Well, hello, he is *my* brother! She seems to have forgotten that. Anyway, to change the subject, how was the ride? Did you get the fruit jars to Binna and Ningali?'

'Yes, I did, and it was a good morning's ride. I even bypassed an echidna! Frightened poor old Neddy. But Binna told me a funny story about an echidna and a turtle. She is such a good storyteller. Umm . . .' Lisa looked at her aunt.

'Umm what? Go on. You suddenly stopped.'

Lisa gulped. 'Ningali was down at the river the other day and met some Aboriginal boys who were camped down there. She asked where they were going and they said they were heading north to work with their friend Billy on a large cattle station, Angus Downs, or something like that. Said there was plenty of work up there until the next shearing season, and they needed a couple of fellows. They said some of the stockmen had been fighting. One got into a serious fight and maybe lost his eye.'

'That does not sound good at all. The overseer would have a job on his hands if that was happening,' said Zena.

'Well, one boy apparently pulled a knife, so the other boy punched him hard in the face, causing damage to his eye. He ran off after he was injured. That's why they needed more jackaroos. But Aunty . . . those boys in the fight, they were Billy and Jimmy.'

'Billy!' exclaimed Zena. 'And Jimmy?'

'Yes, it was Jimmy who pulled a knife, and Billy hit him.'

'Dear God. Wait till Alan hears this news. It's amazing this bush telegraph. For how big this country is, especially out here, news travels fast.' They both looked up at the sound of Alan's bike. His lanky frame came up the stairs, and he stepped into the kitchen.

'I'm done for the day. Gave myself an early mark. Too bloody hot, and the flies were about to carry me away. Is this a women-only gathering?'

'No, Alan,' Zena smiled, 'Just telling Lisa the latest from the detectives. I'll fill in you later, but suffice to say, the Ash fellow is in a cell, or remand centre, confessing his guilt, and the other monster, Lenny, is on the run. Jim Adler had set up an office out at the Girls Home with Lynette Harrison and another female constable to take statements from the girls. So, overwhelming evidence, really, and the magistrate refused bail. I only hope there will be an investigation into that Girls Home and perhaps the other institutions like it. It's very sad, the atrocities that have occurred, and such an abuse of power. The places should be exposed for what they are and closed down.'

'That's bloody great news. How do you feel, kid?' His eyes darted to Lisa.

'Rabbits in the spotlight,' grinned Lisa.

'Damn right,' Alan said, the smile never leaving his face.

'I don't know who is grinning the widest, you or Lisa,' continued Zena. 'But the other news is that Lisa heard Billy is working up north, and Jimmy was on the same station. Got into a real scrap. Jimmy pulled a knife and Billy belted him. Seems Jimmy lost his eye with a solid punch.'

'Shit! Who told you this?' demanded Alan.

'Ningali,' interrupted Lisa. 'She met with some Aboriginal boys down at the river, and they told her they were joining Billy at a place called Angus Downs because they needed extra help at the station. That's when they told her about the fighting.'

'We had trouble with Jimmy last season. Hot headed and volatile and definitely jealous of Billy with this little lady. Always thought Jimmy was a bad egg. He had the propensity to do damage, but Jack always kept him under control. Well, he won't be back here this coming season. Have to let Jack know when he calls. A bloke is gone for a few hours and comes back and the place is full of news,' said Alan, grabbing a beer from the fridge.

After taking a long swig, he added, 'So, Lenny is on the run. I'd love to know where the bastard is hiding. I'd like to pay him a visit. He can't hide for very long. The coppers will be onto him when he surfaces, that's for sure, and apart from our judicial system, these blokes will have to face the inmates, who get great enjoyment dishing out punishment to paedos.'

'What do you mean, Alan?' asked Lisa.

'Prisons are full of all types of crims, Lisa, but anyone who harms a child in any way, well, their lives are made a living hell by their fellow inmates. In prison, paedophiles are considered the lowest in the prison hierarchy. I'm sure the screws turn a blind eye when a paedo is being bashed.'

'How do you know this?' asked Lisa.

'My copper mates told me. The inmates who commit crimes against children are harassed on a regular basis, and they get beaten, tortured and some have actually been murdered. So, even the toughest criminals are unforgiving when it comes to crime against children.'

Lisa could only hope so.

After dinner, she retired early. As she closed her eyes, peace washed over her. Justice was coming. Her thoughts turned to Billy. She knew where he was working. *Please keep safe.* Sleep came over her, and Billy appeared in her dreams. He was riding Jed and he swooped down on her, his lovely brown arms curling around her.

SEVEN

A SUITOR COMES CALLING

The day spread out before them as they got ready to head out in their separate ways. They had done a quick search for the missing bridle, to no avail.

'It's getting hot early now, Zena. Summer, and the heat is expected, but we could do with a bit of rain,' said Alan as he lit up a cigarette just outside the Tack Room. 'I can't find that bloody bridle, it's got me beat, Zena, and a little worried.'

'I know. How does a bridle just up and vanish? The dogs would alert us to a car if anyone was hanging about, unless we were out in the far paddocks. We wouldn't hear anything then.'

Lisa interrupted. 'The dogs always bark, Alan.'

'Yeah, but it's a different bark alerting us to strangers to the ones where they're just trying to get our attention.'

'I'm really upset about the bridle as it was my birthday present, and I know I put it back above the saddle,' reiterated Lisa vehemently.

'It's okay, kid. Relax, it'll turn up,' encouraged Alan. Lisa wasn't so sure.

A cloud of billowing red dust became visible as they stood chatting. Zena surmised, 'Land Rover. Think it's Mitch Walker.'

They watched as the vehicle made its way to the compound gates. 'Morning all,' said Mitch as he came through the gate. 'Glad I caught you all at the one time.' His broad smile was directed mainly at Lisa.

'Here's the invite to my nineteenth birthday bash,' he said proudly, handing the envelope to Zena. Saturday 20th January from 6.00 p.m. Hope to see you all there.'

'We would be delighted to come, Mitch,' said Zena. 'I don't think we have anything on, but I'll check and give Kate a call to confirm.'

'What are you up to today, Mitch?' asked Alan.

'Probably the same as you – fencing, checking the boundaries. The kangaroo culling by the shooters seems to have kept them and the dingoes under control, even though we don't get many dingoes. But I've got a funny story. You'll enjoy this one, Alan,' beamed Mitch.

'Well, fill us in then, because you seem to be bursting at the seams to tell this yarn,' commented Alan.

'Me and the crew had camped out, after herding some stock, and decided to stay down by the river, have a swim, catch some dinner and light a fire . . . the usual. We took on a young jackaroo a month ago, Gerry Daly, skinny kid who looked like he needed a good feed, only sixteen years but said he liked to work hard. I had my doubts – thought he would break in two with a bit of physical work but you give them a shot. Anyway, around midnight we hear this sort of scuffle, and Gerry was poking at a King Brown snake with a stick. The bloody snake was attempting to get in his swag. That was the last we saw of Gerry Daly. He took off at morning light never to be seen again!'

Mitch guffawed loudly. Zena and Lisa's faces were one of shock, but Alan and Mitch could not stop laughing. 'Bloody funny story, alright,' said Alan as he slapped Mitch on the back.

'Um . . . Anyway, Lisa, I was wondering if you'd like to come and see our property, Woodside. I can pick you up and bring you back.'

All eyes shifted to Lisa, and she felt embarrassed. Mitch had suddenly put her on the spot with his request. She felt almost trapped and didn't like the sensation. It brought back unpleasant memories of having no power. Her aunt looked pleased with the idea though, as did Alan.

Lisa stammered a response. 'Well . . . well, I guess so.'

'That's great then. What about tomorrow if you're not too busy. I can pick you up early morning and have you back by lunch time. There's a lot to see, and Mum will have some morning tea.'

'Sure,' Lisa said, folding her arms across her chest.

'Fantastic, I'll pick you up at 8.00 a.m. then Lisa.' Mitch was beaming as he got back into the Land Rover. He gave a toot and took off in the dust.

Lisa had not really warmed to him the first night they met, and it had made her angry when he called the Aboriginal kids boongs. *I guess it won't hurt*, she thought. But she felt apprehensive.

'It'll be lovely,' said Zena. 'I know you will just adore their property. Kate has a beautiful home. She's a keen decorator and has purchased antiques from all over the world. Money is not a problem for the Walkers.'

'I just don't feel that comfortable with him. He seems to overpower me . . . or something,' murmured Lisa.

'It's only for a few hours, and Kate will make you feel very comfortable. It gives you a chance to see another working property that's much bigger than Woori,' explained Zena.

Lisa nodded grudgingly.

'Come on, before it gets much hotter. We'll see you later.'
Alan took the ute with Zena and headed off.

◊

'The boy seems keen on our Lisa, darling wife,' Alan chuckled.

'Yes, he does, a little too keen. Not so sure about Lisa though. She certainly did not like his comments about the Aboriginal kids.'

'He was just generalising,' said Alan. 'I'm sure there was no malice. Everyone . . . well, lots of people do call them boongs. Anyway, they'll sort it out themselves. If she doesn't like him, then that's the finish of it. No chemistry.'

'The problem is, Alan, her chemistry is with Billy. You saw for yourself, and my gut instinct tells me that Billy is coming back. I just feel it.' Zena could see Billy clearly in her mind and the way he interacted with Lisa. He would no doubt have grown more into a man. A little bit older. A little bit wiser.

'Connections are made with the heart, Alan, not the tongue. Billy is all heart. Mitch was born with a silver tongue. The ladies in town all swooned over that boy before he left for overseas. Mitch can have any girl he wants,' said Zena.

'I hope it's not going to be a bloody triangle. Don't need any love issues during a busy season,' harrumphed Alan. 'First it was Jimmy . . . now bloody Mitch.'

'You're thinking way too far ahead, Alan. We have another six to seven months before the next shearing season comes around, and we have way too much ahead with other things. We need to keep focused on the pending police investigation not a jolly love triangle.'

They both nodded in agreement.

◊

Lisa was sweeping, her back to the door of the Tack Room, but spun around swiftly when she heard something outside.

'Is anybody there? . . . Hello.' Silence. A cold shiver ran down her spine as she craned her neck for the source of the noise. There was a presence of someone, something. Lisa stood still, just for a moment's freezing silence, and then forced herself to walk to the door. As she tentatively stepped outside, the glare of the sun made her squint, and the dogs were barking madly.

'Sit down,' Lisa yelled as she tried to quell their noise, but there was no doubting the sound of a horse in the distance, moving away.

Was there someone here or did I imagine that?

Lisa suddenly felt frightened and ran up the back stairs into the house, locking the door.

It was midday when Zena and Alan appeared. 'Bloody hot out there,' he protested as he threw his hat on the table.

'Get your things done, kid?'

'Yes, all good. I just came in for lunch and then school lessons. But I felt scared when I was in the Tack Room. I thought I heard someone outside.'

'What . . . what do you mean?' asked Zena.

'I was sweeping when I heard a noise outside. I went out there to look around, but no-one was there . . . but then I thought I heard the sound of a horse . . . sort of in the distance.'

'That's odd, Lisa,' said Alan. 'Were the dogs barking?'

'Yes, but they always bark. And, really, I never know what they are barking for. But that's why the sounds were sort of hard to hear. The dogs wouldn't shut up.'

'Yeah, but as we discussed . . . there's the friendly attention bark and a more aggressive bark. Which one was it, kid?'

'I . . . I just don't know. All I know is that I felt someone was there,' admitted Lisa.

'Okay, I'll go and have a look around the place, take the ute and see if I spot anyone. Be back shortly,' stated Alan.

Zena came over to her niece and gave her a hug. 'Well, I don't know who would be wandering about here, Lisa, but it seems very odd. Maybe someone was looking for Alan. I know I'm guessing, but right now, we have bigger hurdles to face. By the way, I know Mitch put you on the spot today, but how do you really feel about heading out to Woodside?'

'It's okay, Aunty. It's just for half a day. I do feel nervous, but I don't know really why. Maybe he's getting too close, and I just don't trust strangers, especially men. He's always so confident and and he . . . he just seems to take over. But as you said, it would be good to see the place. It does sound amazing.'

'Have a think about it. If it makes you feel really uncomfortable, it's maybe not a good idea at this stage,' said Zena.

'No, all good. I have said yes. Maybe it's my past haunting me, and besides, you know the Walker family very well. As you said, you've been friends for a long time.' Lisa paused. 'But then, my father and mother thought they knew Lenny too.'

Zena hugged her tighter. 'You'll be fine, Lisa. Kate is and has been a wonderful friend. And she'll be there the whole time. On another note, I'm going to make a call to Des late this afternoon. You said he usually gets home around fourish?' Lisa nodded.

'Let's hope he picks up or otherwise I'll get another round with the Dragon Lady. Despite her venomous spray the other day, I still need to broach the adoption. She said she doesn't want you back, but that was in a fit of rage. I really have to ask her formally. I have no doubt Agnes will say yes. Then it's a matter of getting their written agreement. Fingers crossed.'

'I hope he picks up, Aunty.'

'Me too. I may make more progress with my brother. Just a thought too before you head off. If you really feel uncomfortable going tomorrow with Mitch, just let me know. You don't have to do anything you don't want to do. It's no problem to give Kate a call.'

'No, I'll be fine, Aunty, but thank you.' They both looked up at the sound of Alan's ute.

'Anything?' asked Zena as he came inside.

'Nothing, not a soul to be seen . . . are you sure you heard a horse, Lisa?'

'Yes, I think so, but as I said, it was hard with the dogs barking. It was like in the distance, sort of moving away.'

'Well there's nothing about . . . so let's not worry for now. I'm off for a siesta while this heat sticks around but I'll be back out there after a snooze. You know where to find me.' He ducked off to the bedroom.

◊

Despite Alan's comments, Zena was worried. They lived so remotely and left all the doors and windows open of a night. She made a conscious note to lock the doors from now on. Her thoughts turned to the dreaded phone call she knew she had to make that afternoon.

It was 4.30 p.m. when Zena glanced at her watch. Des should be home. Zena drew a deep breath. *I'm going to make that phone call now. Des, please pick up. I just have to get your dual consent.*

Zena dialled nervously. The phone rang out. *Damn,* she swore to herself. *I'll try again just before five.* She felt a flutter in her stomach as the next half hour ticked away.

Okay, Zena, here we go again. On the third ring, Mark answered. Zena breathed a sigh of relief. 'Hello, Mark, it's your Aunt Zena.'

'Hello,' he greeted, happiness resonating in his voice. He was such a good kid, heading into his teens now at thirteen years of age.

LINDA DOWLING

'How are you? I hope your father told you that you are welcome to come to Woori any time. We'd love to see you, and I
can fly you up, Mark. Your sister would love to see you.'

'Umm, no . . . Dad did not mention that, but I'd really love
to visit,' he bubbled into the phone.

*Sod, he hadn't even told the boy. This was either Des's or Agnes's
doing.* 'Okay then, mention it to your parents, and I'll speak to
your father again about it, he probably forgot to tell you. Is he
there? I need to speak to him about another matter.'

'He's just got home. We dropped Mum off at Janine's place
about thirty minutes ago.'

*Bravo, Zena thought. Better than expected. Des will be on his
own, with no interference on the sideline from Agnes.* She heard
Mark call out to his father and then the phone was picked up.

'Hello, Zena.' There was annoyance in his voice. 'I thought
Agnes told you not to call. The house is in a bloody turmoil. I
have hysterical women everywhere. It's driving me bloody mad!'

'Yes, I got a mouthful from Agnes the other day, and I
would not have bothered you except that I'm ringing informally
to ask you something about Lisa.'

Des cleared his throat. 'Christ, what is it now? Just bloody
well get on with it.' He didn't bother to keep the agitation from
his voice.

'Agnes said she didn't want Lisa back again, and Alan and I
would like to take legal guardianship of her, well . . . it's really
kinship adoption. You would relinquish all parental rights to
her, but I need you to both sign a written agreement. I'll get my
solicitor to draft a letter and start the process. I know you don't
want her back, and I also know she doesn't want to come back
to Fairfield.'

Des grunted into the phone. 'I'll discuss it further with Agnes, but in view of the current events, I think it's a bloody good
idea. No-one wants her back except Mark, and probably the
dog. But I know Agnes will want to speak to you herself.'

Zena rolled her eyes. 'I wonder if you ever think about the words that tumble out of your mouth, Des. This is your daughter, your own flesh and blood.' Silence.

Zena continued. 'I think it's in everybody's interests that we instigate this adoption, Des. As I said, I'll talk to my solicitor and get it underway. Is there anything you want to say or for me to tell Lisa?'

'No, just get on with it. I don't need a third hysterical female venting their opinion. Two in the house is bad enough. I have really had a gutful of bloody women. It makes a man mad!'

'One other thing, Des, before I go. You didn't mention to Mark about coming up to Woori. Why not? I know it didn't just slip your mind.'

Hesitation. 'Not a good idea at this stage,' he said abruptly.

'But Des, they are—' He slammed down the phone.

Zena finished the sentence. 'Siblings.' She resolved to call her solicitor the next morning.

Zena returned to the kitchen and began setting the table when Lisa appeared. 'Hey, that's my job'.

'It's okay, Lisa. I needed to get my mind off the phone call.'

'Oh . . . . what happened?' Lisa sat down, preparing for bad news.

'The usual. Des was belligerent and devoid of emotion. He wants to talk to Agnes about the adoption process. He basically consented, but I'll give it a few days and see if anything comes out of my call this afternoon. Agnes may just agree. One can only hope, darling girl. Oh, there's the bike, so Alan is just about to come up those stairs.'

'What's new?' said Alan as he washed his hands under the kitchen tap.

'As I told Lisa, just the usual nonsense with my brother and his hag of a wife. But at least I got to speak to Des without Agnes interjecting on the side. Agnes was out, consoling poor old Janine. But he feels us adopting Lisa legally is the right thing to do. He said he didn't want another hysterical female in the house! The sad part is that Mark picked up first, and Des had not even told him about the idea of him coming up here.'

Lisa looked despondent. 'It's been so long, Aunty. I'm sixteen now and Mark is thirteen. That's close to two years that we haven't seen each other. They know how close we were!'

'That's the problem, Lisa. Agnes is doing this deliberately and probably enjoying every minute of it. Trying to keep you separate, but they can't do this forever. Something will eventually give. I have tried so many times to get Mark on the phone for you.'

After dinner they sat on the verandah, watching the sunset. It was bold and rich in colour. 'Sunsets are truly a gift of nature,' said Alan. 'I never tire of them . . . and like people, they're all different.'

'Neither do I,' said Zena, smiling. 'That poem by Emerson is so fitting.'

'What's that, my dear?'

'Every sunset brings the promise of a new dawn.' They all watched the bright red circle sink slowly into the horizon, the darkness spreading across the plains, dipping into its folds like an unmade bed.

Lisa sat in silence with a mixture of emotions. Her own parents didn't want her, but the two people she was sitting with right now wanted her to be their own and to look after her. It was a paradox. Lisa thought about all the girls who had been sent to Girls Homes just because they were not wanted by their own parents, or a new stepfather or stepmother had rejected them. They were all deemed uncontrollable for the slightest err. The decision to abandon them never seemed to be questioned by the authorities; it was just an awful accepted thing. The girls were just sent away. Lisa hated that word: uncontrollable.

'Cat got your tongue, kid?' asked Alan.

'No, I was just alone with my thoughts for the moment. Happy and sad at the same time. I wonder why my parents, who were supposed to be my caretakers, don't want me. Have never really wanted me. Why did they have me if they never wanted me? I just don't get it. Even a cat will take its kittens.'

EIGHT

DEATH BECOMES HER

Mitch was true to form. The Land Rover pulled up at exactly 8.00 a.m.

Zena glanced at Lisa. 'Could have set my watch by that boy. You good to go?'

'Yep, fine. A little nervous but interested to see their property.'

'You'll like Kate. Have fun, just enjoy yourself. I know it's not Billy, but Mitch can be a friend. My fun for the day is calling Agnes this morning. Des would have talked to her last night. Not a call I want to make, but if I call now, she'll be at home on her own. I need to confirm with my solicitor that I have spoken to both parties and that they're in agreement. He can then send his letter.'

'Off you go now. I may have some news when you get back. Give Kate a hug from me.' Zena watched as Lisa headed down the back stairs. Mitch was in view and smiled as he saw Lisa. They walked to the compound gates, and Lisa turned back to wave to her aunt.

Mitch greeted her warmly. 'Morning, Lisa, good to see you,' he grinned as he opened the car door. 'Got lots to show you, and Mum has made a chocolate cake for morning tea. My favourite. Hey, you look nice . . . and you smell good too!' Mitch sniffed the air. Lisa shrank into the seat as he walked around to the driver side. His comments made her feel uneasy.

'I'm looking forward to showing you Woodside,' he said as he slid in next to her. He seemed to fill the whole car.

'Thanks, Mitch. I'm looking forward to seeing it. Alan said the place is amazing.'

'Sure is.' Mitch flashed a broad smile and gunned the Land Rover.

◊

Zena was glad she had the house to herself. This phone call would be like going into battle. How she hated talking to that woman. She took a deep breath as she dialled. On the sixth ring, she was about to hang up, when the receiver was finally lifted.

'Hello, Agnes speaking.'

'Hi, Agnes, it's Zena. How are you? She felt the iciness penetrate down the phone line.

'I thought I told you never to call again!' Agnes yelled.

Zena could envision her pinched lips and scowling face. 'I'm just calling to see if Des spoke to you about the kinship adoption. Lisa is doing very well, and it's clear you don't want her in the family home.'

'I don't give a flying fuck how she is doing! She has ruined people's lives with her lying and accusations. My daughter is a wreck, and her husband is no doubt going through hell. He has shot through, and who wouldn't with those bloody detectives snooping about. She's a lying little bitch. I'd like to wring her neck.'

Agnes's voice became even shriller and she spoke so quickly that she seemed to gasp for breath with each passing word. Zena persevered.

'Agnes, it is up to the detectives and the courts to prove the allegations made by Lisa. I strongly doubt that she is lying—

Her words were cut off as Agnes talked over her. 'Don't bloody well call here again! Do you hear! I am about to have a nervous breakdown myself. I don't want to know about her. She is no daughter of mine. I should have drowned her in a bucket when she was born. Send the fucking adoption papers, we will both be glad to sign!'

The line went dead. Zena cradled the phone to her ear and stared at the wall. *I tried to be pleasant*, she thought as she put the phone down and shook her head in dismay. Those two were not fit to be parents.

'What's up, darling wife?' said Alan as he came into the house. 'You don't look too happy.'

'I am, really. I got what I wanted. I just spoke to Agnes about Lisa. The usual screaming. Lisa is a lying bitch and we are to send the adoption papers. At least I can now say I spoke to the two of them, and they are both in agreement. The only thing I'm worried about is Mark. Just how do we get him up here? Lisa misses him, and they are close siblings. Why don't they see that?'

Alan put his arms around her. 'People will think and do what they want; it's impossible to change that. You've done all you can, so no more talk of this. Just let the cops do their job, and Jeff our solicitor can get the ball rolling with the adoption process. When the cops prove what those mongrels have done, Agnes will have to eat her bloody words, and then hopefully you can get Mark up here.'

'Some people never believe though, Alan,' whispered Zena.

'True, but Agnes and Des may with time, and we can still get the boy up here. There's also the phone. Lisa can call him, you know. Call him every night if she wants.'

'Yes, I guess there are other alternatives until we get him up here. I'll call my solicitor now and get this process going.'

Zena discussed the matter with her solicitor, Jeff Plowright, for well over an hour. He made notes as she spoke, and by the time they had finished, he had a good idea of the situation and what needed to be done. What a relief. Such a capable man. He handled all their affairs and would do everything right, and quickly.

As she sat on the small stool next to the phone, it suddenly rang, startling her. 'Hello . . . this is Zena Smith.'

'Gosh, that was quick,' chuckled Detective Collette.

Zena laughed. 'I was sitting next to the phone, Andrew. Literally just got off it.'

'Very good. I just wanted to give you an update.'

'I could do with some good news, so tell me what's happened?'

'As you know, Detective Adler took nearly twenty statements from the girls currently in the Parramatta Girls Home and provided this information to the prosecutor. I have to say that he is a pretty tough guy, and you really have to have convincing evidence when you present to him, but when he read the statements from the girls, his face said it all. He looked at me and said it was truly horrifying.'

'I am so glad it's black and white, Andrew. Abuse of power, horrific and humiliating treatment of the young girls. We have opened Pandora's box,' said Zena. 'What is particularly sad and also disgusts me is that a lot of the girls were young Aboriginal girls, taken from their homes.'

'Yes, the whole institution is disgusting, and I couldn't agree more . . . We are just the tip of the iceberg,' admitted Andrew. 'Some of the girls said in their statements that they were taken to other sections of the institution and shared around with the male officers and their friends. This was run by Child Welfare, and they got away with it for so long. I truly have to shake my head.'

'I don't know where the best interests of the children were, Andrew,' sighed Zena, her mind reeling.

'I don't know either, Zena. Anyway, Superintendent Ash was already in remand as I told you, but the collation of this material makes it pretty clear Lisa was telling the truth. The matter will still go to the district court when a date has been set, but I am so pleased Lisa will not need to attend now.'

'That is good news, and I'm buzzing after hearing that, Andrew. I guess that Ash bloke realised there really was no way out. Bravo,' said Zena.

'Yes, Zena, overwhelming evidence. So many girls, and their statements were all taken individually. All had received the same sexual abuse of some form. Lisa started the ball rolling, and Jim said some cases were even more sickening. One girl said it was a hell hole and another said she was sent there at the age of five. With this Ash monster, it was like a smorgasbord. All those young girls unprotected. If it weren't for Lisa, it would have continued for a long time. There will no doubt be an investigation into the Girls Home with possible closure. Sometimes there is a Royal Commission. I hope so. Their innocence has been stolen,' said Andrew gravely.

'Lisa was pleased when I told her what had occurred to Superintendent Ash after we last spoke. But why do men do this, why does it happen?' asked Zena.

'Who knows, Zena. Power, dominance . . . I can tell you as a detective, we see all manner of things, and I still shake my head. I can recall a book I read way back. It was by a guy called Albert Kinsey. He was a biologist and sexologist, but it was written in the mid-1950s, and he stated that a quarter of girls under the age of fourteen years reported that they had experienced some form of sexual abuse, including exhibitionism, fondling or incest, at rates roughly similar to those reported today.'

'That's awful, Andrew! When will it ever stop?'

'It's more out in the open now than ever before, but you will always get the predators,' replied Andrew soberly.

'Any news on the other one as yet?' asked Zena.

'We had a sighting on the South Coast, down near Merimbula. The local police saw his number plate, but they got stuck behind a semi-trailer on a winding coastal road, so they lost him.'

'Merimbula? Gosh that's a long way from the western suburbs,' said Zena, puzzled. 'I went there many years ago for school holidays. Such a beautiful sleepy beach town. I wonder why he would head that way?'

'Well, as you said, it's sleepy, so he's probably lying low, but we will catch up to him. He cannot hide forever.'

'Thanks, Andrew. You have made my day. Keep me posted. I'll let Lisa know when she gets in.'

'No problem. Just let her know it was only due to her that we have been able to halt this abominable system. She has saved a lot of further hurt to the girls there. From the information we have gathered, there was mental and severe physical abuse as well as the use of pharmaceuticals to control the girls' behaviour. The girls were reluctant initially to provide information as they all seem to have these feelings of shame. This absolute shame that they did something wrong, and they feel so guilty. It really is shocking. No wonder they turn to drug addiction, prostitution and suicide. We will have a tough time trying to follow up the girls who have been released.'

'Yes, that is the one thing Lisa kept saying, that she felt so ashamed and that everything was her fault. Where do we go from here?' asked Zena.

'We just finish the prosecution process. If I hear anything else, I'll let you know . . . it's just a matter of waiting for the dis-

trict court to hand the sentence down,' said Andrew, his sombre voice running down the phone line. Zena thanked him and
they disconnected.

It was nearly 1.00 p.m. when Alan came in for lunch. His face
was sunburnt, and he looked tired.

'I think some iced water and a sandwich is in order, Alan.
You look buggered.'

'Trying to get the water pumps to the stock working, bloody
hot in the shed. Like a sauna.'

'What's wrong with the pumps?' queried Zena.

'Nothing. Absolutely bloody nothing. Those Southern Cross
pumps are just about fail proof,' replied Alan.

'You know the cut-off switch to the diesel motor always stays
on, so it pumps water to the stock. No reason ever to turn the
bloody thing off. Well, the switch was off, and if I wasn't so diligent checking the pumps, we would have bloody dead sheep
everywhere!'

'God, Alan, what is happening! Are you sure you didn't accidentally bump the switch?'

'Yes, I'm sure . . . bloody sure. It's the last thing I look at
when I leave the shed, that the switch is on, then I close the
door,' advised Alan.

'Something isn't right, here. First the saddle and bridle and
now switches to our pumps suddenly being turned off. What
do you think? I mean really, Alan, these things just don't happen without some human intervention,' stated Zena.

'Someone is definitely hanging about. Lisa is not imagining
things. That saddle of hers looked like it had been dropped, as
if someone had been disturbed, dropped it and then bolted. I
don't know what exactly is going on or why someone would be
doing these things but from now on, keep an eye out, and we
lock doors of a night. I'll put a lock on the Tack Room and

bring Buster and Dougy from across the bore to inside the compound. They are not savage but their barking may scare anyone off and alert us.' Alan exhaled deeply and ran his hands through his hair.

'We just have to deal with it and hope I catch the bastard. Anyway, I saw a car heading this way . . . saw the red dust before the car. Mitch's Land Rover, I'd say.'

'Probably bringing Lisa home. He was here on the dot at 8.00 a.m. Be interesting to see what she thought about Woodside and if she enjoyed Mitch's company. Maybe best not to say anything about the pumps, it might spook her,' said Zena.

Zena heard the phone ringing again. 'I'll get it, Alan. See if Mitch wants a cool drink or . . . well, you know. Just offer him something. I'll just get this call.'

Mitch left, and Alan sat talking to Lisa about her day.

'It's so big Alan, bigger than Woori. Mitch said just over 30,000 acres. His mum . . . Kate . . . is really lovely, and her house, everything was so French. The home had such high ceilings, tall windows with these beautifully panelled walls. One room was painted yellow like butter, and when the light streamed through the window, it looked like gold. I thought I was in heaven! Their floors were like ours, polished woods and beautiful Persian and Oriental rugs. There were all these glistening mirrors and interesting pieces of furniture and so many oil paintings,' Lisa exclaimed breathlessly.

'So, I gather you enjoyed yourself,' remarked Alan.

'Yeah, I did. I surprised myself. Mitch talked so passionately about the land and how Woodside had been in the family for three generations. He knows a great deal about farming and sheep and did Polocrosse, so he must be good in the saddle too' said Lisa.

'Well, kid, you may have a new riding partner, maybe get a few tips from Mitch,' grinned Alan.

'I'm glad I did go. I was hesitant but Woodside is a beautiful property, and it was a perfect day to wander around and sit with his mother, Kate. I could not believe how long their driveway was though and all the eucalyptus trees that had been planted along it. It's amazing. So big compared to Woori, and so many staff. Mitch explained why they need eight extra help-ers. Too much for them on their own, with dogs, sheep, cattle and the horses, not to mention maintenance and fencing. He said the staff look after the property when the Walker family want a break or a trip.'

'Yeah, that's a good idea. I find it so bloody difficult to leave Woori for that very reason.'

'Mitch said he could help with that if you wanted a short break or even a longer trip, now that he's back.'

'He's a good boy, Lisa, and just next door. I think Kate would love to see grandchildren someday,' Alan said with a wink.

'Oh,' Lisa said with surprise. 'Not too sure he should be looking in my direction then!' As Lisa finished the sentence, Zena appeared. She was solemn, her face was drained, and Lisa knew instantly something was wrong.

'What's up?' asked Alan, as they both turned to face her.

'That was Des. I don't know how to say this, Lisa, there is no easy way.'

'What, Aunty! What's wrong?' Thoughts raced through her head. *Superintendent Ash! Lenny! The whole investigation! Am I go-ing to court? My brother?* Fear gripped her. She thought the worst and began to panic.

'Tell me!' she blurted, rising from her chair, urgency in her voice.

'Your mother Agnes just passed away. I tried to speak to her today but she was belligerent and eventually hung up. Her breathing on the phone was very laboured, but I put it down to anger . . . The way she huffed and puffed.'

Lisa's face twisted and her cheeks paled. A stunned silence filled the room momentarily. Her mouth fell open with surprise, and her lips moved as if she wanted to say something but couldn't. Her heart was beating wildly in her chest as a gamut of emotions tore through her body. Shock, and to her horror, some form of slight relief that the powerful hurt this woman caused would never raise its head again. Her words came tumbling out.

'What! Dead. Dead! I can't believe it. Dead! God, she was so horrible, no love, nothing, and now gone! My mother. Dead!' Lisa wailed, shaking her head from side to side.

Lisa's anguish was apparent as Zena took her hands. Lisa was silently screaming. The tears slowly fell down her cheeks like an unbroken stream. She was suffocating with each breath, trying to hold in her pride.

Her voice was broken. 'I feel . . . so, so . . . numb, Aunty. I don't know what else to say. My mother is dead. I know she didn't love me . . . never wanted me, but she was my mother. Why? Why didn't she love me? What did I do to make her hate me for all my life?' Lisa's breath hissed out through clenched teeth. Now she'd never know.

Zena held her niece until silence filled the room. Lisa had no more strength, and when she finally spoke, it was a mixture of punctuated words and more tears.

Lisa wiped her eyes and looked at her aunt. 'What do I say? What do I do? I'm angry that she didn't love me and angry I didn't get to say goodbye, but she wouldn't have wanted me near her anyway. She made that perfectly clear.' Lisa felt wretched inside. Her voice was raspy now. 'It could have been so different. Why didn't she love me like she was supposed to?' Lisa grappled with her thoughts.

'What was the cause of death?' asked Alan.

'Massive heart attack. She was dead by the time she hit the kitchen floor.'

'Did she mention me at all when you spoke on the phone?' Lisa's voice was hoarse.

'No, she didn't mention you really, and the phone call I had with her was very difficult. Do you want to go down to Sydney for the funeral, Lisa?' asked Zena. 'You realise you'll run into Janine and Des.'

Lisa considered this before replying. 'Yes, I know that, Aunty, but I really want to go. I may be able to see my brother. It's been so long.' She stared listlessly at the wall and began to tremble. There were too many emotions flooding through her right now.

'Des is going to call me when the funeral arrangements have been made. What about we ask Des then about Mark, and perhaps he can come up for the school holidays. But I need to choose my timing about that. It's a little sensitive at this time, but he may be okay with a different discussion. Best to test the waters. I don't want to be there consoling him for the loss of his wife and then blurt out can we take Mark for a holiday.'

Lisa nodded. 'I understand. But it would be so good just to see my brother and spend time with him.'

Over dinner, despite the situation, they talked about Woodside. Zena watched Lisa's body language. She kept rubbing her arms when Mitch's name was mentioned. *She is not really comfortable*, Zena thought. *Billy. He is always there.*

Zena kissed Lisa goodnight after they cleared the table. 'You have an early night, darling girl. Alan will give me a hand. It's a miserable time to lose your mother, particularly as I'm sure there were so many things you wanted to say to her, but paying your respects at her funeral, despite the treatment she handed to you over the years, is a sign of maturity and integrity. I am so proud of you, Lisa. Try and get some sleep, honey.'

◊

In bed that night, Zena turned to Alan. 'I didn't have the heart to tell her what Agnes said on the phone.'

'Nothing to achieve with that,' agreed Alan.

'How was Mitch? Sorry, I didn't get to chat with him. He must have been in a hurry?'

'He was in a hurry, but from watching him when he walked Lisa to the back stairs, the poor bugger is besotted. A grin from ear to ear. I'm sure he would have loved to come in and stay a bit longer but he had to get back home.'

'Strange how some people get so many hurdles thrown at them in life. Lisa has had so many hurdles to jump. It's a wonder she hasn't gone off the rails. First the horrific abuse from two men, then the investigation, forbidden to see her brother, the death of her mother, what next? But I hope 1972 is a better year for her. She'll be seventeen. You never get two horrible years in a row,' announced Zena.

'By the way, that reminds me. It's December now, and jewellers get busy around this time. I will have to take those opals from Old Harry into town to Bill Carlton, the jeweller, and get the earrings made. I was thinking either for Christmas or her birthday,' said Alan.

'Great idea, Alan. I can't wait to see them on her. A Christmas present would be good. That was so very generous of Harry. I will miss the old bugger this coming season. Everything changes, doesn't it?'

'Yes, darling wife, nothing ever stays the same.'

NINE

MENDING BRIDGES

By lunchtime the following day, Des still had not called. Zena looked at her watch. *Damn it, Desmond. I'll call. I want to know what's happening.* She picked up the phone and dialled.

Des answered very quickly.

'Hi, Des. It's Zena. How are you? I am sorry this has happened. It must be such a sad time for you in relation to Agnes and everything that seems to be happening at the moment. I want you to know how sorry we are for your loss. Let me know if I can do anything to help. Despite our differences, I am always here for you.'

There was a long pause, and she waited for something abrupt to come from his mouth. 'Thanks, Zena. I know you two did not get on and there was a lot of friction between Lisa and Agnes. She was a difficult woman . . . headstrong and sometimes spiteful, but I loved her in my own way just the same. I am sure these allegations Lisa has made sent her to an early grave. I don't know what to think.'

'Look, Des, I tried to talk to Agnes and said to leave it to the detectives to produce the evidence. They have now actually charged the superintendent of the Parramatta Girls Home, but he broke down and formally confessed. There will be further arrests as other guards were involved in the sexual abuse of the young girls. Statements have been taken from those who are still there, which will be used in evidence. Lisa has suffered the most terrible abuse, as have all those other girls. Young innocent girls, Des, who should never have been sent there. Stepfathers who were raping them at home and then said the girls were uncontrollable; new boyfriends of the mothers, sexually interfering with the young girls, and pregnant girls, all thrown into the one pot. If only Agnes had comforted Lisa or not taken sides and tried to get to the bottom of things initially, with the change in her behaviour, the Girls Home situation may never have arisen.'

'God . . . Zena, is that right?' He sounded devastated. 'Agnes was not one for patience, and taking the time to sort things out wasn't her. Thank goodness she isn't here to hear that information. That would have killed her anyway, just the shock of it.'

'I did try to tell her, Des, but she just wouldn't believe it. The detectives are waiting for a date from the district court so that Superintendent Ash can be formally charged . . . and of course you would know Lenny has disappeared.' Zena touched lightly on the subject.

'Yes, I heard. Why would he run off? Janine is beside herself. As I said to you on the phone, she's hysterical and threatening to kill Lisa for lying and bringing shame to her and the family. She can be nasty, just like Agnes. Sometimes there's no filter on that mouth of hers, and she screams like a bloody banshee.'

'I don't know why Lenny would disappear, Des, especially if he has done nothing wrong. To me, his disappearance points to guilt. It just doesn't look good, does it?' contended Zena.

Des sighed deeply. 'Yes . . . you are probably right. Why would someone innocent take off?'

Zena changed the subject back to Agnes's funeral. 'When is the funeral, Des? Lisa wants to come down with me and pay her final respects to her mother.'

'It's next Wednesday at the Presbyterian Church. A 10.00 a.m. service and then the burial is at Rookwood.'

'Okay, we'll be down on the Tuesday evening,' said Zena.

'Do you want to stay here, Zena? I can bunk in with Mark. You and Lisa can have my bed.'

'Are you sure, Des? That would be great. Lisa can catch up with Mark, and we can all drive to the church. How is Mark taking things?'

'He's a tough kid but understandably upset. But he will, like all of us, get through this. He does miss his sister though. I have to admit that. They were close, and maybe it was wrong of Agnes and me to deny them their connection.'

His voice was tinged with sadness. 'Agnes tried to keep them apart to hurt Lisa. She knew how close they were and every time I brought it up, she thundered me down. I just gave up. Mark requested so many times to call Lisa, but Agnes flatly refused. I know he would like to go up there for a visit.'

Zena shook her head. *Why does it take a death or a tragedy to make things good?* 'Lisa would be thrilled Des, and we are happy to fly him up.'

'That's very generous of you, Zena. I'll tell him tonight that you are both coming next week.'

'Take care, Des. We should be there in the afternoon. I'm glad we are talking again.'

'Me too, Zena. I have been spineless and weak, a failure to my daughter. I deserted her when she needed me the most, but I just went along with Agnes's wishes. It was easier to give in than fight. In retrospect, it was so wrong. She was always the antagonist, our Agnes.'

'It's okay, Des. Lisa will be really happy just at the prospect of seeing her brother. Let's work on that and building relationships.' When Zena put down the phone, she felt that things were finally getting better. *It was like talking to my brother from years back. Marriage changed him along the way, as well as the drink. Maybe he will have a chance to become the person I once knew and loved.*

Over dinner, Zena quietly mentioned she had spoken to Des. Lisa put down her cutlery, trying to take in what her aunt had just said.

'What was he like, Aunty? How did he sound?' pressed Lisa.

'He sounded very sad . . . almost lost. I told him we would head down there Tuesday evening. The funeral is the following day. We are bunking in with them at the house.'

Lisa looked shocked. 'In the house . . . my old house!'

'Yes. I thought it would be a good idea. I can change this, Lisa, if you're not comfortable. But it was Des who suggested it.'

There was a silence as Lisa drank in the information and the fact that she would be stepping back into the old house.

'You'll get to see Mark and be able to spend more time with him, Lisa. But I can book a hotel if you prefer.'

'It's okay, kid, to speak your mind,' Alan interjected.

'No, no, it's okay. I guess . . . No, it was just the shock at the thought of going back there but you'll be with me, Aunty.'

'Always. Let's see how you feel when you get there. If you feel so uneasy, then we can easily find alternative accommodation. I have to say Des was different on the phone. He may have done a lot of self-assessing. Sometimes death changes things. The other good news is that Des has agreed to let Mark come up here.'

'Oh, Aunty, that's wonderful!' Lisa brightened. 'It's been so long since I last saw him. He would have grown, just like me. I can't wait to see him. Why did it take the death of my mother for all this to happen?'

'Exactly, Lisa. I thought the same, and you know, I think your father did too.'

'Will he like me or what do you think he will say to me . . . or . . . ' Lisa's voice trailed off.

'I think things will be a lot better . . . and really, what's not to like about you! You have matured and grown so beautifully. Maybe, it might be initially awkward, but things have a way of sorting themselves. Catching up with your brother will be fabulous, but you also have to deal with the funeral, your father and Janine.'

Lisa looked at Alan. 'I will be the rabbit in the spotlight.'

'Not at all, kid. The only one you have to look out for is Janine. She'll be on a mission, that one. Like a wild haired terrier.'

Lisa shuddered at the thought.

TEN

THE FUNERAL

It was early Monday morning. The sun was just showing her face, and the silhouettes of the cockatoos in the sky were majestic as Alan loaded their bags into the Zephyr.

'Travel safely, my girls.' Alan kissed them both goodbye.

'I'll call you, Alan, but please keep an eye over your shoulder. I know nothing has happened since the issue with the pump switch, but promise me you will lock the doors at night,' pleaded Zena.

'Promise . . . Anyway, I have the savage Buster and Dougy prowling around the compound at night.'

Zena laughed as she got into the Zephyr. 'Those two would lick anyone to death.'

The drive to Sydney was good for both Zena and Lisa. There were no interruptions on the long stretches of road. The conversations they had were therapeutic. Fears were discussed about the pending visit, the funeral, confronting Janine and of course the police investigation.

'We'll stay Monday night at the Hydro Majestic, Lisa. It's a glorious hotel in the Blue Mountains with views over the spectacular Megalong Valley. It's a little treat for both of us as I know you think you are heading into another storm with your father. You will adore it there. You feel an affinity for the Aboriginal people, Lisa, so . . . Megalong is an Aboriginal word for "Valley under the Rock".'

Lisa smiled. 'I bet the ladies know this place, Aunty. Funny, Dad always called the old house the Fibro Majestic.' Her thoughts turned to Binna and Ningali and the stories she had heard when sitting with them. *I wonder if they have stories about Megalong?*

When they pulled into the driveway of the hotel, the afternoon sun over the valley was breathtaking. Hues of blue and purple streaked across the spectacular rock faces like an artist's canvas.

'Wow, look at this place, it's incredible!' breathed Lisa.

'Yes, it's spectacular, Lisa. Truly ethereal. One of my favourites. Built in the late 1800s and opened around 1904. It has wonderful views over the Megalong Valley. It was built by Mark Foy, a wealthy retailer. Very art deco and Edwardian.' Zena pointed to a dome.

'That was bought in Chicago and shipped to Australia, and then incredibly, dragged up here by bullocks and reassembled. It was apparently built to be a sanatorium, like a health spa, but it failed, something to do with mineral spring water. There was none, so he imported an awful-tasting mineral water from Germany. Shame really, as he finally sold the hotel. During World War Two, one of the buildings here was turned over to the US troops as a hospital. An extraordinary history, really. Come on, let's check in. I'm famished,' laughed Zena.

Dinner was in the main dining room, which was very old world with chandeliers and views over the valley.

'It's almost otherworldly, Aunty, this atmosphere,' Lisa admired as she stroked the white damask table cloth. 'The silver cutlery, the beautiful glasses and the waiters seem to hover and do everything for you.' Her mind wandering, Lisa thought about the weevils in her food at the Girls Home and the dining room with the other girls.

'Hey, you,' said Zena. 'You just left . . . where were you?'

'I was just thinking, here I am sitting at this beautiful place and not so long ago, I had porridge with weevils.'

'I know. It's been a major transition for you, and you have been seriously challenged for all your young years and are about to be so again, by just seeing your father and Janine,' admitted Zena. 'It will be tough, but once you cross the bridge and get started, it will be easier for all of us. Especially you. Des will be just as nervous, Lisa. There was something about his voice on the phone that I have not heard in years.'

'What was that, Aunty?' asked Lisa.

'Compassion.'

After dinner Zena spoke before curling up into bed. 'That scrawny little girl with the dark circles under her eyes has gone. Be strong and confident. You have done nothing wrong and your father knows that now. I told him about the statements from the other girls. I would say he is truly remorseful. Try and sleep. I am right next to you if you need me.'

When they woke and Lisa looked out from the windows, the sunrise over the escarpment was spectacular. *I think this must be like heaven. Up here with the spirits. Valley under the rock.*

'You're awake,' said Zena as she yawned and stretched.

'Sorry, Aunty. I tried to be quiet but I just had to look at that view again.'

'Well, you look, and I will jump in the shower. We need to get moving as Sydney traffic is different to our sort of traffic.'

After a light continental breakfast, they headed towards Sydney. Zena realised how much she hated it. *Bloody traffic. Bloody impatient idiots.* Lisa grew much quieter as suburbia loomed before them and houses ran back to back for miles, with the long roads, cul-de-sacs, street signs and lights that ran through the once-sleepy suburbs. It was all tar and cement as they drove into the suburbs.

Lisa thought to herself, *Getting closer to home. My old home.* She shivered.

Her aunt interrupted her thoughts before they could run away from her. 'Not a kangaroo to be seen. How are the nerves, Lisa? I would say we will hit Fairfield in about fifty minutes. It will be a bit different to the Hydro Majestic. You'll be sharing a bed with me!'

Lisa laughed. Her aunt's humour broke the tension slightly.

'I have butterflies. And yes, I'm so nervous, Aunty. I hope my father sees me differently. I just hope he can find love in his heart, but on top of all of this, I am so looking forward to seeing my brother.'

'Your father said he was sorry when we spoke. It seems Mark had also asked so many times to speak to you on the phone but as I said, Agnes flatly refused. He said at one stage she pulled the phone out from the wall and hid it. She just wanted to hurt you. Strange behaviour for a mother, but let's not dwell on that now.'

They turned on to a long tar road, which was familiar. 'Home,' Lisa murmured. 'The road to my old home.'

'Yes, here we are, Lisa. Fairfield.' Lisa swivelled her head around, taking in all the houses. The paddocks that were once empty and green were now filled with houses. The long road that used to be dirt was now tarred.

'This is the road to home but . . . everything has changed!' exclaimed Lisa.

They pulled into the old driveway. It was late Tuesday afternoon and a dog was barking. 'It's Cassius! He's still alive.' Lisa's eyes lit up. 'Will he remember me?'

'Of course he will,' reassured her aunt. 'Dogs don't forget those they love.'

They parked the car and walked up to the front door. It felt strange to knock on the door after all these years.

The door opened slowly, and her brother Des stood before her. He had visibly aged. 'Hi Zena, it's been a long time, too long. Thank you for coming.'

Zena stepped into the hallway, and it had a strange musty smell. 'Lisa is just behind me, bringing the bags.'

Zena kissed Des on the cheek. He seemed very tentative. Lisa carried two bags and stood frozen as she looked at her father in the doorway.

'Dad,' she whispered, and thoughts of yesteryear flashed through her mind. The beatings, the lack of love, the punishment. She felt her heart racing as if it would burst through her chest.

Zena extended her arm. 'Come, darling. It's alright. I'm here.' Lisa's father stood in awe. Lisa was now a young woman and growing into a real beauty. She was no longer scrawny, but had a real presence about her. *Is this the same girl my wife had no time for, even hated? My daughter.*

Lisa moved towards her father and aunt, her legs no longer a part of her body. They felt so heavy. Her palms were damp with sweat. A thousand awful memories flooded her mind as she slowly put the bags down.

'Hi, Lisa. It's good to see you after all this time,' her father said. She was wary and although her instinct was to go to him, she kept her distance. As she came closer, she extended her hand. It was a weak handshake, almost as if she was frightened to touch. To connect.

'Just put your bags in the room up there, it's our old room, and I'll put the kettle on. Mark is at school but will be home in a couple of hours. Which will give us time to chat.'

As she moved towards the bedroom with the bags, Lisa felt herself gag. The carpets were worn and the place smelled old. It was a place of sorrow, and a place where she felt haunted by her own unhappiness. She felt the wind go out of her sails. She wanted to be back at Woori.

When Lisa came out of the bedroom, she sat down, and saw the sorrow in her father's eyes. She looked at the chair he was sitting in and had visions of the electric cord. Too many horrible memories.

Zena placed her hand over his and said, 'I'm sorry for your loss, Des. She was a tough lady, but you stuck by her.'

'Yes, I did. It will be different without her, but I guess you adjust. But I am so sorry about the lack of contact between you, Mark and Lisa not being able to speak to each other and the events that have taken place here. You can get caught up in your own mess.'

He looked at Lisa, his eyes watery. 'It's probably too late to apologise, Lisa. Nothing can take away what you have suffered, here and at that Girls Home. Agnes was so convinced you were lying. Please forgive me. I don't know what else to say.'

Lisa was stunned. Her father, a grown man, was asking for her forgiveness. Redemption.

'Umm, Dad, I . . . I just don't know what to say; things are all jumbled and there's so much pain inside me.' She felt her lips tremble.

Zena stepped in. Her voice was soft and calming. 'We have a lot ahead of us and we accept that there has been ignorance, pain and suffering for all people, but especially endured by Lisa. But we are here now for Agnes and to pay our respects.' *Even though I couldn't stand the bloody woman.*

Lisa gulped, and the tears filled her eyes. She looked at her father's sorrowful face.

'For now, let us try and heal. We have a long way to go and we have to get past the funeral,' said Zena.

Des nodded with deep sincerity.

'What about the funeral arrangements? Is everything sorted?' asked Zena.

'Yes, all sorted. As I said, the service is at 10.00 a.m. tomorrow at the Presbyterian Church and then down to Rookwood Cemetery for the burial.'

Zena spoke. 'I just wish Agnes had been alive to see the truth, Des, and what has evolved from the police investigations. It has been a horrendous time with the investigation, and with Lisa reliving the abuse and all the explicit details. But not only for her, the other girls as well. She has suffered both physically and mentally at a devastating level. She has been seeing a psychiatrist for counselling, which has been invaluable. No girl, let alone anyone, should have been subjected to the abuse she endured.'

Lisa sat silently. She could hear the anguish in her aunt's voice and saw the shame in her father's eyes. He put his head down and openly wept. 'I am so sorry, Lisa. I was never there for you. I was so weak. I should have protected you.'

Lisa could only gaze at him dully.

'But Des, there is a positive. If Lisa had not been sent to the Girls Home, maybe the abuse of those girls would not have been discovered for a long time. The tremendous, long-standing abuse will now be out in the open. The girls will also hopefully get the counselling they deserve, although I am sure some girls will just scatter to the winds.'

The three of them sat in the little kitchen, all affected by the lost years, mistakes and the process that was now evolving. Life was taking a different course.

Des finally spoke. 'Agnes was bitter to the end about what Lisa had said. It ate her up. She lashed out at everyone. She was inconsolable when she heard about the allegations Lisa had made against Lenny, and she wanted to strike out at everyone. Living with her was a nightmare. She gravitated towards Janine and the two were as thick as thieves, feeding off each other's misery. As I said, Janine wanted to kill Lisa, even speaks of it now. It's been terrible. I worried for Mark under this atmosphere. I have to say since her death the house has been very quiet and peaceful.'

'I can imagine it must be quiet, Des. You know as well as me that Agnes was a hurricane and could take the wind out of your sails with her cutting words. I say this respectfully at this time, but I wonder if she didn't bring herself to an early grave. She just was filled with so much hate. It was unnecessary and bordered on evil. Lisa was devastated that she was prevented from speaking to Mark. It's a sorry thing, death; it brings our mistakes to the fore. Makes us realise what we should have or could have done,' said Zena.

'Life lessons. We make terrible mistakes sometimes. How do you correct these?' asked Des sincerely. 'I'll do my best, that's all I can do. Anyway, Mark should be home soon. You will be surprised when you see him, Lisa. He loves swimming and took to the water like a fish. Knocked the weight off, and he won't let me near his hair anymore. He turned thirteen two weeks ago.'

Lisa so wanted to see her brother. She could not envisage a sleeker version of him. Excitement filled her thoughts. She wanted to give him a big hug.

'I saw Cassius at the side gate, Dad. Can I go see him?'

'Sure, Lisa. He's getting on though now. Has arthritis in the back legs but is still a great watch dog. Can't even get a bloody newspaper delivered. Everyone is still terrified of the old boy.'

Lisa rose from her seat and walked towards the back door. *Will the dog remember her?* When she got to the back door, to her right were the bunks she had shared with Mark. She shivered. It seemed so long ago.

Lisa pushed the back door open, and Cassius lay on the grass. She noticed the chooks were all gone.

The dog looked at her through his glassy aged eyes. 'Hi Cassy, here boy,' she called. The old dog had trouble getting up but his wagging tail said everything.

Lisa ran down the back steps and fell to her knees. He jumped all over her and then rolled on his back. 'Oh, so you do remember me?' She felt the tears falling down her face. 'You were my best friend,' she said as she scratched his stomach, relief flooding through her. How she had missed him.

◊

Zena tentatively broached the subject of Mark. 'Des, how do you feel about these up-coming school holidays? Mark could come to Woori and stay for a few days. As I mentioned, we can fly him up. You are most welcome to come as well.'

Des didn't even hesitate. 'That's a good idea, Zena. Mark would love some time out with his sister, and of course, you and Alan. Your offer is tempting, but I was thinking of taking off down the coast. I just need some time alone to think about what to do with myself.'

'What do you mean, Des?' Zena pressed.

'Oh, whether to stay here, whether to move down the coast. It means changing Mark's schools at age thirteen, and more upheaval. So it's a lot to think about. Agnes didn't want to move and certainly wasn't into any travel, so it will be nice to hit the road for a change.'

'I think that's a great idea. Mark is your priority, particularly his education. Lisa's was interrupted. I have her with School of the Air Australia completing her Higher School Certificate, albeit in a moderate way, but I am just thinking about a twelve-month period of really polishing her education in a private school as a boarder. Education is empowering, and I think this would be of great benefit. The difficult part is getting her to agree or even leave Woori. She just loves the place. A real bushy.'

Des nodded. 'I'm sorry I was so rude on the phone, Zena. I was surrounded by hostility here, and it often impacts on everything, but it's so good just to sit and chat with you now. It's long overdue, and just looking at Lisa, I am so grateful to you and Alan . . . what you have done for her.'

'If only Agnes had been . . .' Zena sighed.

'If only Agnes had not been such a bitch,' said Des, finishing off the sentence.

'Yes . . . you summed it up, Des. But once Lisa settled, there was never any problem. It was her anguish and the way Agnes treated her that was an issue, but the main thing was the sexual abuse from Lenny. That was the trigger. Let's not think about the mistakes or the unpleasantness it created. We can leave this behind. We cannot change the past but we can always change as we go forward.' There was a noise at the front door and Mark walked in.

Zena gasped. 'Why, good Lord! Look at how tall you've grown, and where is all that chubby puppy fat?' She stood up and hugged Mark. He was so pleased to see her and was lost for words.

'What a good-looking young man you are, Mark, and your father tells me you've grown gills.' That was an ice breaker. Mark laughed. 'Yes, I love to swim now, Aunty Zena; breast stroke is my favourite.'

'So I've heard,' laughed Zena.

'How is my sister? Where is she? asked Mark, dropping his school bag.

'She, like you, has grown . . . and into a beautiful young woman. You'll find her just outside the back door. I think the dog has something to do with it.'

Mark walked to the back door and looked through the screen gauze. His sister was no longer scrawny, and like him had grown and filled out.

'Hey, you,' he called out. Lisa stopped patting Cassius and looked up. Her mouth flew open. Mark flung the door open and ran down the back steps. Their hugs were fierce, and tears streamed down their faces. The world that was once lost to them was now open.

'Oh, I have missed you,' cried Mark as he squeezed her.

'Me too,' smiled Lisa through her tears. She held on tightly, not wanting to let go. Cassius jumped at the pair of them, barking with joy.

Mark stood back and wiped his eyes. 'I tried so many times to call you, but Mum wouldn't allow it.'

'Me too. Aunty tried so many times to get you on the phone, but anyway . . . Wow! Look at you now!' exclaimed Lisa as she wiped the tears with the back of her hand.

Mark was suddenly pensive. 'It was so hard living without you, and then I heard all the horrible things that happened to you, which our mother said were not true. There were days I just shut the world out. I think it was why I took to swimming. Up and down, up and down, that pool, and so solitary. You don't hear anything when you swim.'

Lisa touched his hand. 'I am sorry if I caused you any pain, Marco.'

He kissed her lightly on the cheek. 'You caused me no pain. I wish I could have prevented your pain and the things that happened to you. I know what Lenny did to you. I heard them talking, and I knew something was going on way back then. I could sense your fear. You changed. I wish you had told me. I would have done anything I could.'

Lisa sighed. 'Yes, I know, but you were only ten, Marco. I wish I could change all that but the police have taken over and one of the men has been brought to justice, but Lenny is still on the run.'

'Dad said as much. Janine will be at the funeral. She is horrible and refuses to believe anything.'

'I'm prepared. I've grown stronger, and I speak my mind.'

Mark laughed. 'Gosh, it is just so good to see you.'

'I can't wait to have you come to Woori. It is such an amazing place. Just so special. Words cannot describe it. The animals, the land, the Aboriginal people. It's home,' said Lisa passionately.

'You bet. I look forward to it.' Mark was overjoyed. 'We best head inside. I feel sorry for Dad. He was hen-pecked most of the time, especially the last two years. Mum never stopped ranting. It was like living in a volcano. Every day it would erupt. He's grieving in his own way, but I have to say, and this is awful, the place is so peaceful now. Come on, let's see what is happening in there.' They linked hands and then walked into the house.

Zena delighted in seeing them together again. 'Your father was just chatting about you coming to Woori for a few days over the school holidays. Now that you are a fish, you might prefer an ocean trip, but it would be great to have you on the farm, having fun with your sister. There's lots to do. What do you think?' asked Zena.

Mark showed no hesitation. 'Gosh, that would be great. I would love that.'

'Okay, I'll sort it out with your father and get it all organised. Fly you up. Let's get dinner underway. We have a sad day ahead of us. Let's not forget to think of that,' said Zena, gritting her teeth. She was still mindful it was her brother's wife, and respect was needed.

Mark and Lisa were clearly enjoying their time together, although the funeral hung heavily in the air. Seeing Janine was going to be difficult for Lisa.

'I think we should get an early night. It will be a big day, and funerals are never pleasant. It is a celebration of a life. We may not have agreed with everything Agnes said and did, but we will pay our respects,' said Zena.

'Thanks, Zena. I appreciate that,' said Des.

Mark and Lisa cleared the dishes and sat in the lounge room with Des and Zena. It was mostly conversation around Woori and the wonders of the outback.

'Wait till you see the emus chase the car, Mark, and of a night, you can see the emu constellation. The Aboriginal people say the emus were the creator spirits that used to fly and look over the land.'

'What's an emu constellation then?' Mark asked.

'Well, because we have no city lights, when you look up at the stars, you sort of look to the left of the Southern Cross and you can make out a darkish cloud between the stars, which is the emu's head, and the neck, body and legs are like long dust lanes stretching across the Milky Way. It's so beautiful; I'll show you. My friends Binna and Ningali say the position of the emu in the sky tells them when to collect the emu eggs.'

'That's a lovely story, Lisa. Who are Binna and Nin—?' queried Mark.

'Ningali.' Lisa laughed. 'They are Aboriginal ladies who tell these magical Dreamtime stories. They believe the sun is a lovely old lady who gets up every morning and puts on her red ochre, which is why we get the red sunrise. They say she lights a stringy bark tree and carries it across the sky, giving us all the light and warmth. And the moon, he is the male, and he is big and round and fat like the full moon, but he is lazy.'

'I can't wait, Lisa. I just can't wait. You make it and these stories sound so special,' Mark said excitedly.

'It is!' exclaimed Lisa.

Des looked across at his sister. He looked just as mesmerised as Mark.

'Right then, is everyone ready for bed? I'm ready to hit the sack. Lisa, you are my roommate. Please don't snore. I have had a big day of driving,' her aunt jested. Zena kissed her brother and Mark goodnight.

Des held Zena's hands. Words were not needed. He was grateful she was there.

Des came over gingerly to his daughter. 'Goodnight, Lisa. Thank you for telling us your wonderful stories and thank you for having the courage to be here.' There were a thousand things Lisa could have said but the words would not come out. She looked into her father's eyes and could see his pain. 'Night, Dad. See you in the morning.'

After getting ready, she slipped into bed next to her aunt. It felt strange sleeping in her father's bed. This was also her dead mother's bed. Zena must have read her thoughts.

'You're very restless, darling girl. It's just a bed. Yes, your mother slept in it, but you are here and present. It's your bed for the moment. I know there are so many memories flooding your head. Most of them bad, but I'm here. We need to get through tomorrow, so try and rest up. You were wonderfully courageous today. Respectful and gracious. I think your father can see the amazing person you are and have always been. Sleep tight.' Zena squeezed Lisa's hand in the dark, and Lisa was grateful that sleep came quickly.

The clock next to her said 6.10 a.m. Zena looked at her niece who still slept. She yawned and stretched, the movement stirring Lisa. 'Morning, Aunty.'

'Morning, sweetheart. How did you sleep?'

'Mmm, not bad, I guess.'

'Do you want to see if the shower is vacant? One shower between four is a problem. I'll go first.' Zena grabbed her robe and headed to the shower. She was followed thereafter by Lisa. There was no sign of life from Mark or Des.

After dressing, Zena looked at her watch. 'Let's go and make some noise; they should be up and moving about or we'll be late.'

Lisa knew exactly where everything was kept and took charge of the kitchen. It was familiar territory albeit a weird sensation to be back there. 'Hey, you,' greeted Mark as he wandered out, face marred with sleep. 'I'm ducking in for a quick shower.'

'What do you have for breakfast? I can only find Corn-flakes,' said Lisa, shaking the packet.

'That will do, and some toast with honey.' Mark scooted off.

Des came out, still in his dressing gown. 'You girls look very smart.' His face was weary and sad. He'd obviously had a poor sleep.

'The bunks are not the best for sleeping, are they?' He looked so contrite.

Lisa gave her father a sheepish grin. 'No, Dad. They are not real good, but hey, we managed.'

Zena handed him a cup of tea. 'Mark is in the shower, so drink this. We had best move, Des. Only just over two hours before the service.'

'Can you imagine if I was late for my own wife's funeral? I am sure Agnes would find a way to strike me down from wherever she is resting.' They both chuckled at that.

'I'll drive', offered Zena. 'It's easier. You won't have to concentrate, Des.' They were all ready by 8.30 a.m., and Des gave directions to the church. Silence filled the car, but it was not an uncomfortable silence. It was like everyone was engaged in their own thoughts. Lisa sat in the back with Mark and felt cocooned by his presence.

'Today will be a difficult day,' Zena said softly. 'Not everyone in this car was treated well by Agnes. But it is a funeral, so let's try to remember that Agnes gave birth to Mark and Lisa and had a good husband. My brother.'

Des reached out and touched her hand. *Even though he did the wrong thing so many times, he's still my brother.*

Zena thought of Janine and wondered if she would talk to her and Lisa at the funeral. Maybe. Maybe not. She hoped Janine would keep control of her emotions in terms of Lenny. She was as vindictive as Agnes. If anything, apart from the sadness of a funeral, it would be an interesting day.

When they entered the church, the coffin rested at the front of the altar. White roses were placed on top. There were around twenty people, most of whom Zena did not know. Mark pointed out Janine to her as they all walked in together, sitting in the same pew.

◊

Janine was a bitter-looking woman, and Lisa was shocked by her appearance. Although only twenty-eight now, she looked much older. The stress had clearly taken a toll on her physical appearance, which could only be described as haggard. Her thin, cruel lips had the same look as Agnes's. Her wiry hair still resembled a Brillo pad.

It was a fairly quick and sombre service, and the minister spoke eloquently. Des had asked him to read the eulogy, which he and Mark had written. As Zena listened, she thought what a lot of shite, especially the part about Agnes being a most charitable soul.

Following the service, people gathered outside. Zena stood with Des and watched as Janine suddenly made her way over to Lisa, who stood next to Mark.

Mark went to offer his condolences to Janine, but she suddenly lunged at Lisa, grabbing her jacket. Her face contorted with rage. 'You fucking little whore. You killed our mother. You should not be here. Our mother hated you. I hate you. You have driven a wedge into this family and my marriage. I want to fucking kill you. I will kill you. Do you hear! I don't care what happens to me as long as I see you dead and the worms eating you. I will follow you . . . follow you to your fucking grave!' The mourners turned in disbelief. Lisa tried to pull away, but Janine slapped her hard in the face.

Lisa was stunned and her face stung. Her father, followed by Zena, quickly stepped in. 'That will be enough, Janine. Stop this.' He grabbed her hands and pushed her away. 'It's a funeral for God's sake.'

Janine backed away clutching at her shirt. Spittle formed at the corners of her mouth. She glared at Lisa and spat, 'Mark my words, you little bitch. You are not getting away with what you have done. I will make you pay!' Her anger shook the ground as she strode off.

The murmur of the crowd was embarrassing. 'Come on, let's get away from here. Are you okay, Lisa?' asked Zena, ushering her towards their car.

'Yes,' she whispered as she held her hand to her face. 'Just . . . Just humiliated and embarrassed. What will people think? And I think I need some ice for my face.'

'People will only think of Janine's poor behaviour today. Who behaves like that at a funeral? Come on, we will head to Rookwood Cemetery now,' said Zena.

Des nodded. 'Yes, and that will be the end of it. Agnes specifically requested no wake.'

They drove for about fifteen minutes and pulled up at a freshly dug hole in the grounds of the cemetery.

The minister was already present and delivered the last commendation and farewell. Des watched as his wife was lowered into the ground. Ashes to Ashes, Dust to Dust. He threw one final white rose onto the coffin. Lisa was numb and stared at the coffin. Mark cried softly. She was still their mother.

On the drive home, Mark's eyes were red from crying. Des sat silently next to Zena in the front seat.

As they pulled up at a set of red traffic lights, Zena spoke. 'I never thought Janine would react like that. Most unexpected.

Janine is consumed with hate, and her behaviour today was so upsetting and entirely inappropriate.'

'Yes, but as I said, she has been hysterical since Lisa made the allegations about Lenny,' said Des solemnly.

'How will she be if Lenny is charged and the allegations are proven in court?' asked Zena.

'A lunatic,' said Mark.

'Janine is very fiery . . . like her mother. I am sorry, Lisa. I had no idea she would react in that way,' apologised Des.

'Me neither, Dad. I was so shocked.' Lisa could still feel the sting on her cheek.

They drew closer to Fairfield. 'This is an odd thing to say,' said Des. 'As there was no wake, I thought I would get some takeaway for tonight. Save us cooking. I know you don't feel like much now but you may later, and it's just a matter of re-heating. Agnes always liked this Chinese restaurant in Fairfield. It's called the Ginger Jar. A bit of a final touch. The last hur-rah. Just us. What do you think?'

'I think that's perfect, Des,' agreed Zena.

A half-smile crossed his face. 'I would always buy Chicken Chow Mein on the way home from the pub. Always saved my neck when I walked in the door half pissed with the Chinese grub. That or a bottle of oysters.'

'Great. Steer me to the Ginger Jar then, Des. I know Agnes didn't want a wake, but a small dinner for her tonight with the four of us and her favourite Chinese food would be almost symbolic.'

Des gave directions to the restaurant. When Zena got out of the car and walked towards the entrance, she turned and looked at Des, pointing her finger at the restaurant. Des smiled and nodded. The place did look a bit dodgy.

Zena walked back to the car. 'Are you sure this is a restau-rant that is functioning, Des?'

'Yes,' he laughed. 'They don't give much priority to being flash. "Shanghai Charlies" Agnes called them. Said they cooked the local cats for meat.'

'That would be right. I can hear that coming from her mouth. Okay, I won't be long.' Zena disappeared through the front door.

'Aunty Zena is so lovely, Dad. Beautiful and kind,' said Mark. Lisa smiled. She knew what he meant.

'Always been like that from as far back as I can remember. Bringing stray animals home, always helping those who needed help. I am so glad you both came down for the funeral. I needed to mend some broken bridges. I don't know how I will ever stop feeling remorse for my actions as well as Agnes's brutality. I have done so much wrong,' Des said sadly. Lisa didn't know what to say.

Zena reappeared with a few white plastic bags. 'Smells good,' she declared as she jumped into the driver's seat. 'This will make you swim faster, Mark.' The air was clearing of the funeral tension.

'Okay, Mark, your turn. Direct me home, please.'

Over dinner, the four of them sat and told stories of Agnes, good and bad, and some of them had Des laughing.

'She was a stupid bloody bitch at times, but I was a right bastard when on the drink. To her, to you, Lisa, and the discipline I gave was harsh and cruel. I really had my beer goggles on. You look back and see your errors. I wish I could turn the clock back. The drink changes everything, your whole personality. Those were my dark years, and the years I caused everyone pain, including myself. I would wake up and feel like shit. The things I did. The things I said.'

He looked across at Mark. 'Stay away from the drink. It never does anyone any favours. It can turn your life upside down.'

'Everything is better in hindsight, Des. I have seen wonderful stockmen over the years do the same. They come back to work for the season and are so alcohol affected that we have to get rid of them. But the fact that you have just said this is recognition and an admission of what has happened. We cannot change the past but we can do better going forward.'

'Wise words, Zena.' Des looked at Lisa, who seemed to be dumbfounded by what he had just said. 'I'm sorry, Lisa, the things I said and did. I wish I could take it all back.' Des choked up and then stopped.

Lisa's emotions were rising, and she felt a lump in her throat. She had never known compassion from her father. But he had said sorry so many times during their visit.

Zena took control. 'It's been a long day, and we have a lot of travel to do to get home. An early night is needed, so time for bed. We'll be up with the birds to get back to Woori. It was a good service, Des, and fitting that we finished off with a serve of Chinese.'

Zena kissed her brother goodnight and gave her nephew a strong hug. Lisa did the same. She could not remember the last time she kissed her father.

'We'll see you both in the morning. Goodnight,' said Zena.

Lisa followed her aunt to the bedroom and sat on the side of the bed. 'You were amazing, Aunty.'

'It's a funeral. Despite what she has done, it is a matter of integrity. Always remember that. What Janine did was outrageous. What a horrible person. I can still see her thin, cruel lips shouting obscenities. Be interesting when her husband is brought to justice. But for now, let's try to get some sleep.'

That was easier said than done. Lisa tossed and turned, still seeing the angry face of Janine and the coffin. Chills ran down her spine when she thought of Janine's words. *She wants to kill me. She is just like Agnes.*

◊

During the morning, Zena discussed flying Mark to Dubbo with Des.

'We will have Christmas together, Zena, and then he'll head up in January if that's okay with you,' said Des.

'What do you think, Mark?' he asked as he turned to the boy.

'I so want to go, Dad.' His face was beaming.

'Just let me know the date a week in advance, Des, so I can arrange a flight. We look forward to having you at Woori, Mark. Just call when we get back and we'll work out a date that suits you.'

'Well then, time to hit the road.' Zena shook her brother's hand and kissed him lightly on the cheek. 'Do what you want to do, Des. There's nothing stopping you now.'

Lisa looked at her father. Sorrow was etched in his eyes. 'I can never forgive myself, Lisa. I should have protected you. I failed to save my own child. Had I not been drinking so much, had I not been so spineless . . . '

Lisa bit her bottom lip; the words would not come out. She was about to burst into tears. So many mistakes, so much hate over the years, and now so much mending. She wondered what life would have been like had her mother loved her and if there had been no alcohol-fuelled violence.

'It's alright, Dad. We will get through this.' Lisa hugged him and felt his chest heaving.

'Goodbye Marco, see you soon. Big hugs.' They extended their arms. Lisa didn't want to let go. 'See you at Woori.'

ELEVEN

EVADING CAPTURE

Zena drove straight to Bathurst rather than staying overnight in the Blue Mountains. The Hydro Majestic had been a treat; the motel in Bathurst was adequate and comfortable for an overnight stay.

During the journey, they had discussed the death of Agnes and Des's remorse.

'His comments were interesting and quite profound in that he seems to be reassessing himself,' said Zena. 'Better late than never. How we found him is what he used to be like before he married Agnes. I don't know whether he started drinking because of her but his personality changed over the years, Lisa. He's off the grog now, so apart from Agnes' death, you are seeing a different side of him.'

'I wonder what family life would have been like if there had been calm and no alcohol,' Lisa pondered.

'Love is a funny thing, Lisa. The heart wants what the heart wants, and some couples do have a love-hate relationship. They cannot bear to be with each other and they cannot bear to be away from each other. It creates a fiery household. But I have seen over the years what drink does to a person. It seems to change the whole personality if it gets a hold of them. As I mentioned to you, Alan and I have seen terrific stockmen one year and when they return, they are a nightmare. Up drinking all night, and their work ethic so affected. It's one of the main reasons Alan hired Jack to oversee everything. Alan got tired of keeping them in line.'

'I miss Woori, Aunty. I'll be glad to see the open spaces.'

'Ditto, Lisa. I'm getting like Alan, claustrophobic in the city. Concrete jungles.'

They pulled into the motel at Bathurst and after settling in, decided to have dinner in their small restaurant. 'The food is simple and plain, but we can get an early night and rise with the birds. I'll call Alan now. It's just after six. He should be in now. Why don't you head to the restaurant and look at the menu. I won't be long.'

'No problem, Aunty. See you there.'

Zena dialled home and smiled when she heard her husband's voice.

'Hi, darling, it's me. How are things?'

'Hot, bloody hot. I didn't call you down there. I thought you would appreciate no interruptions. What was the family reception like?' asked Alan.

'Good. It was a transformation really. Des was very remorseful. He has stopped drinking and apologised to Lisa on so many occasions. I was flabbergasted when he said the house was so peaceful now that Agnes had passed away. It was quite emotional for everyone, but as we agreed, there were lots of bridges to mend. Mark has grown into a fine young man, and I said he could come up this school holiday break. I hope that's okay.'

'Yep, no problem. How was the funeral?'

'Simple service but when we got outside, Janine attacked Lisa, slapping her face and calling her a whore. Put the wind up Lisa when she said she wanted to kill her.'

'What! Are you joking! A bloody funeral and she does that!'

'No, I'm deadly serious. Des stepped in and stopped it, but Janine's behaviour was appalling, let alone that behaviour at her own mother's funeral.'

'She must be as mad as the mother. Is Lisa okay?'

'Rattled, but we got through it. I'm looking forward to getting home. We both are.'

'I'm looking forward to you both being home. By the way, Detective Collette called late yesterday afternoon. He said there was no urgency, but when you got home, he wanted you to call.'

'Oh, did you ask what the nature of the matter was, Alan?'

'I did, but he said he would rather us all be together when he discussed this matter. So, I said fair enough and that I would pass the message on.'

'Sounds ominous. I wonder what it could be? Well, I'm not going to worry as it gets you nowhere. Any more odd things happening about the place?'

'Not a thing,' assured Alan.

'Do you think it's worthwhile letting the police know?' asked Zena.

'No, not for now. Let's just see how things pan out,' replied Alan.

'Okay, your call. We should be home mid-afternoon. I best go. Lisa is in the dining room. Sweet dreams, big hugs.' She disconnected and made her way to the restaurant.

Zena walked towards Lisa's table and sat down. 'See anything you like?'

'Um, I thought the schnitzel looked good with the veg,' said Lisa, showing her aunt the menu.

'Sounds good.' The waitress appeared and Zena ordered.

'How's Alan?' asked Lisa.

'He's looking forward to us coming home, but he did mention that Detective Collette had called yesterday afternoon. Be interesting to hear what he has to say. He wanted us to be there together rather than pass the information to just Alan. Makes sense I guess, instead of repeating whatever he has to say, but I wonder what it can be, Lisa. Anyway, one night's sleep and we will be home.'

'I always think the worst, Aunty. That old feeling in my stomach starts to churn.'

'Best not to worry until you know what it is. Practise your breathing techniques from Dr Tyler. No use worrying about nothing, but my curiosity is aroused to the fact that we all have to be there.'

Lisa changed the subject. 'Do you think there is an afterlife, Aunty? The Aboriginals believe there is,' ventured Lisa.

'Really? I wasn't sure of that part of their culture. Who told you that?'

'Ningali and Binna and the way they described it. I believe it too.'

'Enlighten me,' said Zena.

'They said different groups believe different things. But basically, they go to the Land of the Dead or sky world, you know, the sky. This is where the dead person's soul travels to as long as the rituals were carried out during their life and then after death. This allows them to enter the Land of the Dead. They are very protective of their sacred sites. So they believe in resurrection and that we return again to live another life. You are born, you die, you are born again. I wonder if Agnes will be born again . . . would she come out a different person?'

'God, I hope so,' laughed Zena. 'You've fallen in love with their culture, haven't you?'

'Yes, I so love to sit and hear their stories. Maybe I was once an Aboriginal person in a past life.'

'Who knows . . . maybe,' offered Zena.

It was just after nine when they returned to their room. 'Time for bed now. I'll leave the curtains open so we wake with the light. We can get breakfast along the way. I wonder if Agnes has hit the sky world, Lisa,' pondered Zena.

'Night, Aunty,' said Lisa quietly and closed her eyes. She was exhausted.

It was good to get on the road early. Not much traffic and they only stopped for breakfast.

The big open spaces became more abundant as they watched the houses side by side, with their paling fences and red rooves fade away. The open highway spread before them. They knew home was not that far away. 'Not long, Lisa. Get ready for all those gates and the dust!'

When Lisa shut the last gate, she gave a yelp and jumped. 'I am so excited to be home, Aunty.'

'Me too, kiddo. Let's go. Alan awaits somewhere out there but I would say with this heat, he is probably inside having a cold beer.'

As they came up the stairs, Alan was there to greet them. 'Ladies,' he said as he hugged them and then took their bags. 'Welcome home. What can I get you?'

'I'll get us a cup of tea. I think I drove faster as my curiosity levels have peaked. I want to know the reason for the detective's call. All manner of things have raced through my head,' said Zena as she busied herself in the kitchen.

'Heard about the funeral and Janine's behaviour, Lisa,' said Alan.

'It was awful. I got such a shock. Janine just sort of lunged at me and grabbed my shirt. Her face was so contorted and filled with rage. But when she said she would kill me and follow me to my grave, it sent cold shivers down my spine.'

'I bet, kid. Anyway, it's a long drive out here, and she would have problems finding the joint. So don't lose any sleep.' Alan smiled reassuringly. 'And don't forget, she would have to get past your aunt. Good luck with that, Janine.'

Zena laughed. 'Oh Alan, I'm not as quick as I used to be. Now, while we are all here, let me see if I can get Detective Collette on the line.' Zena moved down the hallway and took a seat next to the phone.

She dialled the direct line and waited. 'Detective Collette. Andrew. Good afternoon, it's Zena Smith. I'm sorry I missed your call yesterday, but I was down in Sydney for a funeral.'

'Yes, hello, Zena. Alan mentioned that. It was your brother's wife, Agnes, I heard. Sorry to hear of this news.'

'It was basically a matter of supporting my brother and paying our respects. The relationship with his wife was always frosty, particularly since the revelations about her first daughter's husband, Lenny.'

'Oh, I see, that's the connection. Yes, I have seen that aggressive reaction many times. They just don't believe it and some actually never do. Funerals though, they are never easy.'

'Anyway, we are all here and I'm following up your call. Is it a good time to continue?'

'Yes, Zena,' Andrew replied, hesitantly. 'The police at Merimbula station were called to the local caravan park yesterday by a woman, Caroline Lockhart, who was in a hysterical state. She resides there with her ten-year- old daughter, after separating from her husband due to domestic violence. Mrs Lockhart had left her daughter alone in the caravan to head into town. When she got back, she could hear strange noises coming from inside. When she flung the door open and stepped inside, Lenny was in the process of raping her daughter.'

'Oh my God, no, no, no!' Zena wailed. 'Monster. Vile Monster! What happened then .... please?'

'Mrs Lockhart started screaming, so Lenny jumped up, pulling up his shorts and rushing past her, knocking her off the caravan steps. Other residents came to her aid. The police were subsequently called, and they came to the caravan park. It was, as you can imagine, very emotional, tragic in fact. A doctor was called to offer sedation for Mrs Lockhart and to assist with her daughter. Fortunately, she did get a good physical description of the assailant and was able to provide this to us.'

'Did you say sedated. The mother or daughter? And where is Lenny now?'

'Well, he is unfortunately still on the run. Managed to get away again. Mrs Lockhart was sedated and then taken to the local hospital. She was quite hysterical but under the circumstances, you can understand why.'

'Oh that poor woman and the little girl . . . where is she? I feel so sorry for both of them. This is tragic news.'

There was a silence.

'Yes, it was tragic for the little girl, and I am sorry to tell you this, but she is deceased.'

Zena's hand flew up to her mouth. 'Oh, God nooooo, no no,' she wailed, shaking her head from side to side. Tears welled in her eyes. She immediately thought of Lisa being exposed to that danger, as well as the deceased child whose life he had ended.

'They are doing an autopsy, but they seem to think he suffocated her to stifle the screams. An accident that was not meant to happen. I'm just not sure. He may have panicked. The police then took the photos of Lenny and did a door knock to the surrounding homes, tenants of the caravans, camping sites and then to the office of the caravan park. The manager there identified Lenny immediately. He was staying in the same caravan park. Needless to say, there was a knock on the door of the caravan where he was staying, and he did not respond. So, he's on the loose again.'

Zena had a vision of the evil bastard, and the little girl cowering with fear.

'You have to get this monster, Andrew!' Zena's face clouded with anger and sadness.

'Yes, we know that . . . before he does something like this again. Small girls obviously play a part in his sexual fantasies. Some rapists panic and kill their victims, just like him. I would say she was struggling and possibly crying, so he got flustered. Probably held his hand over her mouth and nose too long. So, they panic and kill accidentally or sometimes they just kill them to protect their identity.'

'God, I can't imagine what the mother must be feeling right now. Domestic violence and then the loss of her daughter. She will probably blame herself until the day she drops.'

'Yes, Zena, no-one ever gets over the loss of a child. It will, however, make Lisa's allegations water-tight. He has been identified now by the mother and of course, he has now raped and murdered a ten-year-old girl.'

'Tragic in one way, Andrew, that it would take the murder of a ten-year-old child to make the justice system realise Lisa was not promiscuous or the one at fault. This will turn the situation around.'

'Yes, Zena, it will. If you or Lisa have any further questions, please don't hesitate to call.'

'Thank you, Andrew.' Zena hung up the phone.

'Well, we heard part of it,' commiserated Alan as Zena joined them, still shaken by the phone call.

Zena looked at Lisa and spoke with hesitancy. 'He . . . Lenny,' Zena faltered.

'Yes, Aunty . . . go on,' said Lisa, almost fearful of the words that would follow.

'He was caught raping a ten-year-old girl in a caravan on the South Coast, Merimbula. The detective said he must have panicked, and it looks like he suffocated the young girl. Maybe to keep her quiet. Her mother had headed out to do some shopping and left her daughter there. Thank God she came home and caught him literally in the act, because she was able to identify Lenny from photos.'

Lisa was visibly shaken. She wanted to scream but no sound came out. 'Oh no, no, the poor girl.' She squeezed her eyes shut and shook her head, shaking uncontrollably, rocking herself back and forth. Lisa wailed like a wounded beast and banged the table with her fists. 'It could have been me, it could have been me, Aunty . . . another little girl, innocent.'

Alan drew his arms protectively around his niece She was sobbing and leaning into his chest, hiding her face from the world. *It could have been me.*

TWELVE

CHRISTMAS COMES TO WOORI

The mood was sombre in the days that followed after hearing the news from Detective Collette. Zena knew how close Lisa had come to the same fate. Her nightmares had returned and that first night, she woke screaming, struggling to fight off Lenny.

As Zena raced to her room at the first high-pitched scream, she knew a call to Helen Tyler was desperately needed. As she held Lisa in the middle of the night, Zena tried to console her. Her niece was wild with fear and choking on her words.

'Him,' Lisa cried out. 'Both of them, those monsters, tearing at me, trying to take me back to their darkness, their hell holes. It was like they were here in my room, Aunty, their vile acts, the putrid smell, all the horror. And I could feel their hands all over me.'

Zena made an appointment with Helen a few days later, who worked through the tragic loss of the young girl and Lisa's emotions surrounding the death. The counselling and discussions had provided support emotionally and spiritually, but Lisa still felt drained.

The journey home from her session with Dr Tyler was quiet.

'Talk to me Lisa, I am right here for anything you want to say,' Zena said softly.

Lisa felt the tears welling as her emotions tumbled out. 'I couldn't save my friend Julie and I couldn't save that little girl. I keep seeing her in the caravan. I've been there, where she was.'

Zena pulled over to the side of the road. She looked at her niece, so vulnerable and young. 'Yes I know, darling, but you have survived and you must continue to survive. There was nothing you could have done to stop those tragic losses but now, so importantly, you have the chance to stop what is going on right now. Here take this.' Zena passed a tissue.

Lisa wiped her tears away and sighed. 'Yes, you're right, Aunty. It's just hard to get it off my mind.' As they travelled towards Woori, the opening and shutting of the gates was the only thing that kept Lisa focused and moving. She wanted to shut down and hide.

By the time they got back to Woori, it was a clear warm night as the evening colours flooded the beautiful flat plains – pink and orange with long streaks of purple underneath a fading blue sky. Alan sat waiting on the verandah as Zena flopped down onto one of the big lounges.

'Tough day?' asked Alan.

'Tough,' Zena replied. 'Lisa was very quiet heading back here. Who can blame her though? It could have been her life cut short. Monster. And somewhere, still out there.'

'Hey there, kid. Come sit with us,' Alan said when Lisa came on to the verandah. Her face told the events of the day. It was drained, and stress had given her a pale pallor to her usually bright, tanned face. She almost wilted into the chair, avoiding their eyes.

'The stars will soon show their bright twinkling faces. I want to see the Southern Cross and the emus,' yawned Lisa. *I know somewhere Billy will be looking for that too.*

'I feel so tired, and I can't stop thinking about the little girl. The terror and fear, Aunty, that she must have felt. Alone in a caravan and him coming towards her. I know those feelings. The powerlessness.'

Zena reached out and stroked her hair gently. 'Yes, you do, darling girl. Try and hear Helen's words. Use your techniques, and we will let this day go away. The police will catch up with Lenny, and justice will be done. It's too late for the little Lockhart girl, and I just pray nothing happens to anyone else, but his capture and justice is not far away.'

Lisa shivered. 'Do you want me to bring you something to your room or do you want to have dinner with us?' her aunt asked gently.

'No, I just want to be alone with my thoughts.' They sat until the moon rose high in the sky, and when the Southern Cross was in view, Lisa smiled. *The fat man who was the moon.*

'Goodnight, you two. I'll see you in the morning,' said Lisa before making her way to bed.

With wide-open eyes she gazed at the moonlight and the shadows dancing in her room, expecting any moment to see Lenny's face. She felt a strange silence brooding in the house, a silence caused by the villain who still roamed free.

◊

It was still dark when Alan rose the next morning. He returned some three hours later, with a six foot She-Oak under one arm and a large silver garbage bin in the other.

His ute pulled up just after 7.00 a.m. 'Where has Alan been so early, Aunty?' asked Lisa, sipping her tea.

'He wanted a tree . . . you know, our own real Christmas tree.'

They watched him come through the compound gates carrying the large tree. He propped it up in the garbage can and came inside.

'Well done, Alan,' said Zena with glee.

Lisa smiled. 'A real tree, it's lovely. We always had plastic at home. Where did you get it?'

'Down near the river. When you bring it in, Zena, fill the big plastic bucket next to the bin with water and then put that inside the garbage bin. It will keep the tree fresher longer. You may need to put some bricks in to steady the tree.'

Alan sat down and joined in, buttering the toast Zena had just put in front of him. 'I know we have a lot on our plate, and I know the recent events have shaken everyone, but let's try and have a happy time for Christmas.'

'Yes, you're right, darling, I'm sure once the tree goes up and we decorate that and add a few touches in here, we'll feel more like celebrating. We have not really bothered with Christmas while you have been here, Lisa, as there was so much to get through, and we just wanted you to settle. But we have covered so much. What do you think, Lisa . . . are you okay with this small celebration? It's only a few days away?'

'Yes, I agree and I'm fine, Aunty. Christmas was not much of a celebration at home, but now, things feel different,' Lisa said quietly but her thoughts still rested on the young girl. She would forever haunt her.

◊

It was now Christmas Eve and there was finally some excitement in the house.

Alan had kept Lisa busy with the horses. 'It's been a good day, Lisa. You're a natural at this kind of work. You know your father also had a natural affinity with horses and was an excellent farrier before he met your mother. Well, that's what Zena tells me. Must be in the genes. Come on then, let's wash up. Time to enjoy a good meal.'

Zena had cooked all day. She really wanted to make it special, not only to lift the mood but to celebrate Christmas together. She looked up when she heard the motorbike. He knew the girl well; she enjoyed sitting on the back with him but sometimes he went too fast. Probably why Lisa liked it. She smiled. *I do too.*

'The smell coming from this kitchen makes me feel even hungrier, Zena. Not sure about Bing Crosby and his Christmas tunes though.'

Lisa pulled a face. She was in agreement. 'I saw that, Lisa,' Zena laughed. 'Well, I just happen to like old Bing. So you two can suffer in silence. It's Christmas Eve and my indulgence, once a year. Good tree, Alan! It's up now, so we can all decorate it after dinner.'

As they sat around the table, they talked about Mitch's birthday party, which was only just over three weeks away. 'Going to be fun, that's for sure,' commented Alan. 'Kate always does it well. Every party or celebration we have ever been to out there at Woodside is always a big event. Always loads of people too.'

'We'll have to find you something to wear, Lisa, not that white dress you are busting out of. I may have something if we don't get down to Sydney in time,' said Zena.

'I'm not fussed, Aunty,' replied Lisa. 'Anything is fine.'

'Oh, and Lisa, what do you think about driving out to see the ladies and taking them a few goodies tomorrow?'

'Oh yes, yes please!' said Lisa excitedly.

Alan rolled his eyes. 'Now don't tell me they have a Dreamtime story about Santa?'

'Probably,' smiled Lisa.

Zena knew she had pressed the right button. The murder of this young girl had pervaded Lisa's thoughts. They remained clouded and troubled, so a trip to see the healer women would be a good idea for her.

Christmas morning arrived. It was a clear and perfect day. Lisa stretched and lay listening to the birds greeting the morning with their symphony of song. Their music echoed through the golden rays that filtered into her room. Lisa had visions of the old lady putting on her red ochre and lighting up her stringy bark tree, carrying it across the sky.

Merry Christmas to me. Merry Christmas to you, Billy.

Lisa could hear her aunt chattering and laughing, so she quickly swung her legs over the bed and dressed. Christmas jingles filled the house. She wanted to join in on the excitement. It was so different to Fairfield, where the mood was always sombre and conservative. She put Billy's necklace on. *You are with me now.*

'Morning,' she said when she found Alan and her aunt, giving them the biggest hugs.

'Merry Christmas, kid. Santa has made a stopover. I heard the reindeers on the roof last night,' Alan chuckled.

Lisa giggled and ran out to the sitting room where the She-Oak tree stood glowing in the morning light in her fine decorations. Brightly coloured parcels, all different shapes and sizes, were scattered under the tree.

'There are a few there for you, kid,' said Alan. Lisa dropped to her knees, squeezing the parcels with her name.

'Ooooh, can I open them now?'

'Don't see why not,' replied Alan and her aunt together. 'Start with the big ones and work your way down.'

Lisa picked up the biggest box and tore it open. 'Oh, it's lovely . . . RM Williams. What a beautiful jacket. Thank you, Santa.'

'Yep, it's the best, waterproof, not that you need it all that much around here, but good to have one if it does rain. It will also keep you warm, Lisa,' explained Alan.

She picked up two boxes of the same shape and opened the first. 'A new dress! I so hope it fits!' She quickly stood up and held it against her. It was a pale pink taffeta strapless dress with a black print motif. It flared out from her waist. 'I love it, Aunty. It's gorgeous!' She quickly unwrapped the next box, which held a lemon shift dress with white daises on the hem and under the bust.

'I don't know which I love the most! They are both just so beautiful.'

'Well, one is more formal, sort of more dress up, but at least these should fit you better. With Mitch's party approaching, you have a choice now. Come on, two more boxes,' enthused Zena.

The second box was filled with new jeans and t-shirts. 'Just what I need! Where and when did you get these, Aunty!'

'Mrs Dunphy. I told her to get in more stock. She would have gone to Sydney, I'd say. I also got a few things in Walgett while you were seeing Helen. One more to go, this is from Alan.'

Lisa fumbled the tiny package. As she pulled the paper off, she eyed a small black velvet box. She looked at them both and felt the tears springing to her eyes.

'Hey, cut that out, Lisa. This is a happy time . . . stop your blubbering,' joked Alan.

As she lifted the lid, the opal earrings sparkled. 'These are Harry's . . . Harry's old opals! They are so stunning.' Lisa held them to her ears.

'Yeah, we were going to wait for your birthday, but as it's a way to go, we decided we wanted you to have them now,' said Alan. 'Been a tough year.'

Lisa jumped up and ran towards them both. She threw her arms around their waists. 'Thank you, thank you. I love you so much.'

'We'll have to get your ears pierced in Walgett, but go see what they look like in the mirror,' prompted Zena.

Lisa took off and stood at the vanity in her ensuite, gasping at the small stones that shimmered green and blue. She thought of Old Harry. *Thank you, Harry. I will wear them with pride.*

Lisa scooted back to the living room. 'I have nothing for you . . . I can't give you anything and you both have done so much for me.'

'We don't need anything, Lisa. We have each other and we have you, which has been a gift to both of us,' reassured Zena.

'Oh, Aunty. I am so happy, the happiest I have ever been. Thank you for loving me . . . for bringing me here to Woori . . . and everything else you both do for me.'

Zena folded her arms lovingly around her niece, kissing the top of her head. 'Everything will be fine eventually, Lisa. Next year will be a goody. Now, come on, I have a man to feed here, and the ladies know I always come out with something on this day. We're going to take a Christmas hamper for them with a few treats. I'll do a small pork roast and take out a few baked vegetables. They just love my Christmas pudding. So lots to do, and then we can flop in the afternoon, and of course, play more Bing Crosby.'

Alan groaned. Zena swatted him, laughing all the while.

Lunch was a feast. 'I feel so full. I have never eaten so much. My belly is sticking out!' exclaimed Lisa, patting her stomach.

'Enjoy it,' said Alan. 'I look forward to it all year. Zena puts on a good spread, but the queen of all spreads is Kate Walker.'

Zena laughed. 'That's for sure. But you'll see that when we head out there for Mitch's birthday. Not too far off. Help me clear as we need to get on our way. Lisa, grab that esky from the laundry, and I'll load this food into it. No need for ice as it will still be warm by the time we get out there. The esky just makes it easier to transport, and keeps away the damn flies.'

They all jumped into the Land Rover and headed out to see Binna and Ningali. Lisa wondered if they had any news on Billy. She crossed her fingers.

'Well, they have the fire burning,' observed Alan. 'Helps keep the flies away . . . and snakes.'

'They don't believe in Christmas, but they understand we celebrate it, so we don't make a big deal. Just basically bringing some good tucker out to them,' added Zena.

Ningali waved as they pulled up. 'Hey, big boss, how you bin? No see for long time.'

Alan smiled. She was a funny one. 'Ningali,' he greeted as he tipped his hat. He carried the esky up to where Binna sat. He took off his hat and sat down. 'Binna, good to see you, old girl.'

The old lady smiled and held out her hand. 'Boss Alan, I hear your voice. You always welcome.'

Zena and Lisa followed. Binna cocked her ear. 'Aaaah, boss lady and da little one.'

Ningali giggled. She grabbed a hessian bag and placed it on the dirt floor.

'Don't do anything special for me, Ningali, I'm good,' Alan said. 'Got your finest wares out, I see.'

Alan sat on a wooden stump next to Zena whilse Lisa sat cross legged on the hessian bag.

'We've brought you a few things, ladies,' said Zena as she pulled the food out of the esky.

'Somethin' smells plenty good,' grinned Ningali as she rubbed her belly. 'Boss lady, she bin real busy in da cook up.'

Zena laughed. 'Yes, just for you two girls, so please enjoy. I wanted to thank you both for taking the time to talk to Lisa. It's been a long journey for her. Not over yet, but my girl is progressing. A few setbacks of late, but we will overcome these.' She gazed fondly at her niece.

Binna spoke quietly. 'Da baby always welcome. She have da light step now, her voice like da bird, she singin.'

'Yes, Binna, a few ups and downs, but I'm happy. Binna, thank you . . . for all you do.' Zena was so grateful to this woman.

Lisa blushed. 'Do you have any news, Ningali?'

Alan looked at Zena. What was this news question all about? Bush telegraph, no doubt.

'No, we have no news,' said Ningali. 'No Billy news, not since da last time.'

Zena broke in. 'Well, ladies, we celebrate Christmas as you know, and I have brought you some of the food we usually eat to celebrate our religion and the day. I know it's not in your culture, but it's our way of saying thank you. Everything is wrapped up in the esky and still warm, so please enjoy.'

'Thank you, boss lady, we bin eating fine because of you. Lisa, da baby, you come visit us. Sit with us a while,' said Binna.

Lisa grinned. 'Yes I will, as soon as I can, Binna.'

'We like da boss man here,' Ningali giggled as she looked at Alan.

'As cheeky as ever, Ningali. Consider yourselves lucky then,' he joked as he dipped his hat to the two women. They both cackled like children.

'Ningali . . . just one last thing. I know you have a keen eye and you get about wandering for your own bush tucker, and down at the river, that's where you saw those other two blokes who gave you the news about Billy, right?'

'Yes, boss.' Ningali's eyes widened.

'Well, just keep an eye out for me then please, Ningali. A couple of strange things have happened over at Woori, and if you see any strangers, just let Lisa know.'

'Yes, boss. You got trouble?' asked Ningali.

'Yeah, you could say that, Ningali. Just a few odd things,' Alan said.

'Right then, we'll be off and let you enjoy the food while it's warm,' said Zena as she unloaded the tin plates wrapped in alfoil. 'Lisa will collect the plates next time she's out here.'

Binna reached over to Lisa's hand and held it tightly. She closed her eyes and murmured softly in her own native tongue. Her milky eyes opened slowly. 'You must be careful, little one. Someone travel long on da road to find you. They carry bad things in their heart. Be safe.'

Lisa looked terrified and felt the shivers in her spine. She glanced at her aunt, who also heard what Binna had said.

'Binna, what's going on? What do you mean? Who travels here?

'I feel da danger. Keep da little one safe,' Binna said solemnly.

'Come on, Zena, let's go.' Alan pulled at her arm, bidding the two women goodbye.

◊

The women watched as the Land Rover sped off in the dust.

'What you see, Binna?' asked Ningali.

'Bad spirit, looking for da baby girl.'

Ningali stood, swatting the flies away.

'Plenty trouble. Lisa brave, but need dat Billy. He be here to protect her. True.' Even Binna didn't know just how right she was. The approaching danger was deadly.

165

THIRTEEN

MITCH'S PARTY

Everyone was silent at first as they headed for home. Binna's words had jolted their senses. Zena broke the silence. 'What did they mean, Alan? What danger? It's such an odd thing for Binna to say, especially with the saddle having been moved and the pumps suddenly stopping. Who is coming, for God's sake?'

'I know as much as you do,' said Alan, 'Which is bugger all. We'll just keep an eye out . . . keep locking things. Christ! Never had to do that before.'

'It really gives me the creeps,' admitted Zena. 'What else can go wrong?'

'Nothing is going to go wrong. We just need to be vigilant, and anyway, the old lady was probably seeing things that don't exist. Maybe she's getting daft in her old age,' added Alan.

Lisa had kept quiet, lost in her own thoughts, but she wasn't so sure about Binna being daft. She knew what a powerful elder she was, in more ways than one. She knew Binna felt things around her, saw things – and if she sensed danger, then it was travelling towards them.

◇

The night of Mitch's party soon came around. Zena was pleased. It was something to look forward to and at least a festive occasion. 'We best get ready,' fluttered Zena. It's just after 5.00 p.m. and the party starts in an hour.'

'I would really love to just flop on the verandah, it's so hot today . . . and the flies,' moaned Lisa.

'January is always hot, Lisa. They'll be gone soon, so off you go and get ready. We'll have a great time, and there should be a few young people there instead of us oldies to chat to.'

Alan opened a cold beer as he waited for them to get ready. He looked at the dogs through the gauze of the back door. Buster and Dougy were loving roaming around inside the compound instead of being chained up like the other dogs.

'Hey, you two, we are off tonight, so keep an eye on the joint,' Alan ordered as they stood wagging their tails at the bottom of the stairs.

Lisa slipped on her new pink dress, flat shoes, and threw her hair up in a messy bun.

'How are you going in there?' asked Zena as she came into the bedroom.

'Oh, Lisa, that does look splendid. Pink really suits you. Come on, Alan is waiting for us.'

He let out a low whistle as they appeared. 'You both look gorgeous,' he declared, putting down his beer and picking up the keys.

As they pulled up and parked, the paddock was lit up with lights of all different shapes and sizes. Every tree in Kate's garden had lights. 'The place looks like a bloody Christmas tree,' guffawed Alan. Lisa just gazed around her in awe.

A four-piece band was playing country music and 44-gallon drums, which had been cut in half, were filled with beer and champagne. Caterers had been organised and were busy with a lamb on the spit, and the amount of food on the tables already looked mouth-watering. The place was filling with people of all different ages, but Lisa noticed there were a lot of young pretty girls.

'I'm hungry,' laughed Alan.

'Can you wait for a moment, Alan? We need to find Kate and Dave as well as the birthday boy. Look, there they are. Come on you pair, it's polite to say hello.'

Mitch had spotted Lisa already. He took a sharp intake of breath as they walked towards him.

'Happy birthday, Mitch.' Zena handed him the neatly wrapped package, but Mitch couldn't take his eyes off Lisa.

'You look beautiful in pink,' Mitch admired. Lisa blushed. *Here he goes again.*

'You've done an amazing job, Kate. The place looks divine. Very festive and welcoming, and I love all the lights,' gushed Zena.

'Thank you, Zena. I think we are in for a long night; the place is not even full yet. About 150 coming,' said Kate.

'Good grief. I didn't know Mitch had that many friends,' laughed Zena.

'Relatives, mates, family friends and girls, lots of pretty girls.'

'Where are they all sleeping?' asked Zena.

'Behind the house, some have erected tents, some are sleeping in the back of their utes, some have swags. We have put up as many as we can in the house, and we cleaned out the shearing sheds. So where you can find a bed, that will do for one night. Recovery breakfast tomorrow as well, so if you want to come along, please do,' invited Kate. 'By the way, you both look stunning. I'll get us a glass of fizz, Zena, to kick the night off.'

Alan stood talking to Dave about the coming season. He had a beer in his hand and was going nowhere.

Kate returned and handed a glass to Zena. 'Is Lisa allowed one yet?'

'Mmm, maybe one, but it's up to her. She's only sixteen, so she might want to save it for later when we make a toast to Mitch. I'll ask, but she seems to be cornered right now by the birthday boy.'

'Yes, he is quite besotted with her, Zena. Never stops talking about her.'

The two women laughed. 'I may have to rescue her, Kate' said Zena. She noticed Lisa was starting to scratch her arms. She was getting nervous.

'Hey, how is my girl?' asked Zena as she wandered over to her niece. 'Now, Mitch, no hogging! You have to circulate with all the other young pretty things. Come with me, Lisa. I'll get you a drink.' Lisa followed her aunt quickly as more girls moved in around Mitch.

'Thanks so much, Aunty. I had that same feeling of being overpowered. He just kind of zooms in on me.'

'Kate said he is pretty keen on you.'

'Well, look at the selection here. I'm sure he'll find something else to catch his eye,' said Lisa. 'That one there in the red dress seems particularly keen. She's like a fly buzzing around him.'

Zena laughed. 'That's Tess Dunphy . . . you know, Mrs Dunphy from the haberdashery. That's her daughter. She's a bit of a handful. Has some sort of psychiatric condition, something like bi-polar, up and down. I feel sorry for Mrs Dunphy. It's hard as a single mum, husband shot through years ago. Alan said the lads have all paid Tess a visit. She's a bit on the promiscuous side, but she's certainly doing her best to get Mitch's attention.'

'Her dress is so short and her boobs are falling out,' observed Lisa.

'Mmm, learn a lesson, Lisa. Less is more. Elegance always wins, but I agree, Tess is giving it a real go.'

Changing the subject, Zena clapped her hands together. 'Okay. Champagne . . . now or later?'

'Now, I guess. Gosh, I feel very grown up.' Lisa followed Zena to the glasses stacked on a table and poured herself a champagne. The bubbles tickled her nose and as she took a sip, she began to feel a warmth oozing through her body. She enjoyed the taste. 'Take it easy, Lisa. You are under age, but out here, it shouldn't hurt. One or two maximum,' said Zena.

Wherever Lisa walked, Mitch's eyes followed her. 'I get the feeling I'm being watched, Aunty.'

'So I've noticed. Stay with me if you feel uncomfortable. There are more people coming in, so it will be quite a crowd. Always good that way as you can usually duck and weave and find new people to talk too, but that boy is certainly drawing the ladies around him.'

Lisa sat with her aunt and watched with amusement. Tess Dunphy was almost clinging to Mitch now. The girls were all vying for his attention. Yes, he was handsome and wealthy, but he wasn't Billy. *My Billy. He's a natural high for me. I don't care if he's black, I'll wait.*

'I'm just going over to chat to Kate, so I'm not far. Help yourself to some food, darling girl.'

Lisa sat on a chair tapping her feet to the music. *I feel like another glass of champagne. Another won't hurt. It tastes so good. Cool and silky.* Lisa wandered over and helped herself then came back to her chair.

'Is that another one, Lisa?' Zena asked as she sat down.

'Yes. Funny how these little bubbles make me loosen up.'

'Well, that will be quite enough for tonight until we have that final birthday toast to Mitch. I don't want you falling flat on your face. Champagne is meant to be sipped Lisa, not guzzled.'

'It tastes so good, Aunty, and it makes me feel . . . umm not so tense.'

'Well, that's the effect of alcohol for sure. But no more as it will work the opposite way.'

Lisa giggled. 'What way?'

'You will get sillier, lose control or even pass out. Not very flattering. Get the picture?'

Lisa nodded, but the champagne did make her float.

'So, no more, young lady. It's not a good thing at your age,' warned Zena.

'Why does everybody keep telling me what's good for me?' Lisa pouted.

Zena's head snapped around to look at her niece. 'Definitely no more or we leave.'

'Sorry, Aunty. That did sound a bit rude.'

'As I said, no more until we make a toast to Mitch, which should be around midnight. Two and a half hours from now by my watch. There are plenty of soft drinks that have bubbles.'

The music became louder, and a few people got up to dance. A young man suddenly appeared beside them. He stretched out his hand to Lisa. 'Hello, I'm Frank, a cousin of Mitch's. Would you like to dance?'

'Hello, I'm Lisa, and yep, I sure would.'

Zena was astonished. Two glasses of champagne and Lisa had come out of her shell. She remembered what Des had said. The drink changes your personality. She thought she had best stick close to her girl; otherwise, this might turn into a disaster.

Frank was spinning Lisa around, and she was laughing as he did so. Young and flirty. Another young man butted in, and Lisa was swept in another direction. 'I really need to stop this,' Zena murmured. *Not looking good.* She breathed a sigh of relief when Mitch suddenly appeared.

◊

'Sorry fellas, this one is taken.' He took Lisa by her arm and drew her in close to his body. He began to move her around the dance floor. He was mesmerised. Her eyes sparkled from the effects of the alcohol, and he pressed harder to her slender young body. His hand wandered down her back and her soft honey-brown flesh under his fingers made him tingle.

Mitch bent and whispered in her ear, 'I could devour you.' Lisa pulled back slightly, her danger radar suddenly ignited.

'Thanks, Mitch . . . for the dance,' she said as she broke free and moved to sit with her aunt again. Lisa slid into a chair and pointed up at the stars. 'Sky charms fall from there. The spirits are all up there.'

Lisa began to hiccup. 'Oops. . . sorry, Aunty.'

'Stay right here and don't move. I'm getting you some water.'

'Here, drink this,' said Zena as she returned and handed Lisa a glass of water.

'I miss Billy . . . my Billy,' Lisa whispered.

Alan wandered over. 'What's going on, Lisa? You looked a bit wild out there. Certainly the centre of attention. Everyone wants to know who you are. The beautiful girl in the pink dress.'

'Just having fun, Alan,' said Lisa, burping.

'Two glasses of champagne,' added Zena, raising her eyebrows.

'A bit of juice, that'll get your motor started. But no more.' Alan sat down, and Zena was grateful for some extra support.

The night wore on and the music was contagious. Mitch came over after greeting most of the guests. 'Well, Lisa, are you ready for another dance with me?' He extended his hand, and Lisa unsteadily rose to her feet.

He led her out on to the makeshift dance floor. The air was soft and warm but all she could see was Billy's eyes. It was a slow set, and Mitch gently took her into his arms and moved her around the floor.

'You are so dazzling. I just can't take my eyes off you.' Mitch pulled her closer. Lisa could feel the strength in his arms. The champagne had made her relax and she began to move with him.

Dave and Kate joined Zena as they watched the young couple together.

'They make a nice-looking couple,' said Kate as she stood watching with her husband Dave.

Zena nodded. 'Yes, they do, Kate, but they are both still young and I'm not sure if either of them really know what they want . . . she's definitely not experienced at this socialising with boys. But yes, I agree, they do look good together.'

'Billy seems to have vanished from her train of thought,' Alan whispered to Zena.

'Don't speak too fast. Lisa just mentioned him. Just before you came over, she told me how she missed Billy. That girl is counting down the days until the next shearing season. Trust me.'

'That's about seven months away, Zena. Anything can happen in that time,' said Alan confidently. 'If Mitch plays his cards right, he may sweep our young girl off her feet.'

'What are you betting, husband?' asked Zena with a bemused look.

'How about a dance yourself?' Alan suddenly stood up and grabbed Zena by the hand. More people followed and the old wooden dance floor was suddenly full.

◊

Tess Dunphy was brooding as she watched the dance floor from the side. She had already begun to slur her words. It was common knowledge she liked a drink. *That bloody dark bitch, trying to steal my man. Who does she think she is? I fucked Mitch last week. He loves me, not her. I'm going to show her something.*

Tess suddenly strode to the dance floor and yanked hard on Mitch's arm, trying to pull him away.

'Hey, Tess, what are you doing! Stop that,' he demanded as he tried to disentangle himself. Tess would not let go and then pushed Lisa violently, who staggered back.

'Fuck off where you came from, bitch! Mitch is mine!' Her words slurred as she tried to grab Mitch's arm again.

'Tess, stop this!' Mitch shouted. 'Go and sit down!'

'No, I won't . . . Go on, Mitch, tell her. Tell her how much I mean to you. You fucked me last week. You love me, don't you?' She was almost pleading, and it was a pitiful sight.

Mitch stood protectively in front of Lisa until Dave and Alan came to his aid. Lisa was suddenly shocked back into reality by Tess's aggression, and her eyes widened with fear. Terrified, she stayed directly behind Mitch.

'Come on, Tess,' Dave said. 'You've had quite enough.'

She started to struggle wildly. 'Take your fucking hands off me. You bitch, you'll be sorry you done this. Mitch is mine . . . . all mine, ya hear!'

Mrs Dunphy suddenly appeared. Her face was filled with embarrassment.

'Tess,' she hollered. 'Stop this, get a hold of your manners! We are going home.' The young girl seemed to snap to attention at the sound of her mother's voice.

Mrs Dunphy apologised. 'I am so sorry, Dave. She has had too much to drink. I'll take her home now. Can you give me a hand to my car? It's just the other side of this paddock.'

Alan and Dave half dragged and half walked the drunk girl to Mrs Dunphy's old Holden.

Lisa hurriedly made her way to Zena and tried to steady herself. 'That girl is scary, Aunty. I was so shocked by the things she said. Reminded me of Janine . . . that aggression, the way she attacked.'

'Learn a lesson, Lisa. The alcohol was speaking then. No filter to her mouth, and ladies who drink too much are never a good look.'

Kate was standing in disbelief next to her son. 'That behaviour and her language were disgusting, Mitchell. Be careful who you jump into bed with or it will come back to bite you. I hope you used protection. I don't want a call a few weeks from now.'

'Sorry, Mum. I think I need a good stiff rum, and yeah, I carry the rubbers . . . always.'

Kate watched her son walk away. *I don't think I want to hear how many rubbers you carry about, Mitchell.*

Alan and Dave walked back together. Kate had already joined Zena and Lisa. 'I am so sorry this happened to you, Lisa. You have my apologies,' said Kate sincerely.

'I'm alright, Mrs Walker, just a bit of a shock. She was scary, so very fiery, but I think she is in love with Mitch,' replied Lisa.

'How did you go, Dave?' asked Kate as both men sat down.

'Shame it was a bit of a spectacle for Mitch. Sorry ladies,' Dave added, his eyes meeting Zena's.

'I'm sure everyone turned a blind eye,' soothed Zena, trying to reassure Kate. 'Lisa was a bit shaken by her language and aggression, but Tess has gone now.'

'Sorry, Lisa, once again. We had no idea Tess would be like this.' Kate's voice was tinged with embarrassment. She looked over at her son.

Mitch was filling up his tankard with his mates, and there were howls of laughter.

'Young men,' sighed Kate. 'No doubt some of them would have found humour in that spectacle. I'll go and see what needs to be topped up on the table and just mingle a bit.'

'Come on then, we'll give you a hand,' offered Alan as he followed Dave and Zena.

'Are you okay here, Lisa?' asked Zena. 'I won't be long . . . but no more alcohol.'

'Yes, Aunty. I'll find my favourite stars.'

◊

Mitch glanced up to see Lisa sitting alone. He wandered over and sat down. 'Sorry about before,' he apologised as he sipped his rum. 'Yeah, real sorry you had to see that, Lisa. Tess and I used to date but not anymore.'

'But she said you . . . you, well you had your way with her only a week ago.'

'Yeah, big mistake,' grimaced Mitch. 'I won't ever be going there again.' He changed the subject.

'Can I get you a drink, Lisa? A champagne? I'll get you another one.'

'No thanks,' replied Lisa, feeling slightly out of touch, a funny tingly sensation running through her body. She remembered the jab of Valium at the Girls Home and how it made her lose control. *Stop, Lisa. Think.*

'Beautiful night, hey Lisa,' said Mitch.

'Yes, I can see the Southern Cross. It has a special meaning for me. Billy told me all about the Southern Cross.' Lisa let her head tip back, closed her eyes and gave a relaxed moan. She could see Billy at Goobang, and a warm smile crept across her face.

'That's a contented look. I think any moment you're going to fall asleep,' complained Mitch. 'Why does the Southern Cross have a special meaning?' he asked curiously.

'Because it was when the Sky King walked the earth. Binna and Ningali told me many stories, and Billy took me to Goobang. He's my friend and has taught me a lot.'

'What? Sounds like you've been mixing with the boongs too long. That's the second time you have mentioned this bloke

Billy. He must be special because your voice softens when you say his name. Is he a darky too?'

Lisa's eyes flew open, and she felt herself bristling. She jumped unsteadily up and stood facing Mitch, her hands on her hips. 'Boongs . . . darkys, what is that supposed to mean? Don't you mean Aboriginals? They're not boongs or darkys. They are people.' Her voice was raised and she was getting angry with him, drawing many glances in their direction.

'Hey, sit down. I'm just joking. I've always called them that. I don't mean anything by it,' he said sheepishly. He knew he had upset the girl and clearly crossed a special boundary.

'Sit down. I'm sorry. I apologise. I didn't mean to offend you'. *Shit, that is two outbursts from two females. What a night. Bloody boongs, bloody women, and who the fuck is this Billy?*

Lisa took a few deep breaths and noticed her aunt walking towards her. 'Everything okay, here?'

'Fine, Aunty. We were having a conversation about my *Aboriginal* friends.' Zena saw the fire in Lisa's eyes and thought it best to change the subject. 'Kate was looking for you, Mitch. She needs you to make a speech and cut your cake.'

Mitch looked at Lisa. He did not want to leave on this note and knew he had deeply offended her. He made his way through the crowd. *Boy she went off like a sky rocket. I'll have to remember not to call them boongs. Bloody boongs. I've always called them that.* He went to find his mother.

Dave and Kate motioned Mitch to a small table which had a huge cake on it. Dave rang a small bell, and the conversation stopped.

'Thank you all for coming here to celebrate Mitch's nineteenth birthday. We are so proud of our son and his achievements. We could not wish for a finer son. We'd like you to charge your glasses and make a toast with us.'

Dave began a rendition of Happy Birthday, and when it finished he said, 'To Mitch,' and raised his glass.

'To Mitch,' the guests replied as he cut the cake.

'Thank you, everyone, for coming. I'm the lucky one having parents like Kate and Dave. Please enjoy yourself. The night is young.' He wanted to get back to Lisa and stopped by the bar to fill his tankard. His mates joined him and they told him to skol.

'Come on, mate,' his cousin Frank said. 'Skol. Australian tradition on your birthday mate and also have to get you pissed, real pissed.' Mitch took the tankard and drank it down, rum dribbling from the corners of his mouth. He wiped it away and felt the jolt of alcohol.

He banged the tankard on the table and his mates filled it with rum and coke again. Three rum and cokes later, too much singing and a lot of back slapping, Mitch started to feel the effects.

'I want to see Lisa.' His voice was slurry. 'Yeah mate, she's a real beauty,' agreed Frank. Mitch pushed Frank's arm off his shoulder and weaved his way across to Lisa, who sat with her aunt.

'Uh oh, Alan. Typical Aussie boy birthday. Get pissed, vomit, and the next day they don't remember a thing. Look at the way he's walking.'

'Yep, a bit shaky in his boots,' chuckled Alan, amused.

'I think it's time to go. Come on, Lisa, we are heading home.'

As they stood, Mitch reached them. His breath smelled strongly of rum.

'Beautiful lady, I was wondering if I could see you tomorrow.' As the words tumbled out, he lurched forward.

'Hey, where are you going?' Mitch spluttered. 'Stay here. I want you to stay here. You have to stay. It's only early. I feel mad Lisa, with wild delirious bliss!' He held up his tankard and shouted to the sky.

'We have to go, Mitch,' Zena said politely. 'It's just after midnight and something tells me you have had too much to drink.' Mitch grumbled something and headed back to his friends, stumbling a little.

When they reached Woori, Lisa was glad to get home. 'I think I had too many champagnes, Aunty. I have this giddy, floaty feeling.'

'Oh, really. I stopped you at two, so where did the rest come from?'

'Mitch, but it wasn't his fault. I liked it, but now I feel woozy.'

'Well, you can sleep it off and learn a lesson, my girl.' She walked Lisa to her room, where she flopped on the bed. Zena removed her shoes. She was asleep before Zena got to the door. 'Night, hun. Hope there is no headache.'

Alan was sitting in the kitchen when she came out of the room. 'Asleep now but I think more likely, she just passed out. Probably the most alcohol she has ever consumed. Not good at that age. I hope she has a headache. Teach her a lesson. I should have watched her more closely,' Zena admitted.

Alan nodded. 'They did look good together when they were dancing. You have to admit that, and despite his rum consumption tonight, he usually does the right thing. Not sure about the Tess behaviour, though. The boy has obviously been sowing his oats. But that's what young boys do. Still, Lisa is young and she still has a lot to deal with, so certainly, we both don't want any problems from Mitch. If he oversteps the mark, I'll be the first to have a strong word with him. He may be able to get the local girls to meet his needs but Lisa will not be on the agenda.'

'I know most of the girls there tonight would think Mitch a catch. But Lisa would not have been one of them, and you are forgetting something, Alan,' reminded Zena.

'What's that?' He lit up a cigarette.

'Billy. He is always there.'

'Yes, I agree but I think that boy Mitch will do everything to win her over. As I said, the shearing season is seven months away. Anything can happen in that time.'

'He can try. My money is on Billy,' affirmed Zena.

FOURTEEN

THE MORNING AFTER

Lisa woke around 3.00 a.m. Her head was thumping and her was mouth dry. She looked at the creased pink dress that she had fallen asleep in. 'Oh no,' she groaned as she rubbed her head, 'My beautiful pink dress.'

'Ugh, my mouth feels rotten. How could my father do this again and again?' The room was spinning, and she began to gag. She raced for the bathroom and threw up. After removing her dress, Lisa lay on the bathroom floor and fell asleep on the coolness of the tiles.

The laughter of the kookaburras greeted the morning light with their riotous call, echoing across the plains. Lisa sat up and leaned against the bath, her head throbbing. 'Oh, this is so not good.' She pulled herself to her feet and washed her face, looking in the mirror. Her eyes were bloodshot and the nausea still lingered. After rinsing a flannel under the cold water, Lisa lay back down on her bed. It was just after 5.30 a.m.

There was a soft knock at the door. 'Come in,' Lisa croaked, and her aunt entered with a cup of tea.

'Well, well, how are you feeling? I can see not that good if you're holding a cold flannel to your head.' Zena took it and ran it under the cold tap, placing it back on Lisa's forehead.

'My head hurts, Aunty,' Lisa moaned.

'Not surprising. You are only young and not used to alcohol. You were in fact illegally drinking. I blame myself for your headache. One drink would have been sufficient.'

Lisa rolled on her side. 'I know. I'm sorry, Aunty. I hope I didn't embarrass you or Alan or me.'

'No, you were fine, Lisa, but Kate will have a job with Mitch this morning. He was well into the rum and the girls when we left.'

'The bubbles made me tingle and I sort of let go a bit. It's funny how alcohol makes you forget your problems.'

'Yes, but when the effect goes away, the problems are still there. Just remember, too much of that stuff can also make you let go and then make the wrong decisions, which can create even more problems than you already had. Think of your father.'

'I did. I won't ever be like that. Mmm, thanks for the tea.'

'Mitch is quite smitten with you, Lisa. He told Alan as much. He wants to see you.'

Lisa covered her face with her hands. 'Why is he smitten?'

'You'll have to ask Mitch that. And as I said, no harm in being friends. You are both still so young. Be good to have some company to ride out to the river or see a movie though. But you need to put him straight and clarify it's just a friendship, and should he seek anything else, he would need to move on. Alan and I discussed this last night while you were snoring. You certainly don't need any problems from Mitch. You have been through too much, and pressure from a male is not what you need.'

Her conversation with Mitch suddenly flashed through her mind. 'Aunty, he said that word again.'

'What word?' queried Zena.

'Boongs, Aunty. He has this thing where he calls the Aboriginals boongs. And darkys. I challenged him about it. Gosh, I just remembered that. I wouldn't want a friend who talks about them that way. It's just not right. I hate it.'

'Don't shut the door on him because of that, Lisa. A lot of people around here do call them that and they don't mean any malice, but I guess there are some that do. I don't believe Mitch is seriously being racist or derogatory by those comments.'

'How can you be sure, Aunty? He says it so easily,' rebuffed Lisa.

Zena looked at her niece and softened. 'You know, Lisa, you're right. How do we really know someone's inner thoughts? It's just that I've known the Walkers for a long time and have never heard Kate or Dave speak awfully about any race. So keep an open mind. Mitch is just a friend but if you don't like his opinions or the way he thinks, then you don't have to associate with him. But having some young company out here is not a bad thing. I'm going to get you a piece of toast and something for that head. Have your tea. I'll be back.'

When Zena returned, Lisa was sound asleep. She left the tea by her bedside and the headache pills and quietly closed the door.

'Asleep?' Alan asked.

'Yes, sound asleep. I should have watched her, Alan. I feel so bad. I'll leave a note for her. We need to finish off those lambs before the heat of the day kicks in.'

It was midday when Lisa woke again. She was disorientated in time and place but her headache was almost gone. After taking a bite of the cold toast, she threw down the two pills with a glass of water and got under the shower, letting the cold water run over her. *That feels better.*

She hung up the pink dress after checking for damage. Phew, there was none. She loved this dress and would have been upset if it were ruined. She pulled on her shorts and threw on a shirt before heading to the kitchen. She saw the note: 'Your chores are all done.'

Lisa breathed a sigh of relief. No chores and no school lessons. She looked up when she heard a car pull up. Buster and Dougy were barking loudly. It wasn't the ute, but Mitch's Land Rover. She frowned. She was alone. For a moment she thought she would not answer the door, but he bounded up the back stairs and banged loudly, peering through the gauze screen of the door.

'Hi, Mitch,' Lisa said tentatively.

'Hello, you. Nice to see you up and about. Thought I would just drop by and see how you are,' said Mitch.

'You too. I wondered how you were going. Thought you would have a very sore head!' snickered Lisa.

'I did, but I recover quickly,' said Mitch, grinning. 'I was wondering if you wanted to go into town next weekend and have dinner with me, maybe see what's on at the pictures. We can have dinner at the RSL?'

Lisa scratched at her arms. That familiar feeling was creeping in. She paused. *I feel trapped.*

'I will have to ask my aunt. I'm not sure. My brother may be here.'

'Sure, Lisa. That's fine. No rush. Thought you may want to get out and have some fun. I do like you, and it would be great getting to know you more.'

Lisa felt her heart beating faster, but the sound of the ute made her breathe a sigh of relief.

'Oh, here they are now,' said Mitch as he turned to greet Alan and Zena coming up the stairs.

'Hi, son, glad to see you're not suffering the effects of the rum,' said Alan, throwing his hat on the table.

'I sure did, but as I just told Lisa, I recover quickly. Umm, I headed across here because I was hoping to catch you all together. I just asked Lisa but I wanted to ask your permission as well. I'd like to take her to the RSL next Saturday for dinner and maybe a movie, if anything decent is on.'

'Oh, that's nice of you to ask permission, Mitch,' said Zena. She looked at Lisa and could see she was not at all receptive, but it was hard to gauge her mood accurately. She was probably still hung over.

'We'll talk about this later, Mitch, and let you know. We've just come in for lunch,' explained Zena.

'Well, I best hit the road. Have to get a few things tidied up over there,' said Mitch. 'Looks like Woodstock instead of Woodside. So, just give me a call, Lisa, if you want to go.'

Alan saw him to the door.

'See you, Mitch,' said Alan as he took off down the back steps. 'Hope she says yes,' he sung out. The boy had dauntless optimism.

'What do you think?' asked Alan. 'I am sure there would be no danger. Do you good to go out instead of sitting at home with us night after night. Have a think, but I can tell you now, if there is any trouble, I will personally shoot him. I know the Tess episode was ugly, but young boys do get about, Zena.'

'I'm not so sure, Alan,' pondered Zena. 'It is your decision, Lisa, but I am not wholly in agreement, maybe because of what you have been through, what lays ahead, or just because of a whole range of things.'

'But what do I say if I don't want to go?'

'That's easy, Lisa. You simply say no, perhaps another time. But as I said, it's up to you.'

Lisa nodded. 'My mind is on a lot of things, and we haven't made any plans for Mark's stay as yet either.'

'Yes, I know that, Lisa. But Des was organising a date and said he would let me know. So, if you want to go next Saturday, then fine. But if a situation crops up like this, the easiest way is to always tell the truth. Yes, you would love to go, or no, you are not ready to see people at this stage. If you lay your cards on the table and speak your mind then he will know exactly where he stands.'

'Okay,' agreed Lisa. 'It's just after 3.00 p.m., Aunty. I'm going to brush Noir and give her a lunge. Not up to riding. I'll see you both later.'

As she lunged the beautiful mare, her thoughts turned to Mitch. It would be nice to get out but she still had that uncomfortable feeling always inside her. *I wish I could trust . . . trust men. Maybe start to try. But I don't have the same feeling of safety with him as I did with Billy.*

Lisa let Noir off the lunge lead, fed her some hay and then headed back to the house. Dusk was washing the colour from the sky, and she wanted an early night.

'Hey,' said Lisa as she entered the house.

'All good with Noir?' asked Alan, looking over his reading glasses.

'Good, she is so easy to handle.'

'Because she's smart. I'll wait until later to put her into foal. Sometimes the young mares reject the foals, and as I said, I don't want to have any problems, she is too valuable.'

Alan glanced sideways at her. 'So, have you made any decisions about Saturday night?'

'I would like to go, just to sort of get out. I don't want to be rude by saying that, but I have to get over my nerves. As Helen said, regain my sense of safety and trust. But that apprehensive feeling always seems to surface. It did in the kitchen today when I was alone with Mitch. Maybe that scratchy feeling will always be there.'

'Going to take time. You've been through a lot. Go, only if you feel comfortable, but absolutely no alcohol,' cautioned Alan.

Lisa looked chagrined.

'Zena is having a snooze, so let's set the table and get things ready.'

Alan grabbed some knives and forks. Before long, Zena appeared, rubbing the sleep from her eyes. As she sat down, Lisa announced, 'I've decided I will go out with Mitch. As you said, he is just a friend and hopefully my nerves will not get the better of me being on my own with him.'

'I think you've made the right decision. There's nothing to be afraid of. But getting to know a few of the locals around your age is a good idea. Make it clear to Mitch it's just a friendship. It concerns me that since coming here, you have really only been with us, and that is a good thing, considering what you went through, but it would also be nice for you to get out. That is why the yes side of me comes calling. Don't forget there are the B & S balls too, which are all great for socialising, but not for a couple of years yet,' said Zena.

Lisa looked puzzled. 'What are they?'

'They're a lot of fun and bring back some good memories,' said Alan. 'Bachelor and Spinster balls. They are for the country kids, eighteen years and over. You dress up in formal gear and large volumes of rum are usually consumed by the silly boys. The balls start at night and go until the early hours of the morning. Country music is played and the ball was sort of organised so country kids could hook up with a partner. Then everyone usually sleeps in their swag on the back of their ute.'

'That does sound fun, but I'll have to wait as I'm only turning seventeen this year.' Lisa pulled a face.

'I'm sure Mitch would take you to a B & S ball when you are legal age, Lisa, which is why you can do a few things in between, like go to the movies or have dinner, just as friends. I had male friends when I was teaching. You go make the call, hun. I'll start dinner.'

Lisa wandered into the hallway and picked up the phone, her stomach churning. 'Hi, Mrs Walker, it's Lisa. Thanks for a great night last night.'

'You are most welcome, Lisa. Come over any time. Mitch said you may call. I'll just get him for you.' She could hear Kate calling out and finally he picked up.

'Hi Lisa, I'm glad you called. I was about to hit the sack,' laughed Mitch.

'Me too. Umm, I have thought about next Saturday night, and my answer is yes.'

Mitch let out a whoop. 'Fantastic. I'll pick you up at 4.00 p.m. If the picture is no good, we can just have dinner.'

Lisa gulped. 'Just one other thing I want to tell you, Mitch, without hurting your feelings – it's just as friends. You know, a friend date.' She chewed her bottom lip anxiously. It was the first time *she* had told a man what she wanted.

'That's fine, Lisa. Good way to be. I'll see you Saturday. Look forward to it.' Mitch put the phone down. *Friends sure, for now, but I am going to make you mine.*

FIFTEEN

FAREWELL, OLD FRIEND

It was January 1972. Only seven months to go until the start of the shearing season. Lisa looked down at the quartz stones next to her. She had laid Billy's necklace around the stones. The day he gave them to her was so clear. His lovely brown hands carried the necklace like it was a string of diamonds. To her it was. She reached out and touched it. Bush things.

It was nearly 6.00 a.m. and she could hear her aunt moving about. She stretched and looked out her window. Dougy was barking at the other dogs across the bore and would then run back to the side of the house, not far from her window, trying to dig. Lisa called out to Dougy, and he came running to below her window and then ran back, still scratching at the dirt in the same spot and barking. 'Oh, what is it Dougy . . . why are you barking so early!' Lisa jumped out of bed as there was no way she was going back to sleep with all that racket. Throwing on some clothes, she headed out to start the day.

'Morning, everyone. Dougy is barking and scratching at something under the house.'

Alan looked over his glasses. 'Yeah, Lisa, we can hear him. Buster is probably annoying him. Maybe he's lying under the house to get out of the heat.'

Zena thrust a bag into her arms. 'Here, take these old bacon bones and throw them to the dogs when you get on your way.'

Lisa grabbed some water and headed down the back stairs with the bones. She whistled, and Dougy came bounding, but there was no sign of Buster.

'Buster, here boy.' Lisa whistled as she walked to where Dougy was scratching, bending down to peer underneath the house. She let out a piercing scream and stumbled back. 'Alan! Alan! Please come quickly,' she yelled, backing away. He was already on his feet when he heard the scream, and he scurried down the back stairs with Zena following.

Lisa stood back with her hand over her mouth, shaking as she looked in horror at the dog who lay so still under the house. Alan spotted the blood on the grass and fell to his knees. 'Buster, Buster, here boy.' But Alan knew by the glassy stare that the dog was dead. He reached in and pulled Buster out by his front legs, letting out a sigh. 'He's dead, Zena. My big old Buster is dead.'

'Oh, Alan,' cried Zena, the tears springing to her eyes. 'What's happened . . . snake?'

Alan ran his hands over the dog's body and then turned him on his side, where a stab mark was clearly visible. 'Oh, God no, Alan,' moaned Zena as she turned her head away. Lisa stared in shock, her chest heaving.

'My big old Buster, someone did this to you. You obviously crawled under the house to die. If only Dougy could talk.' *Bastard, bloody bastard who did this.* Alan felt a stab to his own heart. He remembered being given the pup by one of the Aboriginal stockmen about a decade ago. A jet black cross of a few different other breeds but he had a lovable nature.

'Alan, will you please call Michael Raby! I do think the police should be involved now,' pleaded Zena. Her arm was around Lisa, who wept softly.

'What are the police going to do? It's a dog,' said Alan remorsely.

'Yes, a dog, but all the same, the dog has been murdered. Someone has intentionally killed the dog!'

'You're right, a call is appropriate. For now, both of you go inside, and I'll bury Buster. I'm also going to electrify the compound fences of a night.'

As he shovelled the last of the dirt on the grave, Alan wiped a tear from his eye. 'Goodbye mate, you were one of the best.' When Alan came inside, he made the call to Michael Raby but was advised he was on leave.

'What did Michael say?' asked Zena.

'Nothing, he's on leave,' informed Alan. 'I've left a message for him to call me when he gets back.'

The following two days, they all kept busy doing chores and avoided any conversation about Buster. Saturday was two days away, but Lisa knew it was too late to change her plans with Mitch.

'I really don't feel like going now, Aunty,' grumbled Lisa.

'Look, it was awful finding Buster like that but not going out with Mitch will not alter what has happened. It'll be good to get out, Lisa. Buster's death was a shock to us all, but as Alan said, we definitely know someone is about and he or she, for that matter, will make a slip or we will sight them and make an identification. For now, we just have to wait for that slip. Alan is a patient man but the dog's death has wounded him deeply, wounded us all, but he's waiting. Trust me. Pity the poor bugger when he does make that slip.'

SIXTEEN

FIRST DATE

Lisa wore her lemon dress with the daisies and waited nervously until the Land Rover arrived at 4.00 p.m.

'Set a clock by that bloke,' remarked Alan again.

'Have a good time, sweetheart. We'll wait up for you.'

Lisa waved as she went down the back steps to greet Mitch. Zena and Alan stood on the landing.

'Wow . . . you look terrific,' Mitch beamed.

'The curfew is 8.00 p.m., Mitch. She is not eighteen or legally able to drink yet, so be aware of that rule in a public place. Basically, John the Publican should not let her in. But it's only a meal, so we have cleared it with him. May I remind you that you both need to be on your best behaviour, and no alcohol for Lisa,' said Zena, speaking gently but with insistence.

'Not a problem, you two,' replied Mitch. 'No movie tonight, so dinner and straight home.'

They watched them drive off. 'I hope she'll be okay, Alan. She was nervous, and Mitch . . . well, Mitch always gets what he wants.'

'Come on . . . stop worrying. He would be a fool to do anything wrong. Tess Dunphy is a different girl, but we have known Mitch and his family for many years. He may have sown a few wild oats, as young boys do, and there are girls that are happy for them to do that, but he's not sowing any with Lisa. We made our point.'

As they drove, Mitch spoke about Europe and travel and all the places he had been to. The different rainfalls, different soils, sheep and cattle. He made it sound so interesting, and his love of farming was quite clear. He had an engaging charm, and Lisa found it easier to talk to him as the drive continued. He bounded out of the car with every gate. Nothing seemed to be a problem.

'Did you have many girlfriends in Europe?'

'Hey, that was way out of the blue. What made you think of that?'

'Oh . . . I was just curious and wondered what European girls are like. Was there anyone serious?' Lisa was inquisitive.

'No, all the time I was there, despite having fun, I was homesick, and I wanted the open lands and the smell of the bush. But the girls did keep me entertained.'

'Entertained how?' asked Lisa.

'You are too curious, young lady. Suffice to say they helped my education,' said Mitch, who burst out laughing. Lisa's un-ease started to creep back in. He seemed so worldly and cocksure compared to her.

'I don't find that amusing, Mitch. Entertained? You mean women entertaining you . . . is that what you mean?'

'I'm sorry Lisa, it was a bad joke,' apologised Mitch.

'I don't find any humour with women entertaining you. Women are not for men's amusement.' Her voice was suddenly cold.

A stony silence filled the car, and Lisa sat with her arms folded.

Mitch knew he had crossed a boundary and thought quickly to change the subject. 'Hey, there's a good horse sale on in a couple of weeks. We should go. Alan mentioned you had a new saddle but that you just need a new horse.'

'Yep, I know. I've been riding Neddy, but he is so old now. I think one day he'll drop dead under me. Alan told me about the sales and the old horses and how they go to the abattoirs for a can of dog meat. He said there are also the new horses that can still go to the abattoirs, which is when you can grab a bargain. The young ones he said are grog money. It's awful.'

'Yeah, I hate it too, Lisa. They get the mare in foal, keep the foal for twelve months, run it through the sale yards and then straight to the slaughter house. Grog money as you said, but we have picked up some good stock horses there, so who knows, we may bag a bargain for you.'

They pulled up in front of the RSL.

'Here we are, young lady. Just before 5.30 p.m.' Mitch came around and opened the car door for her. As they went inside, she looked at the same spot she had sat with Billy and felt a wave of sadness.

Inside, it was very quiet. 'No queue tonight. I like it better when your aunt and uncle play. At least the place is lively then, but tonight, I think just the opportunity to sit and talk is a good thing. At least we're not rushing off to do anything. What do you want to drink, and yes . . . I remember, no alcohol.'

Lisa smiled. 'Just a lemon squash, Mitch.'

'Well, you head over to that lounge in the corner, and I'll bring this over. The kitchen opens at 6.00 p.m. so we'll have a drink first and then some tucker.'

He sauntered over to the bar, and the girl behind the bar clearly flirted with him. Lisa wondered where the grumpy barmaid, Elaine, was. John the Publican may have given her the boot. From where Mitch stood at the bar, she could see his physique was strong and muscular. His shoulders were broad, his wide back tapering down to a small waist. Not unlike Billy. It was clear, Mitch was certainly very physically attractive to women. This was evident at his party and what she was seeing here at the club.

'Here you are, wash the dust down,' he said, handing Lisa her drink. Mitch tossed down a schooner. 'That hardly touched the sides,' he laughed and went back for a rum and coke. The barmaid was doing her best to get Mitch's attention. As he sat down, Lisa had an amused look on her face. 'You like to flirt, Mitch, it seems the girls are like bees to honey with you.'

Mitch gave her a roguish grin. 'I like women, Lisa . . . and they seem to like me. Can't help it if they want to flirt. Sometimes I enjoy it.'

'Well, lucky I am not one of those types. Someone has to keep you grounded.'

'Look forward to it, Lisa,' he smiled. He wondered if she might be a little jealous. He hoped so. 'We can maybe wander into the restaurant now, if you like. We'll just finish our drinks and the doors should be open by then.'

Lisa actually felt comfortable. He wasn't crowding her space and made no move to touch her or hold her hand. It was like he knew she was nervous about male company. *Had Zena told him?*

'So, how long will you stay at Woori?' asked Mitch.

Lisa was surprised by the question. 'Indefinitely. I'm not going anywhere. I want to breed stock horses with Alan.'

'So you don't have to go home, then?'

'No, I am not going home.' Her voice was a little louder with a flash of annoyance, and Mitch knew he had touched on something very sensitive. 'I'm staying here, at Woori. It's my home.'

'Sorry, Lisa, I thought it was an extended stay. So are you lucky enough to have any brothers or sisters?'

'Yes.' She brightened, 'I have one brother, I think I told you, and he's coming up here for a visit. Hopefully in the next few days. I am so excited to show him Woori.'

'What about your parents?' Lisa bristled again and her discomfort was obvious. 'No, my father is not coming, and my mother is dead.'

Mitch felt the whoosh go out of her sails again. Another sensitive point. He quickly changed the subject. 'Look the doors just opened for dinner. That's good as I'm famished!'

Relief came over Lisa's face. She didn't want to answer any more questions about her personal life. What would anyone think if they knew what had happened to her?

Lisa followed him to the dining room, and a cheerful lady in her mid-forties came over and handed them the menus. Lisa looked at her name tag. Bonnie. The room was dated, and Lisa's shoes stuck to the carpet, sticky from alcohol. The patterned carpet screamed at them and the red velvet chairs were stained and worn.

'Can I get you something to drink first?' Bonnie asked as she pulled out a pen and small notebook. 'Rum and coke and . . .'

'A small lemon squash will do me, thank you,' said Lisa.

'Be right back and then I'll take your food order.'

Mitch looked around. 'Boy, it could really do with a makeover. Should get Mum in here.'

Lisa laughed. 'Yes, Mitch, I'm sure she could do much better. You do have a lovely home.'

'They do good steaks here with a mushroom sauce. Do you want to try one?'

'Okay, I'll take your recommendation.' She smiled and was actually relaxing. Bonnie the waitress returned and lingered a bit longer, chatting to Mitch. Her eyes darted to Lisa, whose face was clearly expressing agitation.

'Well, I best take your order,' said the waitress and then moved on quickly to the kitchen.

'Another star-struck female?' quipped Lisa.

'Jealous?' teased Mitch, his piercing blue eyes dancing at the mere thought.

'No way, I find it amusing. Very amusing.'

Some people waved to Mitch as they sat down. 'You seem to know everyone, Mitch,' observed Lisa.

'Just being in the same spot for so long and it's a small town. It's not hard, Lisa. But it's also a problem when everyone knows you . . . they also know your business.'

Mitch could see she was settling in herself. *Mum was right. Patience. There was a nervousness about the girl, which also blended in with a shyness.* He had certainly touched on some sensitive points tonight, and he knew eventually things would evolve between them so she could explain her feelings about family and living on the land with her aunt. During dinner, he purposely avoided any topic involving family. When he mentioned horses and Polocrosse, her eyes lit up. Lisa was like a sponge and took it all in.

'You clearly love being in the bush, then. You never interrupted me once,' jested Mitch.

'No, I didn't. So, I need to see you ride now, Mr Polocrosse.'

'You're on!' he almost shouted. It was Lisa asking to see him now.

They finished the meal, and Lisa looked at her watch. 'We best go now, Mitch. I don't want to be late home. I know my aunt will be sitting there waiting up for me.'

'Yeah, sure,' he acknowledged as he came behind her and pulled out her chair. He wanted to throw his arms around her and pull her to him but gently took her arm instead.

As they headed to the front doors, Tess Dunphy and a few other girls who were at Mitch's party suddenly walked in. Lisa wanted to move away from the girl whose cold eyes stared hard at her.

'Well, well. Fancy running into you two here. Having a cosy dinner, Mitchell?' asked Tess sarcastically.

'That's enough, Tess. Have a good night, we are just on our way out.'

'Don't waste any time, do you?' Tess spat, as she glanced at Lisa. 'You're not his type, baby doll. He'll get sick of you and come back to me. You look as boring as bat shit to me. Don't forget to call, Mitch. You know my number. Baby doll won't put out like me. You know you love my bed. It's so cold without you,' Tess sang out in a sing-song tone. Mitch glared at her while Lisa seemed to shrink beside him.

'Come on, let's go.' He protectively walked Lisa to the Land Rover.

'You okay, Lisa?' Mitch queried, gently.

'Tess frightens me. I get the feeling she'll erupt and go berserk or break something. Her eyes are cold but I know one thing for sure, she clearly likes you, Mitch . . . lots. Maybe that's her anger. Seeing you with someone else. Even though we're just friends.'

'Like I said at my party, there is nothing in it. Sure, I've had a physical thing with her but there are not many guys around here who haven't. Tess will find someone, but that someone is definitely not me. Come on now, ready when you are, only twenty-five gates to go,' he quipped as he held the car door open for Lisa. The drive home was punctuated with long silences. Lisa's mind was definitely elsewhere. She had clammed up. He felt like punching bloody Tess Dunphy.

Mitch saw the last gate come into view, and his heart dropped. Lisa would get out of the car, and he really wanted to just take her in his arms and taste her mouth, slide his tongue between her lips. Her innocence and the fact that she seemed immune to his charm and looks were driving him insane.

When they pulled up at Woori, the moon was full and the Milky Way stretched above them. Dougy came barking up to the compound fence. Lisa could see lights on inside the house. Her aunt was waiting.

As he opened the car door for her, Mitch pointed to the stars. 'What a sight. I never get tired of seeing that.'

'Nor I, Mitch. That's the difference being in the city and out here . . . all these beautiful stars.'

'Lisa, I really enjoyed myself tonight. I want to be your friend. Your best friend in the whole world, if you'll let me. I want to get into that private world of yours, the one you keep trapped in your head. I know a lot goes on in there.'

A reluctant smile spread across her face. 'It's good having a friend, Mitch.' He took her hand very slowly and felt how tiny it seemed. He placed her hand against his lips. His mouth was soft and moist. He lowered his head to her neck, breathing in her scent. The girl was intoxicating. Mitch drew back slowly and met her eyes. 'You know I like you . . . very much.'

'Yes, I like you too, Mitch, but as I said, you're a friend.' Lisa could feel the tension rising in her body. Maybe going out with him wasn't such a good idea.

'Okay, but I wanted to tell you that . . . well, about my feelings for you, but yes, I can also be a friend. Maybe . . . maybe we can do it again some time. Just friends?'

'Sure, Mitch.' Lisa's eyes darted away from those piercing blue eyes. They were not the chocolate pools she longed for. 'Um . . . thank you. I had a good night but I really must go now.' His big hands came up to hold her face and he gently kissed her on the mouth. Lisa pulled back, somewhat surprised. Friends didn't kiss each other on the mouth.

'Good night, Lisa.' Mitch watched her go inside. 'I'll call you about that horse ride,' he called out.

'Night, Mitch.' Lisa hit the outside lights.

'Hey, hun, we're in the sitting room,' her aunt called out as the Land Rover drive away.

'How was it?' queried Zena.

'It was okay, but on the way out of the RSL we ran into Tess Dunphy who said awful things. Mitch behaved all night until we got here. Then he kissed me on the mouth, which didn't feel right . . . not good at all. It was just so sudden, and I really was not expecting it.'

'That Tess Dunphy is a spiteful girl. Don't listen to the things that come from her mouth, Lisa,' said Zena.

'What is this kissing bit?' asked Alan.

'It just happened so quickly, and he brought his hands up to hold my face and then he kissed me.'

'Do you want me to say something to him?' asked Alan. 'What do you feel, Zena?'

'I think a quiet word would not go astray, Alan. Clarify it is just a friendship. Lisa is young, and he is more worldly and knows exactly what he's doing. We will handle this, Lisa, so don't lose sleep or become anxious. He just needs to be set straight.'

Alan nodded in agreement.

'Well, when you were out, Des called. Mark will be here in two days,' smiled Zena.

Lisa let out a whoop. 'Gosh, that is wonderful. I'm sooo happy! I'm off to bed then.' She kissed them both goodnight and almost skipped to her room.

◊

Mitch arrived home just before 8.30 p.m.

'Oh, Mum, you're still up.' Kate was curled up in a leather chair.

'Yes, can't sleep, Mitch, until I know you're home safe. Have a good night?' asked Kate.

'Yeah, Mum, apart from running into Tess Dunphy. Copped a bit of a spray.'

'Vile girl. Mitch, you need to stick to girls with a better character. Stay away from Tess.'

'Yeah, Mum . . . good advice. When I dropped Lisa off, I just wanted to stay with her. I want to be with her. I haven't felt like this with any girl. I don't know what it is . . . it's just her. Her powerful magnetism. I feel like my heart will burst out from my chest. Her beauty, her shyness, her mannerisms . . . just everything. But you know, I asked a few personal questions, just sort of chit chat, and it was almost like she retreated.'

'Oh, what sort of questions?' asked Kate.

'Like how long she was staying and about her parents. It was like she didn't want to answer and got a bit defensive.'

'Patience, Mitch. I have a feeling if you rush this girl, you are going to fall flat on your face.'

'I want to make her mine,' Mitch almost growled.

'That is as plain as the nose on your face, Mitchell. Remember what I said. Patience.'

'Mum, that's not one of my virtues when I really want something,' Mitch said wistfully as he kissed his mother goodnight.

As Mitch lay in bed that night, he envisioned Lisa's beautiful face. He couldn't get the feel of her lips against his out of his mind. *I want to be the friend you fall hopelessly in love with. I want to know your secrets, your private world that you keep locked away. I will make you mine. Girls just can't resist me. You'll see.*

PART TWO

SINISTER INTENT

SEVENTEEN

A STRANGER LURKS

'Aunty, I'm going to ride down to the river today. I haven't seen our two ladies for a while and I miss them. I really want to see them before Mark arrives. I'll have a swim and then head back, but I'll get everything done before I go.'

'I don't really want you riding out there alone, Lisa . . . and I don't have anything for you to take. You know I always like to send something to them but you haven't given me any warning.'

'Yes, I know, sorry, Aunty. It was kind of a spur of the moment thing and anyway, nothing has happened since Buster, so maybe that person . . . well, maybe they've gone. I really want to see the ladies and I really want to have a swim.'

'Okay, I know there's no stopping you, but please, just be careful and have a good look around before you get in the water. Promise me,' said Zena.

'I promise,' replied Lisa.

As she galloped towards their humpy, Lisa could see the two figures sitting in the distance. *Good, they are both there.* She looked forward to sitting with them.

'Hello, ladies,' Lisa sang out cheerfully as she tethered Neddy.

Coming over to the humpy, Lisa squatted down next to them.

'How have you been?'

'Bin good, missus,' said Ningali.

'Any news about anything, ladies?'

Ningali glanced at Binna. 'No, we hear nothing. Quiet Lisa.'

Lisa's face dropped and there was silence. She had somehow hoped they had news of Billy. Lisa took a deep breath. 'Please let me know if you hear of anything, Ningali.'

'Yeah, we tell you, little one. You want Dreamtime story from Binna? You stay?'

'I wish, Ningali, but no, I can't stay. Aunty doesn't want me to be out here for long.'

'Need no things, got plenty tucker. You come back when you have da time,' said Ningali.

'Thank you. I felt like a swim today. I'll catch you through the week. My brother is coming tomorrow so I'm very excited. I'll bring him out here to meet you.'

Lisa hugged Binna and Ningali. 'Bye, ladies.' She waved as she headed towards Neddy. Lisa mounted him and squeezed his flanks to go harder, breaking into a canter and then a steady gallop. Lisa wanted to feel the speed and the power of the horse. Most of all she wanted to get to the river and feel where she had lay with Billy.

When Lisa arrived at her usual spot, it was quiet, and danger was not evident as she looked around. *It seems safe.* The water was cool and refreshing, and when she sat on the bank after a swim, her thoughts turned to Billy and Goobang. *I wonder if I could find that place on my own. No. Dangerous, and I would probably get lost.*

Lisa looked around quickly when she heard a noise in the bush. Footsteps, like twigs breaking under foot. Someone was there. Trying not sound too nervous, she called out, 'Hey, who's there? I know someone is there. Is it you, Billy?' She remembered the last time, when he had sat watching her.

Lisa tentatively got to her feet, holding her small towel against her body. She suddenly felt frightened. 'Who's there?' The light wind rustled the trees. It was an eerie sensation, and her mouth felt dry. *I need to get out of here.* Lisa recalled the words of Binna. *Someone is coming . . . but who?*

Lisa quickly made her way to Neddy, dressing quickly over her wet costume. The noise had stopped but fear was striking at her heart. She suddenly did not feel safe. She dug her heels into Neddy's flanks and took off. *Danger was here.* The ride home was hard on Neddy. Lisa never let up. Fear carried her all the way to back Woori. As she pulled up at the gates and rode Neddy to the Tack Room, Alan came out.

'Whoa there, what's the hurry, kid? Heard the hooves before I saw you. Neddy, the poor old boy, is in a lather. What's up?'

'There was someone there, Alan . . . someone was there, I swear it,' Lisa jabbered, swinging her legs down off the horse.

'Take your time, young lady. What's going on? Who was there?'

Lisa caught her breath. 'I was swimming, and then I sat, just quietly. I heard a noise, like someone walking towards me. Step by step over the dead leaves and branches. I just got out of there and then I remembered Binna's words, someone is coming for me.'

'Look, calm down, Lisa. You are safe now.'

'What's going on?' Zena was at the back door.

'There was someone there, Aunty, at the river, and they wouldn't answer me when I called out'. Zena came down quickly, the terror clear in Lisa's eyes.

'Are you sure, Lisa? I should not have let you go . . . I told you I didn't like you going out there alone.' The angst was clear in Zena's voice.

'Yes, Aunty, I am sure . . . definitely . . . someone was there. I heard their footsteps on the leaves, the sticks. They were cracking.' Zena looked worriedly at Alan.

'Well, what are your thoughts? Saddles moved, horses galloping away in the distance, pumps not working, dead dogs and now this?' said Zena, visibly upset.

'I think you do not go to the river alone, Lisa. That is clear. I'm expecting Michael Raby to call any day now. We may not be the only ones being spooked. Maybe the neighbours and other folk around here are also experiencing a few issues,' Alan speculated.

'Come inside, Lisa, you're shivering. Let's get you out of those wet clothes,' said Zena, although she knew Lisa's shivers were not from being cold. It was from fear.

◇

He stood and looked at the spot where she had been sitting, squatting down to pick up a wet leaf. It made him hungry to watch her swimming and see the water roll over her beautiful brown skin. He had watched her towel the moisture from her long legs. He could feel her mouth against his and imagine her nakedness. He touched his erection. She would be back. He would be waiting.

EIGHTEEN

MARK'S ARRIVAL

As Zena and Lisa waited excitedly at Dubbo airport, Lisa could barely contain herself. She was eager to show her brother around Woori and all the things she had learned. Across the tarmac, a tall young man strode towards them, grinning from ear to ear.

'There he is, Aunty,' Lisa squealed as she started running towards him when he came through the airport doors.

'Hey, you.' Mark dropped his bag and gave his sister a big hug.

'Aunty Zena.' He kissed her cheek lightly.

'How was the flight, Mark?'

'Good! It's such a great feeling to see things from the air. I was so excited. My very first flight!' enthused Mark.

'Well, let's hit the road. We can talk and catch up as we go,' said Zena. After making their way through the small airport, Lisa sat in the back of the Zephyr and let Mark have the front seat. 'I'll get the gates as well,' stated Lisa.

'Gates?' Mark queried.

'Yes,' Lisa gushed. 'There are loads of them.' By the time they hit Woori, Lisa's voice was getting hoarse from talking but she had filled Mark in with everything to the last detail. As they came through the final gate, it was early afternoon.

'Is that it, Lisa?' Mark pointed, amazed at the size of the homestead.

'Yep, that's home,' Lisa said proudly.

'It's like a palace sitting in the middle of nowhere. So much space compared to our fibro shack, Lisa.'

'I know,' agreed Lisa. As they came through the back door, Alan was astonished at the boy's transformation. He was no longer the fat little boy with the crewcut who never stopped eating. He was indeed a young man stepping into adulthood.

'Welcome, Mark. Welcome to Woori. We look forward to having you stay.' They shook hands.

Khartoum suddenly raced by. 'Wow! What a magnificent horse,' exclaimed Mark as his eyes followed the big stallion galloping into the distance.

'He is a real beauty. Let him off most afternoons. Stretches his legs.' Alan laughed.

'You should see Noir, Aunty's black mare, she is just as lovely. I've been riding her and working her. We may put her in foal to Khartoum,' said Lisa.

'Can you ride, Mark?' asked Alan.

'No, but I would love to learn. Let me see now, motor bikes and horses. Can I do all of that in a few days?'

'Of course you can,' Lisa blurted. 'You may get a sore bottom like me, but it wears off quickly.' Mark smiled at his sister's enthusiasm. What a different girl.

'I can't believe how quiet it is,' said Mark. 'All I can hear are birds and sheep in the background, and of course the dogs . . . so many dogs!'

Zena nodded. 'Yes, it's why we love it out here, Mark. Lisa will show you to your room and then we can take a drive in the Land Rover.'

'Sounds good,' he said happily as he followed his sister down the hallway.

'Boy, this is an amazing place, Lisa. This room!' Mark said throwing his hands up to the ceiling. 'Makes our bunks look pitiful, and you . . . you look so happy.'

'I am, Marco.' Lisa flopped on the bed. 'The bush, the Aboriginal people, their stories, I find it all intoxicating, and of course being here with Aunty and Alan is bliss. I've so much to show you.' Lisa looked away momentarily, thinking about Fairfield.

'I'm glad everything is good now, Lisa. I was so worried about you, especially when Mum would not let me talk to you,' Mark said solemnly. 'Anyway, no sadness talk. I'm ready, let's go! Show me what has taken your heart.' He took her hand.

Like Lisa, the vastness of the bush, the peace and the wide open plains made Mark just as happy. It was powerfully reassuring.

'I can see why you all love it out here . . . it really is beautiful,' marvelled Mark.

'Yeah, although the bush and living on the land can be cruel at times, they will have to carry me out in a box. We are all living in a place we love,' said Alan.

'Let's head back to the house now. Tomorrow is another day. Mark can have a look at Noir. Maybe you can lunge her, Lisa, and let Mark see her conformation and gait. She moves beautifully, which is why we are all excited to have her in foal to Khartoum,' said Zena.

'We can give you a bike lesson before dinner, Mark . . . if you're ready?' said Alan as he pulled the Land Rover up next to the compound gate.

'Yep, just show me the way,' Mark laughed.

Alan pulled the motorbike out for Mark and showed him how to start it. 'Bit of a job sometimes but the boot gets her going. I'll wheel it out through the gates,' offered Alan. 'Here, hop on and have a go.'

On the first circle, Mark tipped the bike and hit the dirt. He dusted himself off and got on again.

'Off you go,' shouted Alan, the sound of the motorbike setting all the dogs off barking. Mark did a few more circles at low speed and then took off, the dust billowing behind him. When he came back to where they were all standing, his face was beaming. 'Bloody exhilarating, except for the bugs hitting my face,' laughed Mark.

'Well done, mate, another lesson tomorrow. But right now dinner and a cold beer awaits this dry old throat,' said Alan.

Just as they sat down, the phone rang. 'Excuse me,' apologised Zena. 'Alan, I'll have a gin and tonic, please.'

Zena ducked down the hallway, picked up the phone, and knew the strong masculine voice instantly. 'Oh hello, Mitch. Yes she is, just with her brother Mark, who we picked up today from the airport, so she is buzzing with excitement. Just a minute, I'll get her for you. Give my regards to your mother and father.'

'Who's Mitch?' Mark asked.

'The boy next door,' said Alan. 'Quite keen on your sister.'

'That gin and tonic looks good, thank you, darling.' Zena sat next to Mark.

'You have done a great job, both of you, with Lisa. I just can't believe it's the same girl . . . my scrawny sister,' said Mark, the emotion evident in his voice.

'It wasn't hard; she just needed love and someone to listen to her, and of course justice for the horrible things that occurred to her. There is a lot coming up on the horizon that she still has to deal with,' said Zena.

Mark looked embarrassed. 'I just knew there was something going on when we were at home . . . if only she had told me. I would have stuck up for her or maybe whatever I did would have prevented her going to that Girls Home.'

'You were only young, Mark, so don't give it a second thought. The blame is elsewhere but let's not spoil the night by discussing that. Suffice to say, Lisa has endured a great deal, which we are working through, but the police are well onto it. That Girls Home was a shocking place.'

They all looked up when Lisa returned. 'I invited Mitch over the day after tomorrow as he wanted to meet Mark.'

'That's lovely,' said Zena.

'Nice guy?' queried Mark.

'Yes, but like all young men, he has to keep the brakes on. Mitch and his parents live on the property next door and he happens to be a bit smitten with our girl,' said Zena. 'But they are just friends.'

Lisa blushed. 'What do you think, sis?' probed Mark.

'Hmm, I like him, but just as a friend,' Lisa replied, fidgeting.

Zena stood up. 'Dinner is ready, if we can all make a move to the dining room, going a bit formal tonight,' she smiled at Mark.

The conversation flowed and Lisa excitedly told Mark about Billy as well as Binna and Ningali.

'Slow down, kid,' laughed Alan. 'I want to hear what the boy has to say.'

'It's okay, Alan, I love to see her energy and to hear her laugh,' said Mark. 'I've missed it so much.'

'So, any ideas regarding your future, Mark?' asked Alan.

'Just looking at all my options, I guess. I know Rotary have good Exchange Student programs, so I'll source that when I get home. Maybe pick a country next year. My teachers said that the Rotary exchange was now across most countries. It's a great idea. The United States has always fascinated me, and it's lucky

I have great teachers who encourage this exchange system. I do want to see more of the world.'

By 10.00 p.m. Lisa began to feel weary. 'Time to hit the sack, I think,' said Alan. Lisa has a big itinerary tomorrow for you, Mark.'

Zena nodded. 'You two head off.'

'Thank you for a lovely evening and for having me here. I look forward to tomorrow,' said Mark, kissing his Aunt Zena's cheek.

'Night, sweetheart, it's lovely to have you here,' responded Zena.

Lisa followed Mark to his bedroom door. 'Have a good sleep, Marco, it's truly the bee's knees having you here.'

He bent to kiss her cheek. 'Ditto, sis. I can see why you love this place.'

◊

The day was full, and laughter was their friend. Horses, chores, motorbikes and yabby fishing, and Lisa never stopped talking. 'We have to head in after catching these yabbies, Mark, as Zena wants to have lunch down at the river. I was there the other day and got a bit spooked.'

'Why spooked?' asked Mark.

'I just had this feeling someone was there, so I took off quickly and gave poor old Neddy a good run. But some other peculiar things are happening around here, so Alan is waiting to speak to the local copper, Michael Raby.'

'That's not good, especially being so remote,' said Mark.

'No, it does feel a bit spooky at times. My Aboriginal lady friends, the ones I told you about, they live near the river, so if we are going that far, we'll kill two birds with one stone. We can call in and meet them, so you get to meet two of my favourite people, and I can show you the river as well. It is such a peaceful place, and I love to swim there.'

Zena had their lunch packed and was ready to go. 'Got a bucket of yabbies, Aunty,' said Lisa, holding up the catch when they came inside.

'Well done, you two. Dinner tonight then,' she replied.

'That was fun,' said Mark. 'But some have very big nippers.'

'They do, and it's quite easy to lose a finger. Just put the bucket in the laundry, Lisa, and throw a towel over them.'

Alan arrived and they took the Land Rover, heading towards Binna and Ningali, Lisa chatting all the way about the Dreamtime stories Binna would tell.

'That's them there.' Lisa pointed.

'They live in that?' asked Mark, surprise in his voice.

'Yep, sure do,' affirmed Lisa.

'They are very resourceful, Mark,' informed Zena. 'The Aboriginal people have roamed this land for 60,000 years. I help the ladies with food and a few other things, but basically they fend for themselves. Like Lisa, I adore them both.'

Ningali stood and waved. She turned to Binna. 'Little one, she bring da family, got da car full,' she cackled.

Mark was introduced to them and they all sat down. Zena had brought some jars filled with fruit, much to Binna's delight.

'Hello, my friend,' said Binna, her milky eyes vaguely making out Zena's form.

'He your brudder? Nice em lookin, this one,' said Ningali, giggling.

'How are things out here, Ningali? No strange sights?' asked Alan, changing the subject.

'No, boss. I bin lookin' out but no see nuthin.'

'Lisa was swimming down by the river the other day and thought someone was there,' mentioned Alan.

'Me bin fishin, nope see nobody but me look again . . . always keep lookin for da boss.'

Alan laughed. 'Thanks, Ningali. We are heading that way now, just to show Mark the river and more country, so I'll have a look around myself.'

Binna spoke softly, taking Zena's hand. 'You rememba what I say about da bad spirit.'

'Yes, Binna,' said Zena nervously. 'We are watching out. Thank you for your advice, my friend. Right then, we must be off. Take care, ladies.'

As they drove off, silence had entered their vehicle. 'What was that all about?' Mark asked.

'Like I explained, I thought someone was out at the river, and I called out but there was no answer. I was sitting quietly, and it was like the sound of someone's feet walking over broken sticks,' said Lisa.

'That would give me the creeps,' agreed Mark.

'Yes, we are all on alert, Mark. It gives us all the creeps. We have never had any trouble out here before, none whatsoever, so it has us all worried,' said Zena uneasily.

'I'm going to have a wander around while we're out here,' commented Alan. 'I don't want anybody to wander off or anyone to be on their own while we're here.'

'You are scaring us all, Alan!' exclaimed Zena. 'We're supposed to be having a picnic out here. You sound like Agatha Christie!'

'Just being cautious, my love.'

When they arrived, there was a gentle breeze running through the tall gums, the scent of eucalyptus filling the air.

'What a lovely spot! No wonder you like coming here, Lisa,' marvelled Mark. 'And the water is so clear.'

'Yes, it's beautiful.' Her thoughts wandered back to Billy when he sat watching her. It seemed so long ago.

'Let's walk the edge of the bank. I've locked the car. Keep your eyes out for old fires, camp sites, footprints, anything that may look like someone has been here,' instructed Alan.

They walked deliberately, looking for over an hour, Lisa and Mark wandering up and down the bank as the group moved along, finally stopping for lunch. Zena passed the sandwiches around as they sat on the small blanket she had carried.

'Hoof marks here, Alan,' said Lisa. 'But who knows how old they are.'

'Well, no camp sites, and no food tins, no skeletons of dead animals . . . nothing . . . niente! Certainly, nothing to indicate someone has been out here long-term or even short-term for that matter. I was hoping in a way, I would find something. May solve some of the mysteries of late. Come on, let's head back to the Land Rover,' said Alan.

As they got closer to the car, Alan stopped. 'Fuck!' he yelled as he started to run towards it.

Zena stood rooted to the spot. She could see one of the rear tyres had been slashed.

As Alan changed the tyre, his anger punctuated the air. 'I will get this bastard. One thing is for sure, we know he or she is still here, and I am betting it's a he. I just don't think a girl would do this, and a girl would not be hanging out here on her own. I'll come out here with Michael Raby and the dogs. They'll pick up the scent. Come on, let's head home. I'm sure Michael is back at the police station tomorrow.'

◊

He watched as the Land Rover pulled away and smiled. I know the river and the land better than you. You won't find my tracks. Even that Ningali, she's too stupid to find me. Too sharp for her. I watch you and your family, especially my prize. I'll take her. She'll be mine.

◇

The chatter on the way home was much quieter. The event had created a sombre tone, which carried over to dinner.

As Lisa said goodnight to her brother, he spoke. 'Don't worry about today. I'm sure Alan will get to the bottom of it. I just want you to be careful out here. Anyway, I look forward to meeting Mitch tomorrow. One more day with you too. Night sis.'

'Night, Marco, see you in the morning.'

◇

When Lisa woke, everyone was up. She could hear the chatter in the kitchen, and the smell of toast wafted into the air.

'I can't believe I slept in,' yawned Lisa as she kissed her aunt and brother good morning.

'You must have needed it, darling girl,' said Zena. Lisa could hear Alan's voice down the hallway.

'He's talking to Michael Raby. Here, sit down and have some breakfast, but not much as Mitch will be here at noon for lunch.'

'Got your beauty sleep then, sis, have to look your best,' Mark said, teasing her. 'I'm looking forward to meeting him.'

'He is just a friend, Marco . . . nothing more. He is okay and comes from a good family but . . .' And her sentence drifted off.

'Okay, tell me, you are keeping something from me,' Mark teased.

'It's Billy, and he is coming back for me.'

Mark noted her face radiated when she mentioned this boy's name.

'Well then, sis, I look forward to meeting him too,' Mark smiled.

Alan hung up the phone and joined them. 'And?' asked Zena as he sat down.

'Yeah, seems there have been no reports from any neighbours or anything like we have experienced. We are the only ones. Michael will head out here tomorrow, and we'll ride out to the river.'

'Ride?' asked Zena.

'Yep, we're taking all of the dogs to try and pick up any scent. Whoever is out there knows the bush . . . real good. I need that strong sense of smell from them as the dogs can pick up on anything. Might scare the bugger away, hearing all the hounds. But I'm going to leave some of the dogs closer to the house from now on. And a few around the compound, so I'll move their kennels and only leave the hunting dogs across the bore. The dogs we use for pig hunting, especially Bear, are much more savage than the likes of poor old Buster. So they are coming too when we head out.' He sat down.

'Okay, let's get organised and get things done. I want to sit back and enjoy lunch with Mitch,' said Alan.

Lisa and Mark took off in the ute to do the usual chores and were back just before eleven.

'Hi Aunty, can we do anything?' Lisa asked.

'Nope, all under control.' Zena hovered over setting the kitchen table.

'Let's shower then, Marco, and freshen up. I always feel pig smell on me after being around those animals.'

Mark laughed. 'Yes, not the best smell, Lisa. I've never seen pigs that big. I guess you eat them?'

'We do. No supermarkets out here unless you want to open all the gates and do the long drive into town.'

◊

Alan looked at his watch. 'Yep, five minutes to twelve. Said it before and I'll no doubt say it again. Set a clock by that boy.' They all sat on the verandah and watched Mitch tear down the road towards the house.

'He's in a hurry,' laughed Mark.

Alan joked. 'The boy knows two speeds, stop and fast.'

When Mitch came up the back stairs, he carried two bunches of roses.

'Oh, how lovely,' exclaimed Zena as he handed her the white bunch. 'No doubt from Kate's garden. Tell her I said thank you, Mitch. I'll just grab a couple of vases.'

'And for you, Miss O'Connor, pink.' He gazed tenderly at her face. Lisa felt herself blushing. Mitch was doing his best to impress.

'Huhmmmm,' interrupted Alan, 'May I have your attention please.'

'Oh, yes, sorry, Alan,' said Mitch.

'May I present Mr O'Connor . . . Lisa's younger brother.'

Mark smiled. 'Mark will do,' he said as he shook Mitch's hand. 'Nice to meet you, Mitch. I have heard a lot about you and your family.'

'And I have heard a lot about you too, Mark.'

Zena arrived with the white roses in a vase and placed it on the dinner table.

'Perfect. They look gorgeous, Mitch. I've put the pink roses in your room, Lisa,' said Zena. Mitch smiled, he was happy Lisa would see these in her room as a reminder, hopefully of him.

'Okay, if everybody can please sit, anywhere you want, lunch will be served. Alan, can you organise drinks, please. Mitch said he only has a couple of hours as his Dad wants him back,' mentioned Zena.

As Alan fetched the drinks, Mitch sat down next to Lisa, and Mark sat opposite. He watched the chemistry between the two. There was no doubt where the young man's heart lay. He hung on to every word his sister said, and his eyes danced when she spoke. *I like him, Lisa.*

'Help yourselves, everyone,' said Zena as the food was carried to the table.

'Yum,' said Mark. 'What a fabulous spread . . . thank you so much.' Zena kissed the top of his head.

Alan then asked, 'Mitch, have you had anything go missing or any odd occurrences over at Woodside?'

'Umm . . . no. Why?' enquired Mitch.

'Well, I won't spoil lunch but suffice to say, Lisa's good bridle went missing, tyres have been slashed, we've had a murdered dog and a few other things happen. Can you and the boys over there keep an eye out, and if you do see something strange, let me know.'

'Murdered dog!' spluttered Mitch.

'Yeah, but we can talk about that later,' said Alan, not wanting to discuss it in front of Mark.

It was a good lunch with much laughter, the looming worries and strange occurrences forgotten for the moment.

'Well, I must be off,' said Mitch. 'Zena, wonderful and wonderful. Nice to meet you, Mark. I hope you'll come again soon.'

Mark stood and shook Mitch's hand. 'I hope so, Mitch. It was good to meet you.'

'Lisa, please see Mitch out,' suggested Zena.

'Okay, Aunty.' She followed Mitch down the stairs.

'Thanks for coming, Mitch. I'm so happy you met my brother. He means the world to me.'

Mitch's arms gently pulled Lisa towards him. 'I could see that . . . and you, little lady, mean the world to me. I cannot get you out of my thoughts. You even invade my sleep.'

Lisa did not pull away. Her body felt a strong sensation of something . . . maybe relaxation. Maybe because she was in a better place. Maybe because she was just so happy her brother was here. Mitch bent to kiss her, and Lisa lifted her lips up to him, ever so slightly. 'Thanks, Mitch. It was good to have you here.'

'I'll be on my way, Princess. I'll call you,' Mitch shouted, his exuberance filling the air.

A thousand mixed emotions flooded Lisa's mind. Everyone liked him.

Later that evening, Mark came to Lisa's room. 'I've had a great time, Lisa, and it was nice meeting Mitch. I like him. A confident guy, and he clearly has great affection for you. But, I want you to be happy after all you've been through, and be with someone who really cares for you.'

'Yes, I know, Mark. He is pretty good but you are yet to meet Billy.'

'I'll say good night then. Homeward bound tomorrow.'

NINETEEN

THE HUNT

The drive to Dubbo airport seemed to take forever. 'I so wish you could stay, Marco. I hate to see you go.'

'Ditto, sis, but I have to get back for school. Dad and I have a few decisions to make.'

'I can call you now, Mark . . . even every day,' Lisa said eagerly, 'and give you all of my news.'

'That would be great, Lisa. I look forward to your calls. Be good to Mitch. He's a nice person and he would watch out for you, take care of you.'

'I know,' replied Lisa. They unloaded Mark's bag and sat with him until the plane arrived. Sadness racked Lisa's body.

'It's okay,' comforted Zena. 'There are no barriers now, Lisa. Mark is free to come up, you are free to go down and free to call. Freedom for both of you.'

The boarding call was made, and Lisa hugged Mark ferociously. 'Please come back soon.'

'Yes, please do,' said Zena, giving her nephew a warm hug. 'You are always welcome, Mark.'

They watched him walk through the doors, and as he turned to wave, Lisa felt her heart break.

'Lisa, you are not losing him, he is just heading home and he will be back. No barriers now, remember. Come on, the Zephyr awaits. And Alan. Don't forget, he's riding out to the river today with Michael Raby and the dogs.'

'Oh yes, Aunty. I want to go with them.'

'Time to move then. You are not leaving me out of this either. I asked Alan to saddle Noir for me.'

As they reached Woori, the police vehicle was parked at the gates to the compound.

Alan was talking to Michael as he saddled up the four horses.

'Did he get off alright?' asked Alan.

'Yes, no problem. Michael, this is my niece, Lisa,' introduced Zena.

'Lovely to meet you, Lisa.' Michael extended his hand.

'Heard of the problems here and that there may have been someone at the river the other day,' said Michael empathetically.

Lisa nodded. 'I also heard someone here, when I was in the Tack Room and yes, then down at the river. I haven't physically seen anyone, but I just know there is someone. And Buster our dog is dead, and I'm sure Alan told you about the tyre . . . and my bridle is missing and . . .'

'Hey, kid, slow down,' Alan said. 'Have already filled Michael in. Let's just ride out and see what we can find, young lady. Let's get on our way.'

'Are you sure you want all the dogs off then, Alan?' queried Zena.

'Yes, absolutely sure. Lisa, go let the dogs off, all of them. I particularly want Bear, my best tracker,' said Alan.

'What if we can't get them back? They'll turn feral and start killing lambs in the season. Then you'll have another big problem,' commented Zena.

'Got a bag of meat and bones here . . . they will follow us all the way home.'

Michael laughed. 'Yeah, Alan, them and every bloody bush fly. Good luck with that, mate. I am staying well behind you.'

Lisa crossed the bore and one by one let the dogs off as well as the ones around the compound fence.

'God almighty . . . what a bloody noise!' laughed Alan. 'Madness!' The dogs jumped the bore and swirled around them, barking madly.

Zena rode Noir, and Alan was on Khartoum. They watched as Michael threw his leg over old Tidgy. 'She was a great mare in her day, Michael, nice and comfy ride on her.' Lisa giggled as she mounted Neddy. Michael looked anything but comfortable.

'Okay,' said Alan as he whistled the dogs, who excitedly ran ahead.

'Feels like a fox hunt, Alan. Reminds me of when I was in England,' laughed Zena. 'Really, Alan . . . all these dogs.'

'It's fun, Aunty, although I know we are looking for something sinister, but gosh, all these dogs and all this noise!' Lisa exclaimed.

The humpy came into view, and they waved to the ladies.

'Will we stop, Aunty?' asked Lisa.

'Not today, darling girl. Let's just get the task at hand over with. Binna and Ningali would be wondering what is going on though. You can let them know when you see them next.'

They rode on and the dogs ran excitedly around them, some lagging behind, their noisy collective barking almost shaking the trees and sending the cockatoos screeching.

◊

He lay silently until he heard the noise of the dogs in the distance. More than one. He knew he had to move fast. They would be upon him. Bastards. Bloody bastards. They would have the hunting dogs. Pig dogs, picking up every scent. He began to make a move. You bring plenty trouble for me now . . . this time. Too many dogs, but I come back for my prize. I want her. You don't stop me next time. She gunna like me. I gunna make her feel good. Better than Billy. Bastard Billy. I get you too. For now, too dangerous. Big trouble with the dogs. They're onto me. I'll be back. You win . . . for now.

◊

Alan watched the dogs go crazy, up and down the banks, scratching and sniffing. Bear, his Rottweiler-cross, followed a trail into the distance along the river bank. 'He'll be back, he always comes back,' said Alan. 'Let him see what he can find. He's certainly onto something.' He dismounted Khartoum and wandered over to where the dogs were getting excited. Alan looked at Michael Raby, who showed his concern.

'Yep, someone has been out here. The dogs are up and down here, really going berserk. Whoever it is, is down here away from where most people would swim or fish . . . much more downstream. He would have heard the dogs . . . for sure. He should be scared. The pig dogs don't mess around,' said Alan.

'You are probably right, Alan. He certainly knows the bush and is on foot. Aboriginal?' asked Michael.

'Don't know. He may have tethered a horse someplace else. But for now, I would say he is moving quickly and on foot.' Alan's eyes looked in all directions.

'The dogs tell us someone has been here. I will periodically come out here with a constable and check the area. If he's still hanging about, this little visit will keep him on his toes,' said Michael.

'I'll ask Ningali to come down further along this way when she's out here, Alan, and see what she finds. Don't forget, those ladies have great bush knowledge,' reminded Zena.

Alan shook his head. 'I'm not happy with that, Zena.' His voice rose sharply. 'If someone is still here, I don't want to jeopardise her safety.'

'You're right, Alan.' Fear suddenly clutched at Zena. If anything happened to Ningali or Binna because of her request, she would never forgive herself.

'Nothing to see and nothing to find. We may as well head back. I would say the dogs alerted anyone out here anyway,' said Michael.

When they got back to Woori, there was a feeling of relief. Although they did not find anything, they were confident their presence was felt. Whoever was out there would know they were onto them.

'Thank you, Michael. Please keep us posted on anything, no matter how insignificant, if you do go back out there,' said Zena.

'Will do. Been a long time since I was on a horse, my thighs will thank you tomorrow. Good luck getting the dogs bedded down,' added Michael.

'All good, mate. None have left me. The aroma of bones and meat has given me a following,' chuckled Alan as one by one they all trooped in, exhausted from the run.

Michael laughed. 'I'll let you know of any issues. A good day. Will leave you to it now.' He headed towards his police vehicle.

Alan moved into the Tack Room and grabbed a long piece of rope. He looped it through the collars of the dogs he needed to go across the bore.

'Lisa, grab these six dogs and chain them to the kennels I've placed around the compound. I'll head across the bore with this lot.'

Lisa could only hope that they had scared away whoever had been making all the trouble. But in her bones, she didn't think so. *I just know you are still out there. Whoever you are.*

TWENTY

THE SEASON APPROACHES

The months passed, and no further incidents occurred around Woori. Alan had decided to shear in spring. Lisa turned seventeen in August, and she only wanted a very quiet affair. The three of them celebrated alone, and Lisa adored the new bridle as her birthday present. Her old one was never found. Mitch became a frequent visitor to Woori and constantly worked on the friendship aspect. Alan had a quiet word about his advances and nothing further happened in this regard. He showed Lisa his prowess with Polocrosse and tried to teach her French, much to Lisa's torment and laughter. Sunday lunch at the Walker house was almost on a regular basis, with Zena and Alan often attending.

Things had settled emotionally. Lisa continued to see Helen Tyler every fortnight, and although pending court appearances were still on her mind, and Lenny was still managing to evade the police, there was a zest to her step and voice. Was it Mitch, or a growing confidence, or just getting older. Life was good, and everyone was pleased at the growing friendship between Mitch and Lisa. The boy hadn't put a foot wrong.

One morning over breakfast, Alan produced a list. 'We have two months before the next season. We need to cover the usual things before it's upon us,' said Alan.

Zena nodded. 'Comes around quickly . . . so quick.'

'I can't wait,' said Lisa excitedly.

'Jack will call any day now. I need to tell him about Jimmy as well as a few other things. Wonder what happened to that boy. Shame really, he had such potential. I don't know much about Jimmy or his background. Maybe that's got something to do with it. I remember a conversation with Burnu a few years back. He said there was often violence in their culture and they had to fix the problem themselves. He said blackfellas were killing blackfellas and killing themselves. Even said women may have been executed for coming onto the ceremonial grounds if the young men were being initiated. Bloody sorry business,' said Alan.

'It is a sorry business, Alan. I feel so much for them. They have high mortality rates, which is so tragic and scandalous. I just can't believe that the majority die before they reach sixty-five. I know it differs regionally, but even with the babies. It's lucky they live. I so wish things could be different for them . . . that they could be given equal opportunity with everything. I take my hat off to Bill Grayden. He was the catalyst for change over in Western Australia. That started in 1957 and it's gradually building, although a lot of people don't like it,' added Zena.

'Nope, and that continues,' replied Alan. 'You will never get it perfect and although things are changing, I don't think we will see it all end before our time on this earth. I think Charles Perkins leading that Freedom Ride in 1965 generated a lot of interest, particularly as he was the only Aboriginal student at Sydney university.'

'But fortunately we have people changing things. Shirley Andrews . . . she has done a lot to establish equal pay for the Aborigines,' ventured Zena.

'Do you remember that story up in Cairns?' asked Alan.

'Vaguely . . . something about labour exploitation?' said Zena.

'Yeah, those two black boys had been working on a large cattle property since they were ten. Became really skilled, been there for fifteen years, and the only money they had was five pounds at Christmas and five pounds to go to the local races! What happened to their bloody wages for fifteen years! Wherever Billy and Burnu are working, I hope they are being treated fairly and getting paid,' remarked Alan.

'Billy is a smart boy, and between you and Jack, you have given him great advice over the years, and Burnu is no fool. I'm sure they will be alright,' said Zena. 'There is one other thing that really disgusted me though.'

'What's that?' queried Alan.

'The way the white stockmen would come back to the camps when the Aboriginal stockmen were still out working with cattle or sheep, and these white men took advantage of the Aboriginal women. Binna and Ningali told me stories of this. Maybe that's why they stayed here, for safety, but apart from that issue, Ningali's ex seemed to enjoy knocking her about,' said Zena.

'Jack will have none of that going on here. You know that. Things are getting better within their culture, although I know with the different states and tribes they have their own fighting and problems as Burnu said. Blackfellas killing blackfellas.

'Now you have distracted me, Zena! We could go on about it all day, but now, on with planning for the season.' Alan spread his notes over the kitchen table.

Lisa sat listening to their discussion. 'I hope what you said was true, Aunty, about Billy being alright. No-one should take advantage of these people.'

'As I said, Lisa, Billy is smart, and he knows what we have been paying him, so I'm sure he will be savvy on what to expect in his pay packet,' reassured Zena.

The discussion was finished and their plans were made. 'I'll leave this list next to the phone. Just have to wait for Jack's call. Okay, the day is beginning, so let's get on with what we need to do.' Alan rose from his chair.

'After my chores, Mitch is coming over. He wants to ride out to the river. Is that okay? I will be with someone, so I'm not alone out there, and I want to call in and see the ladies.'

Zena looked over her glasses. *That's a first. Taking Mitch out there to meet Binna and Ningali.*

'You okay with that, Lisa, being out there alone with Mitch?'

'Yes, Aunty. I have grown very fond of Mitch these past few months and I do trust him. He tells me how much he really likes me . . . all the time, but he is . . . well, he never tries to go any further, and I have made it clear we are just friends. So I do feel safe, and he does make me laugh.'

'On your way then.' Zena glanced at Alan. 'I'll pack a few greens and fruit you can take out there. Throw a few sandwiches in the bag for you and Mitch.'

'Great.' Lisa scooted away down the back stairs.

'I may win my bet, dear wife. She has grown fond of him, even taking Mitch to meet the ladies.' Alan plonked his hat on, the smile never leaving his face as he headed out.

'I am not so sure, my love,' murmured Zena softly to herself. Although Alan had chipped him about making any advances towards Lisa, she always felt like Mitch was ready for any opportunity. But she didn't see a smooth course with Billy due to the racial issues. Mitch seemed to be playing all his cards right. Perfect. *Just one problem – too perfect.*

Mitch pulled up just after eleven, his horse trailer attached. Zena came out to say hello as she watched him unload his big chestnut gelding.

'Morning, Mitch. Good day for a ride. That's a fine boy you have there.'

'Indeed, Zena, he moves beautifully. You should ride him one day. Is Lisa ready? It's a great day for a swim. Maybe a bit chilly.'

Mitch badly wanted to get closer to Lisa, physically, and he had played the same scene over in his mind for the past few months, swimming and seeing her with very little clothing on. He knew she loved to swim. But his mother's words still resonated in his head. *Patience.*

'There she is now.' The ute pulled up at the gates. Lisa bounced out. 'Woohoo, I can't wait. Wow, he's a beauty, Mitch. Big.'

'Yeah, seventeen hands. You'd need a ladder to get up on Almondo.'

Lisa smiled. 'I'll just wash up and grab my bathers.'

'That calico bag is on the kitchen table, Lisa. Sandwiches and water for you and Mitch, and the rest for Binna and Ningali.'

'Thanks, Zena. That's very kind of you. I didn't think to bring anything,' admitted Mitch.

'All good. What time do you expect to be back?' queried Zena.

'Maybe around three or four . . . is that okay with you?'

Zena nodded as Lisa bounded down the stairs.

'I'll leave you to it then. Alan has Noir saddled for you, Lisa – just behind the Tack Room in the yards. Have a great time. Mind how you go. I might take you up on that offer, Mitch, after the season. He really is a magnificent horse,' said Zena as she headed inside.

Lisa disappeared and returned with Noir, the calico bag thrown over the saddle. 'I am so excited, Mitch. I can't wait to get to the river.'

Mitch was the same. He was hoping to take things further, to feel her against him. He groaned inwardly at the mere pleasure of the thought. She had relaxed with him, and he felt they were getting closer. He was feeling confident.

'Let's be on our way then, Lisa.' Mitch hoped somehow this would be a turning point. A time for intimacy.

As they rode, Lisa chatted to him more about her Aboriginal ladies.

'They are so important in my life, Mitch. These wonderful women who roam this earth and give me great spiritual comfort and healing. I have benefited so much from their stories and their cleansing ceremonies.'

'Not too sure, Lisa, but I'll give it a go. Why do you need cleansing or healing. What's that all about?' Mitch tried not so show his reticence to affiliate with the Aboriginals. He felt uneasy.

'Oh . . . . it's just a ceremony they do, but all I know is that it makes me feel at peace and my soul feels really cleansed, like I could float away. Aboriginals see themselves as part of nature and that all things natural are a part of them. All the things on the earth they kind of see as part human and that everything has a soul.'

'You believe that, Lisa?'

'Oh yes, yes I do. I love their culture, and it's told through the ideas of dreaming. Their belief is that long ago, these creatures started human society. These creatures, these great creatures, are just as much alive today as they were in the beginning. They will never die. They are always part of the land and nature as we are. Our connection to all things natural is spiritual.'

The humpy came into view, and Lisa pointed excitedly. 'Look, Mitch, they are both there. I so love sitting with them. Come on.' She spurred Noir to their camp.

Ningali looked puzzled as Lisa pulled up Noir, tethering her to the tree. She had never seen this young man before. 'Binna, she bring da white boy. He plenty powerful lookin.'

'Hello, ladies,' Lisa greeted, walking towards them carrying the calico bag.

'Aaah, little one, be good to see you, and you bring da friend.' Ningali eyed him suspiciously. He seemed a huge young man as he followed the girl.

Mitch did not feel comfortable, and he tried not to show his feelings in the situation. Sitting with two black women was not his choice. *Sitting with bloody darkys that had no teeth. Christ!*

Lisa introduced him. 'My friends, this is Mitch. He lives on the property next door to us.' Ningali extended her hand, which Mitch shook very reluctantly. Binna stared at the outline of his frame, which filled their humpy.

'Ladies, happy to meet you. Lisa has told me all about you on the way out here.'

'You wanna sit, Mitch?' asked Ningali.

'Come on, Mitch. It's okay, they don't bite.' Lisa smiled as she patted the ground.

'Where you two headin?' asked Ningali.

'To the river, I want to swim and I'm not allowed to go alone, so Mitch will be with me today. Do you have time for a story? I was telling Mitch how great they are, Binna.'

'Yeah, we do dat for you, little one. I tell you the Dreamtime story, about da two special people.'

Lisa sat mesmerised as Binna continued. 'Dey have great feelings for each other. Toonkoo and Ngaardi. When Darama, da Great Spirit, come down to da earth, he make all da animals and da birds. He give em all names and he make Toonkoo and Ngaardi. One day, Toonkoo say he go hunting and Ngaardi stay at home and get da bush tucker. She wait and wait but Toonkoo never come home. She worry and cry, da big tears come down her face. Dey so big, her tears make da rivers and da creeks dat come down da mountain. She wait all day but he never come back. But Toonkoo still hunting and he get da kangaroo. He look up and see Darama, the Great Spirit, watching him, so he chuck da spear at Darama, but da Great Spirit caught it. Darama bent it and he chuck it back at Toonkoo and dis became da boomerang. Toonkoo angry with Darama so he get taken away and put in da moon. When da full moon came up, Ngaardi was crying but she see her man Toonkoo in da moon. She go to da mountain and lay down. She say if ever Toonkoo come back, she leave her heart for him to find. Today, her heart is the red flower called da waratah.'

'Oh, I love it. I so love it. I know the flower – the red waratah!' Lisa took Binna's hand and squeezed it. 'Aunty gives you these.' She handed over the calico bag. 'We have to be off now. Thank you so much.'

'Yes . . . thank you,' Mitch said awkwardly, getting to his feet. *This stuff gives me the creeps. Fucking Dreamtime shit.* Mitch was glad to leave.

'Wasn't that wonderful, Mitch,' said Lisa, brimming with happiness. 'Now when I see a waratah, I will think of that lovely story.'

'Yeah, sure was, Lisa,' he replied.

◊

As they rode out of sight, Binna turned to Ningali, her eucalyptus branch slowly swatting at the flies. 'Trouble. His voice cold. Bad for da little one.'

Ningali nodded. 'He look powerful, Binna, but his heart grow da thorns not da flowers.'

◊

As Mitch and Lisa reached the river, the warm sun beat down on them. 'Oh, I can just feel that water's coolness,' said Lisa.

'Let's tether the horses then and hit the water.' Mitch couldn't wait to see her in fewer clothes and felt the heat spread into his body.

'Okay. You go up that way to change, and I'll be down here,' said Lisa, suddenly feeling some hesitation. *I'm okay. It will be okay. He is a friend.* She quickly changed behind some bushes and wrapped the towel around her body, stepping gingerly out. Mitch was already in shorts.

'Are you ready?' He wanted to pull the towel away from her body. He could already see her long, slender brown legs.

'Right then, last one in is a rotten egg.' He ran for the water and dived in. 'Come on, it's beautiful, coolish but great!' he yelled as he floated on his back.

Lisa dropped the towel, and Mitch raked his eyes over her form, studying her lovely body. Such a small waist, and her breasts sat high. He wanted to devour her. To cover her mouth with his.

Lisa quickly hit the water after dropping the towel, a little embarrassed. Mitch sensed her vulnerability, which only turned him on more.

'Lisa, don't be shy,' Mitch soothed as he swam towards her.

'I just feel a little odd, swimming with you here today. And you need to stop staring!'

Mitch laughed loudly. 'Sorry, Lisa, I can't help myself. Beauty is beauty, whether it's a woman or a horse. Got to take it all in, you know.'

Lisa smiled timidly. 'Hey, it's not that deep here,' she said as he reached out for her.

'Come to me, Lisa. I'll throw you up high.'

Lisa paddled towards him. 'Here, put your foot in my hands.' He threw her into the air. Lisa squealed and went under, coming up laughing.

'No way I could do that to you!' Mitch swam after her and they quickly did the same again, Lisa spluttering and squealing.

'No more, Mitch.' But she was enjoying every minute of his playfulness. 'I'm getting out.' She quickly swam towards the bank.

'Aww, come on.'

'Nope, I'm drying off.' He watched her intently. She was breathtaking but was completely unaware of his sexual attraction to her. *I so want you. I want to feel every part of you.*

'Come on, Mitch, we have to head back.'

He leisurely swam back to the grass where Lisa now sat.

She watched his huge frame walk towards her. He was very different to Billy, but there was no doubting his physical presence.

'Can I sit next to you?' he asked.

'Just for a moment,' Lisa giggled. 'As I said, we have to get going.' She nervously looked into the distance.

'Look, look at that . . . isn't that magnificent!' Lisa pointed to the sky. Just above them a great eagle soared.

'Spirit bird, keep me safe,' prayed Lisa.

'That's a very Aboriginal thing to say,' commented Mitch.

'Maybe, and yes, you are right, I have heard that from a very dear Aboriginal friend, but I so love their sayings and stories, just like the one we heard today. Amazing. And I love the red waratah as a flower.'

Mitch took her hand. 'I want to stay here with you. This is, well, I just love this. Just us. You know I care for you, and my feelings grow stronger, Lisa.' He moved his hand to her chin and lifted her face towards him. He could feel her trembling.

'Don't be afraid. I will never hurt you.' He pressed his lips gently to hers, and Lisa let him linger, feeling his hunger.

Something stirred in her heart. She could feel him wanting more. *I must stop this. I do like him. But things are getting confusing.*

'Mitch . . . I do like you. I so enjoy our time together, but for now, can we please keep it as just our special friendship.'

'I understand, Lisa, but seeing you like this and being with you like this . . . it's driving me wild. I so want to go further.' He kissed the nape of her neck softly. Lisa closed her eyes, the sensation driving into her body.

'No, Mitch, we have to go.' Lisa felt his tenderness, but knew she must stop.

She quickly stood up, nervously clutching the towel around her. Mitch followed and stood staring down into her eyes. He drew her softly by her shoulders closer to him. 'My beautiful friend,' he whispered as he kissed her forehead softly. Lisa rested her head on his chest momentarily, enjoying the moment. He was mesmerising and working his way into areas she had kept closed.

'Right then, Mitch,' Lisa said, pulling away. 'I have to get changed, get out of this wet cossie. You go that way.' She pointed in the opposite direction to where they stood.

'Me too, Lisa. Nothing worse than riding in wet clothes.' If only she knew how he wanted to pull that wet cossie off her, throw her to the ground and make love to her. He was using every part of his being to keep from doing so. She was not like any other girl he had met before. There was something about her though that told him she'd been terribly hurt, and this hurt, Lisa kept locked away, hidden. *I will find out . . . she can be sure of that.*

Lisa pinned her damp hair up and threw her hat on, feeling more comfortable fully clothed. 'Are you ready, Mitch?'

'Indeed I am.' He stepped out from the bushes. 'I'll grab those ponies and we'll be off.' *Patience, but I can feel her warming to me.*

TWENTY-ONE

NO PLACE LEFT TO RUN

It was not far from midnight, almost the end of his shift, when Detective Jim Adler came into Andrew Collette's office. 'Good news, mate,' Jim said as plonked his chubby frame into a chair.

'Oh . . . what's that?' asked Andrew, raising his eyebrows.

'Just got off the phone to our mates down in Eden. Got a sighting of that bastard Lenny down there. A local copper, off duty in his own car, picked up the number plate, and is tailing him as we speak. So, the prick won't know it's a copper behind him.'

'That's not that far from Merimbula, the last place he was seen,' said Andrew. 'That's great bloody news.'

'Yeah, he pulled into a servo, so our boy followed him in there and used the phone box to call in. By now, he should have back-up,' smiled Jim. 'Not long now, Andrew.'

'I was just about to knock off and head home, but I'm going nowhere. Come on, let's get a coffee and sit tight,' said Andrew as he made his way to the kitchen.

◊

Lenny was aware he was being followed. Or maybe it was just a coincidence. It wasn't a police car but he kept his eye on the rear vision mirror. It was late, his usual time for any movement, as he pulled into the Eden Caravan Park. As he turned off the main road, the Landcruiser kept going. *Safe. All good.*

He travelled further into the caravan park until he came to his rented van, reversing into the annexe of the caravan. As he did so, he saw the headlights of another vehicle suddenly coming down the same track, which shone brightly into his eyes.

'Turn your fucking lights down, mate! You're on high beam, fucking blinding me!' yelled Lenny. Probably some boofhead back from fishing. The caravan park was full of them. He was about to get out of the car when coming up the driveway towards him, another vehicle with strong headlights headed in his direction.

Both vehicles came to a halt, and the lights from their vehicles pointed directly at him.

Lenny squinted at the direction of the lights. Suddenly, a strong male voice came through a speaker. 'Lenny Wilkinson, step out of the car. Please come out into the light with your hands up.'

Lenny froze. *Bastards. Fucking Pigs!* There was no way he was going to do that. Two officers began walking towards his vehicle with their torches shining directly into his face. Lenny shielded his eyes. *Bastards, I have to get out of here.* Lenny pressed hard on the accelerator and drove straight for the two men, gaining speed. He had to make the main gate and get out of here. They were onto him.

'Get out of my way, pigs, or I will ram you!' roared Lenny as he swung his car at one of the men. They both jumped to the side, landing in bushes, and called on their walkie talkies to the officers waiting at the front gate.

As Lenny slowed to turn the last corner of the caravan park, he was confronted with three cars, lights flashing and a row of men, guns drawn. He hit the brakes hard and stared at the line of men in front of him.

'Stop or we will shoot. Game's over, Lenny. Now get out of the car,' said a tall man with a strong voice.

Must be the main pig. I'm fucked. Well and truly. Lenny looked along the line of men who were standing in front of the main exit. He knew the shock he would inflict on Janine when he was found guilty. He could hear his heart thumping in his ears. Fear had taken hold, and the beads of perspiration were trickling down his face. Life in prison was not for him. He sat in his car, staring at the police.'

'Come on, Lenny, game's up. Just come in quietly.' The same voice was trying to talk him in.

Lenny smiled. He knew what happened in prison to men like him. Beaten by the prison guards and the other prisoners. There was no way out. He pressed his foot hard on the accelerator, the tyres spinning. The police yelled to stop but as his car proceeded towards them, they began firing multiple shots through the windscreen, scrambling from the fast-moving vehicle as they did so.

The fusillade of gunshots echoed deafeningly through the stillness of the night. Lights switched on around the caravan park.

Lenny's car came to a crashing halt, slamming into a tree. As the police got to his vehicle, they knew he was dead. He was slumped over the wheel. Multiple shots had ripped through his chest, clearly showing entry and exit wounds. A bullet had also punched its way to his neck, causing a gaping hole, the blood spilling out from an artery.

'That alone would have caused death,' said Senior Constable McGregor, pointing to the neck wound.

'Was he guilty, Mac?' asked another constable.

'From the information and reports we received, guilty as,' replied McGregor. 'A right sick bastard. One less for the system if you ask me. Got no sympathy for these types. Monsters who prey on children.'

'You guys stay here,' ordered McGregor. 'I'll have to go back to the station and make a report. You'll need to cordon off this area and keep the public away. I'll call for an ambulance when I get back to the station for removal of the body and let the Sydney detectives know what has happened.'

Andrew Collette picked up on the first ring.

'Detective Collette speaking.'

'Detective Collette, it's Senior Constable Jamie McGregor here . . . from Eden Police Station.'

'Yes, hello, Jamie,' replied Andrew.

'We got our man, not how we would have liked, but he ain't going nowhere.'

'I see.' Andrew looked up at Jim, who sat directly opposite.

'What happened?' asked Andrew.

'We followed him into a caravan park and he got past the first two guys who had asked him to exit the vehicle. When he got to the front gates, he stopped when he saw the line of blue in front of him. We again asked him to exit his vehicle. But our fugitive just hit the accelerator and headed straight at us. Must have realised the game was over and prison loomed. He certainly could not get past us. We fired into the windscreen, and his car ploughed into a tree, but mate, he was dead or almost by the time he did that. Took a lot to his chest but the bullet he took to the neck hit the artery. Just about to do my report but wanted to let you know.'

'Thanks so much, Jamie, I appreciate it. I can go home now. No use telling his victims at this time of the morning. He has a wife, so she'll have to know as well. Thanks, mate, for the promptness. If you can send up a copy of the report, that would be great.'

Andrew let out a large exhale. 'One less, Jim. You know, even though I say that, nothing makes sense. Young girls traumatised and even dead. Relatives traumatised . . . lives ruined, and for what? I'm going home too. Tomorrow is another day. I want to do this personally, Jim, that is, call both women. I don't want another police officer they don't know calling to explain what has occurred.'

'Yeah, good idea, Andrew,' agreed Jim. They walked in silence to their cars.

'Goodnight, Jim. Breaking the news to Zena and Mrs Lockhart will be a priority. I am sure all parties probably wanted to see justice served, but hopefully they are consoled by the thought that Lenny will never harm again.'

◇

Detective Andrew Collette arrived at his office for the afternoon shift and found the reports from Senior Constable McGregor on his desk. He knew his first call was to the local police station, closest to Janine. Police officers would have to advise of her husband's fatality. That was not going to be easy. Through the glass of his office, he saw Jim sit down. When he looked up and waved, Andrew beckoned Jim into his office.

'Morning Jim, how did you sleep?'

'Like a big baby, never have had any problems in that department . . . and you?'

'Yeah okay, but the shooting did play on my mind. I wondered if Lynette and yourself might like to pay Janine a visit to advise her of Lenny's death. You both know the case and history. It might help if this poor devil has any questions. Grief does strange things to a person.'

'Yeah, that's not a bad idea. I don't mind. I know the constables usually do this, but if you want to work it this way, sure, no problem.'

'I'll get clearance,' said Andrew, 'and let you know.'

'Have you spoken to Zena Smith or Lisa as yet?' queried Jim.

'No, I thought I would call Caroline Lockhart first. It hasn't hit the media as yet, but it won't be long.'

'Alright, I'll leave you to it, Andrew. Just let me know if you want me and Lynette to head out to the burbs to deliver the news.'

Andrew gave a thumbs up, and Jim closed the door to his office.

'Bloody paperwork, I hate it, but that was the last official call. Just one more.' Andrew shuffled the papers and stepped out of his office.

'All good, Jim, you have the green light. You can take off with Lynette whenever you like. I'm going to call Zena now.'

'Okay, I put Lynette on alert . . . I'll go find her and get out there. Delivering this news, it's never easy.'

'Nope.' Andrew went back to his office. He took a deep breath before dialling. It was Zena who answered.

'Hi, Zena, it's Andrew Collette. How are things?'

'Splendid, Andrew. Things are good, and we're looking forward to this coming season.'

That's great, Zena. Do you have a moment? I have some news for you . . . about Lenny.'

'Oh, do I need to sit down?'

'Probably,' advised Andrew.

Zena sat on the small stool and leaned her back into the wall, expecting the worst. *Here goes, this will be bad.*

'Go on, Andrew . . . please,' said Zena tentatively.

'The police tagged Lenny down at Eden, heading into a caravan park late at night. Basically, he was asked to exit his vehicle, he refused, and then tried to ram the police officers.'

'Dear God . . . what a fool.' Zena gulped hard and brought her hand up to her throat. 'And?' asked Zena.

'Lenny would not stop, he planted his foot on the accelerator and got past the first two cars, but we had officers backing up at the front gate as well. They asked him to get out of the vehicle when he stopped. He obviously sat there making a decision. He made the choice to hit the accelerator and tried to ram the police officers. No choice except to shoot. He sustained fatal wounds to his chest and neck.'

Zena tried to hold the vision of the man's death in her mind.

'Are you there?' asked Andrew.

'Yes of course, I am . . . just,' exhaling loudly, 'shocked, I guess . . . numb. I have no pity for the man but there is that question of *why*? He was so cruel, and a murderer, but why?'

'I know what you mean, Zena. No-one really never knows why. We have Lynette and Jim on their way to tell Janine. Thought you might need to prepare yourself if she calls. It's not hit the media as yet, but I'm expecting it on tonight's television. I also called Caroline Lockhart. She has had the same reaction as you.'

'If only we could bring her little girl back,' said Zena as she felt the tears welling in her eyes.

'I'll leave you to break it to Lisa, better than us.'

'Yes, Andrew, thank you . . . thank you so much.' Zena hung up the phone. She sat staring at the wall in the hallway, dabbing her eyes. She would tell Lisa after dinner. But she was glad the sonofabitch could never harm another young girl again.

◊

'This won't be easy Jim . . . I have a feeling about this one,' said Lynette as they drove to Janine's home.

'They never are, Lynette, bringing news of death into a home,' Jim replied, somewhat detached.

They knocked on the door, and it was opened slowly.

'Hello, I am Constable Harrison and this is Detective Adler. Are you Janine Wilkinson?'

'Yes, I am . . . what is it?' Her eyes suddenly widened. 'Do you have news of my husband?'

'Yes, Mrs Wilkinson, we do. Would you prefer us to come in?' asked Lynette.

'Oh yes, sorry . . . please do.' They stepped into the house. It was dark and the blinds were drawn, letting very little light into the house. Newspapers were strewn everywhere and half eaten food lay on plates around the house.

Janine noticed the look on Lynette's face. 'I haven't been motivated to clean up. Not since the lies about my husband.'

'There is no easy way to tell you this, Janine,' said Lynette softly.

'Tell me what!' she barked, pulling her cardigan tighter to her chest, her mouth pinched with anger.

'Lenny, your husband, was shot and killed early this morning, just after midnight by the NSW police down at Eden. He resisted arrest, despite the police asking him to step out of his car, and tried to ram the constables attempting the arrest.'

Janine's face crumpled then contorted as she let out a strangled cry of rage. She suddenly spat out, What . . . what! You bastards fucking sit there and tell me this shit!' Janine lunged at Lynette and tried to slap her around the face. Jim stepped in and grabbed her wrists.

'Stop this, please, Mrs Wilkinson,' he commanded as he pushed her back into a lounge chair.

Janine began to wail and sob loudly. 'Get out . . . get out of my fucking house, fucking useless pigs. This is all her fucking fault. She killed my mother and now my husband!'

'The coroner's office will be in touch about bringing the body back to Sydney for funeral arrangements. Good day, Mrs Wilkinson. We are sorry to bring you this news' said Jim as he followed Lynette to the door.

◊

Zena had told Alan quietly, so that he was prepared. Lisa chatted on about the horse sales Mitch had told her about. 'They are on next week, Alan. Can we go? Mitch said you can often get a bargain hack. If you get Noir into foal, I will only have old Neddy or Tidgy.'

'I don't see why not. Sounds like a good idea to me. Zena also wants to buy a few good mares. We understand there could be some stockhorses up for sale.'

'Excellent. Umm, am I missing anything here?' asked Lisa.

'Nope . . . why, kid?'

'Well, you two seem rather quiet tonight. Is everything alright?' As Lisa finished the sentence, the phone rang.

'I'll get it,' said Zena. 'I've had enough to eat, Lisa. Will you clear when you're finished, sweetheart?'

Lisa nodded. Her eyes followed her aunt as she walked to the phone. As Zena sat down, she had a feeling it would not be good. 'Hello, this is—'

'Shut up, you fucking shut up! You and that little bitch have killed my husband.' Janine's screams poured into the phone. 'I said I would get her at Mum's funeral and now Lenny is dead, I am going to hold that promise. I hate you, I fucking hate both of you . . . I am coming to finish that little bitch off. She has ruined my life!' The phone was slammed down.

Lisa instinctively knew that the reason for her aunt's quietness over dinner was something to do with that call. She looked at Alan. 'You know something too, don't you, Alan?'

'Best to let your aunt tell you, Lisa. It is bad, but in a strange way, there is some good, if it can be described at that.'

Zena stepped back into the kitchen. Her face was pale, and Alan reached for her hand as she sat down.

'Do you want to do it here or in the sitting room?' asked Alan.

'Might as well do it here,' said Zena.

'Will someone please tell me what is going on!'

'Calm down, kid, and let your aunt catch her breath.' There was a hint of irritation in Alan's voice.

'Lisa, that was Janine. She has been told of the news by the police earlier today. Lenny was shot and killed early this morning. He was resisting arrest and tried to ram the arresting police officers.'

'Oh my God!' Lisa's face contorted into a tremulous expression as she tried to take the news in. It was of disbelief but she also felt a gamut of emotions: shock, numbness and anger. 'Then it's all over. He's dead!'

'If you see it that way, yes,' replied Zena. 'He was cruel, a murderer, we all know that, and we will never know what drove him to do the things he did. But, the good in this situation, if I can use that word, is he will cause no further harm to anyone and of course, the matter is closed legally for you in this regard.'

'I would say he knew he would be found guilty, no question,' said Alan. 'And the prospect of being jailed was evident. Remember what I said about the crims having their own justice inside?'

Lisa nodded, recalling the conversation.

'That bloke knew what he was up against, and in the end, took the coward's way out,' said Alan.

Lisa struggled with a tide of emotions. 'So, what did Janine have to say?'

Zena winced. 'Could have sworn it was Agnes on the phone. The usual venom, swearing and vengeful comments. A person reacts to death and grief in their own way, but I am sure she still believes Lenny is innocent. Andrew will do a follow-up call on his next shift and then a report will be sent to us. But right now, I think it's time for bed.'

It was a long time before sleep came to Lisa. She saw Lenny coming towards her when she was a frightened young girl, tasting the old fear. She wondered if he had been seized by a panic and fear in his final moments. *I hope so. Bastard.*

TWENTY-TWO

TOPI

Alan was up early with Lisa. They were joining Mitch and his father for the horse sales. Lisa was keen to get a new horse, and Alan wanted some stock horse mares. They all agreed before they went to bed that Lenny's death would not alter any of their plans.

Detective Andrew Collette was true to his word and called the following day. Zena was aghast when he described the actions of Janine attacking Lynette Harrison upon receiving the news about Lenny's death.

'If it wasn't so horrible, Andrew, I would laugh,' said Zena. 'Poor Lynette. But Janine did call here last night, with all manner of threats. Initially it was unnerving, but I'm good now, or as good as can be.'

'The coroner should release Lenny's body next week then she can make the funeral arrangements. I assume you won't be attending, Zena?'

'No, Andrew, I would find that most distressing. And I have no intention of paying that child-molesting murderous monster any respects. I also think avoiding Janine permanently is in our best interests. By the way, when is our friend Mr Ash going to court?'

'Another reason I'm calling. The district court has set a date for sentencing on the seventh of July. As I said, he has confessed. The statements were just too overwhelming against him, so Lisa will not have to attend. I don't think she would want to face him . . . would she?'

'No, not at all, Andrew, but I'll let her know the date. Thank you so much for everything. It has been challenging, but hopefully with this last hearing, we can close a horrible chapter, for everyone involved.'

'Indeed, Zena. But I'm glad the perpetrators were caught, and that they are not roaming free to do as they want with young girls. How is Lisa handling the news?'

'There were a few emotions . . . shock, numbness and then anger. She wanted to see Lenny go to jail. Alan said he took the easy way out.'

'Yeah, we all said the same. But jail is the last thing they want. Let me know if I can do anything else, don't hesitate to call.'

'Thanks, Andrew. Give my regards to Jim and Lynette.' She put the phone down.

Zena looked at her watch. They still had a few hours out at the sales. It would be interesting to see what Alan brought home. *Keep busy, Zena.* She looked at the phone. She wondered what Kate was doing and without any hesitation, Zena dialled her number.

'Well, hello, this is a surprise,' greeted Kate.

'Do you feel like a cuppa? We have a few hours until they're back,' said Zena.

'Absolutely, come on over. We can sit and have a chat.'

When Zena arrived, Kate had the table set with her finest crockery. 'Looks lovely, Kate, but I would have been happy to have tea in a tin mug.'

'Zena, please sit down, it's always lovely to see you here.'

Kate poured and handed Zena the plate of finger sandwiches. 'Wonder what they'll bring back,' mused Kate.

'Who knows, but I want to get a good horse for Lisa. She is wearing poor old Neddy out. Alan wants to put Noir in foal around August, and I want to get on to our breeding program.'

'Sounds like a plan.' Kate paused. 'Are you happy with Mitch seeing Lisa?'

'Yes Kate, even though they are both young, but I wanted to touch base with you about that, while they were not here.'

'They seem to be getting on fine now, Zena. I think Mitch was rushing your girl and of course, that makes people go the other way.'

Zena nodded. 'Yes, absolutely. Lisa is more relaxed now, but she's a young girl who will need time. Lots of time and friendship with Mitch is all that she wants right now.'

'Zena, I agree, and I told Mitchell as much. Whether he can exercise that is a matter to be seen. As you know, he did have a few girls hanging off him before he left for overseas, and after his party, the phone rang hot. I had to tell the girls the same thing. He is not available, or he's not here right now, but I will take your number. The most persistent one was Tess Dunphy. Still calls. Just won't take no for an answer.'

'Lisa said that they ran into Tess at the RSL the other week, and Tess gave them a bit of a spray,' added Zena.

'I heard about that. Mitch told us too. Wicked girl. And she certainly made a spectacle of herself here at his party. I feel sorry for her mother,' said Kate. 'Anyway, I was astounded when Mitch came home the other day and said he had been sitting in a humpy with two black ladies listening to a Dreamtime story. Dave nearly fell off his chair.'

'Lisa does love the two Aboriginal ladies who live out towards the river. So do I, Kate. Their stories and their ceremonies are truly unique. The women are gentle and beautiful souls. They have helped a lot with Lisa.'

'Oh, in what way?' asked Kate, intrigued.

'Lisa came to us when she was rejected in the family home. Her mother was a bit of a tyrant. Dead now, but Alan and I basically took her under our wing. She just needed love and support.'

'Mitch did mention that he felt she kept many things hidden, that she kept control over her emotions. But, he is totally smitten and said Lisa was not like anyone he had ever met. How does Lisa feel?'

'Look . . . um, Kate, yes she does hold her cards close to her chest, but of late Lisa has really warmed to Mitch. No harm in having male friends, but she is in no rush for anything other than friendship. The fact that she took Mitch to the humpy and then down to the river is really a big step for her. She does have trust issues.'

'I see. Would you mind if I pass the trust thing on to Mitch?'

'No, not at all.'

'It may help him steady the brakes. Mitch has never wanted for anything, and everything has been in easy grasp, with the exception of this gorgeous niece of yours. He has had a lot of young women, and they all seem to be attracted to him. He's never had to pursue.'

'Always a first time, Kate,' said Zena.

'Anyway, to change the conversation, how is your season shaping up?'

'Pretty good,' replied Zena, 'although I doubt it will be as good as last year. It might come close, but we'll see at the end of it. How about you?'

'I would express the same opinion. We were thinking of taking off somewhere after the season. Are you interested? Our boys can look after Woori for you.'

'That sounds wonderful, Kate, but I'll have to run it by Alan and, of course, Lisa.'

'We were even thinking about a week at Palm Beach,' winked Kate.

'Now you've really got me. Be lovely to sit and watch the ocean. My biggest problem is Alan. He would worry being away, especially if he brings back a few new mares from the sales, and that coupled with the odd things happening of late, I just don't know. Maybe he will agree knowing your boys are watching Woori.'

'The events of late would have me worried too, I have to say,' agreed Kate. 'Dave filled me in.'

'Yes, they were very disturbing, especially the dog being killed and the tyre slashed out at the river. We keep the doors locked of a night now,' admitted Zena. 'Well, I best be off. It was lovely just catching up without the boys around.'

'Any time, Zena.' Kate walked with her to the door. 'Don't worry about those kids either, Zena, everything always sorts itself. I know Mitch would be very upset if Lisa was not interested in him . . . he is not used to getting knocked back, but for every stale cracker there's a piece of mouldy cheese.'

Zena laughed, she always enjoyed Kate's humour. 'Quite right . . . and for every pot there is a lid.'

It was late afternoon when the stock truck drove in. Zena could hear horses whinnying and knew Alan was bringing home new blood. She took off down the back stairs eager to see what he had purchased.

'How did you go, Alan?' Zena queried.

'Very well! I think you will like these girls.' He entered the truck with Dave to lead the horses down.

Zena could see a young, gangly horse. 'That does not look like a stock horse to me, Alan.'

'It's not, Aunty!' Lisa said excitedly. 'He's mine!'

Mitch butted in. 'My fault, Zena. He came into the ring with his beautiful gait, and we all knew he was off to the abattoirs. Lisa loved him, and when you see his head, you'll notice it's a bit Arabic, and he moves beautifully. I couldn't help myself. I bought him . . . for her.'

Lisa was beaming.

'Mitch, that is very extravagant of you,' said a surprised Zena.

'No, I wanted to buy something special for her, since her bridle suddenly went missing and old Neddy's getting on now. She has to have something fast to keep up with me and Almondo.'

Lisa came and stood by Mitch's side, and his arm slowly came around her shoulder. They watched while Alan and Dave unloaded all horses and tied them to the cyclone fence.

'Yes, I can see why you bought him,' agreed Zena. 'Handsome boy, make a nice hack for you, Lisa, and what treasures you have found, Alan.'

Zena ran her hands over the three young mares. 'Beautiful big rumps on them and outstanding conformation. Lovely chestnut with four white socks, two lovely bays. They just need a bit more condition. Well done, husband.'

'Think we have the breeding program sorted. These girls will throw beautiful foals to Khartoum,' said Alan proudly.

'Do you want to stay for dinner?' Zena asked Mitch and Dave. 'I can give Kate a quick call to join us?'

'Thanks for the offer, Zena, but we'll be on our way. Need to do a few things,' said Dave.

Mitch turned to Lisa. 'Enjoy your new pony, Princess. Thought of a name as yet?'

'Yep . . . Topi.' Lisa said excitedly.

'Wherever did you get that name?' Mitch was bemused. 'It's an African word for a highly social and fast antelope. So, Topi will be very social and very fast. My beautiful girl, only you could come up with a name like that.' He kissed the top of Lisa's forehead.

Smitten alright . . . in love I would say, thought Zena.

'Right then, leave you to it and we'll be on our way,' said Dave.

'I'll call, Lisa,' said Mitch as they watched the Land Rover take off.

'Good lad, knows his horse flesh too, Lisa. Let's get these ponies around into the yards behind the Tack Room. Give them a good feed and keep them here while we get a bit of condition on them,' said Alan.

'Very generous of Mitch to buy you a horse, Lisa,' acknowledged Zena.

'I know,' Lisa replied shyly. 'I felt a bit embarrassed, but he wouldn't take no for an answer. He is very good to me and I really like him, but just as a friend.'

As they sat on the verandah that evening after dinner, it was peaceful for everyone. They stayed until the last magnificent glow of the orange sun disappeared, bringing on the night.

'I'm going to bed now. Want to be up early to lunge my new baby,' said Lisa, grinning from ear to ear. She kissed both of them goodnight and ambled down the hallway to her room.

'I wonder if there was no Billy, would she be taking it further,' commented Alan. 'They had a good day, both enjoying each other's company.'

'Maybe . . . who knows, but as I have said so many times to you, Billy is always there. I went over to see Kate while you were all away. She mentioned the fact that Mitch is very smitten, well, we all know that, but she said he is not used to getting knocked back. Always gets his way. I hope he thinks he is not on terra firma with Lisa because of the purchase of that horse. If Billy does come back, I just don't know what will happen.'

'I have a feeling someone will get hurt,' added Alan. 'As I said, I don't want any bloody triangles. The season is six weeks away. Come on, time to hit the sack.'

TWENTY-THREE

TRUE COLOURS

The phone rang early, and Lisa, who was already up, jumped to answer it. 'Hello, this is Lisa.'

'Well, well, young lady, this is Jack. How have you been going? I wondered if you would still be about. Thought the heat and the flies may have made you pack your bags and head back to Sydney.'

'No way, Jack,' Lisa giggled. 'I'm staying put. I've got a new horse and I'm looking forward to helping this season.'

'Splendid, young girl. Now, is Alan about? Got lots to discuss,' said Jack.

'Yep, I'll get him for you. I can hear him in the kitchen now.' Alan poked his head around the hallway. 'I'll take it from here, kid,' he grinned as Lisa handed him the phone.

'I'm getting so excited, Aunty. It's really happening, the season is nearly here.'

'Yes, darling girl, it is, and I know what you are thinking and why all the excitement. Have you thought that Billy may not be back? He's working up north and probably doing a great job. Often the managers try to keep them if they are solid workers.'

Lisa's face dropped. 'No! Billy said he would be back and that I had to wait. He will be here, Aunty. I just know it. Him and Burnu. They will come back. Even Binna said as much.'

'Alright, settle. We'll have to wait and see what transpires. They all know the date to be back here, end of August to start first week of September. We'll soon find out who has contacted Jack. Sometimes, they just turn up on the day with their dogs and lubras. It is just their way, Lisa.'

They heard Alan hang up, and he came back into the kitchen with his list that had sat by the phone.

'Well?' prompted Zena.

'Got the usual crowd, but there has been no response from Billy,' said Alan as he looked at Lisa.

'No, that's not possible! He is coming. I just told Aunty that. Don't say he is not coming, Alan . . . he is!' Lisa shouted, and then took off down the back stairs.

'I just mentioned to her that there may be a possibility that Billy won't be back. But she is adamant he will be. I know she will be heartbroken if he doesn't show, but things always sort themselves, don't they?' said Zena.

'Maybe a good thing. I just don't know. I do like Billy. But I just can't see what sort of relationship they can have. Anyway, Jack was in good form. Told him about Jimmy. He said he could see that coming. Just a matter of time. Still feel for Jimmy, he had a lot of talent. Anyway, I'll go find Lisa. Come when you have finished your breakfast. The new mares and Topi will cool the situation and keep her busy.' He kissed Zena's cheek before heading out to find Lisa.

Alan walked purposefully to the yards, hoping Lisa had cooled down. 'Hey, kid,' he called out as she stood grooming the young coloured horse. 'Calmed down yet? Thought you were going to blow the roof off.'

'Yeah, guess so, but why does everyone think Billy will not be back! He will, Alan. I just feel it. I know it.'

'Alright then, we will leave it at that. Billy and Burnu will be here. They have just forgotten to tell Jack.'

Lisa smiled.

'That's better, now let's get on with the job of lunging and checking out our new horses. Get yourself busy and don't mope. Zena will be down shortly.'

◊

When Mitch came in for lunch with Dave, Kate looked exasperated. 'What's up, Mum?'

'Oh, it's that damn girl, Mitch.'

'What girl?' asked Dave.

'Tess Dunphy. She has called three times this morning wanting to speak to you. I can't fob her off any longer with the excuse you are not here, Mitch. You will have to speak to her or I will call her mother. She is a damn pest.'

Mitch laughed. 'Sorry, Mum. Yep, she is hard to get rid of, bit of a rash, that one. I'll handle it. Make a call. Leave it with me.'

'Can you do it sooner rather than later then? I don't want to be your secretary anymore.'

'Okay, I'll do it now. Just let me get something to eat first. I'm famished and I don't want to talk to her on an empty stomach.' Mitch rolled his eyes. *Bloody girl. Wish I had never fucked her. Thinks we're engaged.*

After lunch, Mitch walked into the office. He reluctantly dialled Tess's number. *I am so dreading this.*

'Hello, this is Tess.'

'Hi, Tess, it's Mitch. Mum said you've called a few times.'

'Yeah, I have. Why don't you return my calls? I've been calling all the time . . . since your party.'

Her voice sounded petulant, but Mitch knew he had to stop any further interaction.

'Look, Tess, I'm sorry. I have been busy but I really don't want you to call anymore. Okay? I have to be honest with you. I am not interested in you as a girlfriend.'

'What! You bastard. Busy . . . busy with what? Your stupid boong-loving baby girl. You think you can fuck me and then dump me. Well, you are wrong! You don't come around here late at night or call me when you want your load relieved and then never talk to me. I'm not rubbish, you know. It's not gunna last.'

'What's not going to last, Tess?' Mitch was curious.

'You and that bitch the people in town have been seeing you with. Wait till her boong friend comes back. Took him to the pictures, you know. All dreamy and gooey with him. My girlfriends saw them. She will boot you out and then I will have the last laugh at you Mr Big Shot. Idiotic cretinous bastard!'

Tess slammed the phone down, and Mitch blew out a long whistle. *Wolf bitch.*

Kate looked over her glasses when Mitch came into the kitchen. 'Tough?' she asked.

'Not too bad . . . but boy, she was angry. Anyway, I hope that's the end of it now. But she did say something strange.'

'Oh, what was it? probed Kate.

'Something like Lisa was a boong lover and she had been seen at the pictures with a blackfella.'

'Well, the black kids are allowed to go to the picture show, Mitch, but they have their own section,' reminded Kate.

'Lisa has this special affinity with the Aboriginal people, Mum, a bit like Zena and Alan, and she mixes easily with them. Those two old birds down by the river, they fill her head with Dreamtime stories. Gave me the creeps, and I could not wait to get out of there. Dark as, no bloody teeth and they could do with a wash. Must have been her friend Billy at the pictures. She keeps talking about that blackfella,' grumbled Mitch. *Bloody Billy.*

'Well, I wouldn't worry too much, son. The job has been done, and I hope that wretched girl does not call here again or I will be speaking to her mother. I suggest you keep your trousers on.'

Dave couldn't help but laugh, and Mitch joined in.

'Oh, stop it, you two,' Kate smiled. 'Zena called in her for a cuppa while you were all at the sales. She mentioned Lisa had trust issues, so my caution for you to have patience was right on the money.'

'Yeah, thanks Mum. But you know, there is something deeper than that, a lot deeper. They almost cocoon Lisa, and she . . . she keeps things hidden. Lisa is very defensive about anything personal.'

'Zena said as much. Had a troubled family home, which is why they took Lisa under their wing.'

'I would love to know what that trouble was, Mum. Every time I ask something personal, she clams up. If you like someone, it is sort of a natural thing to talk about your background, your family.'

'Yes, I agree, Mitch, but for now I would leave it well alone. You said you are making progress and that she's warming to you. I am sure the rest will evolve in its own natural course.'

Mitch's curiosity was reaching a peak about the girl. *I want to know more, and I will find out.*

When the house was empty the following morning, he reached for the phone book, yellow pages, and ran his finger down Private Investigators.

TWENTY-FOUR

ENDINGS

The new mares had settled in nicely, and Alan was getting ready to show Noir and the new additions to Khartoum.

'Coincide with the season starting, Lisa. Boy, we are going to be busy.'

Lisa was now riding Topi and had been to the river and back with Mitch on a few occasions. The young horse moved beautifully, and Lisa looked forward to every ride.

After finishing her chores, she headed up to the house for lunch and heard the phone ring. 'Can you get that, Lisa? I'm just in the laundry,' Zena sang out.

'Hello, this is Lisa.'

'Morning, Lisa, it's Andrew, Detective Collette.'

'Oh, hello. Good morning to you.'

'How have you been, Lisa?'

'I'm good, keeping busy . . . Um, getting ready for the season.'

'Good to hear. Would Zena be there? I just need a quick word.'

'Sure, Andrew. She's just walking towards me now . . . er . . . thank you,' said Lisa, putting the phone down.

'I'm starving, Aunty. It's Andrew,' she said as she scooted to the kitchen.

'Hello, Andrew, and good morning. I'm always hesitant to ask the question, how are things. I always feel something bad is going to be said.'

'I guess people associate police calls with bad news. On this occasion, I have good news and bad news.'

'Oh dear, here we go again. I'm not sure what I want to hear first. I'll go with the good news, Andrew.' Zena sucked in a soft breath and felt her mouth go dry.

'Good news. Well, the Ash fellow was sentenced to life imprisonment, so he will die in jail.'

'That does make me smile, and that is good news!' proclaimed Zena, relieved. 'I have not an ounce of pity for him . . . a monster of cruelty and lust.'

Andrew continued. 'Yes, I have to say I am very pleased he did confess, Zena. The barristers really do tear strips from the complainants. Lisa would have been a mess,' admitted Andrew.

'I've heard that before and I didn't want to go down that road either. Now, the good news has been delivered, what is the bad news?'

She heard him breathe a heavy sigh and then clear his throat. *This is not going to be good.*

'Well . . . two days ago, there was a train accident, a fatality. Shocking, really. The train driver could not stop and said that the woman made no attempt to move, just stared at the train bearing down on her.'

'What's this got to do with us, Andrew, or for that matter, Lisa?' queried Zena.

'The woman who was killed was Janine.'

'Oh my God!' exclaimed Zena. The hair on the back of her neck bristled, and a shiver coursed down her spine. She slumped onto the chair next to the phone.

'Sorry, Zena, bringing more bad news to you. Des has identified the body. Her car was parked at Parramatta station and a small purse was in the pocket of her dress, which contained her ID. She was killed instantly.'

Zena was trying to take it all in. Why hadn't Des called if he had identified Janine? She didn't like the woman, but this was so bloody tragic.

'Thank you, Andrew,' said Zena, trying to gather her emotions and thoughts. 'I'll call my brother and then I'll speak to Lisa.' She blew out a deep breath. Her head was beginning to pound.

'Sure, Zena. I seem to always be the bearer of bad news. Let me know if there are any issues,' said Andrew as he put the phone down.

Lisa noticed her aunt's shocked expression as she sat down opposite her in the kitchen.

'I can tell something bad has happened and I heard you say, "Oh my God!". I can feel my heart beating out of my chest, Aunty. Tell me quickly what it is. I just know it involves me.'

'Andrew had good and bad news, Lisa. The good news is that Superintendent Ash has been sentenced. Life imprisonment, so he will die in jail. There was overwhelming evidence, his confession of guilt and all those statements as well as your own.'

Lisa's mouth dropped open. After the initial shock, she felt the pleasure, warm and hot, burning and mixing with the gratifying feeling that justice was done. A delighted shock. She enjoyed the darkness of her thoughts. 'I have waited for this day for so long, Aunty. I hope he rots in prison, and I hope the prisoners do to him what Alan told me they'll do. Bash him, make him feel pain and give him some of his own medicine . . . for what he did to me and all the other girls.'

Lisa gritted her teeth. 'I hope he begs for mercy and there is no mercy, just lots of pain and humiliation.'

She paused and looked at her aunt. 'I feel so much hatred, but now this . . . it feels like I have come full circle and that bastard will get what he so deserves. But I have a feeling there's more. Go on,' said Lisa tentatively.

'I understand, Lisa . . . this is a relief. I feel the same, sweetheart. But the good news is that there will obviously be further investigations. Perhaps a Royal Commission? Who knows, but that is the highest level of investigation. Certainly, the Parramatta Girls Home and all the other institutions should be investigated. I hope it results in closures for these types of places, and those who committed crimes against the innocent are brought to justice.'

Lisa couldn't hide her delight. 'So, you have told me the good news, Aunty, but you have yet to divulge the bad news. So tell me.'

Zena closed her eyes and swore softly. She wondered what Lisa's reaction would be.

'Okay. The bad news. Well the bad news is that Janine has taken her own life, committed suicide.'

Lisa caught her breath and then bowed her head. She knew what her aunt was going to say wouldn't be good. *I don't feel any sympathy for Janine though.*

She waited a few seconds and then looked at her aunt. 'How did she do this, Aunty?'

Zena looked unsettled. 'Janine stood in front of a train. Andrew said she made no attempt to move, and the train driver could not stop. It was two days ago. Des has already identified her body. I don't understand why he hasn't called. Maybe grief and shock . . . who knows? But I will call him when I gather my senses.'

Lisa shook her head, still trying to get the image of Janine being hit by train out of her mind. She shuddered. 'I really feel numb, and I have to say I have no sympathy for either of them. I hated Ash, and Janine was so like Mum, refusing to believe me and always . . . always totally resenting me. Janine was a tragic figure, but I really don't feel anything for her. She made her own decision. It all could have been so different. Their actions, hers and Mum's . . . it changed my whole life and caused me so much pain. Although I am happy now, every day, I have to push the terror down that they caused me. I don't feel for these people.'

For once Zena was lost for words as she processed what Lisa had just said. A quietness filled the room. Lisa felt her aunt's distress for her.

'I think a ride on Topi to see Binna would clear my mind. Be good for me. I'll go and saddle up now. Do you have anything you'd like me to take?'

'I'll throw in some vegetables I picked from the garden this morning,' said Zena, her voice brisk and controlled.

'Do you need to speak to Helen Tyler as a result of this news?' asked Zena.

'No, I can wait for my next session,' answered Lisa, the resolution and emotional detachment in her voice concerning Zena, although she wasn't the least bit surprised. Those two women had been the bane of Lisa's life. She couldn't say she was sad about their fates, either.

◊

Lisa hit the road at a ferocious speed. Her own breath was loud in her ears, the sound of Topi's hooves drowning out every thought. It took her a moment to separate the sound of his hooves striking the earth from the pounding of her heart. She galloped on until the humpy came into view. As she tethered Topi, Ningali sung out. 'You in da big hurry, little one?'

'Sort of,' said Lisa, grabbing the calico bag.

'We see you ride past a couple of times. Got da new horse. He very pretty, go like da wind,' smiled Ningali.

'Yes, he is very fast. His name is Topi.'

'Aaah, you sit with us now.' Binna patted the ground.

'Some vegetables,' Lisa said as she handed the calico bag to Ningali.

'Troubles, little one?' asked Binna.

'No, not really . . . just difficult news. Someone we know has been killed, and another person . . . a person who was very evil has been sent to prison.'

'Dis news bring sadness?' asked Ningali.

'No, not really. The evil person did a lot of bad things to me and other girls. He is locked away, and I will never see him again. That makes me feel better inside. The other one, she was related to me but she chose to die. It doesn't cause me sorrow. Her intentions towards me were malicious, and I believe she had a bad heart.'

'I hear da troubles in your voice,' added Ningali.

'We do maybe smoking ceremony or maybe healing for da spirit,' said Binna. 'Use my hands, remove da pain. We do da panpooni.'

Ningali began to break up the branches of the bloodwood tree, placing them into their small fire. The smoke began to fill the humpy.

'We do da smudging,' said Binna. 'Put your hands in da smoke. It carry to your body and help da heart and da mind and da body. Move da bad spirits,' said the old lady soothingly.

Lisa closed her eyes and relaxed, the smoke drifting into the air. 'Now you lay down,' instructed Ningali.

She felt their hands move over her back and up to her head, a calmness and serenity of mind and heart sweeping over her. Sleep came as she curled into a foetal position. She rested for a good hour.

While Lisa slept, Ningali pointed to an approaching vehicle. 'Boss lady, she driving fast, Binna.' The old lady nodded. Her friend was no doubt looking for Lisa, who slept peacefully.

Zena looked relieved when she saw the tethered horse. She pulled up and waved to the ladies.

Lisa stirred and rubbed her eyes, half-sitting up. 'Aunty? Sorry, I fell asleep.'

'That's okay, darling girl. You must have needed it.' Zena sat down next to Binna.

'We do da cleansing using da bloodwood leaves and den da hands. She sleep, da little one, like da baby.'

'Yes, I see, it's alright, I just needed to know she was safe. Just a relative . . . well, sort of died in a most disturbing manner, so it is a bit to process. Not so much her passing as this person was always awful to Lisa and caused a lot of problems.'

'She be orright. Take da bad spirit away,' said Ningali.

Lisa smiled. 'Thank you, Binna . . . again.'

'Yes to both of you, thank you,' said Zena.

She turned to her niece. 'Do you feel like heading home now, Lisa.'

'Gosh, Aunty . . . yes. Topi needs water, I did ride him hard.'

'That's okay, I have a jerry can and a bucket. We can do that before you head home,' offered Zena.

'Thank you, my friend.' Zena held Binna's hand softly. 'Vegetables in that calico bag, Ningali, sure you will put to good use. We'll be off then.'

Lisa hugged her two friends fiercely. 'Bye, ladies,' Lisa said with a warm smile. 'I'll see you soon.' She followed her aunt to the back of the Land Rover, where she grabbed some water for Topi. The horse drank thirstily.

'Right then. See you back home. I called Des, by the way, and I also told Alan about Janine and Superintendent Ash when he came in for lunch.'

'Oh . . . did Des . . . did he blame me?'

'No, sweetheart, not at all. He was just in his own shock. He didn't have the greatest of relationships with Janine, and I don't think anybody apart from Agnes did. It is just the way she died. Suicide is always a shock. Des was going to call us tonight, but I beat him to it.'

'I don't want to go to the funeral, Aunty.' Lisa's voice was firm.

'It's okay, all understandable. I didn't expect you to. It's almost a relief, really. I found her death threats to you frightening, and when people lose control of their minds, anything can happen. She was at a loose end, and I think really capable of anything. But Des has it under control. You may like to call him and Mark yourself tonight after dinner.'

'Yes, I will. I was due to make a call anyway just to catch up with Mark.'

'Good, hun, let's be on our way. I feel as if we have closed another awful chapter. Give me a good head start or the dust will choke you and Topi.'

As she rode towards Woori, Lisa's thoughts turned to Billy. *Not long now. I so miss you. I wish you were here now. So much has happened since I last saw you. Endings and new beginnings.*

As Woori came into view, Mitch's Land Rover was pulling up just outside the compound gates. He turned to wave at the galloping rider as he got out of the vehicle.

'Hey, what brings you here?' Lisa asked as she pulled Topi up.

'Just heading back from Carinda, thought I would pop in and say hello, see if you want to ride tomorrow?'

'Let's head inside then. I'll check and see what Alan has planned. Just let me hose Topi down and give him a biscuit of hay.'

Mitch followed Lisa around to the yards, his eyes never leaving her. He felt a powerful need to pull her to him, to kiss her, to feel her body against his. He was finding it more and more difficult to contain himself whenever he was with her.

'All done, let's go inside,' smiled Lisa.

'Well hello, Mitch,' greeted Alan as he folded his newspaper. 'What are you up to?

'Had to pick up a few things in Carinda, so I thought I'd pop in and say hello. See if Lisa wanted to ride down to the river tomorrow.'

'Don't see why not,' said Alan. 'Zena is just freshening up. She won't be a moment. I've got to get the big boss's seal of approval.'

Mitch grinned. His father was always saying happy wife, happy life.

'The afternoon is better for me,' added Lisa. 'Be back in a jiff.'

'Would you like a cold beer, Mitch? Just about to have one myself and am making Zena a G & T.'

'Sounds good. I hope I'm not intruding,' apologised Mitch.

'No, not at all.' Zena stepped into the kitchen. 'Walls are paper thin, Mitch. It's all good. Why don't you stay for dinner? We would love the company.'

'Sure, love to. I had best call Mum then and let her know I'm here.'

'The phone is in the hallway, you make the call and I'll just check on dinner. If you want to shower or wash up, the bathroom is two doors down from the phone.'

'Thanks, Zena. I will do that. Always dusty on the road.' He headed off down the hallway.

'Nice work, darling wife.'

'Don't be daft. I am not matchmaking . . . just being polite. It is what it is and it will brighten the place up, and not to mention take Lisa's mind off the news we received today. Even though it's such a relief that that brute of a superintendent will be spending his life behind bars. Bastard. It's almost too good for him after all he's done to those girls. Especially to our niece. I hope they castrate him in there.'

'As I told Lisa, the crims will have a field day with Ash. Men who molest children get no mercy. He would be in a world of pain right now. Things will be brutal and vicious for him. Men who practice vileness get no mercy. No escape. I can hear him howling and screaming already. My heart breaks,' said Alan sarcastically.

Really, it's like a chapter closed then . . . Agnes, then Lenny, Mr Ash and now Janine,' remarked Zena. 'All deserved, I must add. But at least Lisa can start putting the whole sordid ideal behind her.'

Alan nodded. 'She deserves to have a good life, unmarred by those bastards. We reap what we sow. To me, all of them have met their own justice.'

'I don't know if she'll even fully heal, but she's got a much better chance of it now with us, Alan. I so hope so, for her sake. I am, well we all are, very satisfied that Ash got life imprisonment and will never see a free day. And the inmates will crucify him in there—' said Zena, not finishing her sentence.

'Right then,' said Mitch as he came into the kitchen. 'Scrubbed clean and Mum notified. What can I do?'

'Nothing, just sit yourself down. Alan is getting you a beer and we are heading out to the verandah. Sunsets are our thing. Lisa is just washing up, so relax. No rush for anything.'

Mitch followed Zena out and sat down, his big frame relaxing into the softness of the lounge. Alan handed him a beer. 'Thanks, mate,' said Mitch, taking a big swig. 'Nothing beats an icy cold beer at the end of the day.'

'Nope,' he agreed as he handed Zena her gin and tonic. 'Here's our girl now,' said Alan as Lisa joined them, taking a seat next to Mitch.

'Can I get you something, Lisa?' asked Alan.

'No, I'm good. I'll call Mark before dinner and catch up on the news.'

'Give him my regards,' said Mitch. 'Hope he's back up here soon.' As Mitch finished the sentence, the phone started ringing.

'I'll go, it might just be him,' said Lisa, springing to her feet. Her excited voice as she picked up told them it was Mark.

'Where was home for Lisa?' Mitch queried.

'The western suburbs, Mitch, out near Liverpool, a suburb known as Fairfield. Her mother passed away not that long ago, but her home life was . . . Lisa may have told you, fairly traumatic,' replied Zena.

'No, she hasn't really told me anything and just sort of clams up when I ask. Why was it so bad that you had to bring her here? If I know, maybe I can understand her more.'

Zena nodded. 'I think she will tell you in her own time, that is, when she's ready, but suffice to say, alcohol and physical violence were prevalent.'

'Okay, I see. Mum said she had trust issues, which is why I don't rush her . . . with anything emotional.'

'Your mum is a smart woman, Mitch, and I would heed that advice. But by her being with us, she has learned to trust and voice an opinion without being punished. Physical and mental abuse on young children does take its toll, and recovery is usually a protracted course. Some never recover. But the Aboriginal ladies you met, and a professional counsellor Lisa sees regularly, have all played a part in the healing process. Alan and I are grateful to them all.'

'But what could those Abos do? They aren't doctors.'

Zena's back stiffened. 'Those Aboriginal ladies, more so Binna, are powerful healers, and if you would care to read about what they do and how they connect the spirit to the earth and realign the soul, you may find yourself surprised.'

'Yeah, Mitch, you would be amazed with their natural cures and the way they see things. They make a poultice for inflammation. Turned this non-believer into a believer, and I have seen Lisa improve with their smoking ceremonies,' said Alan.

There's that raw nerve again, Mitch observed. Zena's voice had become bolder and clearly she loved the boongs too. *But I have the three things I need now: Her name, date of birth and where she lived.*

Lisa bounced in, and Zena was grateful her presence broke the line of conversation.

'How were they?' queried Zena.

'Good, although they are both shocked with what has happened but are processing everything. I will call tomorrow and speak to both of them again.'

'Is Mark alright Lisa?' asked Mitch.

'Yeah, he's fine, it's just that . . . ' Lisa's eyes danced furtively. 'A relative died a few days ago.'

'My condolences then, to you all. I am sorry for this news,' said Mitch.

'Right, let's get dinner underway before it gets too late,' interrupted Zena. She had a bad feeling all of a sudden and just wanted to get the night over with. *My gut feeling tells me Mitch is probing for a reason. What are you up to, Mitchell Walker?*

TWENTY-FIVE

WOLF IN SHEEP'S CLOTHING

The next day Mitch waited until his parents left for town and had the house to himself. He nervously dialled the number, Dean Jones, Private Investigator. A pang of guilt stabbed at him. *I just need to know, Lisa.*

A young woman answered. 'Morning, you have reached the office of Dean Jones, private investigator. How can I assist?'

'Yes, good morning. I have a confidential matter that I would like investigated. Who can I speak to regarding this?'

'What is your name, please?'

'Mitch . . . Mitchell Walker.'

'Right then, I shall put you through to Dean Jones. One moment please.'

The voice on the other end was gravelly, the type of voice you hear from chronic long-term smokers. 'Morning, Mr Walker, it's Dean Jones. How can I help you?'

'Morning, Mr Jones. I have a highly confidential matter I'd like investigated, and I just need a few background details. This person doesn't provide much information and I want to know more. It is actually someone that I am kind of seeing but she never provides any details of background or family.'

'Of course, we can handle that type of enquiry. Always wise to know what you are dealing with. So, I just need her details, name, date of birth,' stated Dean.

'Her name is Lisa O'Connor. She is currently residing with her aunt, Zena Smith, on a property out past Carinda. Her date of birth is the 16th August 1955, and she grew up in a suburb called Fairfield.'

'That is all the info I need. So what do you want to know?' asked Dean.

'She came to live with her aunt due to problems in the family. I just want to know what problems. I really like this girl, but I am clueless regarding personal information and when I do ask, it causes her to become defensive.'

'Okay, got the picture, leave it with me. My fees are $15 per hour.'

'That's fine, Dean. I'll leave it with you. So what happens now?'

'I will make some enquiries. Sometimes I can access information quickly and sometimes it can take a few weeks.'

'Look, it's not urgent, and I would rather you get as much information as you can,' said Mitch.

'Very good. I'll call you when I have a report prepared,' said Dean.

'Actually, no, I would prefer no phone calls, unless I make them to you,' replied Mitch.

'Right, I'll get onto it. Perhaps you can call in a week's time?'

'Perfect,' said Mitch. 'Thanks for your assistance, Dean.' He hung up the phone. *We shall see, young lady . . . we shall see.*

He looked at his watch. Time to do a few things around the place and then hitch up Almondo in the horse trailer for the ride down to the river. The shearing season would be upon them soon enough, and Mitch knew the time spent with Lisa would be much less.

When Mitch arrived at the gates, Lisa was ready. Topi was tethered, and Zena stood chatting with Lisa. He saw the calico bag and winced. *Bloody stopover with those boongs.*

'Hi, you two. Great day for a ride, Lisa.' Mitch flashed a wide grin.

'Sure is. I'm ready. You have kept me waiting,' she said playfully. Lisa mounted Topi and threw the bag over her saddle. 'A quick stop on the way, Mitch.'

'Yeah sure,' said Mitch, but Zena thought the smile was forced. *Why do I get the feeling sometimes that he has a very large, artificial smile?*

'Safe travels, hun. See you when you get back.' Zena watched them disappear down the road, her feelings a little on edge. She was no longer sure she could one hundred percent trust Mitch's intentions.

◊

It was a slow canter to the humpy, and Lisa was happy in her thoughts as the ladies came into view. 'Can't stay too long,' grumbled Mitch. 'It's already just after two.'

'Yes, I know. I'll just take these bottled fruits up to them,' replied Lisa, pulling off the calico bag. 'You stay here and hang on to Topi.' She made her way over to the humpy.

'Hello, ladies, I brought you your favourite.' They both sat cross legged, the remnants of a fish recently eaten on their tin plates.

'Have you been down by the river, Ningali?' asked Lisa.

'Yep, me go for da maugro. Binna like da fish.'

Lisa laughed. 'I can't stay as it will be late getting back, but I'll be out again on my own and have more time with you. Take care, my friends.'

◊

281

'Lisa have da happy heart. Season start soon. Billy be back,' said Binna.

'But not for sure,' added Ningali.

'He be back, come back for da little one,' repeated Binna.

'What about dat big white rooster . . . what she gunna do with dat bloke?' asked Ningali.

'Plenty trouble with dat boy, he not good for her. He gunna get hurt, him have da thorns inside,' warned Binna as Mitch and Lisa rode off.

◊

When they got to the river, Mitch smiled. *Good, finally on our own.* He wandered down to the river after tethering the horses and put his hand in to feel the temperature.

'It's cold, Lisa. Don't really feel like getting wet . . . do you?'

'No, let's just sit for a bit and take all this beauty in. This place always feels so peaceful.' Lisa lay back on the grass, her hands behind her head, looking up at the sky.

'I should like to build a home right here.'

Mitch came to sit by her side. He gazed at her hungrily as he shifted onto his side, his head resting in his palm. 'I could look at you all day and never get tired of it. I will build you a house, right here if you want.'

'Oh, Mitch, don't be silly,' Lisa said nervously. His fingers traced the side of her face very gently, gliding down towards her chest. He wanted to bury his face between her breasts and felt his erection stir. Lisa stopped his finger.

'Mitch, that makes me feel uncomfortable,' cautioned Lisa, sitting up.

'Sorry, Lisa . . . just can't help myself. It's what you do to me, and I won't be seeing much of you when the season gets underway. Now that makes me sad.'

Lisa rolled her eyes. 'It's only for a short time, Mitch, and the season's so much fun. The place comes alive with all these people. Black, white, kids and dogs, a great mixture. I'll have to come over to Woodside and see your crew. I didn't last season but I suppose your routine and work is just the same as ours. Alan said it will be the usual chaos at our place. Old Harry who came last time won't be here. He's the old chap who died.'

'Yes, I heard about that. Dad said he was a top old bloke.'

'He was . . . gave Alan these beautiful opals, blues and greens. Alan had the jeweller make them into earrings for me. They are so gorgeous.'

'They probably match those beautiful eyes of yours.' Mitch moved closer. 'Lisa,' he whispered, fluttering kisses down the side of her neck. She caught her breath. The softness of his kiss and his confidence told her that nothing in this world would stop him from getting what he wanted.

'Stop there, Mitch . . . please,' pleaded Lisa.

'I don't want to.' He continued to kiss her, his tongue flickering out to taste her skin. His touch was searing.

'No, that is enough! Now please stop, we need to go!' She jumped to her feet. His kisses were intoxicating and this was no place to lose control. His presence was overwhelming and her body reacted with both terror and a lust so strong it made her head spin.

The moment was broken, but Mitch was sure her body had responded with a surge of desire, which she pushed away.

'Sorry, Lisa, really sorry. I just lost control,' conceded Mitch as he gritted his teeth. His mind coursed with lust, raw and insatiable.

'You are right; it's time to go.' They headed back to Woori in silence, and it wasn't an amicable one.

TWENTY-SIX

POINT OF NO RETURN

Mitch kept a low profile for the next few days. He could not bear the thought of Lisa turning him away but he ached to have her. *Let things blow over a bit.* Kate would be calling Zena to see if they wanted to come over for lunch on Sunday. He hoped Lisa's anger towards him would have passed by then.

It was now Friday. He wanted to call Dean Jones to see if he had any information. After breakfast, Mitch excused himself and went to the phone in the office. Dave had left the house, and Kate was busy in the kitchen. As he dialled the number, he so hoped some information had been gathered.

The same young woman answered. 'Yes, Mr Walker, I will put you through.'

'Hi, Mitch,' said the gravelly voice. 'Glad you called . . . we have a fair bit information on your lady friend. Very interesting history for one so young.'

'Like what?' asked Mitch.

'Police record, indecent sexual allegations, and then being sent to one of those institutions for reform.'

Mitch gasped. 'Shit, are you for real?'

'Certainly am, son. Have a report here, which I can post with my invoice.'

'No, that's not necessary. I'll come in this afternoon and collect it as well as pay your fees. Thanks, Dean. I should be in late afternoon.'

Mitch sat in stunned silence. *Who was this girl? So sweet and innocent. Police record! No wonder she shuts down when you try and ask things.*

He strode into the kitchen. 'Mum, I'm going to head into Walgett. Want to get a few things before the season starts. Let Dad know where I am.'

'Sure, darling. By the way, I'll be calling Zena to see if Sunday lunch is okay for them,' said Kate.

'Sounds good.' He kissed her on the cheek and grabbed his keys.

The drive into Walgett gave Mitch time to think. Yes, violence in the family along with booze, but why would she have a police record? And then there was the sweetness and the innocence, portrayed so well. Her fright at anything sexual, yet sexual allegations were in the reports. But the other day at the river, she looked like she was about to let him take her. For one split second, there was no resistance. He felt a rush of pleasure.

When Mitch arrived at the office of Dean Jones, the young receptionist greeted him. The air in the office was musty and smelled strongly of stale tobacco. It looked like it could do with a good clean.

'Hi, Mr Walker. Dean said to give you this. It's your report. He has left for the day and this is his invoice.'

'Okay, thank you,' said Mitch as he paid in cash.

His hands trembled as he held the large white envelope. He wanted to tear it open but waited until he sat in the privacy of his car. He pulled the photos out. Police mug shots, Lisa

O'Connor charged with stealing, destruction of property, assaulting police officers. *Whoa!* Then off to the Parramatta Girls Home, deemed uncontrollable by her mother. Accusations against her brother-in-law, molesting her, sexual penetration. Mitch's eyes widened . . . sexual penetration?

He stopped for a moment and took a deep breath. *Fuck . . . you are not a virgin. No wonder everything has been hidden. This report is like opening up Pandora's box.*

Mitch stuffed the photos back into the envelope and threw them in the glovebox. He had best get a few things. He wandered into a clothing store, picking out a new shirt and then hit the newsagents for some magazines regarding agriculture. As he headed for home, his thoughts wandered. *I wonder what the brother-in-law did and if she enjoyed it. But Christ, how old was she? A minor, and where was the brother-in-law now?* Nothing made sense.

He passed Woori on the drive in and saw no trace of anyone. *I hope Sunday is on, Lisa. I want to see you.*

Mitch pulled the envelope out of the glovebox and put it into the clothing bag before bounding into the house. The information was like pieces of a jigsaw, and he wanted to explore it further.

'Hello, darling. Get what you wanted? asked Kate.

'Certainly did,' Mitch beamed. 'A new shirt for Sunday . . . did you call?'

'Yes, and they are coming. They'll be here around noon.'

Two more sleeps and I will sit across the table from you and know exactly where you have come from and what you have been up to. My girl, I know some of your secrets.

◊

Lisa felt nervous as she dressed. Mitch had not called since the incident at the river. He did apologise, and she had known he was showing his real feelings more and more. But even though she did like him, Billy was in her heart. He would be here soon. *I'm waiting, Billy. Please come soon.*

Kate was the welcoming hostess as usual. 'Welcome, everyone, lovely to see you. Lisa, you are looking gorgeous.'

'Something smells bloody good, Kate,' commented Alan.

'Beef Wellington,' grinned Kate.

''What can I help with?' asked Zena.

'Nothing really, all under control, maybe a further thirty minutes and we'll be set to go. Time for a drink!' said Kate. 'Let's join the boys, shall we?'

'Where's Mitch?' asked Lisa.

'Just getting ready, Lisa. He was last in, even bought a new shirt for today,' said Kate proudly.

Zena noticed Lisa was scratching her arms. *That's not a good sign. She hasn't done that for a while. Something is bothering her.*

'Oh, there you are,' said Kate as Mitch moved forward to shake Alan's hand. He sat opposite Lisa in one of the oversized arm chairs and a thousand pictures ran through his mind. Mug shots, her lying naked on a bed with some other man. Her brother-in-law, for fuck's sake. How disgusting. Here she sat so demurely, her eyes downcast. His smile was cunning, and his eyes glowed with lust.

'New shirt, Mitch?' asked Alan.

'Yep, bought it just for today.' His eyes bored into Lisa's, who had finally looked up. 'What do you think, Lisa? Do you like it?'

'Sure . . . it looks fine, Mitch, really suits you,' she replied nervously. There was something in his manner, almost like a cat with his shifty eyes.

Lunch was no different to their usual get-togethers. Lisa gradually relaxed. One glass of champagne, and the warmth settled her nerves. Maybe she felt uneasy due to his advances at the river. But Mitch was jovial, and their chatter mainly centred around the pending season, just weeks away, and if they had enough staff. Zena chatted excitedly about the breeding program with her new mares.

It was time to go. 'Alright, lovely ladies, we need to hit the road. Have to hay up, and Jack is calling tonight if I recall correctly from our last conversation.'

'Fabulous lunch, Kate.' Zena kissed her cheek.

'Hey, Lisa, one more ride before the season begins, and then I won't bother you anymore.' Lisa felt put on the spot. 'I'll even get Mum to make something for your lady friends.'

Kate shot Mitch an odd look. 'Lisa's Aboriginal lady friends, Mum.' He knew that would be a clincher.

'Um . . . sure,' Lisa replied. 'That's very nice of you, Mitch, and . . . thank you, Kate.'

'Great, I'll call when I have a few spare hours this week,' smiled Mitch.

Lisa breathed a sigh of relief. She was almost certain he would want to go tomorrow. Mitch was not giving it any urgency, as he would normally do, when suggesting a ride out to the river. 'Call you when I have a few spare hours.' That remark was odd, different. Mitch always had a plan. *Maybe when we get home I should tell Aunty what happened at the river. Or maybe just leave it. Only one more ride and Billy will be here.*

That very thought cheered her soul.

As they got into the Zephyr, Zena turned to her niece. 'Everything alright, hun? You were a little quiet, and I noticed you scratching your arms.'

'Yes, Aunty, I'm fine, just nervous or rather excited about the season. Lots on my mind.'

'Yeah, kid. I can't sleep for the excitement,' said Alan. 'I'm sure Jack will have all the latest details when he calls tonight.'

The phone rang early evening and Alan picked up, chatting to Jack for well over an hour. When he came back into the kitchen, he could see Lisa was eagerly waiting for his news.

'Well?' asked Zena.

'All good. Cookie is back and he promises new menus. Got a new bloke, a jackaroo from up north called Kev. Apparently he's a great shot, which is good news now that we don't have Jimmy. That boy could shoot an eagle without us even seeing it in the distance. So, I'll be interested to see what this Kev fellow is like. Apart from that, no other news,' said Alan.

'And Billy . . . what about Billy and Burnu?' queried Lisa.

'No news, kid . . . but they all know to be here the fourth of September to start. So, that means they are welcome to wander in end of August to set up, get organised or whatever they need to do to get going on that official date. Some of them just wander in without any prior contact. It doesn't matter. There has never been a surplus and we have never been short. Everything seems to sort itself.'

Lisa felt a tinge of sadness. Maybe her aunt was right. Maybe she would never see Billy or Burnu again. 'Okay, I'll say goodnight and see you in the morning.' Alone in her room, Lisa touched the quartz stones. *Please come back to me, Billy.*

◊

Alan had a hot breakfast ready when Zena came in. 'What a surprise . . . how lovely. Any reason?' Zena asked as she lifted the sizzling bacon off the heat.

'Should hold us until late afternoon. Bacon and eggs seems to stick to your sides. I just want to keep Lisa busy and not break the momentum with the mares and Khartoum. Got a list of things for her to do. I just have a gut feeling she needs her mind taken elsewhere and she loves working with the mares.'

'Good idea. She does seem to be out of sorts or her mind elsewhere. The next few weeks are going to be tough for her . . . not knowing, and I understand that,' added Zena. Lisa just then stumbled in, all tousled hair and sleepy eyes.

'Morning, sweetheart, Alan was just saying he would be keeping you busy.'

'I want to be busy . . . busy with the mares. I'm looking forward to it, actually. I have come to understand horses a lot more and the importance of good stock horses. So I guess, it is as you said, my education continues in the equine industry.' She helped herself to the hot breakfast.

'Indeed, Lisa,' said Zena, but she knew the girl's heart was heavy. *Good act, darling girl, but you don't fool me.*

'What will you be doing today, Zena?' queried Alan.

'I want to get a wriggle on with pre-cooking a few things to help Cookie. I'll freeze these, but I just think initially, there will be a lot of sadness for him without Harry, so I'll throw in a few extra specials to lift the mood. I may come up when and if I get done here. Also, I wanted to go over some sheet music. With the warmer weather coming and the extra people flooding in for the season, no doubt John the Publican will be calling for a few Saturday night dates to advertise the RSL.'

Alan kissed Zena's forehead. 'Come on, Lisa, let's move.' He beckoned her out of the kitchen.

As they pulled up in the ute, Alan took Lisa's hand. 'If anything makes you feel uncomfortable today, just let me know. Because we are live serving, sometimes the stallion and even the mare will display aggressive behaviour, but he is usually a pretty good boy. Nevertheless, I have the restraining equipment if need be.'

Lisa nodded her okay as she got out of the ute. Alan instructed, 'Just bring the mares around to this yard as well as Noir, and I'll go and get Khartoum.'

Khartoum was prancing by the time he arrived with Alan. 'Yep, he's ready. Did you know, just like us, they have an affinity for a mate?'

'No, not really,' replied Lisa.

'Well, just to make sure this little lady is ready, I'll check her reaction to his presence. If she turns her head and moves her tail to one side, lowers her croup and then urinates, she is in active heat and ready to breed. But, if she squeals, lays back her ears, or worse, tries to kick and bite, it's probably too soon or too late.'

'Gosh, all that info . . . I never knew,' exclaimed Lisa.

'Lots to think about, Lisa. You have to take the teasing and the whole process slowly then let the mare have time to decide how to react. Rushing is bad management, and I also let them stay close to each other for a few minutes after mating rather than separating them immediately. It respects the social bond while allowing the stallion to recover fully. Romantic, hey kid.'

Lisa laughed. 'I would also say thoughtful, Alan.'

When Alan brought Khartoum into the same yard, Noir began to react and swish her tail. 'Hold her firmly, Lisa, and talk to her.'

As Alan brought the big stallion up behind Noir, the mating seemed rather brutal, but then it was all over very quickly.

'Looks so odd, Alan.'

'Yeah, I agree, but after you have seen a few, it's nothing really. Just nature,' he said calmly.

When they had finished with the last mare, it was well past lunch time. 'Time for a cup of tea and see what my lovely wife is up to,' said Alan.

As they headed up to the house, Lisa was quiet. 'Okay? Not too confronting for you?' Alan probed.

'Oh no . . . . I'm alright with that. It was as you said, nature, but you are so kind in how you considered the feelings of the mares and how they would react.'

Alan knew instinctively that Lisa was making comparisons to her past situation. 'You will be fine, Lisa, and so will those four-legged ladies.'

Lisa half smiled. Alan was right. When they came inside, Zena was pulling out a tray of scones. 'You bloody bewdy,' Alan sang out. 'Just what a bloke needs.'

The jam and cream were already on the table, and Zena loaded the scones off to another plate. 'Yum,' said Alan as Zena poured the tea. She then turned to her niece.

'Good day down there, Lisa?'

Yes, Aunty, so interesting. Alan is a great teacher. I hope they are all pregnant.'

'Me too,' added Zena. 'They'd have gorgeous foals . . . by the way, Mitch called. He wants you to call him back.'

'Uh . . . okay, thank you.' Lisa was sure he would want to go to the river. She had felt more relaxed with him over Sunday lunch, so maybe he had understood how she felt. She enjoyed his company but their last outing had made her uncomfortable. This would definitely be their last ride.

'You go and make the call, Lisa, unless you want any more.'

'Gosh no, I am so full! They were delicious.'

'Right then, we'll clean up . . . off you go.'

Mitch answered on the first ring. 'Hello, Lisa, thanks for being so prompt. I was just on my way out, glad you caught me. I wanted to know if you'd be up for a ride tomorrow or the day after? Almondo is getting a bit fidgety, so he needs a good gallop.'

She hesitated in her response. 'Sure, Mitch, that sounds fine. Topi is the same way too. There's something about those long rides, isn't there. They just stretch out.'

'Sure is. So, what time would suit you? Tomorrow or whenever? You pick.'

'Tomorrow is good, around two. But just a ride out and then back.'

'Yep, no problem, Lisa. I'll see you then.'

When Lisa hung up the phone, she felt confident she had asserted herself and directed how the day would be for both of them.

Zena looked up when she came into the kitchen.

'We're riding tomorrow but it will be my last ride with Mitch for a while.'

'Oh, why's that?' queried Zena.

'Because I'll be riding with Billy,' Lisa said confidently.

The following day, Mitch was right on time. Lisa watched his trailer pull up. Topi was saddled, and Lisa sat waiting outside the compound gates, somewhat apprehensive. Would Mitch behave?

'Hey, you.' His long, lanky frame got out of the Land Rover. 'Looking forward to this.' He flashed one of his trademark grins.

'Yes, me too. And Topi. He wants to get going, he's so fidgety.'

Lisa watched as Mitch unloaded Almondo and then she mounted Topi.

'Almondo is almost dancing, they just know when they are about to run,' laughed Mitch. 'Nearly as fidgety as your bloke.'

'Bit like teenagers, they want to run and play,' said Lisa.

'Ready when you are, young lady. Oh, by the way, Mum didn't have time to make anything for your friends.'

'That's okay, Mitch. We will just ride out and back. No stops today.'

They hit the road in a thunderous gallop. It felt good, and Lisa waved as she passed the camp of her Aboriginal friends. *Not today, my dear friends. Tomorrow perhaps.*

Mitch galloped at a breakneck speed, his big gelding pounding the road all the way to the river, his hooves biting into the soft earth. Topi excitedly followed but as fast as he was, he was no match for the long-striding horse. They pulled up in a lather of sweat, heady and exhilarated. The joyousness of the ride had got to Lisa.

'That was bloody great. Boy oh boy, can this guy move!' said Mitch, sliding off Almondo's back.

'He sure can, Mitch. What a wonderful stride. Topi and I ate your dust all the way,' she said, laughing. 'I need some water.'

Lisa dismounted and went to the water in her saddle bag. 'Good idea. The horses may need a drink too. Let's just walk them down to the river, give them a drink,' said Mitch.

'Topi is really huffing and puffing . . . might sit a spell, Mitch. I'm still mindful of his age and bone soundness.'

Mitch was pleased with the idea. He thought for certain she would not even get off Topi when they hit the river. He so wanted to sit and be alone with her.

'Yep, we don't want him to snap any bones. I'll tether them up here to these trees, now that they've had a good guzzle.'

Lisa looked at her watch. 'Perhaps ten to fifteen minutes, and then I want to get home.'

'Sure thing, Lisa.' He made his way to sit down next to her. There was a pensive silence.

'Heard from Mark?'

'Yes, all good. I'm hoping he can get up here again this Christmas and stay longer,' said Lisa.

There was a gentle breeze, which blew her hair softly over her face. Mitch brought up his hand to push her hair back.

'Are you going to behave?'

'Maybe . . . maybe not,' Mitch said smugly.

Lisa glared at him and as she made a move to get up, he suddenly forced himself on her, the blood rushing to his heart, his desire for her flaming so intensely. He held her firmly, pushing her to the ground, his lips seeking hers hungrily as his hand slipped under her shirt and felt her breasts.

Lisa struggled violently and waited for him to release her. A cry escaped from her lips. She wiped her mouth, her face burning, then she turned towards him with a lightning swing and slapped him hard across the face with such force, it shocked Mitch cold.

Lisa jumped to her feet. 'Don't ever touch me like that or do that again.'

'I'm sorry, Lisa,' Mitch said, running his hands through his hair. 'For fuck's sake, I'm in love with you, I want to be with you. I want to make you mine. I can't play this friendship game anymore. I want to be your lover and give you pleasure. I want to be everything for you.'

Lisa stomped away, walking towards Topi. Mitch stood up and began to walk after her.

'Stop, Lisa. Stop! For Christ sake, listen to me. I know you are not a virgin. I have information and I know about you. I have tried to take things slowly, but I just . . . you make me wild and crazy with desire. I want you so much.'

'What do you know?' Lisa scowled, turning to face him, the anger and terror bubbling within her.

Mitch was now cocky. He had her attention. 'I know you may have had sex at a very young age. Are you a virgin, Lisa? I know you have a police record as well.' He slowly walked towards her, a sly grin spreading over his face.

Shock began to register on Lisa's face as she felt her safe world being ripped apart.

'So, there is no reason to play this sweet little virgin game that you do. I know you want me, I felt it the other week when we were out here. You were ready to give it to me.'

Mitch lunged at her, and a brief struggle ensued as Lisa tried to free herself. His voice was half coaxing and half scolding, and his mouth crushed hers with such ferocity she could hardly breathe. Then she felt his mouth and tongue move down her neck. 'Stop it, Mitch, stop it!' She drove her knee hard up into his testicles.

Mitch reeled back in agony, his hands resting on his groin. 'Fucking bitch . . . whore, fucking boong lover. You will be sorry you did this. Everyone is going to know about you.'

Lisa ran for the horses and as she mounted Topi, she looked at Mitch and spat on the ground. She dug her heels in and headed for home. *Run, Topi, run, as fast as you can.* As Lisa galloped past the humpy, she knew the ladies would see her on her own. No doubt their curiosity would be peaked and no doubt Ningali would have questions.

Mitch felt the anger rise in him. He touched his face where he had felt the force of her slap and the ache of his testicles. *You'll be sorry, you little tease.*

He waited for the pain to ease and then mounted Almondo. *Stupid bitch. I need to fuck someone. I am over the ache in my balls. Tess Dunphy, expect a call.*

As he galloped by the humpy, he felt the eyes of the women upon him.

◊

'We see da baby on her own . . . now we see dat big white rooster, he trail behind. Bin trouble out by da river. Plenty trouble,' informed Ningali.

'We find out, proper true,' said Binna. 'Dat boy trouble to her.'

TWENTY-SEVEN

WHAT GOES AROUND

It was late afternoon by the time she cantered Topi into Woori, and the ride home had settled Lisa's nerves. She wiped her mouth and spat the taste of Mitch into the red earth. *Bastard! Do I tell Aunty or just let it be? Calm and settle. Think logically, Lisa.*

After hosing Topi and giving him a biscuit of hay, she gathered her senses in the Tack Room, cleaning her saddle and bridle. The cats stretched lazily on the stacked hessian bags. 'What a life you guys have . . . no problems except to keep the rats and mice under control.' Lisa suddenly laughed nervously, 'I just tried to keep a big rat under control.'

It wasn't that funny really. She bit her lip. How did he find out that information? It began to gnaw in the pit of her stomach. *I need to tell Aunty, but will it affect her relationship with Kate?* Lisa sighed and stood in the doorway, looking towards the house. *I need to find my rock.* She strode off, looking for her aunt.

The house was empty but there was a note on the kitchen table: *Up at the shearing sheds. Z & A.* Lisa raced back down the stairs and jumped into the paddock basher, zooming towards the shearing sheds. Mitch's horse trailer was still at the gate, but she knew he would not be far behind.

'Someone's in a hurry,' drawled Alan, nodding in the direction of the approaching ute.

'So I see,' replied Zena.

'Good ride?' asked Zena as Lisa pulled up.

'Yeah, sort of . . . no not really,' Lisa mumbled, her head bowed.

'What do you mean sort of and not really?' pressed Zena.

Lisa paused. 'Mitch made a pass at me.'

Zena looked at Alan, who stopped what he was doing. 'What sort of pass, kid?'

'Kissing me and sort of holding me forcibly, but I kneed him in his crown jewels.'

Alan laughed loudly. 'That will stop him, no doubt about that.'

'Stop laughing, Alan. I get the feeling this is no laughing matter,' concluded Zena.

'And . . . he put his hands under my shirt.' Lisa paused. 'Then he said he knew about me, and asked if I was a virgin and said I had a police record.'

Zena's brow furrowed and an increasing feeling of unease seeped through her mind.

'How the devil did the little prick find this info out?' demanded Alan, angrily.

'I really don't know, Alan, but it makes me as mad as hell. Obviously been snooping but why, for what gain?' huffed Zena, seething at the personal intrusion.

'Oh please, Aunty, don't make a fuss. I would never have told you if it meant losing your friendship to Kate or causing further problems for any of us,' pleaded Lisa.

'I will get to the bottom of this. Kate and I have been good friends for a long time and ditto for Alan and Dave, but this behaviour is way out of line. It's bloody inappropriate and needs to be tackled head on. This is basically sexual assault, Lisa, when someone touches you without your consent. The boy has no right to do this, spying on you and then making unwanted and forcible advances, to you or any girl, for that matter. Who does he think he is!' raged Zena. 'I am getting madder by the minute. I have always said Mitch has never lacked for anything and he always gets what he wants. Is this the only time he has made a pass at you, Lisa?'

'No, Aunty.'

'What! Good God, Lisa, why on earth haven't you told me this?'

Lisa began to feel overwhelmed, and tears welled in her eyes.

'Oh, darling, I'm sorry. You are not to blame and please don't be upset, but he needs to be taken to task about his behaviour.'

She kissed Lisa's cheek. 'Everything will be alright.' Her voice was soothing.

'We'll head back to the house, Alan. I'm taking the ute. See you at home.'

'His horse trailer is still there, Aunty,' said Lisa.

'Well, with a bit of luck, I'll give him a piece of my mind if I see him,' Zena seethed. *Oh . . . I just wish!*

When they got back to the house, the trailer was gone. 'Well, the bugger has collected his gear and gone. Come inside now, Lisa. I'll call Kate tonight.'

Alan lit up a cigarette and sat back down on a stump of wood. *Should sort it out, man to man, give him a right bashing.* After stubbing out his cigarette, he cranked the bike up and headed home.

Zena was in the kitchen, getting dinner. 'Where's Lisa?'

'Cleaning up. It's not so much the pass, although she was rattled by it . . . it's more the info he has managed to get his hands on,' said Zena.

'It's a guess, but I would say a good guess, the boy has paid someone to dig a bit deeper. My only question is why,' said Alan.

'Exactly. As Lisa said, she knocked him back before, and she has not been that forthcoming with personal info, nor have we, but we don't have to. So, the big boofhead has hired someone. She is our niece, she is a good girl and we don't have to provide any more information to him or anyone else for that matter!' said Zena angrily.

'True. I'd like to sit with him a bit. That face would not look so pretty afterwards.'

'We are not resorting to any violence, Alan.'

'Who said anything about violence, just a good clip under the ear would let him know I was pissed off. But I also wonder if we should let it go and tell him he is not welcome here as we know what has happened. And if he rings, we just say she is not available,' said Alan.

'No, he needs to be told rather strongly that his behaviour is contemptible - not only forcing himself on two occasions, but the possible improper use of personal information. I will speak to Kate after dinner, and she can deal with it.'

When Lisa appeared, she looked drawn. 'Stop worrying, sweetheart. I will let Kate deal with this. She is a lady with a lot of integrity, and I know she will tear strips off Mitch without it affecting our friendship. So, sit and try to eat something. You haven't done anything wrong, but he certainly has, the stupid bloody hormonal twit.'

'I don't get guys or men,' Lisa sighed.

'Just a thought.' Zena hesitated.

'What thought?' asked Lisa.

'You stopped seeing Helen Tyler a couple of months ago, your decision and only you know how you feel but with all this, do you need any professional support?'

'No, Aunty. I'm fine in that regard. Thank you, and if I do, I will let you know.'

'Let's go eat, before it gets too late. You have to make that call,' said Alan, rising from his chair.

After dinner, Zena began to clear. 'You go, dear wife, and make that call. Lisa and I will keep busy. There are a few books on breeding in my study I want to show her.'

When Zena dialled the number to Woodside, a thousand memories flashed through her mind and the fun she had had with Kate and Dave, as well as Mitch, over the years.

'Hello, this is Kate Walker.'

Phew, Zena thought, *my prayers answered.*

'Kate, it's Zena. Have you got a moment to discuss something that has raised its head.'

'Certainly, Zena. It sounds serious by the tone of your voice.'

Kate sat and listened, her face turning pale.

'Oh dear, I am horrified Zena,' cried Kate, the incredulity in her voice evident. 'Please pass on my apologies to Lisa. Dave and I will take it from here, and of course, this does not affect our years of friendship. Mitch is just a stupid young man. He hasn't even come home yet after his ride with Lisa. We thought he must be there with you. He must have stopped over somewhere. But where? Don't worry, my friend, be assured that when he does get home, he's going to rue the day he was born.'

Zena looked pleased when she hung up. She knew Kate would have no hesitation in dealing with the matter. But it was a difficult and delicate situation.

'How did you go?' asked Alan as Zena came to the door of the study. Lisa's eyes were fearful.

'Kate was shocked but she was going to wait until he came home from wherever he is before grilling him,' said Zena.

'He's not been home yet?' asked Lisa.

'No. Probably out prowling about, although I would not imagine there was much to find in Carinda,' said Zena.

◊

Kate had heard Mitch's car pull up in the early hours of the morning. It was nearly lunch time when she stomped into Mitch's bedroom. The curtains were still drawn, and the rum smell permeated the room. She also noted the whisky bottle and empty glass on the bedside table, his clothes strewn on the floor.

'Time to wake up, Mitch. I need to discuss something with you,' scolded Kate as she pulled open the curtains, the light filtering in. Her son lay half-naked on his stomach, and she gasped when she saw the scratch marks on his back. *Where have you been, Mitch? And better still, with whom?* She groaned inwardly. It had better not have been with that Dunphy girl.

'Come on, wake up!' Her voice was more authoritarian. 'Come on, I said wake up!' Kate prodded his ribs.

'What's up?' He rolled over, half-sitting up, facing his mother, his voice parched and hoarse. Mitch covered his eyes and then flopped back, his temples pounding. He closed his eyes for a short time but the stabbing pain in his head and the burning of his throat only intensified.

'I will give you more than head hurts in a minute if you don't wake up and listen to me.' The harshness was still present in Kate's voice.

'I spoke to Zena on the phone last night . . . she was quite upset, and I don't jolly well blame her!'

Mitch knew in an instant. *Shit. I'm in trouble now.*

'May I tell you now, Mitch, that you are a very lucky young man. Lucky because if Lisa wanted to, she could charge you with sexual assault. You did place your hand up her shirt. This is disgusting and despicable behaviour, and you of all people should know better. You jeopardised the friendship we have with Alan and Zena, and you hurt their niece in a way that is reprehensible.'

'But Mum, she has a police record.'

'I don't care if she has a police record! I am sure there are reasons behind that but the fact that you went deliberately snooping for information is unforgivable!' Kate's voice was shrill with sheer anger.

'Now get up and out of bed. Your father is disgusted . . . we both are! We never raised a son to act like this . . . ever!'

Mitch moaned and rolled over. 'Get dressed, Mitch . . . and wherever did you get those marks on your back?'

Mitch's memory suddenly recalled him fucking Tess Dunphy. It was wild sex, and he had been hungry for her. Tess never let him down, and they went well into the early morning hours. He was physically drained but inwardly smiled at the pleasure she had given him. She rode him hard, but even as he climaxed, his only thought had been of Lisa.

Kate slammed the door and left him lying in bed. He knew he would have to face his father when he got up and be forced to bear the humiliation. *Time to face the firing squad.*

Mitch made his way into the kitchen. His parents sat together at the table, their mood very subdued.

'Mitch,' said his father gravely. 'Your mother told me what has happened, and I am speechless, almost shaken to my core that you could do this. You have behaved abhorrently, and this is not what I would expect from a son of mine.' Dave looked ready to explode. 'What's wrong with you!' he demanded.

'My apologies, Dad . . . Mum. I just lost control. It won't happen again,' apologised Mitch despondently. He was desperately sorry for the pain he had caused his parents.

'What were you thinking!' his father's voice grew louder. 'We all have urges, son, and this is something controllable, so don't give me any of your frog shit. You do realise that sticking your hand up a woman's shirt constitutes sexual assault! If Lisa had wanted to, she could have made a formal complaint. And then my boy, you would have a criminal record. Can you understand the gravity of your actions!'

Silence enveloped the room like a thick fog.

'Yes, Dad . . . I can. It was an error of judgement.'

'You can bloody well say that again! Have we given you too much, Mitch, that you expect anything that crosses your path is a given?'

'No, Dad.'

'Well, you are a bloody idiot . . . too old to put over my knee, Mitchell, and too old for the strap, but you are not to see Lisa, call her or go near Woori again. Do I make myself clear?'

'Yes, Dad, quite clear,' replied Mitch.

'Furthermore, it would appear you have done some investigative work, which I cannot for the life of me fathom why. But suffice to say . . . you will not now or ever divulge what grubby information you managed to obtain. There will be no more hurt or humiliation to this family or to our friends. Are you also clear on this point, Mitchell?'

'Yes,' said Mitch, his head bowed.

'Right then, get yourself something to eat and shape up. We need to get on with the business of running Woodside. Kate, please call Zena and let her know that there will be no further problems or issues with Mitch,' said Dave, his anger punctuating the air.

Dave grabbed his hat off the kitchen table. 'Bloody lucky the police are not on their way to see you . . . silly idiot son. And you will write a letter of apology to Lisa,' shouted Dave as he headed out the door.

Mitch was left alone after his mother walked to the office to call Zena. A sense of shame and humiliation crept over him, plucking away at his being, but he knew he had dug the pit of humiliation with his own hands. He would never have Lisa now. *Fuck, I have really blown it.*

◊

Two days after the incident at the river, Lisa was working with Zena and Alan down at the shearing shed and around the men's quarters. A ute they had never seen before approached them. When the driver got out, he introduced himself.

'Hi, I'm Mike Catlin. I work over at Woodside. Kate asked me to give this letter to you.' He handed the envelope to Zena. It was marked 'Lisa'.

'Thanks, Mike. Please tell Kate it's much appreciated.' She watched him drive away.

'It's marked "Lisa", for you, young lady,' said Zena, passing the envelope.

'What can it be?' asked Lisa.

'Only one way to find out, kid. Open it,' said Alan.

Lisa plucked the letter from the envelope and read the neat-ly written words. 'It's from Mitch, expressing his profuse apologies and that he would not divulge any of my personal information to anyone.'

'From the call I received from Kate, and now this letter, you can bet the boy was hauled over the coals. You will see no more of that behaviour, and you will see nothing of Mitch here at Woori, unless specifically invited,' remarked Zena. 'Of which I highly doubt,' her voice filled with disgust.

'The letter covers everything,' continued Lisa. 'His advances, the information he managed to get, and that he will not divulge the nature of it. Here . . . read it, Aunty.'

Zena's eyes scanned the brief letter.

'Well, the boy has done his dash. He won't come around here again, too bloody embarrassed,' announced Alan.

'I am so relieved, Alan.' Zena handed the letter back to Lisa. 'I don't even want to look at him if we should cross his path in public.'

'Do you think I should give back Topi? Mitch bought him after all,' Lisa said.

'No way, Lisa. You have bonded well with the horse. A gift is a gift unless he decides you cannot have the horse, which I highly doubt. He'll be keeping very low, Lisa, and would not want Topi back. He is a lovely horse but really, just a coloured hack,' added Zena.

'Yes, Lisa, I agree,' said Alan. 'Mitch has no use for Topi and I wouldn't give it a second thought. Just bloody glad the season will start in a week. It will take our minds off all this business.'

Lisa pondered what they had just said. Keeping Topi did not feel right, yet she was loathe to give him up.

'We are done here. Everything is set to go . . . the sheds look great. Just need the manpower now,' stated Alan.

TWENTY-EIGHT

A MYSTERY

Jack called at first light. He knew Alan would be up. 'Everything set to go, mate?'

'Yep, sheds and the quarters are looking terrific, Jack, and Zena has helped a lot with cooking preparation in case Cookie is under the pump initially. All organised.'

'That's bloody good, mate. See you in a few days then,' said Jack, his big voice booming into the phone.

Alan was taking a cup of tea into Zena when Lisa appeared. 'Who was that, Alan?'

'Jack. He is on his way. Sorry, the phone probably woke you up,' said Alan.

'I was awake anyway; my mind is churning. So glad Jack is on his way.' Lisa beamed.

'Getting excited too, kid. I want to check those mares and Noir to see if they are in foal. I hope so as now is the best time to get them in foal.'

'Why is that, Alan?'

'The mares will carry their babies for eleven months, so August this year they are pregnant until July next year. Just getting out of winter, with spring on the way, so not too hot for the foals.'

'How do we check they are in foal?' asked Lisa.

'I knew you would ask a question like that, but not so early in the morning,' Alan groaned. 'Well, since you have asked, I put my hand in the mare's rectum and check her uterus for indications that she's pregnant. The sign is usually the size of her uterus and the nature of the swellings on her ovaries. So I sort of gently palpate the area.'

Lisa pulled a face. 'Glad it's your hand and not mine. Yuck.'

'Well, you might have to do it one day, so you better watch and make notes.'

After breakfast, they headed to the home yards where Noir and the new mares were kept.

Alan walked quietly around the mares, talking and stroking them as he did so. He put a halter on Noir and then tied her head to the railing. 'I keep them here, Lisa, to watch the first semester of gestation but also to condition the new mares. Have to look after our girls.'

'Ready? You're up next, Lisa, so watch carefully,' said Alan, placing the long glove on his right arm. 'We are looking for a very small bulge at the base of the uterine horn. Maybe about an inch. You must be very careful so as not to perforate the rectum.'

'Eeeww,' Lisa said as she watched his arm slide in nearly up to his shoulder.
'Yep, I would say fairly confidently, this gorgeous lady is in foal. Zena will be pleased. She so wanted Noir to be in foal. Want to give it a go? No pressure,' said Alan.

Lisa grabbed a glove and started pulling it up her arm as Alan tethered the next mare. 'Okay, now remember what I said, just slide it in very slowly . . . . very carefully. See what you can feel.'

'It's very warm.'

'Of course it is, you're inside her.'

'Um . . . I am just not sure, Alan.' She gently withdrew her hand.

'That's okay, Lisa, you did good. I'll finish the rest,' agreed Alan.

Lisa watched fascinated as Alan did the same procedure on the other mares. 'Yep, Khartoum has done his job. All our girls are pregnant. Let's go tell Zena. She will be thrilled.'

They could hear the piano playing when they pulled up outside the gates. 'That's a lovely sound, my woman on the piano.'

Lisa smiled. The sounds of the piano did float over Woori gracefully.

'Putting the jug on,' Alan sang out as they came into the kitchen.

'Splendid, Alan. I was just about to do the same thing. So, how are the girls?'

'All pregnant, all in foal, Zena, including Noir.'

'Oh, that's wonderful,' exclaimed Zena as she joined them. 'Our first bit of good news, and just before the season. It's an omen I'm sure, Alan. Going to be a good one for us this year.'

Lisa piped up. 'I have to exercise Topi today, Aunty, and I wanted to ride out and see the ladies. Is that okay?'

Zena pondered this for a moment. 'Sure, I doubt that you will pass Mitch on the road, and there have been no problems. All quiet so I guess all good, but please avoid the river. Just go to the camp and back.'

'Deal,' promised Lisa.

'You can take these, the last of the carrots and sweet potatoes I dug out.'

'Great, Aunty. I'll finish what I need to do and go early afternoon.'

Alan was in the Tack Room when Lisa appeared. Dougy was barking and wagging his tail as usual. There indeed had been no further things removed or strange occurrences since the dogs were closer around the compound and inside the gates as well.

'This bloke doesn't want to leave here,' Alan said, patting Dougy's head.

'He is such a sweet dog, Alan. Darling Dougy with his big wagging tail.'

'Yeah, good mutt, but so was Buster,' Alan said wistfully. 'Ready to go?'

'Yep, just get my bridle and saddle.'

'I'll get Topi for you and bring him around.'

Lisa reached for her saddle and plonked it on the rail as Alan walked towards her with Topi. 'Getting well-muscled from all the feed, riding and lunging, Lisa. He looks good.'

'I know, wait till Billy sees him,' she said excitedly.

'I'll open the gate for you. See you when you get back,' said Alan as Topi danced on the one spot waiting for the gate to open.

'Better move, Alan,' Lisa shouted as she zoomed past, the horse picking up speed rapidly. He was as excited to hit the road as her. Lisa breathless with delight. They rode hard underneath the blue sky, which seemed to be held together by a stitch-work pattern of fluffy white clouds.

Lisa knew now why her aunt loved horses and riding. It was a combination of fear, trust and adrenaline as well as the human and animal connection. *I must get her to ride Noir with me before the season gets underway.*

Lisa slowed Topi as they rounded a bend, and the humpy came into view. No-one was visible. *Oh, I hope I haven't missed them for some reason or they are out and about.* As Lisa tethered Topi and walked towards their fire, she heard someone stir. It was Ningali.

'Aaah da little one. Ha, you catch me and Binna . . . we bin sleeping. Tired catching da fish. Up early today.'

Binna sat up and rubbed her eyes. 'We wait for you, mebbe problems at dat river with da white boy.'

'Yes, I had a few things happen, Binna. The white boy got a bit forward, but I handled it,' confided Lisa.

'Dat big white rooster, he got da spurs, he gunna be dangerous,' warned Ningali as she wagged her bony finger at Lisa.

'Oh Ningali, you are funny – big white rooster,' Lisa laughed. She looked at the fish that lay across the hot coals on a piece of wire. 'Smells good! You did well, Ningali,' said Lisa. She froze momentarily and then she suddenly stepped back.

'Eh, you go da pale colour and jumpin around,' said Ningali.

'Oh, I looked across there and saw that brown thing, that thing lying over there and thought it was a brown snake.'

'Dem snakes don't come so close to da camp with da fire,' cackled Ningali. 'But I don't like 'em. Dey got da evil eyes. See 'em down by da river sometime, get plenty scared so I move.'

'Alan told me that the eastern brown snakes are the second most deadly snake in the world and that their bite will kill you in under half an hour. I hate them.' Lisa shivered.

'Yeah, proper true. Big boss, he dun tell da truth, da browns dey very bad,' added Binna.

'What is it then, lying over there?' asked Lisa, looking closer.

'Dat bridle, me out by da river, and I go downstream to a different spot. Way down stream, get me plenty good deep hole. But it stink down there. Strong smell. Plenty strong stinky with so many flies. So I go look. Da horse, him lay dead, and da maggots dey already do da work. But I take da bridle, lookem good.'

Ningali picked her way around the fire and lifted up the bridle, handing it to Lisa.

'Oh my goodness, that's my bridle!' Lisa exclaimed.

Ningali looked at Binna. 'This is mine, my bridle! On what horse, Ningali?'

'Oh, he be da browny colour, like da earth. He bin dead mebbe a few days. Da stink travel on da wind.'

Lisa suddenly felt spooked. How did her bridle get on a horse that now lay dead down by the river?

'I will have to get back and tell Alan and my aunt. This is not good news, ladies. My bridle went missing and now it turns up on a dead horse. I'm sorry, I wanted to stay longer, but I will have to take the bridle back to them.'

Lisa squatted down and took Binna's hand. 'Stay safe, both of you. I will see you again soon.'

They two women watched as Lisa hurried back to Topi and mounted him swiftly.

'Da badness come . . . bad spirit. It all around,' said Binna. 'Sorry days, dey lie ahead.'

TWENTY-NINE

THE SEASON ARRIVES

Yesterday, Lisa had been numb with shock when she saw the bridle, but today, her mind was painfully active.

'What do you think, Alan?' asked Zena.

'I really don't know, but it's clear that someone took the bridle from our Tack Room to use it on their horse, a horse that is now dead down by the river. Obviously, they have no use for it and are on foot or they would have taken the bridle.'

'That means that they or him or her are still about, Alan,' Lisa exclaimed, the wheels of her mind churning.

'We don't know that, but with the extra people about for the season, and the dogs close by, we may see something. Just keep doing what we're doing. Lock the doors of a night, keep an eye out and don't forget to also lock the Tack Room. When everyone is here, we may take the dogs down to the river again.'

'Good idea,' agreed Zena.

'Anyway, Jack is here tomorrow and then the place will start to fill. Be good to have people around again,' said Alan.

◊

It was late afternoon when the old Holden ute came through the last gate. 'Nothing has changed,' Jack said to himself. The big man loved working at Woori and always looked forward to the season with Alan and Zena. He kept driving to the big house and saw the dogs around the compound fence. *Well, never seen that before, so something has changed.*

Jack pulled up at the compound gates and looked around. He was puzzled by the movement of the dogs so close to the house.

Lisa was with Alan catching yabbies when they heard the car pull up. 'Company, kid, let's go. The big bloke is here.'

Lisa grabbed the bucket, which was nearly full, making her way to the house, her legs carrying her as fast as they could.

'Jack,' she squealed, and ran towards him, dropping her bucket as she flung her arms around him, so glad to see him. He saw Alan not far behind and waved.

'Hey there, you are squeezing me to death, young lady,' protested Jack, a great big guffaw of a laugh rocking the surrounds. He grabbed Lisa by the shoulders and extended his arms.

'Whoa, let me look at you . . . what a little beauty, not that you weren't last year. But you have grown and geez, I have to say, you so resemble your aunt.'

Lisa blushed. 'It's so good to see you, Jack. I have been waiting and waiting and waiting!'

'Good to hear,' said Jack, beaming.

Alan caught up to them. 'Yes, we have been waiting. How are you, Jack?' They shook hands vigorously, their sheer joy of seeing each other again showed on their faces. 'Zena is up at the house.'

As they made their way to the back stairs, Zena stood waiting on the landing at the back door. 'Hello, Jack,' said Zena 'So good to see you.' She kissed Jack on the cheek as he came inside, and he gave her an enormous hug.

'Missed you lot, great to be back at Woori. How are things?' queried Jack.

'Real good, Jack, except for a few odd occurrences,' said Alan.

'Like what, mate?' asked Jack as he thirstily enjoyed a beer.

'Lisa's bridle went missing, and it was found by one of the Aboriginal girls on a dead horse when she was out fishing by the river. One of the dogs here was stabbed and crawled under the house to die.'

'Stabbed! Fuck! Sorry, Zena! But that's not good shit, mate.'

'Nope, as I said, Buster crawled under the house to die. Old Dougy out there wouldn't leave him alone, scratching and digging, which is why we found him. But the smell would have alerted us anyway. So, keep your eyes peeled, and let the crew know when they get here that if they sight someone that is not part of the crew, to let you know. Whoever it is, they are still here. We thought it may have been just someone wandering about or passing through, looking for something to nick, but I now think otherwise. Maybe Buster the dog got in the way of what he was trying to do. Dunno. Wish dogs could talk. Anyway, I'm clueless to this stranger's reasoning or why they are creating such violence and fear. Stuff like that doesn't happen out here,' said Alan.

'Yes, it's odd, Jack . . . very odd,' added Zena. 'Keeping things locked now. Never had to do it before.' There was a touch of sadness in her voice.

'If you have time one afternoon, I thought we might head out to the river with the crew and take the dogs if it's okay with you. We did that before with Michael Raby, the local copper, and after that, things quietened down,' revealed Alan.

'Yeah sure, mate. It's all a bit bloody queer if you ask me. Is that why you've shifted the hounds?' asked Jack.

'Yeah, hoping the barking will scare anyone off. They bark most of the time, but you know if someone is about that they don't know as it's a different kind of bark. But I'm sure whoever it is, they are coming and going down by the river. Food and water.'

'Well, I'll keep an eye out. Might be a bit of fun if we catch him while we're here,' said Jack.

Zena frowned and shook her head. 'Men! Come up for dinner when you've settled in down there, Jack.'

'You bewdy, will do . . . what time?'

'About 6–6.30ish.'

'Good, gives me time to have a look about and scrub up. See you in a little while,' grinned Jack as he headed down the stairs.

'Oh, I am so glad he's here . . . they will all be here. I am so excited,' said Lisa.

'Yep, can see that, kid. Calm down, you need to have your thinking cap on to help with the season. Bring those yabbies inside so Zena can see what we caught.'

'Sorry, Alan. I left the bucket outside. I'll go get it.'

Lisa came back up with the bucket and handed it to Zena. 'That will do nicely, Lisa . . . Well done. Our entrée.'

◊

Over dinner, Jack was his humorous self, swore like a bullock driver and told many funny stories. Lisa hung onto every word.

'The crew should all start to arrive over the next few days. Organised chaos. They all know this year's starting date is the fourth of September.'

'Very good. So you say this new bloke, Kevin, is a good shot? I'll be interested to see just how good a shot. Be hard to beat Jimmy.'

'Yeah, shame about that boy, amazing eyesight. Suppose right off the rails now,' said Jack. 'Was it the grog?'

'Don't really know, but he won't get work again on any station again, which will really cut into him. For all his temper and eruptions, he was bloody good at what he did, and of course an expert marksman. So, how did you hear about Kevin?' pressed Alan.

'I was working up in the Isaac region, not far from Clermont. In the pub having a few yarns when the locals told me about this blackfella, Kev, who could shoot a shilling off a cow's rump with not a scratch to be seen. Said he was hanging about town looking for work. A bit far-fetched if you ask me, no-one can shoot like that. So I said, "How do I find this bloke?" They told me to wait around until it got dark as he always seemed to show up outside the pub, asking for work. So, I was leaning against this post, and all I saw was a set of big white choppers smiling at me in the dark. So, I said, "Who goes there?" and this bloke says, "It's me, Kev, boss." Still all I could see were his teeth. So we got to chatting, and he said he left the last joint because the manager there didn't treat him too well.'

'It's not uncommon, Jack. I worry about all these young lads getting mistreated and underpaid,' said Zena. 'I don't understand people's reasoning or the discrimination. If a black man or a white man does the same work, then it should be equal pay. It has been such a struggle for the indigenous people. At least in the end, they were granted equal pay . . . . that was in 1968, I think. There was something on the ABC radio advising of a new board or something like that being set up. I am sure it was the Department of Aboriginal Affairs. Long overdue, but at least something is being done, and they are making some ground.'

'Yeah, I worry too, Zena. Can't believe bloody Queensland though. The only state that did not abandon laws that discriminate against Aboriginal people. But they will have to give in. All the other states have. Stupid.'

'That's a concern. Billy and Burnu were apparently working up there,' said Zena.

'I'm sure they'll be fine, Zena,' reassured Jack. 'Both smart men, and they know their wages and worth from working here. But getting back to Kev. He's a funny bugger, got a way of putting things. I asked him to show me his shooting prowess. So he picks me up at the pub, and we go out bush in his ute. Oh yeah, wait till you see his you-beaut ute, and anyway, I pin a tin wheel with a black spot in the middle and tell him to shoot at the spot. Pulls out this Remington rifle, a 223, and away he goes. Bloody amazing. Every shot was dead on in the centre of that round black spot. No other marks, every shot was in the exact same spot! Every shot!

I asked why he was looking for work because clearly he wanted to work, hanging around every night at the pub. Kev simply said, "I likem keep busy." He's not a young bloke . . . it's hard to pick their age, and some of them don't even know how old they are. But his shooting skills would be an asset to any property. Said about his last boss, and I am quoting Kev now, "He bin treat me like a dog alla time".'

Lisa started to giggle. 'Is that how he talks?'

'Yep, you gotta catch on quick. Real pidgin. You will like him, Lisa. I sure as hell do. Top bloke. Well, I best be moving. Great dinner, Zena, as usual. Can't beat a good home-cooked meal. Steak and veg will get me firing tomorrow.' Jack smiled. 'I will say goodnight. I bet when I get down there, someone will have moved in or will be setting up. Anyhow, will see you in the morning, Alan, to go over a few things.'

'Sounds good, I'll catch you then, Jack. Thanks, mate, great to have you here.'

As Lisa lay in bed that night, she looked at the little necklace on the bedside table Billy had given to her. *The season is really here. Billy is coming. Nothing else matters.*

THIRTY

NEW JACKAROO

Over the next four days, the slow trickle of workers kept building until Woori was a full house. The stockmen had their own camps, and gunyahs had their lubras, piccaninnies and dogs. The same shearing crew, ringers and roustabouts had descended upon the men's quarters, and Jack was pleased to see familiar faces.

Cookie arrived in his old station wagon as cheerful as ever, despite Old Harry not sitting in the front seat, and he promptly hung up his dinner bell. Old Ben with his bandy legs helped unload the wagon, and he could not stop yakking to Cookie. Ned, one of the shearers, arrived just after Cookie and quickly advised of his new tunes on the harmonica.

Alan stood with Jack early one morning watching the group grow. 'Didn't take them long, did it? A moving bloody caravan,' grinned Jack.

'Nope, everyone seems keen to work, which is good,' replied Alan. 'Any news on Kev the shooter.'

'Nothing as yet, Alan, but I would say he's on his way. He is somewhere out there, for sure, and I might be wrong, but he did not look like the type of bloke who would let you down.

Good strong handshake and keen to work, so he will be here. I'd put money on it.'

'And my last question regarding crew,' said Alan.

'I know exactly what you are going to ask, Alan. Known you for too long.'

Alan looked amused. 'Go on, tell me, you big bastard, if you know me so well.'

'Nope, nothing on Billy or Burnu, but they did rock up last year just two days before. You know these blackfellas don't seem to have a word really for goodbye or don't understand keeping in touch. They just turn up. If they are making their way down from the north, they won't be in a rush. And you have started the season slightly earlier this year.'

'Hey, Alan, old mate,' Cookie called out, wandering over.

'Good to see you, Cookie. Zena and I are pleased you came back, not the same without Harry but you know, you are part of the furniture. Got those opals made up that Harry gave me into a pair of earrings. Sure Lisa will show you while you are here. My lovely wife has cooked up a few things for you too, just to help things get off quickly and to a good start.'

'Bloody gem, that one, and how is the young niece?' queried Cookie.

'Growing. Quite accomplished now as a rider. Got a new horse too, fancy coloured thing. Can turn on a twenty-cent coin and goes like the clappers. She should be down shortly when she's finished her chores. Breaking her neck to get down here.'

'Are the two young Aboriginal boys coming?' queried Cookie.

'No mate, well maybe one . . . Billy. Jack seems to think he will show up with Burnu, but Jimmy is a definite no.'

'What's happened? He was a bloody good stockman.'

'Yeah, he was, we all saw that. But Jimmy was volatile and always ready to erupt, and there was that rivalry and jealousy last season between the two boys, so maybe it's a good idea he isn't coming. We heard he was working at the same place as Billy up north, and they got into a real bad scrap, which ended up with Billy giving him a good belting.'

'That don't sound like Billy,' said Cookie.

'No, it's not,' agreed Alan. 'But the idiot Jimmy pulled a knife in the scuffle, which is why Billy belted him. Connected to his eye though, and rumour has it, Jimmy may have lost an eye.'

'Shit, boss, that's no good. Stupid black bastards. Always knew Billy was a strong bugger but he was always kind of, easy-going sort of, you know what I mean, nothing seemed to bother him, just like his old man, Burnu,' said Cookie.

'Yeah, real stupid, Cookie, but no-one is going to stay calm or mellow if there is a knife at their throat. Anyway, look at us white blokes, we get up to the same. Good and bad amongst us all,' added Alan.

It was the noise of an engine that made them look towards the last gate leading into Woori.

'What's that friggin' thing! Got a bloody big motor under that hood by the sound of it,' said Cookie. 'Not seen that rig before, canary yellow with a few hand-painted orange flames.' Both men started to laugh.

'What the hell is that, Jack?' asked Alan.

Jack had heard the car and knew who it was as the bright yellow ute headed across the paddock towards them. He had seen Kev's tall frame behind the wheel as the ute got closer, and Kev flashed his broadest grin.

'Gentlemen, meet Kev, our new stockman,' introduced Jack as the ute came towards them.

'Crikey, where did you find that or him or whatever!' said Cookie. 'Bet he will be a bloody useless bugger.'

'At a pub mate . . . and you will have to eat your words, Cookie, of that I am sure,' guffawed Jack.

'Yeah, looks like the type of bloke you would find in a pub,' replied Cookie.

All eyes were on the yellow ute as it leisurely pulled up at the sheds. Even the lubras from the black's camp had all come out to gawk at Kev and the noisy ute. They were almost childlike, giggling and shrieking, the excitement infectious as they pointed to the tall, lanky stranger.

'Kev, over here,' Jack said as he beckoned him over. Kev got out of his ute and took off his battered hat. He was dark and his brown eyes danced as if amused by everything and everyone, and as Jack said, he had a good set of choppers that lit up his face.

'Alan, this is Kevin, our new stockman. He's a great shot and happy to assist in any way. Good, hard worker he tells me.' Kevin extended his hand, which Alan shook firmly.

'Pleased to meet you, Kevin. Make yourself at home. Jack will show you around the place,' said Alan.

'Yeah, boss, call me Kev, alla fellas tell me dat my name. Do plenty hard work, proper true,' he grinned as he looked at Alan.

'I'll put a cracker up your bum, mate, and light it if you don't,' said Cookie. Kev's eyes flew open at the older, wiry fellow.

'Just joking, mate,' laughed Cookie as he extended his hand. 'I'm the cook, that's why they call me Cookie.'

Kev looked pleased. 'Cook boss, be runnin' da campfire, do plenty big cook up?'

They all laughed. 'Yeah . . . do plenty big cook up,' replied Cookie.

'Me shoot em grub for ya, kangaroo, goanna . . . what dem fellas like?'

Cookie looked shocked. 'What! Eat kangaroo . . . not bloody likely.'

'It's alright, Kev, plenty of tucker here, no need to go out and shoot anything,' said Jack as he patted Kev on the back. 'Come on, I'll show you where you can sleep if you don't want to join your mates in their camps over that way. Up to you where you set up.'

'He seems a good one, Alan,' added Cookie.

'Yeah, a replacement for Jimmy. Not as young, maybe late forties, but he has all that experience. He's apparently a great shot according to Jack, so if he matches Jimmy's skills in that regard, and you never know when it's needed out here, as well as keeping the stock moving for the shearers, I'm a happy man.'

'That Jimmy, something about his eyesight that was superior to us. I never seen anything like it. If he has lost an eye, it would be a tragedy in terms of his shooting skill or for that matter, anything. Thank goodness the bloke upstairs gives us two of everything. But that Jimmy, he could see what we couldn't see. I remember a blackfella told me years ago that an emu's eyes enhance the spiritual vision, and that men often tied some sort of stone to their beard to enhance their sight or the spirits . . . something like that. Jimmy must have hung stones in his beard to see the way he did,' added Cookie.

'Yeah, he was unbelievable. Anyway, Zena will be down with Lisa, and she will let you know what she's organised in terms of food. Other than that, it's business as usual, Cookie. I'll kill a beast and bring it down for you to roast for the season party tomorrow. The girls have salads and spuds wrapped in foil, so we are set to go. I'm just joining Jack. If you need me, you know where to find me.'

'Sure thing, Alan, time to get busy, great to be back,' said Cookie as he headed to his small kitchen.

Ned had staked a claim on his sleeping arrangements already and sat on a timber plank playing the harmonica. It was Kev who sat down next to him.

'Pleased to meet ya,' said Ned.

'Me likem da music too. Got da geetar in da ute. Me bring em, play da songs, mebbe get em nice lubra, likem da voice,' said Kev, flashing a big grin.

'You be careful, mate, which lubra you attract, don't want no trouble here, most of those lubras are taken, but there's an old girl here called Buckaroo Mary, maybe the only single one. Always here every year with the crew, for as long as I can remember. Pretty feisty. Comes along with her daughter, sort of just hangs about. But you really don't want to mess with her though.' He pointed. 'That's her over there. As I said, she is probably the only lubra not taken, mate, but bloody hell, it would be like jabbing a spider with a stick,' said Ned laughing.

'Me want no trouble, me work hard for da boss. Me go get da geetar.'

Ned smiled. Kev was already wanting no trouble and wanting to work hard. He would fit right in.

'Nice guitar, mate, now let's hear you play,' said Ned as he wet his lips and began a few tunes on the harmonica. To his surprise, Kev's voice wasn't half bad, and the tunes from his guitar were melodic. He certainly had an audience now with the lubras appearing once again as well as the piccaninnies. Even the dogs had stopped barking.

They looked in the distance at the coloured horse galloping towards them, and an old ute followed slowly behind. Ned and Kev stopped playing.

'That's the boss lady in the ute, she's a real beauty, treats us all pretty good,' said Ned.

'Who da young one, on dat horse, dat real beauty . . . lookem too good to be true.'

'Ha Kev, you bet, it's the boss lady's niece. All the blokes love her, she is very kind and as sweet as they come,' said Ned.

They went back to playing their songs and watched as Zena and Lisa arrived. They carried bowls of food from the back of the ute into the men's eating area. 'She does that all season, helps Cookie, and her tucker makes us all fat,' laughed Ned.

'No seen dat before, food at da other stations taste like shit, mebbe is shit. Kev get skinny on dat shit tucker.'

Ned laughed. 'Not here, mate.'

Zena walked with Lisa over to the two men. 'Who have we here, Ned?'

'Me Kev.' He took off his hat, his face beaming.

'Well, lovely to meet you, Kev, and welcome to Woori. This is my niece, Lisa.'

'Hello, Kev.' She stood looking at his huge teeth. So perfect and white. Usually the blacks had various teeth missing.

'Nice tunes you two were playing,' said Lisa.

'Yes, it won't go astray for our pre-season kick off,' added Zena. 'We will see you tomorrow afternoon for our official opening. Hopefully, everyone will be here by then.'

'What dat pre . . . Dat mean kicking da balls, like some kick off?' asked Kev.

'Ned laughed. 'Geez mate, not likely, unless you want to have a game of soccer. It means we have a big cook up, plenty tucker, play some music and get shit faced. Eat and drink as much as you want. They always do it here at Woori. Then the next day, it's down to business, no mucking around.'

'I just get da tin plate at dem other stations. Dog food on da plate. Treat us blackfellas like dogs alla time.'

'Not here. You won't want to leave, and I guarantee you will be back next season.'

Lisa scanned the area for any sign of Billy. Nothing. Her heart felt heavy. She turned quickly when her name was called. 'Oh look, Aunty, it's Cookie.' She ran towards him.

'Hello, my girl.' They hugged each other. Zena followed her niece. 'Missus,' Cookie greeted her as he took off his hat.

'You two look as lovely as ever,' said Cookie.

'I am so pleased you came back, Cookie, we all are. Couldn't do this without you.'

'Thanks missus, got a few new recipes, keen to try on this lot,' revealed Cookie.

'I'm sure they will appreciate it, Cookie. I've prepared a few things as well. I'll bring them down as the week passes. No room in the fridges here if I bring it all down at once. Just some beef casseroles, lasagnes and pasta dishes. Those things stick to the men's sides,' laughed Zena.

'Come on, Lisa, I know who you're looking for. There has been no sign of him yet. Let's join Alan and then head back to the house. Big day tomorrow, – your chores, then in the kitchen helping me. Have to keep busy, keeps your mind off things,' said Zena.

'Bye, Cookie, see you soon,' said Lisa. She hadn't given up hope about Billy yet.

THIRTY-ONE

START-OF-SEASON PARTY

It was late afternoon, and the beginning of a beautiful sunset was about to commence. Lisa and Zena were busy preparing food. Alan was ahead of them and had already left to help Cookie with the slain beast.

'I thought of something the other day, Aunty, and it slipped my mind. Finding my bridle so suddenly distracted me.'

'Oh . . . what's that?' asked Zena.

'Why don't we invite Ningali and Binna to some of our get-togethers? Maybe they would like the company of their people.'

'I have never thought of that, Lisa . . . yes, you may be right. I always get the feeling they are happy in their own company but I guess no harm in trying. It's too late now for our pre-season party, but maybe during the season, we can ask them.' Lisa nodded.

'Okay, that's about it. Let's load it all onto the back of the ute. Just grab those fly protectors, Lisa. They are just over there folded up on the sideboard. We need to make a move now. Follow me with some food, whatever you can manage, and tuck the fly covers under your arm for when we get down there.'

With the ute packed, they headed unhurriedly towards the shearing shed. They could see the gathering of men and hear the music as well as the dogs barking. Woori had come alive again. Lisa's heart was beating faster. *Please let Billy be there, please.*

As they pulled up, Alan and Cookie came to assist. 'Just take all the bowls, Cookie, and throw them on the table under the lean-to. The fly covers can stay down here, we will always be using them,' instructed Zena.

'Looks delicious,' praised Cookie. He suddenly stopped. 'Oh, what have we here.' The dazzling of the opals in Lisa's ears caught his eye. 'Harry's bloody opals!'

Lisa put her hand to her ear and smiled at Cookie. 'Yes, I thought I would wear them here tonight for Harry.'

'He would be proud, Lisa. They look beautiful. I remember the day we found them. Bloody beautiful.'

'That was a very nice gesture Lisa,' said Alan, coming up behind them. He helped carry the last bowl of food.

'Well, I'll make a quick toast and then let's get on with it.' Alan put an arm around Zena.

Lisa looked quickly around. Nothing. She felt for the necklace that Billy had given her. *Please come, Billy, even if you are a day or two late.*

With the speech over and the welcoming of the new addition, Kev and Ned began to play. It lifted the mood as the piccaninnies and lubras laughed excitedly. They were well underway, and the beer was flowing, the moon rising above them. The sound of a horse whinnying close by made them look in the direction of the last gate. Two figures on horses were at the last gate.

Lisa slowly got to her feet, her body trembling. It was Jed. She could tell the big, beautiful horse anywhere, who danced and fidgeted at the gates. A tall figure in a black hat dismounted and opened the gate. Tears welled in her eyes as she looked across at her aunt.

Zena stood with Alan and Jack, a champagne in her hand. 'Bugger me,' said Jack. 'It's old Burnu with Billy.' The two men rode in a steady trot towards the gathering.

'Bloody great sight, seeing them,' remarked Alan.

The riders approached, and they could all see that the boy, like Lisa, had grown. Zena looked at the powerful-looking young man riding towards them, his well-built, commanding physique apparent under his shirt.

'Hard work has been good for him, Alan. Think we are going to have a problem,' whispered Zena.

'What sort of problem?' Alan whispered back.

'Well, it doesn't help that the boy comes back, almost a man, and I have to say, so physically attractive.'

Alan started laughing. 'I'll have to admit, he does look good sitting up on that horse.'

'Have a look at our girl over there,' nudged Zena. 'She hasn't blinked. I best go join her, Alan, before she faints.' The two men rode to the black's camp first, where they tethered their horses. The lubras all started chattering in their own tongue.

As Billy walked towards Alan and Jack, it was clear his body was as hard as the grim plains in Queensland he had worked on. He radiated a confidence. The boy was now a man.

Burnu next to him had clearly aged, but the old man still had an aura of spiritual force.

'Good to see you both. We thought you may have missed the boat,' grinned Alan, shaking their hands.

'Bin travelling slower, mebbe horse goin' lame. Good to rest her now,' said Burnu.

'Long ride, Burnu, from up north. Take one of our horses and give your mare a good rest during the season. No problem to do that for you,' said Alan.

'Boss man Jack, good to be back,' said Billy as he shook his hand.

'Too right, mate. I was worried you both would not get here. I had heard you were working way up north. Heard of the trouble too with Jimmy. That bloke is not here and won't be coming back to Woori. Alan and I stand firm on that one,' Jack said.

'Yeah, plenty trouble, boss. Jimmy don't like take orders from me, and one day he just lit up, pulled the knife, so I hit him, mebbe too hard, boss, but he sort of dived into da punch,' admitted Billy.

'Well, you are both here now, tired no doubt, so make yourselves at home. Do what you need to do, grab a beer and some tucker,' said Alan.

'Plenty hungry,' chuckled Burnu as he walked over to say hello to the other crew.

'Good looking boy, Alan,' commented Jack as they watched Billy head towards Lisa.

'Yeah, it's a worry, Jack . . . a real worry. She talks about him all the time. Now he comes back as an even a better version of himself.'

Jack barked out a laugh. 'Can't play with nature, Alan. Come on, let's get a beer. The last one hardly touched the sides.'

◊

'Oh, Aunty, he's coming over.' Lisa squeezed Zena's hand tightly.

'Yes, I can see that, darling girl. Calm down.' *This season is going to be a worry.*

'Boss lady,' said Billy, bowing and holding his hat to his chest.

'Hello, Billy, it's lovely to see you and Burnu. We thought you may have not made it. Well, I will leave you to it,' said Zena. 'You okay, darling?'

Lisa nodded, mesmerised by the boy who stood in front of her.

'Grasshopper,' Billy said softly, his hand lightly touching her shoulder.

'Oh, Billy, I have missed you so much, and I was so frightened you would not be here. As soon as Lisa began to speak, her lips trembled and tears began to fall. 'I just didn't think I would ever see you again. It was a terrible feeling.'

'It's okay, Grasshopper. I said I would be back, come back for you.' Billy so wanted to take her in his arms and hold her but a thousand eyes were upon him. 'We go sit.' Billy pointed to a hay bale against the shed.

Lisa followed Billy and felt the rapid beating of her heart. She so wanted to be alone with him and tell him all the things she was feeling.

'Come sit, Grasshopper, and tell me your news,' motioned Billy.

'Gosh, where do I start! Well, I have my new horse Topi now, who I ride nearly every day. He is so fast and turns in such a short circle. We got him from the sales, and he was about to go to the abattoirs.'

His velvet brown eyes never stopped watching her, amused by her chattering and childlike manner. Billy rested his hand over hers as they sat together, the warmth from his touch tingling her skin.

'You hear 'bout Jimmy?' asked Billy.

'Yes, I was so frightened when I heard that news. I never liked Jimmy much, he always felt so dangerous. Ningali told me about it because she ran into some men down by the river. They were heading your way. Did you like working there?'

'Yeah, dat station okay and dey wanted me to stay,' said Billy.

'Oh yes, Aunty said as much . . . but you came back.'

'For you . . . my grasshopper,' smiled Billy.

By the time the evening was drawing to a close, it was like they had never left from last season. Burnu had been talking with Zena and the other crew and watched as his son sat with Lisa, their eyes never leaving each other.

'I have to say hello to your father, Billy,' said Lisa.

'Burnu is tired, getting old now. I had to stop many times on da road.'

'He looks well though, Billy.'

'Yep, but da pace, it wear Burnu down. He get slower and slower, and by da end of day, he tell me he is buggered.'

'I am just so glad you are both here.' She rested her head on Billy's shoulder.

Kev nudged Ned as he watched the beautiful young white girl with the dark boy.

'Who dat darky . . . he be with da boss lady's niece? Makim big trouble,' said Kev.

'No Kev, it's alright. They knew each other last season. They got a special bond, those two,' said Ned. 'And he ain't that dark, well not as bloody dark as you, mate. His mother was white,' said Ned.

'He da creamy. Da girl, lookem plenty happy. Dat boy make her shine,' observed Kev.

'Yes, mate, I got eyes too, you know. Get used to it. He is extraordinary as a stockman, great skills. Once you get to know him, you will like him. We all do. Commands a lot of respect. Maybe take over Jack's job when he retires.'

'Lookem forward to it, brudder. Mebbe teach me a few tricks. Time to pack up my geetar.'

'Yeah mate, that was a bit of fun playing with you. Looks like we are the last to leave, apart from those two. See you in the morning,' said Ned.

Zena walked over with Alan to where Lisa sat with Billy.

'Don't get up. Have either of you eaten? You have been doing a lot of talking over here,' Zena smiled. 'We are going to pack up here now. So, if you want to grab something, the time is now. I'll just throw the empty bowls into the back of the ute and cover them over to stop the flies. I can wash the dishes up in the morning, Lisa. No hurry. Any leftovers will be in the staff fridge, Billy. I'm sure someone will wake up hungry through the night. Great to have you here, and Burnu. Our girl has missed you.'

'Thank you, missus. Billy bin missin' her too.'

'Don't make it too late, Lisa, as Billy has been travelling all day. Eat something and we will see you shortly,' said Alan.

Billy smiled and stood up. 'Thank you, boss. I will get Lisa back to the homestead not too late. I use Jed.'

'Okay, we'll see you in the morning,' said Alan.

◊

Alan spoke first as they drove back to the house. 'Wise to leave them there alone, Zena?'

'Don't see why not, Alan. She has been busting her britches to see him, so you cannot halt his or her feelings. As I have said all along, there is this chemistry between them. I know they will not do anything foolish. I have chatted to Lisa about this, so let's not overthink the situation.'

'Nope. Boy likes girl. Girl likes boy. Simple,' said Alan.

'Not so sure about the simple, Alan,' said Zena, 'but our girl deserves some happiness with someone who will treat her right, whether black or white.'

◊

The ride on Jed back to the house, her arms wrapped tightly around his waist, the smell of Billy under the stars, was exhilarating. *The stars, they carry your sadness away.*

They stood in the pale moonlight at the compound gates. Billy slowly cradled her face in his hands and proceeded to kiss it lightly, first her forehead, then her cheeks and finally the corners of her beautiful mouth. How he had hungered for that mouth. His next kiss was soft and lingering, and this time Lisa responded to his kiss eagerly, almost crying from excitement.

'I'd best go, Billy. I so just want to curl up with you. Never leave you,' said Lisa softly.

'Go, Grasshopper, I see you in the morning,' said Billy as Lisa closed the gates, looking at the figure who galloped away into the darkness.

◊

Billy closed his eyes. She not only belonged to him but was part of him. He had been waiting his whole life for her. He knew their meeting had been written in the stars.

THIRTY-TWO

CRACKSHOT

Alan headed down to have a coffee with Jack. Zena had loaded him up with two slabs of fruit cake. He had always enjoyed Jack's company but knew one day he would lose his services. That would be a very sad day.

'How are things, mate?' Alan asked as he pulled up. 'The crew bonding? Ready to get going?'

'Bloody terrific, Alan. That new bloke Kev has taken a real shine to Billy, and they never stop talking. I gotta say though, poor old Burnu has slowed down.'

'Well, I'm sure he wouldn't be here if he didn't think he could cope.'

'True, so true,' conceded Jack. 'How are things over at Woodside, did they get the same crew as last year?'

'Not sure, I must ring Dave and see how they've started this season. Had a bit of a run in with his boy.'

'Who, Mitch?' asked Jack.

'Yeah. He made a couple of unwanted passes at Lisa. She kicked him in the balls,' said Alan.

Jack let out a roaring laugh that stopped the lubras chatting. 'Bloody hell, what a story. Feisty thing . . . good on her. He always struck me as never wanting for anything. Sometimes too easy can ruin a kid.'

'Yeah, so we won't be seeing him around here, unless he's invited, but I don't see that happening. Zena was really wanting blood,' said Alan.

'Anyway, from last season, the writing was on the wall, Alan, no room for three. Clear to me. Billy had charmed her or vice versa. We know he's a darky but if people like each other, then that's basically it,' stated Jack.

Alan laughed. Yeah, that's what my wife says.'

'Here comes Billy now with Kev. Have to get him to shoot for you. Maybe later today, just for a bit of fun,' said Jack. 'Can't take my eyes off the bloke when he does get his gun. Not a tremor or a shake. Nothing. Steady as a rock.'

'Sounds good, Jack. I would like to see him in action. What time and where?' asked Alan.

'Say about four. I'll let the other blokes know. Kev is quite proud of his shooting ability,' added Jack.

Billy cantered into the area with Kev not far behind. 'All good up there?' asked Jack.

'Yep, dem lambs up dere, big and proper fat. Good lamb chops, boss,' said Kev as he smacked his lips.

Billy let out the first laugh.

'He's bloody contagious, Billy, that's for sure,' said Jack. 'Hey Kev, I was telling Alan we all want to see you shoot. Are you up to it, mate, just a bit of a fun demo?'

'Only if you want, Kev. I'd love to see you shoot,' added Alan.

Kev nodded. 'Sure, boss. Got to keep up with da practice, no get rusty. What time?'

'About four, Kev. You may have an audience,' grinned Jack.

'Orright, proper true. Me da big star at Woori.' A broad smile spread across his face.

'I'll catch you later then,' said Alan. 'I'll call Dave and see how he's going, Jack. Will let you know if he needs a hand. But no news is good news, and I am sure Dave has it under control over there at Woodside.'

◊

It was mid-morning, and the ute was at the gates. Lisa was back from her chores. No doubt getting them done quickly so she could ride with Billy, who was yet to see Topi.

'Lovely ladies, may I join you?' asked Alan as he sat down.

'Yes of course, darling, what can I get you?' asked Zena.

'Tea and some of that fruit cake would do me well. Going to ring Dave and see how he's faring. He should have enough crew. Always well planned but good to have a chat with him about the season. What are you girls up to?'

'Lisa thought it might be nice to see if Ningali and Binna wanted to come out one afternoon and join us down at the shed. Sort of mix with our crew, and of course, the lubras, some of whom Ningali would know,' said Zena. 'They don't get to see anyone really, except us. I thought it was a good idea.'

'Stuck in their ways, I think, and highly unlikely they would want to move from that shack. I am even amazed you got them to eat vegetables, Zena. Not something in their diets. Now you want them to socialise with us here at the sheds?' laughed Alan, somewhat amused.

'It's just to get them out and see some of their own people, Alan. They have been out at that humpy for so long.'

'You can ask, no harm in that.' Alan looked at the two rolls of fabric across the kitchen table. 'Making something?'

'Maybe,' replied Zena. 'If the ladies do say yes, Lisa thought it would be nice if they had something to wear. I think they have about two outfits that Ningali dunks in the river to wash.

Lisa said they are wearing very thin, with more than a few holes.'

'Yes, Alan, their clothes do have so many holes,' added Lisa.

Alan groaned. 'I will leave it to you both. Going to ring Dave now.'

'We'll head out and see if they want to come over to Woori. I can drive out and then drive them back Alan . . . too easy,' said Zena. 'Or maybe they can sleep in one of our tents. Just need to set it up. There is a three-man tent somewhere in that Tack Room with the other camping gear. I think it's in the smaller room to the left when you go in. You know, that little area you use as a workshop.'

'No problems, will have a look see,' said Alan. 'We're getting Kev to show us his shooting skills around 4 p.m. Maybe the girls will have a laugh at that.'

'Perfect!' exclaimed Zena.

No sooner had Alan finished the sentence than Zena was grabbing things and heading for the door.

'Come on, Lisa, if we leave now, we can make it out there and then be back in time to whip up a couple of dresses.'

'Bloody hell, how do you think you can accomplish that? Maybe shooting won't interest them?' said Alan.

'Bye, Alan,' Lisa sang out. 'I hope they say yes . . . what a hoot!'

Zena threw the two rolls of fabric into the back of the Land Rover and headed towards the black ladies' camp. She hoped they would not be offended if she showed them the material.

It was good to be alone with her niece as they drove towards the humpy. 'How is Billy and things between you two? You were like glue together, Lisa.'

'I just love being with him, Aunty. There is this spirit about him, like Binna and Burnu. This absolute physical presence, and then, the other side, his softness. I haven't seen much of him since the first night as he has hit the ground running.'

'Yes, Jack would be keeping him busy but just remember, no need to rush things. Just take your time.'

'I know, Aunty, but it's hard. Billy makes me feel so many things. I have no fear when I am with him.'

Zena smiled. *I know that feeling all too well.*

'With a bit of luck we might be able to bring the ladies back with us. They can shower and get ready at home. It may be a little odd to them, running water and being inside a house. They probably don't remember the last time they had a warm shower but I don't think they really care. I know they are so different to us. Ningali brings that small bucket back as their wash water from the river, so perhaps this will be a real treat.'

Their humpy came into view. 'Fingers crossed, Lisa. I do hope they say yes.'

'Me too, Aunty. It'd be great having them at Woori.'

They pulled up at the humpy and jumped out of the Land Rover. 'Hello, ladies,' Zena waved and called out.

'It da boss lady and da little one. What dey doing here? Dey drive out and in da big hurry,' observed Ningali.

'I hope no got da troubles,' replied Binna.

Zena followed Lisa and they sat down on the log stumps, the fabric rolls resting neatly on Zena's thighs.

'What bring you ladies here?' asked Ningali. 'You bin in da big hurry.'

'Well, we are having a bit of a do late this afternoon, and we wondered if you would like to be our guests. We have a lot of other lubras and their piccaninnies down by the shearing sheds, lots of fires and music, and Kev our new jackaroo is giving a shooting demonstration. It should be fun. You can stay at Woori. Alan is setting up a tent if you decide to, that is, you don't have to stay in the house . . . and I thought you may like to have a warm shower for a change, Binna. I can bring you back here tonight if you prefer, or early in the morning. Up to you. But Lisa and I would love you to be there.'

'Oh, please say yes,' begged Lisa.

The two ladies looked at each other. 'Shall we go away while you chat?' asked Zena.

Ningali's eyes widened. 'Me likem to go, Binna. Likem da music and to mix with da people.'

'Da little one, she get excited, mebbe say yes,' said Binna.

'Oh please do, ladies. I am just as excited. We both owe you so much,' said Zena. 'But I have another suggestion. We can go now and maybe you can wander around Woori, have a look. It's been a while since you've been there. Have some good tucker for lunch. Rest up a bit. What do you say?'

'Oooh,' said Ningali, nearly squealing as she clapped her hands.

'I have brought these fabrics to show you, but I do not want to offend you in any way. I wanted to make a couple of dresses for you both. It's easy for me to do, if you will allow it. Lisa said your dresses were getting very thin and there are a few holes.'

'Ha! Me and Binna, lookem fancy,' giggled Ningali as she swirled on her stick legs. Binna cackled. It would be nice for them to see their own kind.

'Let's go then,' said Zena. They helped Binna down to the Land Rover and took off in a cloud of red dust.

◊

Alan headed to the Tack Room to find the tent. Knowing his persuasive wife, they would have two extra guests.

But he had to call Dave at Woodside, almost their yearly ritual for start of season. After finding the tent, he went inside to call.

Alan dialled and wondered who would answer. He hoped to goodness Mitch was out working. He breathed a sigh of relief when Kate answered.

'Morning, Kate, it's Alan. How are things?'

'Hi Alan, lovely to hear from you. Things are fine. Just chugging along with more than enough staff. We are lucky like you; the same crew seem to return.'

'Is Dave about?'

'No, he is, as you can imagine, out and about with Mitch and the crew.'

'How is the boy, has he settled down?' queried Alan.

'Yes, he has settled down and is about to be settling down further. He was quite remorseful you know, and realised he had blown any chance with Lisa. Silly boy.'

'Settling down further . . . did I miss something, Kate?'

'No, Alan, this is good and bad really.'

'I hate those sentences, Kate,' remarked Alan.

'Well, you would eventually find out via bush telegraph, so you may as well hear it from me. Mitch is getting married.'

'Whoa! Married! To who? When did this all happen?' Alan sounded shocked.

'Mitch proposed to Tess Dunphy. She's pregnant.' Alan knew by the sound of Kate's voice that she was not happy. She delivered the news in a matter-of-fact punctuated manner. Emotionless, as if resigned to a scenario she could not change or exit.

'Well, congratulations Kate. You are going to be a grand-mother.'

There was a long sigh at the end of the phone, and Kate made no further comment.

'Well, give my regards to Dave and wish Mitch the best. When is the wedding?'

'Six weeks' time. We will have the ceremony and wedding party out here. Just a quiet one, Alan. You would understand if I didn't send an invite to Zena and yourself.'

'Yes, of course Kate.' The sadness was coming in waves over the phone.

'Take care, Kate.' Alan hung up the phone.

Stupid boy – but who am I to say that? Tess may be good for him.

Alan heard the Land Rover pull up. This would be interesting. The excited chatter told him everything. He saw his wife come through the compound gates first with Binna, followed by Ningali and then Lisa. He laughed and shook his head. He came onto the landing and greeted the two women at the top of the stairs.

'Ha dat big boss, Binna, come to greet us,' cackled Ningali.

Binna smiled as she was guided by Zena up the stairs while Alan held the door. 'Now just this way, Binna, and to the right. I'll take you down to your bedroom and Ningali will take over.'

Lisa followed Zena as she opened the bedroom door. 'You can have a kip here, Binna. I am sure Ningali will help you to use the shower if you want to, and the toilet. I'll leave you to it. Lisa will bring in some sandwiches and some tea.'

'Dis fancy room, boss lady. Never seen dis before,' said Ningali. 'Binna's eyes can't see dat much but I tell her.'

'Make yourselves comfortable. Lisa please show Ningali the taps, hot and cold.'

Lisa just beamed, and nodded.

'I know this will feel very strange to you, and I'm not trying to change your ways but the warm running water is something you ladies don't experience very often.'

'Don't forget the ham and tomato sandwiches for the women, Lisa. I'll put the kettle on, so ask them what they need. I'll leave you to organise them.'

'I'll just show Ningali the taps, if she can just stop giggling for a minute,' laughed Lisa.

Zena came back out into the kitchen where Alan sat reading.

'I have to go back up to the sheds in a moment, but I stayed to make sure everything was okay. You know you can't change them, Zena. They are happy the way they live, squatting in the bush. Splash of water in the right places. You know what I mean.'

'Yes I do, darling, but it's just a treat. They can do what they like. It's just great having them here. I have some patterns for dresses that I can easily knock up. Just basic colourful sacks they throw over their heads. Did you find the tent?' asked Zena.

'Yep, and the foam mattresses, just in case they say yes,' winked Alan.

'Sometimes when they mix with their own, they want to stay. I'm hoping, Alan. I don't like them down by the river on their own, not with what has been happening.'

'The other news is . . . I called Woodside and Kate answered.'

'Right, and I have a feeling this is going to be painful. Spit it out, Alan.'

'Mitch is getting married.'

'What . . . married! To whom?' Zena exclaimed, her hand to her mouth.

Alan started laughing. 'That was exactly my reaction and nearly the same words.'

'In six weeks' time Mitch will be married to Miss Tess Dunphy.'

'Oh dear Lord. Did Kate tell you this?'

'Yes. Seems Mitch has Tess in the family way. Said not to expect an invite to the wedding. Just a small ceremony out at Woodside.'

'Oh no, this is Kate's worst nightmare. I must call her but then again what can I say . . . what do I say?' Zena thought for a moment as a slow smile of acknowledgement crept across her face.

'I bet the evening I called Kate to tell her what Mitch did to Lisa, he made a visit to Tess Dunphy. Remember Kate said he hadn't come home? That was the day I rang. Reap what you sow, Mitchell. Anyway, I cannot dwell on that news, suffice to say he won't be bothering Lisa anymore. Now, I have two frocks to make,' said Zena, disappearing into her sewing room.

Alan could hear Ningali squealing, and Lisa was just as loud. 'Someone's having fun,' he laughed as he plonked his Akubra back on and headed out.

Zena emerged carrying four dresses over her arms and walked towards their bedroom. One of each print for the ladies. So easy to make. Loose sacks really. The laughter had died down. Ningali must have gotten used to the bath or the shower. She knocked softly on the door. 'Who dat?'

'It's me, Ningali. Can I come in?' asked Zena.

'Yeh, boss lady. Me and Binna just restin and enjoyin da big comfy bed.' They had scrubbed up well. Lisa had obviously shown Ningali the shampoo and soaps.

'How did you both go with the shower or bath?' asked Zena.

'Dat stuff smell real good and like bein under da waterfall. You got da billabong in dere too.'

Zena laughed. 'It's a shower, and the billabong is the bath. The smelly stuff is just soap, Ningali. I will give you some to take.'

'Binna don't like much. I just help her splash some water, dat all.' The elderly lady sat quietly in the big armchair but a smile lit up her kind face.

'Okay, these are the dresses I made. I have a good eye so I am sure they will fit, and I made them extra loose. This one has green and red, like the bush flowers, and this one is like the earth, brown with the yellow flowers. So you have one of each.'

Ningali looked at the dresses in disbelief. 'Boss lady. I never had dat before. New dress and da colour. Dey pretty.' She ran her long brown fingers over the cloth.

'Binna, look what da boss lady make. She makem real good.'

Zena went over to help Binna get up out of the big chair. 'This way, Binna.' Even with her hazy sight, she could see the vibrant patterns. 'Thank you, my friend.' Her hand reached out to touch Zena.

'Right then, I will leave you two to get dressed. Alan won't be long. I guess Lisa is getting ready.'

'Yeah, da little one, she leave us, say she go to splash up too.'

Zena collected the empty plates and cups and came back out into the kitchen. 'Oh, there you are, Lisa. I've just come from their room. They are so funny, like children, but I will get you to go in there in about ten minutes. Just knock on the door and see if they need a hand, although all they had to do was slip the new dresses over their heads. No buttons, no zips. They may want to keep their old dresses for whatever reason. I'll just go and clean up. We will need to head down there in the next fifteen to twenty minutes. Alan was lining up some targets for Kev.'

Lisa knocked softly. 'Hey Ningali, it's me, can I come in?'

'Da little one, Binna, she come to da door. I gunna let her in.' As Ningali opened the door, Lisa gave a small squeal. 'You both look so beautiful.'

'Yeah, me lookem fancy orright.' Ningali twirled at her vision in the big mirror. She had chosen the green and red print, which looked lovely against her dark skin. Binna wore the earth tones, which made her white hair stand out even more.

'How are you feeling, Binna?' Lisa asked tentatively.

'Feel like not belong but make Ningali happy. Me likem be outside with da nature.'

'Well, let's make our way now, as we will drive down in the Land Rover to watch Kev, the crackshot, and of course dinner is down there too.'

Zena was waiting and turned when she saw the two women. 'You both look lovely . . . I am so pleased you came. I know this feels very strange and rather odd, but by the end of the night, you may feel a little different. I can bring you back to your camp after dinner. It is up to you.'

Lisa helped the ladies down the back stairs, and Zena grabbed her keys. New dresses, no shoes. Have to love these Bush Marys.

Alan and Jack had set up many targets, and the crew as well as the lubras and anyone who was at Woori from the dogs to the kids were all there to watch. Sitting on hay bales, sitting in the dirt, sitting on logs of wood, they were all ready for the action.

Zena pulled up and saw Kev standing next to Alan, a rifle over his shoulder. There were various targets away from the shearing sheds. Bottles and tin bullseyes were what Kev obviously needed to hit. It was going to be fun. Cookie had the big hotplate burning, and the smell of onions and sausages wafted through the air.

Ningali stepped out the back of the Land Rover and then came around to help Binna. Zena pointed to a bale of hay and they made their way to it. It was hard not to miss her long stick legs in the dazzling red and green print.

Alan waved. 'Geez, bloody Ningali doesn't scrub up too bad.'

Kev looked across the paddock and nodded. 'Who dat orright looka? Big Bush Mary.'

'Her name is Ningali. That's her mother, Binna, the old lady with the white hair. They both came about five seasons ago and never left. Their camp is down towards the river. Ningali was with a white bloke, can't remember his name, but he used to belt her, knocked some of her teeth out, so she took off from him after the season. Jack didn't want him back either.

'Ningali called him a lazy bugger, and he was. The ladies have both become good friends of ours over the years. They are very spiritual, and my niece and Zena adore them.'

Ningali watched Kevin closely. Mr Crackshot. Him tall. Him not bad. She smiled. It felt good to be out.

'We are just waiting on Burnu and Billy,' said Jack. 'That dust cloud up there tells me they are on their way.'

Lisa's heart began to race. Another night with Billy. She knew the very beginning of the season was hard work and extremely busy, but things should start to settle so she could ride with him.

They cantered over to the black's camp and let their horses off into a small yard. One of the picaninnies carried a biscuit of hay to them.

Burnu's eyes lit up when he saw Binna, his old friend, and he came across to see the women.

'Ahh Burnu, dat Lisa, she make us get away from da humpy, so we here,' said Ningali cheekily.

'Plenty good to see you both . . . . it bin long time,' said Burnu as he sat on the ground next to them.

Lisa plonked herself on a bale of hay just next to Ningali. Her aunt had brought two fold-up chairs, which she set up for herself and Alan.

Billy joined his father and greeted the two ladies. It was good to see them at Woori. He looked across to Lisa sitting on the bale of hay and wandered over to her. 'Grasshopper, you smell good,' said Billy as he sat down next to her.

Jack nodded in Cookie's direction and he sounded his bell.

'Now I have your attention, let me introduce Kev, our resident crackshot. He will demonstrate today to Alan, and all of you, why he got the bloody job here. Can't ride a horse for shit, so he better be able to shoot.'

There was much laughter. 'I would ask you to be quiet while Kev takes aim at the various targets. For every target he misses, it's twenty-cents into the rum pot, which we will use at the end of season party or maybe on a case of beer.'

'Dat a bloody big price, boss. Kev no miss . . . dat for sure. Likem my money, boss, no lose here. Me gunna use my bolt action Remington 223. She never miss da target.'

Jack smiled. He knew Kev would be right on the money. 'Right, here we go!' Jack bellowed. 'There are a dozen bottles 400 yards away. There is a green stripe around the neck of each bottle. He has to hit that green stripe, twelve bottles, in twenty seconds.'

The lubras threw their hands over their ears as Kev's rifle blazed away. Jack hit his stopwatch. 'Just under twenty seconds.' There was a loud cheer.

Jack walked over to a round, large tin shape and held it up. He then nailed it to the fence post.

'Here we have a bullseye, right in the centre, with the other six other small bullseyes around the perimeter. Kev has to pay twenty-cents if he hits any of the outside targets or misses a target. Again, 400-yards distance, and he has to hit the centre target or he coughs up,' said Jack. 'By the way, the norm is for five shots into an apple at 100 yards. So Kev has three shots, aiming for the centre at 400 yards.'

A battery of shots were fired, the parrots squawking at the deafening sounds as they took to the air.

Jack picked up the round piece of tin that had fallen to the ground and showed everyone. Every shot had hit centre target.

Ningali squealed and clapped. 'He bloody good, orright.'

Ned started to play his harmonica and Cookie started serving the food to the queue that had formed. Zena grabbed the salads she had made and placed them under the lean-to. The hot damper came out and was quickly covered, the smell attracting every bush fly about the place.

Kev walked back to where Lisa was sitting. He looked over at Ningali.

'Hey, you can shoot . . . where you learn dat?' squealed Ningali, getting to her feet. Kev smiled, he was clearly amused by her.

'She da good lubra, but cheeky,' he bent down to tell Billy.

'I heard that,' said Lisa.

'I tell dat to her face, she da good lubra.' He straightened up, looking directly at Ningali. She nervously giggled and slapped her long thin thighs, whispering to Binna, 'Dat one, dat Kev, he proper good.' The old lady smiled her toothless grin. Her daughter was excited.

'Not too much grog, Jack, it's a week night. Tonight's just a bit of fun,' cautioned Alan.

'Yeah, I'm watching, mate. Boy, can that bloke shoot. Hate to be his target,' said Jack.

'I'll go join Zena, give her a hand,' said Alan.

'Darling wife, got you working again?' He ambled over to assist.

'Certainly have, just giving Cookie a break, but while you're here, when did you want to tell Lisa about Mitch and the wedding.'

'Leave it for now; it's not that important to us. We can tell her in the morning. Don't spoil the night. Everyone is having a lot of fun.'

'True,' said Zena, handing Alan a plate with sausages, salad and damper.

'Alright, missus,' said Cookie. 'Had my dinner, so I will take over. You go sit with Alan.'

Zena pointed to the two fold-up chairs she had earlier assembled. 'Look at our girl, Alan, the smile hasn't left her face.'

Billy suddenly stood up and said, 'I'll be back.' When he returned, he held a beautiful didgeridoo. 'Bin playin up in Queensland. Dis sacred instrument, Lisa, date back 40,000 years. I learn for you. Da sound of da didj, it clear out da pain and sorrow.'

When Billy started playing, the camp fell silent. The sounds were haunting and magical, sweeping across the plains like a deep mystical experience. Some of the lubras produced clapping sticks and joined in on the beat.

Ningali suddenly leaped to her feet and started to dance, foot stomping in a mystical way as if recreating the dances of the animals and the birds, her arms extending, her body moving rhythmically to the beat. It was truly an ethereal moment, and Kev watched in awe as the tall lubra swirled in the red dust.

When Billy finished, everyone started to clap.

'Oh, Alan, that was truly magnificent. Aren't we lucky to have this right at our door,' said Zena. 'Simply breathtaking, truly a part of Australia's soul.'

'We are indeed, my darling. That boy is . . . he has this unique oneness with the land and the animals. He's just like Binna and his father. Something spiritual about him, as you always say, and he has these healing powers he seems to have inherited or been taught. Burnu says the boy has the gift, and I believe it.'

Zena nodded in the direction of Kev. 'Think we may have started something here. Kev seems to be besotted, can't take his eyes off Ningali.'

'Well, we have had a few romances over the years, I'm sure this won't be the last,' chuckled Alan. 'At least Kev won't punch her teeth out. Decent bloke.'

Jack's voice suddenly bellowed out. 'Okay, everyone needs to eat, we are about to clear so Cookie can get to bed.'

Zena leaned over to Binna and Ningali. 'Ladies, it is just after eight. Have you made any decision about staying or going? I can take you now if you like?'

'We stay, boss lady. We got da tent . . . over dat way. Boss Alan he bin set up for us. True.'

'Splendid. Well, breakfast is served early, and I will come down and take you back tomorrow. Goodnight, ladies.'

'Thank you, darling, for setting up that tent.' Zena kissed Alan.

'Pleasure, my love. They both look pretty happy. What about those two?' grinned Alan.

'Leave them to it. Billy will do the usual, bring her up on Jed. Don't be too late, Lisa,' Zena sang out. 'Billy has to be up early.'

'All good, Aunty.' Her face was aglow with happiness as she tried to play the didj, much to Billy's amusement. *They make a striking couple*, Zena thought.

THIRTY-THREE

NEW RELATIONSHIPS

Lisa stretched and felt an absolute happiness descend over her. It was a beautiful spring day as the sunlight tipped its head through her room. Things wouldn't be so frantic in a few days, and she would be able to ride Topi with Billy. She sprang out of bed, eager to meet the day. Maybe there might be an opportunity to ride late this afternoon. *Fingers crossed.*

Zena was leaving as Lisa came into the kitchen. 'I'm just heading down to take Binna and Ningali back. See you in a while. I know it's early, but I won't have breakfast just yet. I have a feeling Binna will want to be out of there. See you in a bit.'

As she headed towards the sheds, Zena could see the men up and about. She pulled up closer to where Alan had pitched the tent for the ladies under a peppercorn tree. As she came around to the tent flaps, Binna sat just at the entrance, cross legged, her eyes closed. It was almost as if she was in a trance. Where was Ningali? Zena swung her head around the black's camp. Nowhere. Binna slowly opened her milky eyes.

'Hello, my friend,' she said, her voice almost a whisper.

'Good morning, Binna. I hope you slept well.'

'Me sleepem good, very soft da mattress here.' The old lady patted the surface.

'Is Ningali up and about, maybe looking for food, some breakfast?'

The old lady gave a short cackle, and her frail shoulders shook.

'What is it, Binna? You girls up to something? Can you let me in on your secret?'

'Dat Ningali, she no come back. Not here in da tent. She go with dat Kev.'

Zena burst out laughing and then shook her head. Yes, *Ningali, it's been a long time for everything – dancing, music and men.*

'Well, I will have to find her. What do you want to do? Stay, or I will get Ningali, get some tucker and take you both back?'

'Mebbe, but me wait, likem be with my people and da sisters again.'

'Well, I will get you something to eat. Do you need me to take you to the long drop?'

'No, one of da sisters, she take me early dis morning. She come back too with da grub for me. You no worry, dey being proper good to me.'

Zena was pleased. The lubras were already looking after her. Sisterhood. Now to find that Ningali.

She didn't have to look far. Kev's ute had a swag thrown in the back and a makeshift canopy over the back. Ningali's unmistakable long, thin legs were hanging out of the swag, and she slept peacefully. Empty beer cans were on the ground. Not too many, which was a good sign. Kev had kept it under control.

The shed was abuzz with activity, Binna was being looked after and Ningali was asleep. All good. She may as well head back, she had a bit to do herself and her stomach was saying it wanted breakfast. Zena smiled all the way back to the homestead.

◇

Lisa was up feeding the pigs when she saw the big black horse in the distance. *Billy.* She craned her neck and then waved, but he was too far away. Probably working all those boundary paddocks, the dust was billowing as he moved the sheep. Looked like a willy willy, a dust storm.

Oh damn it, Alan said not to bother the men when they are working but a drive out surely wouldn't matter. Lisa hopped into the ute and drove gingerly towards Billy. She saw another horse as she approached and waved to Kev, who flashed her his trademark grin. Lisa giggled. All she could see was teeth under the big hat.

Lisa sat waiting in the ute. If Billy got what he needed to get done, he would come over. She would stay here as she didn't want to spook those sheep. It was good to watch their horsemanship, ducking and weaving and herding the sheep into a paddock closer to the sheds. She remembered what Alan said. The indigenous stockmen opened up the outback. Suddenly, the big black horse stopped, and Billy took his hat off and waved. He galloped Jed towards the ute.

'Good morning, Grasshopper, me happy to see you.' Billy slid off his horse.

'Me happy to see you too.' Lisa smiled.

'Me and Kev out here working together, he top bloke, got himself some Ningali last night,' Billy laughed.

'What . . . are you serious, Billy?'

'Yes, miss, me serious. Ningali, she like Kev, in his swag dis morning.'

'Oh, I love it, that's brilliant! Wait till I tell Aunty. Um, will you have a full day, I mean will you have any spare time?'

'Billy has spare time today, Grasshopper, maybe we go for ride at three. Bin up real early, so can go.'

Lisa's face lit up. 'That's great! I'll meet you at the compound gates then. Can't wait to show you Topi.'

'Me look forward.' He bent down, leaning into the window of the ute, his big velvet brown eyes searching her face.

Lisa glanced up from under her brows, smiling.

'Would Grasshopper like to kiss me?' he whispered, almost inaudibly.

'Yes, Grasshopper would like to kiss Billy.'

He moved his head gently and planted a lingering kiss on her full mouth, drawing back to gauge her reaction. It was a kiss that seemed to make her so utterly his own. *My grasshopper.*

Her eyes were shining. 'I had best get going then. See you at three, Billy. I will be waiting with Topi.' She blew him a kiss.

The Land Rover was parked in its usual spot. Lisa raced up the stairs and couldn't wait to tell Zena about Ningali and Kev.

'Yoohoo, it's me, where are you? I've got some big news.'

'In the sewing room. I thought I would get rid of these other fabrics just lying around. Enough to make those girls one more each.'

'You are so kind, Aunty. I want to be like you.'

Zena stopped sewing and looked over her glasses. 'But you are, darling girl. So kind and helpful, and your heart is so big, despite what has happened to you.'

Lisa hugged Zena. 'Thank you so much. I just love you and Alan and Woori . . . ooh and just everything.'

'I can see the season is having its effect on you. Now, what is your news, and I will tell you mine.'

'Ningali was in Kev's swag last night.'

'Yes I know, I was down there this morning, early, remember?'

'Isn't that great, Aunty. I saw Billy working with Kev this morning, and he said he was a top bloke.'

'I think we all know that by now. Both Jack and Alan are very impressed. If Ningali likes him and vice versa, then so be it.'

'What is your news then, Aunty?'

'Take a deep breath, young lady . . . Mitch is getting married.'

'Married! God . . . to who! How did you find that out?'

'Alan called Woodside to see how Dave was getting on with the season. He's always done that, nothing new, but it was Kate who answered. She told Alan the news. Getting married in six weeks' time to Tess Dunphy.'

Lisa's mouth flew open. 'Tess Dunphy! Tess Dunphy!'

'Calm down, Lisa, the girl is pregnant.'

The look of shock was immediate on Lisa's face, and her head was swimming from the news.

'It's okay, Lisa, he has obviously been seeing her, and now she is about to have his child. We don't expect an invite to the wedding, either. It's a very small affair over at Woodside. I would say Kate is devastated in one way, she didn't really see Tess as daughter-in-law material. But a beautiful, innocent child has been conceived, so she will make a wonderful grandmother. There is always a positive, Lisa.'

'Yes, Aunty. Well, the good thing is that he won't be bothering me anymore.'

'Whether Tess was in the picture or out of it . . . that wasn't happening. Barred from Woori for life because of his actions with you, and my guess for all his life, he will regret his behaviour deeply. His life has changed; he will now have a wife and child to look after.'

'You were right, Aunty. As you said, everything changes, nothing stays the same. I just hope he will love that child. Anyway, I came in to have some lunch. I'll go check Noir and the other mares before I do and then I'm riding Topi with Billy at three. I am so excited, Aunty,' said Lisa.

'I can see that, my dear. Just be careful when you go out there, as I know you will head to the river. Please keep your ears and eyes to the ground.'

'I will. But Billy will be with me. Are you taking Binna and Ningali back?'

'They seem okay here. I spoke to Binna, and she said the lubras were looking after her and she was happy to be with her people. Ningali was snoring in the back of Kev's ute. I could see her legs sticking out the swag.'

Lisa could barely put two words together for laughing.

'They are happy for now, that's the main thing, but I will go back down when I finish these two dresses and see what they want to do. You go on and don't worry about anything but yourself,' said Zena.

◊

As Lisa sat outside the Tack Room with the cats purring around her feet and Dougy needing pats, she heard the thunder of hooves, and her heart raced. *Billy, he comes for me.*

She grabbed Topi and headed for the gates, closing them just as Billy came to a halt.

'What do you think, Billy?'

'Pretty, Lisa, he is very pretty. Coloured horse.'

'Yes, he is a Pinto, but he moves so fast, Billy. He's only young, so with age, he will get even better. I just love him.' Billy smiled at his grasshopper. She had such a love for animals.

'Let's go . . . to the river and back,' smiled Billy.

'To the river and back. Come on, I'll race you.' Lisa mounted quickly. 'Come on, Topi, as fast as you can.' She dug her heels into his flanks.

Topi quickly picked up speed, his hooves resonating with the earth. Billy wanted to watch Lisa, so he let her have the lead. She was now an excellent horsewoman and rode as if she were part of the horse. Topi worked under her beautifully, steady in his stride. *But you are no match for me, Grasshopper.*

Billy spurred Jed on faster to overtake Topi, and with a word of command, asking for more from the big black horse, his action shifted and his huge stride became more powerful, such that he seemed to fly through the air. He flashed a smile at Lisa and let Jed have his head. As he passed, she was again struck by the graceful way he rode, even at speed.

They rode long and hard until they reached the river, Billy slowing down to a canter, allowing Lisa to pull up alongside. They then rode slowly, talking and laughing, the exuberance of the ride carrying them along.

'That was so great, Billy, I loved it. What did you think of my boy?' she asked as she patted Topi.

'He good horse, Lisa, suit you, no better. Horses and people, they form special bond.'

They reached the river and led the horses down the small track. 'Let them drink now, and we sit.' Billy pulled out a long rope and ran it through the rings of their bridles, then tied it to a tree. 'Give dem boys a long lead.'

They sat on the bank of the river, feeling the coolness of the late afternoon breeze. 'I've so missed you, Billy. I did fear you may not come back. I had heard stories you were doing well in the north.'

'Yeah, me do good work but my heart belong somewhere else.'

'Where?' Lisa teased.

'Belong here with you, Grasshopper. Always. When I was away, I lay awake at night. I hear your voice, kiss your mouth. I feel your wonderful spirit. I want to reach out to you.'

'Yes, I felt the same and then I heard that awful news about Jimmy, and I was so worried for you.'

'Jimmy don't like me being boss, and he just got angry. Jimmy angry all da time. Something eat him up. Da bad spirit. But we don't talk no more about him.'

Billy pulled her face gently towards his lips. His first kiss was light, as if he were testing her. When he drew back, his chocolate gaze mesmerised her, and she eagerly slid into his embrace, welcoming the warm lips that sought hers. Her feelings for him made her giddy, and Lisa ached to feel him, to let him take her where he would. He pulled her into him again, his kisses becoming more urgent.

Lisa gently broke away. 'If we start, Billy, I know I won't stop. It's getting late, and this is not the place. And I really want to take things slowly.'

Billy stood up and pulled Lisa to her feet. His arms surrounded her, warm and gentle, kissing her forehead, neither wanting to break the embrace. Lisa clung to his muscular shoulders. He ignited everything inside her and completely consumed her body and soul.

'Come, Grasshopper, you belong to Billy. I will wait to see you in my bed. We go now.' He took Lisa's hand and walked towards the horses. As they galloped past the humpy, it was odd not to see the smoke curling into the sky but Lisa smiled. Binna and Ningali were at Woori.

◇

He sat quietly. No-one had heard or sensed him. He hissed under his breath. *Bastard Billy, you come back and now you take what is mine. I kill you,* he seethed as he felt for the long-bladed knife.

THIRTY-FOUR

ARTIE GOES MISSING

'Another good season, another good crew. A bloke can get lucky, Zena. Billy and Kev have really excelled, and they work well together. They have this indelible spirit and this fortitude for life as stockmen. It's tough out here and more so in those blistering hot shearing sheds, hard gut-breaking work, and none of them complain, no matter who – the ringers, the stockmen, camp cooks, fencers, shearers, nothing. I am a fortunate man.'

'They obviously love the life just as much as you do, Alan. That's why they keep coming back. I just wish we could do more for them politically or make the public aware of indigenous people, their resourcefulness, knowledge of the country and their skill in working and living on the land. I hope it's never lost. Very philosophical this morning, aren't we?' laughed Zena.

'It's just that they . . . well, they amaze me,' added Alan.

'What's the plan today, same same?' asked Zena.

'Yeah, and a few other things. That bloody old ram Artie is missing, and I bet he has taken a few ewes for company. Billy said the wire fence was broken in sections, up in the far paddock, like it had been trampled, so I bet the old bugger has rammed it. He keeps ramming it until the fencing breaks or until he can get through it. It's a wonder the old boy doesn't knock himself out.'

'I do love Artie,' said Zena. 'I never moved so quickly that day he chased me, and when I jumped the fence, the stupid thing just rammed the gate.'

'He is getting old and cranky, but he needs to be kept in a smaller pen, no wire and no roaming. I wonder if rams get dementia. I'll get Burnu to ride out and see if he can spot him. I'm trying to find him easier jobs around the place, rather than riding in the hot sun herding sheep.'

'Yes, I worry for him, he has slowed down . . . thank you, my darling, for looking after him.'

'How are Binna and Ningali? Still here, I see.'

'Well, you won't shift Ningali now. She has taken up residence in the back of Kev's ute, and Binna, well the lubras know she is a powerful healer, so she is being treated like a queen down there. Those lubras have plenty of bush knowledge, so they go out gathering for her and generally look after all her needs. As Binna told me, she is happy with her people. I hope they stay, Alan.'

'Righto, my darling, don't make me late for work. That breakfast will stick to my sides. Can't beat lashings of pig and eggs.' Alan came behind Zena, who started to stack dishes in the sink and caught her by surprise. He kissed her softly on the lips. 'Love you, I don't say it often enough.'

Zena sighed as she watched him leave, the sound of the motorbike fading into the distance. *Love you too.*

Cookie was dishing out breakfast in the eating area, and Alan was pleased he caught everyone together.

'Morning everyone, Jack has a plan for most of you today. Burnu, can you take Kev and ride out quickly this morning to see if you can find an old ram for me. His name is Artie and

I've had him since he was a wee lamb. He's up on the boundary paddock, closest to the river.' Alan pulled out a map.

'Dat orright, boss, I know da paddock. We go look for him,' said Burnu.

'Artie is a cantankerous old thing and he will ram you if you get too close. And don't think you can out-run him, either of you, or you will feel his curly horns up your arse.' All the men howled with laughter. The regulars knew Artie well.

'Me shootem dead, boss,' said Kev.

'You'll do no such thing or you will incur the wrath of my wife. She loves old Artie. Had him since he was a baby. We will let him drop dead in the paddocks from old age, but he wanders off now smashing and trampling fences, and he always takes a few ewes with him. His harem. So I want him brought down to that steel paddock over by the shearing shed. I can see what the old bloke is up to there. Kev, you may want to take a good rope and throw it over his head. Stay on your horses. You are not going to get close to him.'

'Orright boss, dat fella he gonna be back here, follow me lika dog,' said Kev as he went to find a rope.

'Don't let him get too close, Burnu,' warned Alan. 'Just watch Kev out there, he may get too cocky. Artie is smart and we don't want any injuries.'

'No, boss.' A big smile crossed his face.

The others took their leave and headed out into the day. 'Thanks, Cookie,' the crew said as one by one, the seats were emptied.'

'Go now too, me get da horses,' said Burnu.

It was a steady ride and they both chatted easily. 'You bin here da long time, Burnu?' asked Kev.

'Yeah, never better fella, dat Alan boss, treat us all good. Always come back. My boy, he feel dat too.'

'Your boy, he got da paler skin. Lookem me, black like da night, but dat Billy creamy, not a darky like me.'

Burnu smiled. 'Billy . . . his mother, she white girl.'

Kev's eyes flew open. 'Da white stuff? Ned he tell me something like dat.'

'Yeah, she good lady, meet her on one of da stations I bin working on. Boss don't like mix mix, so we go.'

'Where da mother now?' queried Kev.

'She dead, with da spirits. She die having Billy, have da big loss of blood, hemragge, somethin' like dat, dem doctors can't stop da bleeding. So I take my boy and we stay together. Bin moving round station to station, but all dem white girls dey likem Billy. Da boss ladies always teach him proper good English, readin, writin. I knew dat only good for my boy. But no more talk of da lady . . . his mother. Not good for da spirits.'

Kev nodded. 'Da boy, he likem dat boss's niece. Don't like da lubras?'

'Nah, once da boy see dat girl, she too, she likem my boy . . . well dat was it. Da spirit bird follow her and my boy, he got da healing powers. Dey walk together on dis earth. Me got no problem with dat.'

'Yeah, but it's da whiteys dat do,' added Kev.

'Plenty big problem dat for sure, proper true, but dat won't stop 'em.' Da spirits protect dat two. Lookem up dat way,' said Burnu pointing. 'Dat's Artie's paddock, come on, he gotta be in dat one somewhere. Lookem good now, Kev, and remember what Boss Alan said. He da bad ram, gunna butt you. Stay on da horse.'

Kev started laughing, his eyes opening up wide. 'Me got to stay in da good shape, me got dat Ningali hopping around in da ute.'

Burnu shook his head, laughing inside.

'See da fence line, smashem good. He be in here orright,' said Kev. 'Dere look look, behind da peppercorn tree. He bin standing lookin at us Burnu, proper true. Dat lazy bugger, he got da girls with him.'

'Slowly, Kev,' cautioned Burnu, 'no spookem.' He watched Kev reach for his rope as they headed to a gate, and the horses jumped the broken section of the fence.

As they moved towards Artie, suddenly Burnu saw something suddenly move in his peripheral vision and realised it was a snake, rearing and ready to strike. His horse shyed, then reared, throwing him to the ground, landing him almost on top of the snake. He rolled and tried to scramble to his feet but the snake was too quick. Burnu felt its fangs latch onto his forearm, and he cried out in pain. It came at him again just as Kev reached for his rifle, killing it instantly.

'Fuck, Burnu, plenty trouble now.' He jumped off his horse. Kev looked at his arm, two puncture wounds just below his elbow, the swelling and redness starting to develop.

'Come on, gotta get back to da house,' said Kev, the panic in his voice evident.

Burnu slowly put his hand up. 'No, dat big eastern brown, deadly. Five minutes and I start to meet da ancestors. Me no make it back.'

Kev helped the old man to his feet. He was already experiencing difficulty breathing. Burnu pointed to the peppercorn tree where the ram had been. They had cleared off upon hearing the shot.

'Get me to dat tree, Kev, and sit me against it.'

Kev threw Burnu's arm over his shoulder and half walked, half dragged the older man to the tree. He ran back to his horse to get some water.

'Here Burnu, drinkem da water,' said Kev.

'No,' whispered Burnu, as he held his hands out blindly. 'Da eyes failing now.' He vomited to the side.

'I ride for da help Burnu, gotta do somethin . . . I be back, hold on.' He took off his bandana for a tourniquet and wrapped it around Burnu's elbow. 'I leave da water.'

Kev mounted the horse and took off. It was a good fifteen to twenty minute ride, and he knew the browns could kill in ten to sixty minutes.

He galloped as hard as he could towards the homestead, shouting as he got closer. 'Boss lady, boss lady, help, come quick, boss lady!' He pulled up at the compound gates.

Zena had been in the sitting room and from the window saw the horse galloping at full speed. She was up on her feet already but when she heard the shouting she knew something was terribly wrong.

'Kev, what is it, for God's sake,' she shouted as she met him at the gate.

'Burnu, it's Burnu, boss lady, he be bitten by da snake, dat big bloody brown snake.'

Zena froze. 'Kev, please ride now to the sheds. Alan is down there with Jack. Tell Jack to come inside and alert the flying doctor . . . they may be in the area. He knows how to use our radio. I'm taking the Land Rover.' Zena grabbed the First Aid kit and ran.

'God, please no, please, please, please, no.' The tears were streaming down her face. As Zena got to the top paddock, she could see Burnu's horse. She drove at speed through the gate and screeched to a halt, grabbing the First-Aid kit from the Land Rover. Zena then started running towards the white-haired figure who sat with his back against the peppercorn tree.

She fell to her knees at the side of the old man, but she knew he was on his way to the spirit world. He was nearly gone. He was paralysed, spit dribbling from the corners of his mouth, and vomit covered the ground. His breathing was rapid and she knew he was about to go into cardiac arrest. She noted the two large puncture marks on his forearm.

'Burnu, please, Burnu, stay with us . . . God no, please don't take him away.' Her body trembled with the fear of losing her friend.

'Burnu, Burnu, please, I know you can hear me,' said Zena as she took his brown leathery hand in her own. 'I love you, my friend. I will look after Billy, I promise you.' Drawing his hand to her cheek, the tears spilled down her face. The sound of her weeping was carried on the winds. Alan saw his wife in the distance rocking back and forth under the tree.

Alan pulled up beside the Land Rover and leaped out of the ute with Kev following closely behind. He knew the old man was not in a way, so they ran towards his wife and Burnu.

When they reached Zena, Alan knew the old man was not in a good way.

'Not good?' he cried. Alan fell to his knees next to his wife.

'Oh Alan, he's fading. I don't want him to go.'

Alan put a comforting arm around Zena as she sobbed uncontrollably.

'Come on, my love.' He kissed her forehead lightly and assisted her to her feet. Burnu's head suddenly lagged to the side and his chest stopped moving.

The only sound was the army of flies buzzing and the whimpering from Zena. 'Go peacefully, Burnu,' said Alan.

'My brudder gone now, he go meet da ancestors in da spirit world,' said Kev.

'Where is the snake, Kev?' asked Alan.

'He dead now, dat fella not gunna hurt no-one no more. Got da bugger with da first shot. He fly into da air, dead. He over dat way.'

Zena leaned forward and closed Burnu's eyes. 'Goodbye, my friend.'

Alan walked with Kev to where the snake's body lay. 'Big bastard, nearly seven feet. Burnu never had a chance.' Alan stomped on its head.

'Come on, Kev, help me with Burnu's body. They will want to have a burial this evening.'

Alan moved to the back of the ute and pulled out the tarpaulin. He spread it over the back, leaving an open flap to cover Burnu's face. Kev helped load his body into the back, and they covered him over.

'Kev, can you drive the Land Rover back, and Zena will come with me. Just let Jack know that the RFD is no longer needed. He'll be waiting inside the house. We'll head back to the sheds . . . . come up the both of you when you are done there.'

'Sure, boss.'

No words were spoken on the drive to the sheds. Zena lay her head on Alan's shoulder, her only movement was to wipe her tears away. He knew she was devastated. God help her when Binna goes. He placed his hand on her thigh for reassurance.

'It will be alright, my darling,' Alan said softly.

'Lisa is down at the sheds this morning with Cookie. He asked for some help. She is going to be devastated, so will Billy.'

As they pulled up to the shearing sheds, Cookie and Lisa came out to greet them. He saw the form of the body wrapped in a tarp in the back and put his head down. Lisa stared, trying to understand what was going on.

Zena quickly got out of the car and came to her side. 'What's going on, Aunty? Who is that?' Her voice was quivering.

'Hi Cookie, it's Burnu. Brown snake.'

'Dear God!' Cookie brought his hands to his head.

Alan glanced at Lisa as he gave Cookie the news. She had heard Burnu's name and screamed hysterically, falling to the ground, punching the dirt. 'Burnu, no please . . . not Burnu.'

Alan came to Lisa and helped to her to her feet, holding her tightly, her tears mixing with the red dirt.

◊

'Binna, dat someone screamin, howlin, like da big pain. Come, we go see,' said Ningali as she assisted Binna to her feet. They walked slowly in the direction of the sheds.

◇

'Jack, please go find Billy,' Alan said sadly.

'Sure, Alan. I know where he is.' Jack roared off on the motorbike, his face like stone. This would be hard for the boy. He spotted the boy and waved, watching as he galloped towards him. This was not going to be easy, a moment he would dread for all his life.

'Hey, boss,' said Billy, his face quizzical.

'Mate, you need to come with me now; Burnu has been bitten by a brown.'

Billy's face visibly changed. 'Brown?' He hesitated momentarily before speaking. 'Burnu, he passed on?'

'Yes, mate, you need to come,' said Jack, his voice full of sorrow.

Billy turned Jed towards the shed and spurred the big horse to a gallop as Jack followed slowly on the motor bike.

Lisa's screams had alerted the crew as well as the lubras, and they gathered in a group. Ningali and Binna came around the corner and saw the group. Binna stopped. 'Somethin wrong, sorrow here,' she whispered as they joined the others.

Billy rode back swiftly and pulled Jed up hard, staring intently at the body of his father. He dismounted and came to the back of the ute. His hand travelled up and down the tarp as he spoke in his own words.

Alan joined Zena, her arm around her grief-stricken niece.

Lisa thought her heart would break as she watched Billy move slowly. He turned to look at her, and she saw his grief. She suddenly broke away from Zena and ran to him, throwing her arms around his neck. 'I'm so sorry, Billy,' she sobbed, the tears spilling down her face. Billy kissed her forehead softly. He knew his world was changing. They both turned to listen to Alan.

Alan removed his hat and the others followed. 'I have very sorry news this morning. Burnu was with Kev in the far paddocks and his horse shyed on seeing a brown snake, throwing Burnu to the ground where the snake sprang, and sadly, Burnu was bitten. Most of you know, brown snakes are the only snakes in the world that can kill in as little as fifteen minutes. Burnu, my friend, went out as a warrior and his end was quick.'

Alan looked at Billy, who stood stoically with Lisa. Billy turned to Alan and Zena. 'We look after him now.'

What will you do, Billy? asked Alan.

'We do the burial,' he answered solemnly.

'Billy, we would all like to be present, if that is okay with you.'

'Sure, boss. Billy let you know when da ceremony begin.'

'Lisa, just come this way please,' said Zena as Jack and Kev came to the back of the ute to lift Burnu's body.

'No, I want to stay here . . . please.' The tears were still streaming down her face.

'It's best you come with us, we will come back down.' Zena extended her hand. 'Someone will get word to us, come on, just give Billy some time.'

Lisa got into the Land Rover, and they drove back to the homestead.

'I'll put the kettle on,' said Alan, not knowing what else to do or say. He was guilt-ridden having sent Burnu into that paddock.

'I'll just wash my face,' said Zena, escaping to the solace of her room. The wound to her heart was deep.

Lisa did not move from the chair at the kitchen table, her body in a slumped position, no words leaving her lips.

'They will have a ceremony, Lisa, befitting an old warrior like Burnu. Salt of the earth . . . wonderful mate,' said Alan.

'Why do they die so quickly from the snake bite, Alan? Why can't they be saved?' Lisa wiped the tears with the back of her hand.

'Second deadliest snake in the world, Lisa. You get bitten and then feel fine for a bit but then you start to feel really crook, and the venom proceeds with terrifying rapidity. Paralysis, vomiting, shitting yourself . . . so from fine to dead. It's that quick.'

Alan looked at the First Aid kit on the table. 'Those things are basically useless out here. So please, kid, always be careful. This is just a terrible tragedy. We will hear the lubras wailing all night.'

'Like Old Harry . . . they did that when he died,' said Lisa sadly.

'Yeah, just like that, like Old Harry when he passed on.'

'What will happen now, to Burnu's body?'

'I would say Billy will have a burial. The Aboriginal people honour and dispose of their dead in many different ways. Some sprinkle ochre over the body and then it's usually buried in the ground, sometimes with their possessions, such as stone tools or ornaments, probably Burnu's hat. Some tribes even make special clothes for their dead. We will have fires tonight near the grave, and maybe Billy will build a small earth mound marked by other things like bark from the surrounding trees or things from the earth. The place of burial can be where they happened to be camping at the time. So in that regard, Burnu was camping here. Means we will have him here always, and his spirit will be at Woori.'

'That makes me feel better. I want to have him here. Always. I will miss him so much,' said Lisa as she began to sob.

'Burnu had a full and wonderful life and raised a great son. He would not want to see you crying like this. Here,' he said soothingly as he passed her a mug of tea.

Zena came and sat down as Alan passed another cup to her.

'Thank you,' Zena said softly. 'I guess we wait until someone comes for us. I will just be out back. There are a few things flowering that I can take down.'

Alan just wanted to hold his wife and take away the grief.

'It won't be long, Zena. I would say just over an hour and we'll be back down there. I will leave it to Jack or Billy to make a speech. I'll just add my bit. I will miss the old bugger . . . I feel partly to blame. If I had not sent him up there to find old Artie, he would still be here.' The words choked Alan's throat.

'You can't say that, Alan. It could have been anyone. How many times have we encountered a snake over the years? Loads,' reminded Zena.

It was Kev who appeared at the back door, knocking softly as he removed his hat.

'Boss, da ceremony gunna git goin . . . . Jack tell me to come get ya,' said Kev.

'We're ready, Kev, just been sitting waiting for this. You go, we'll follow in the Land Rover.'

When they arrived, Lisa could see the tarpaulin containing Burnu's body. The crew and the lubras as well as the piccaninnies stood around a mound of earth. A stick was placed roughly in the mound, and Burnu's hat was on top. Lisa realised it was a freshly dug hole, which was to the rear of the black's camp. An open fire was burning with a few peppercorn trees scattered. From there, Burnu could look across the vast plains. Sorrow filled the air, and the lubras wailed softly and chanted. Some stood while others sat, visibly demonstrating their sadness.

Ningali stood with Binna, her arm held tightly around the old lady, who seemed as if she would collapse, the pain too much to bear. She saw the tears roll down their faces.

Billy stood with Kev and the other men, their camaraderie and feelings for the young man evident. Lisa stayed with Alan and Zena, her heart breaking. *Last year Harry; this year Burnu.*

Jack spoke, but the emotional strain at the loss of his friend showed on his face. He held his hat to his chest. 'We are here today for Burnu Garrett, a legend as an Australian Indigenous Stockman. One of the men who opened up the outback, Burnu was strong, fearless, stoic and most of all, kind. A proud man, respected by us white blokes and his people. He was always at one with the land. It is well known that the Aboriginal peoples gave us their stock routes, their knowledge and skills; Burnu did all this and more. Over the years we would sit at the night camps, swapping stories of the Dreamtime. He had me laughing till dawn some days with his funny sense of humour. He was also very spiritual, and none more than me have witnessed and experienced what he could do. His knowledge is not lost though as he has passed this through to Billy, his only son, and so the next generation takes up his wonderful pool of wisdom, custom and bush tradition. Burnu, you will be truly missed. You are part of our history, an amazing person, a wonderful Aboriginal stockman. We salute you.' Jack bowed briefly as if in a bush salute.

Alan stepped forward. 'Burnu, my old mate, we swapped many yarns over the years, and you will never be replaced. The work you did on Woori, we are so grateful, as you provided us with much knowledge about the land and working with the land. I know that most stations would admit that they could not have survived if it had not been for the Aboriginal knowledge and labour. I am one of those. My friend, thank you. The journey to your spiritual ancestors is before you.'

'Billy,' said Jack. 'Are you up for a few words, mate?'

Lisa's lips trembled. She could see and feel his pain.

Billy stepped forward. 'Me lucky to have Burnu as my father. He always fair and kind. Teach me lots of things about da earth. He always say da earth have a living spirit, and he see many things through Dreamtime. He work with dat spirit, spirit of da earth and da spirits of all da life forms. He teach me to understand da spirit of da animals, trees, rocks, water and all other life, seen and unseen. Dey come into da soul. He a great healer and draw da illness out of da body. He love da land, he was at one. My Burnu, my great teacher, my father. We have da ceremony here and send Burnu on his way.'

Some of the lubras brought their clapping sticks and began to click them, watching as Jack, Kev, Billy and Alan picked up the tarpaulin containing Burnu's body. The tarpaulin had been painted in ochre and roped to secure it, and big bunches of eucalypt had been pushed under the ropes. Everyone followed, the lubras clicking the clap sticks, as the body was lowered into the grave. Zena threw the flowers into the grave, and the lubras threw stones and bark. Billy took the hat off the stick and it went down into the grave too.

'Goodbye, old mate,' choked Cookie. 'Won't be the same.' He crossed his heart and looked up at the skies. 'Go join my mate Harry and have a yarn for me.'

Cookie had started the fire to the stove, and steaks, sausages and onions were thrown on the hot plate.

Lisa came to Billy's side. He looked down at her and smiled. 'It's alright, Grasshopper. We own our grief and share it, slowly healing. Burnu join da spirits. Come, we have to celebrate his life.'

He led her away from the grave site. Kev and Jack started to fill the hole in but left the large earth mound where Burnu's head lay. The lubras had gathered rocks and placed them around the grave and then threw the eucalypt branches on the top when the men had finished.

Ned's harmonica played softly, and Billy grabbed his didj. Some of the lubras were up on their feet and joined by Ningali, who led the foot stamping, swirling in the dirt to the sounds of the didj. Others remained seated, using their clap sticks and chanting. They cried in sorrow, sharing their grief. Binna sat on a chair, alone. A solitary figure, feeling the loss and pain of a great friend.

It continued well into the night, Lisa saying goodnight to Billy and leaving him to be with his people. 'See you in the morning, Billy. I am so sorry for your loss.' He watched her walk away with Alan and her aunt, but so wanted to feel her warmth on this long night.

As Lisa lay in bed, she could hear the wailing, the high piercing whines that subsided into moans. They would wail all night for the spirit leaving this earth. Sleep came over her, but all she had wanted to do was stay with Billy.

THIRTY-FIVE

LIFE GOES ON

It was still dark when Lisa decided to get out of bed and drive down to see Billy. She knew where his little tent was, not far from Burnu's grave and away from the other blacks' camp. He liked to see the stars, he said, and not be in the confines of a hot shed. She dressed quietly and grabbed the keys to the ute, quickly heading down the back stairs.

Alan rolled over when he heard the motor start. Zena stirred. 'Was that a motor, Alan?'

'Yes, it's Lisa. I heard her moving about. No doubt she is on her way to see Billy. Go back to sleep if you can, it's still way too early to get up. She will be okay, Zena.'

Lisa pulled up the ute well clear of the camp. She knew she would have to be quiet, so walking the rest of the way was the only solution. She could see Billy's tent under the bright moon and walked gingerly towards it. As she squatted down, she saw it was empty. Fear raced through her heart. Where could he be? She couldn't go traipsing around or she would wake everyone up, so she best head back.' *Billy, be safe.*

Lisa sat in the ute and waited for some time, hoping Billy would have noticed her drive in, but there was no trace of him, and as the sun peeped in the distance, she started the engine and headed home.

The light was on in the kitchen, and she saw Alan and Zena sitting at the table. 'Been somewhere, kid?' Alan piped up.

'I thought I would see how Billy was keeping, but he was nowhere to be seen. Waited down there until the sun started to come up, but nothing.'

'Probably out wandering. I am sure he's fine,' reassured Alan. 'Come on, get some breakfast and go about your business, you cannot change what has happened.'

'No, darling girl, they grieve in their own way. I'm going to call Des, to see how he's going, and also, we are heading into Walgett this Saturday, do you want to come?' asked Zena.

'Why Walgett?' queried Lisa.

'Pick up something for Mitch's wedding. The polite thing to do,' said Zena.

'No, I'm fine here. I'll keep busy and see what Billy is up to. What will you buy?'

'Not sure really, but as I said, it's the polite thing to do. We have known the family for many years.'

'I best get moving, see you girls later. Billy will be fine, Lisa, just give the bloke some space,' advised Alan.

When Alan got down to the sheds, Jack was waiting. 'All good?' asked Alan, pulling out a cigarette.

'All good, they have settled down. The wailing kept us all awake but Billy is nowhere to be seen, and Jed, his horse, is gone as well.'

'Shit! exclaimed Alan. 'Where do you think he's gone? He hasn't pissed off, has he?'

'Don't think so, Alan, although Kev said he was pretty upset, so he may just need a bit of time on his own. Probably sitting under a tree,' said Jack.

'What about his things, have you looked in his tent?' asked Alan, now concerned.

Alan stood up. 'Yep, mate, everything is still there, even his didj. He'll be back. Let's go, things to be done, and we are one man short.'

◊

Zena felt tired as she worked through the morning. Fitful sleep and the wailing had penetrated the night air. She would ring Des now for a chat. He had taken three months leave from work after Janine's death to contemplate his future, sorting out where he was going to live, Mark's schooling and Janine's affairs.

Des picked up quickly, and it was good to hear his voice. 'Hi Des, it's Zena, just calling to see how you are?'

'Yeah fine, Zena . . . all good. Things are settling down here. I must say the police have been terrific, got a lot more respect now for the boys in blue.'

'Yes, they are criticised terribly but when you need them or if something goes wrong, they seem to know what to do and say. Any plans re moving as yet?'

'No. I am just loathe to shift Mark out of his current school or send him to boarding school. Since Agnes' death, and then Janine's, the place is so quiet and settled. There's no angst under the roof anymore. It's sheer bliss, I have to tell you.'

'I understand about the schooling. I had wanted Lisa to continue, perhaps do twelve months at Abbotsleigh or perhaps Loreto at Normanhurst, but she has dug her heels in. Doesn't want to leave Woori. I just think had she gone on to one of those schools, she would have benefited greatly.'

Des laughed. 'She probably wants to follow in your footsteps, breeding horses and finding a nice country boy to marry. Mark was telling me about someone called Mitch.'

'He is way out of the picture now and marrying someone else.'

'Missed the boat then?' queried Des.

'No, not really, the boy got another girl pregnant and as it turns out, we are happy things sorted themselves that way. Lisa is fine about it,' said Zena.

'Zena, the adoption process you discussed many moons ago, we can probably let that be now. Save you legal fees. No need to proceed as it makes no sense. The girl is where she wants to be, she is happy and that is fine by me.'

'Thank you, Des. Lisa has covered a lot of ground. The past year has been one of great loss and change. With moving forward there is no doubt Lisa has an increased awareness of who she is and what she wants to do.'

'Your influence, Zena, certainly not mine, nor Agnes's. You have done a wonderful job. I am indebted to you,' said Des.

'Thanks, Des. Lisa has been an absolute delight. Let me know when you want to come up. It's heading towards October, so that means only twelve weeks until Christmas. As I said, you are both welcome to stay here.'

'Will think about it, Zena. I know Mark will say yes, but we'll discuss it and see what his plans are, as well as mine. Time off from the salt mines has done me good. You can actually get clarity of mind when you stop working,' informed Des.

'You're right. I couldn't imagine teaching again, and you have been challenged with your losses. It's great knowing you can just relax and listen to your head and your heart, Des.'

'Well, give my regards to Lisa and Alan. We will let you know what we're doing. Take care, Zena.'

'Thanks, Des. Talk soon.'

She hoped they both came but somehow Zena had the feeling Des just wanted his own space. Heaven knows that was a luxury previously.

Zena had no sooner put the phone down when Lisa came charging up the stairs. 'Aunty,' she sang out frantically, flinging the back door open. 'It's Billy!'

'What about Billy?' asked Zena. 'Oh God, what has happened now!'

'He's gone. He's gone and so is Jed.' She flopped onto a chair, her head on her arms, sobbing.

'It's alright, Lisa. He has probably just taken off for some peace or a little time out. He'll be back soon, I am sure of it,' soothed Zena as she stroked the back of her niece's head.

'He wouldn't just up and leave without saying goodbye, would he?'

'Of that, I am sure. He's just grieving, Lisa, so try to stay calm. Alan will tell us all about what has happened when he comes in this afternoon. Just keep busy. I'm positive Billy will show up, and soon. How did you find out?'

Lisa lifted her head. 'I saw Kev getting some morning tea and asked if he had seen Billy. He told me that he left very early.'

'Well, there is your answer . . . he has just gone for a ride. Take it easy, Lisa. Billy has a job to do here and losing his father, who was also a great mate, will be tough. Go wash your face and I'll make you some lunch.'

Two days passed and there was still no sign of Billy. Lisa was frantic, and no amount of pacifying from Alan or Zena would make her settle. It was now the end of the week. 'We should get a group together and go looking . . . we should do something,' Lisa said over dinner. 'He may have been bitten by a snake, like Burnu, and lying dead somewhere or injured.'

'We will do no such thing. Billy is a big boy and all of his possessions are still in his tent. Alan has just zipped it up. Try and keep calm, you are not doing yourself any favours. You know he thinks the world of you. Burnu's death would not change that, Lisa.'

'Nope, kid. We all know what great affection he has for you. Sometimes the pressure is just too great after you lose someone in death. It is so final. He will ride in on that big black horse and things will resume as if he never left,' added Alan. 'So calm down.'

'Don't forget we are heading to Walgett tomorrow, so we will be gone for most of the day. Do you need anything or want anything in particular, Lisa?'

'No. I'm good, Aunty. But please, as you drive, can you keep a watch.'

'We will, but Billy will be back shortly. Why don't you get an early night. You obviously have not been sleeping these past few nights and it's showing,' said Zena.

'Yeah, Lisa, bags under your eyes, not looking too cute with those. An early night and stop worrying,' repeated Alan.

Lisa sighed. She wanted to laugh at what Alan had just said but an absolute despondency pervaded her thoughts. 'See you both in the morning then.' She left for her bedroom.

◊

'Where do you think the boy has gone, Alan?'

'Who knows, he could be anywhere. I would say he's just grieving and when he's ready he'll be back. Let's turn in. I'll get up early and head down to the sheds and see if the horse is there, maybe bring her some good news.'

'I hope so, darling,' said Zena. 'We don't need any more bad news.'

As dawn broke, Alan threw his clothes on and grabbed a juice on the way out. He was worried, he had to admit, and sleep was restless for him. He knew how close the boy had been to Burnu. Alan bent down to kiss Zena, who slept peacefully. 'Won't be long, my wife.'

Alan cranked the motorbike up and took off, the sunrise just building. Best time of the day as the richness of the golden rays spread across the plains. The lights were on in the kitchen, and Cookie was humming as Alan pulled up.

'I know what you're gunna ask me . . . and nope, not a single sign. We are all a bit worried now, Alan,' said Cookie.

'I'm heading off into Walgett with Zena. Want to get away and be back early. Can you let Jack know if there is no sign of the boy by tonight, we are all out looking for him.'

'Good plan, boss, I'll spread the word.' Cookie pulled off strips of bacon, throwing them into the sizzling pan.

When Alan got back to the house, Zena and Lisa were up. 'Any sign?' asked Lisa.

'Nope . . . but I told Cookie to let Jack know if there is no sign by the time we get back later this afternoon, we are out looking.'

'Oh thank you, Alan,' said Lisa as she ran towards him and wrapped her arms around his waist. 'We have to find him,' she pleaded.

'Yes I know, Lisa, now please do us a favour while we are gone. Exercise Topi and Noir, check the mares, do your chores and lastly, stop worrying, just keep yourself busy.' He ruffled her hair.

'Have this toast, Alan, your favourite, Cocky's Joy, and perhaps we can go. If we leave now, then we'll have some light at the end of the day,' said Zena.

'Sure thing. Quick shower and shave. You get yourself organised. I won't take long,' said Alan, wolfing down the thickly buttered toast.

Lisa took off in the ute and tried to keep busy, but every thought followed Billy as she scanned wherever she drove. *Where are you? Please come home.*

When she was up with the pigs, they managed to knock their feeder over. 'Oh yuck, that means I have to go in there and walk through all that pig shit and the mud. I'll stink. You guys smell so bad.' Lisa did give a small laugh. 'But you always look so happy in the mud,' she chuckled as she sat there staring at them. What is that saying? *Like a pig in mud. Now I know where that comes from.*

Lisa tentatively opened the gate to their pen and walked across, slipping and sliding to upright the heavy feed stand, the pigs following her and milling around. As she turned, one of the pigs was directly behind her, and she lost her balance, tripping and landing flat on her face.

'Eww, Christ no! Arghhh,' she squealed in disgust. She sat momentarily, her hands in the air. 'Ugggh,' she wailed, the pigs oblivious to her angst, the stench overwhelming. The sound of hooves approaching in the distance made her cock her ear. She scrambled to her feet and stood facing the direction of the horse. There was no mistaking the rider or the horse as they galloped towards her. 'Billy!' she screamed.

As Billy pulled up and looked at Lisa, he started to laugh, and then he couldn't stop. 'Grasshopper, you are supposed to feed dem pigs not get in their pen and play with dem.'

Lisa soon joined in, the belly laughs ripping through the air. It was a pure release of tension at the joy of seeing Billy. She looked down at herself in despair, an exasperated look on her face.

'Oh Billy, I have been so worried, everyone has. Where have you been?'

'Bin clearing my head. Good now. Come on, Grasshopper, you need get cleaned up. You stink,' laughed Billy, dismounting Jed.

'There are some hessian bags in the back of the ute, Billy. Can you please put them over the driver's seat, so I don't get pig shit all over the seat?'

'Let's get you out of dere,' said Billy as he opened the gate for her. As he did so, his boots squelched in the slop.

'Not good feeling,' said Billy. 'Me stink too now.'

Lisa so wanted to throw her arms around him but all she could do was laugh as she walked like a penguin to the ute.

'Can you grab the jerry can in the back there for me and just splash it over my hands and arms please. I'm covered in the stuff.'

'I follow you and meet you at da gates,' said Billy, still amused as she drove off to the homestead.

Lisa stood waiting for him. 'I put Jed around in da home yards,' stated Billy as he walked the big black horse to get a feed.

'I have to get under the shower and now!' yelled Lisa as she kicked off her boots and headed to the Mud Room near the laundry to remove her clothes.

'Billy need to take off da boots and jeans too.'

'Well, come in here, I can wash everything,' instructed Lisa. 'Oh, wait just a minute, Billy. I will go first.' Lisa stripped off to her underpants and threw a towel around her.

'I'm heading to the shower, Billy,' said Lisa as she headed to the bathroom. 'Just take off your jeans and throw them in the tub. There are cookies on the table, and can you switch the kettle on, please. Everyone is in Walgett.'

The smell was nauseating as he stepped inside the Mud Room, removing his jeans and throwing the legs of the jeans under the tap, rinsing them as best he could, the stench permeating the room. He stood naked from the waist down.

'Lisa,' he called out, but she could not hear him. He stepped towards where he could hear the water running. 'Lisa,' he said louder.

'Oh yes . . . yes, Billy, sorry.' She partly opened the shower door to listen.

'Lisa.' He walked closer to the bathroom. 'I washed da bottom half of my jeans, got dat pig smell on me.'

Billy leaned against the wall. The vision of her lovely nakedness through the shower door was intoxicating. His heart beat
rapidly as he listened to the water running and knew he was
losing the battle to control himself.

There was silence. Lisa knew he was just near. Her senses
were exploding with passion and a deep longing that only he
was able to fill.

Billy took a deep breath, a raw, wanting feeling overwhelming his being. His body responded with a surge of desire as he
boldly stood at the bathroom door.

'Lisa,' he said hoarsely, the steam filling the room. He could
see her naked body through the glass, and he stepped into the
room as she slowly turned to face him. His muscular frame
filled the door as she stared into his amazing chocolate eyes,
ablaze with the giddy rush of lust and love. Her hand came out
slowly and pushed the door open as Billy tore off his shirt and
threw it to the ground. Her breath caught at the sight of his
wide muscular chest as he stepped into the shower.

He moved behind her slowly, letting the water splash over
him, and then lowered his head to her neck, breathing her in.
Lisa turned around and tipped her head back, then he leaned
down to kiss her lips.

A tiny voice whispered a warning but she had now lost control. The ache to be with him, to feel him, overrode any desire
to stop or push him away.

Lisa clung to him as his hands roamed her body, and she returned his hot kisses, long and lingering, savouring his mouth
wanting him with the same lust he felt for her. The warm water
felt good running over their bodies, and then his arm came out
to turn the taps off. They stood staring, both completely
aroused, their bodies wet yet burning.

'I've missed you, Billy. I was so frightened.' Lisa's voice was
shaky and soft.

Billy brought his finger to her lips. 'I here now, Lisa. I safe. No need worry, but I can leave now. I don't wanna hurt you or cause trouble.'

'No, I need you, I want you to stay. I was lost and nearly out of my mind when you were gone. I know this is what I want . . . and it's you . . . for always.'

Billy reached for a towel and began to press her body gently, moving down her breasts and along her arms, savouring the beautiful young woman who stood before him. He moved slowly down her legs, kissing her thighs, working his way until he stood up again. With a groan, Lisa leaned into him, meeting his lips, tasting him and feeling his arousal.

Billy picked her up, and Lisa pointed to an open door down the hallway. 'That's my room, Billy,' she said as he walked towards the room, placing her gently down on the bed.

He lay next to her, his body on fire. 'Are you sure, Lisa?' He looked at her, inwardly groaning. Lisa extended her arms to him. 'Yes,' she whispered. 'I'm sure.'

He smoothed the wet hair from her face; she was glistening as he moved to lay on top of her, her legs curling around his waist. Her body was warm beneath his, a combination of firm muscle surrounding her soft feminine curves. His fingers caressed her bare forearms, the sensual touch increasing her pulse. He was enjoying the sensations of her body and the way it moulded to his. Their mouths grew hungrier and Lisa closed her eyes as Billy explored her body, consuming her completely.

Lisa felt his erection ease inside of her, but instead of terror and fear, the warmth of his touch made her body tingle with both need and happiness. She bit his neck gently, the hunger in her screaming to be filled, arching beneath him, her body on the verge of shattering into a thousand pieces. The pleasure was almost unbearable, and then Billy's body shook, and he flung his head back, shouting her name.

Lisa kissed him tenderly, her hands roaming over his body, a feathery touch tracing his jawline and down to his neck. He loved that she was curious about his body. He rolled himself off her and lightly brushed her lips as he threw his leg over her hip. She slid easily into his embrace, and the simple kiss reinforced what she already knew. She never wanted to be without Billy.

'You have awakened my soul, Billy, and you bring peace to my mind. You make me feel safe and treasured.' Lisa was drinking in his healing powers, the strength he gave to her.

He took her in his arms and kissed her. 'Never tell me to leave. Billy bin in love with you since da very beginning.'

They held each other tightly, neither wanting to move. Lisa looked at the clock on her bedside table. 'Billy, we had better get dressed.' She watched him as he stretched, his beautiful body. He pulled her quickly to him, and kissed her hungrily, still feeling the fire in his blood and how warm her body felt beneath him.

'Do you realise you called me Lisa, and not Grasshopper,' she teased.

'Grasshopper,' Billy said cheekily as he ducked the moving towel.

'Come on, we have to shower and get dressed. My aunt and uncle will be on their way home.'

◇

After Billy left, Lisa lay on the bed, feeling the emotion she had experienced with him. There had been no fear as she openly received him. A loveliness she had never conceived of had travelled through her body as pure spirit, and everything that had perplexed her about sexuality had been explained. *I have come a long way.* Lisa touched the necklace Billy had given her many moons ago, and her heart exploded with love.

THIRTY-SIX

YOUNG LOVERS

Billy got down to the sheds late afternoon. The crew gathered around and clearly, they were happy to see him return.

Jack strode over as Billy dismounted. 'Good to see you, son. Cleared your head out there?'

'Yes, boss. Me good to go, feel orright now,' said Billy.

'Great, we have all missed you, and are very pleased to have you back. The little lady up there at the homestead has been down here every day asking if we had seen you. Fretting away,' boomed Jack.

Billy smiled inwardly, hoping they wouldn't notice the dampness of his jeans. He looked down at his boots, the mud still present. 'She be orright, boss. I see her tomorrow or mebbe she come down late this afternoon. Do I have to do anything for you now, boss?'

'No, Billy, just get your stuff ready for an early start tomorrow,' said Jack.

Billy took Jed to the makeshift pen he had made not far from his tent. There was good shade underneath the peppercorn tree. He walked towards Binna and Ningali and made his way to their tent.

'Glad to see you both still here,' said Billy, squatting down.

'Ha Billy. You take off, but me . . . me likem stay,' said Ningali, her eyes lighting up.

'Think Kev has something to do with dat, Binna?' asked Billy.

The old lady smiled. 'Yeah, plenty,' said Binna as Ningali started to cackle.

'Where you bin?' asked Binna. 'You cause da worry, but me know you orright. Da little one, she bin hoppin' up and down.'

Billy laughed. 'Just ridin' and campin', like to look at da stars, quiet out dere, and big moon at night. Make heart feel good.'

'Proper true,' replied Binna.

'I see you again soon.' Billy stood up and walked Jed to his pen.

'You right, Binna, dat boy never leave here . . . me pleased she no go with dat big white rooster,' said Ningali.

As the Land Rover pulled up at the last gate, Alan pointed to the figure in the distance leading the black horse.

'Look, Zena, bugger me, that's Billy. The boy is back. Yahoo, that will make our girl smile. Matter of fact, it makes me smile. Thank God. I just had this feeling he was going off on Walkabout or some ritual.'

Zena breathed a sigh of relief. 'It makes me happy too, Alan. I can't wait to tell her the news; she'll be down here like a rocket. Will we go over and say hello?'

'No, let's get up to the homestead, pack these things away and give her the good news. Maybe we can all come down together and see how the boy is faring. I was worried, have to admit,' revealed Alan.

'Good idea, Alan. Can't wait to see her face.'

Lisa was in the Mud Room dunking her jeans when she heard the Land Rover pull up and footsteps on the back stairs.

'Hello, Aunty, I'm in here. Had a bit of an accident,' said Lisa.

Alan put their groceries on the kitchen table. 'What accident, kid?'

They both popped their head into the Mud Room and saw Lisa scrubbing her jeans.

'What happened? What is that awful smell, Lisa?' queried Zena.

'A stupid sow got behind me. I didn't see her, and as I stepped back and turned, I toppled over, right into the pig shit,' groaned Lisa.

Alan started to laugh and Zena joined in. 'Wish I had seen that, kid,' chuckled Alan.

'Yes, joke is on me, and I am still trying to get the stink out of my clothes.'

'I'm sure that's enough, Lisa. Your hands are red, obviously from scrubbing. Just throw them out on the line in the sun. But we have some good news for you.'

'What's that?'

'Just on the way in, we saw Billy. He was leading Jed to the paddock he keeps him in.'

Lisa did not know whether to feign surprise. She had never lied to her aunt and she was not going to start now.

'Beat you to that news. When I was sitting in the pig pen, he headed towards me. Saw the ute and helped me up. I was so glad to see him, Aunty . . . just so glad.' Lisa's face was beaming.

'Why don't you ask him to come up for dinner with Jack,' suggested Zena.

'Oh, that would be wonderful,' she squealed. 'What time?'

'Say about six, time enough to do a good roast,' replied Zena.

'Come on, you can get on the back of the bike with me. I want to say hello to Billy and see how the day has gone with Jack. Throw those duds on the line, and I'll see you at the gates.'

'Good woman,' Alan said as he kissed his wife.

Lisa hung on to Alan's waist as he zoomed towards the shed. She loved the bike and loved the speed; it was almost as good as riding Topi. She was truly elated as the day just got better and better.

As Lisa hopped off the bike, she walked to Binna's tent. 'Hello, Binna . . . it's me, Lisa. I have come to sit with you.'

The old lady smiled. 'Good to hear da little one, you like da bird singing now.'

'Yes, Binna, I am very happy now, the happiest I have ever been.'

'Dat good, me pleased. Long time since we shared a story.'

'Yes, I know, Binna, but I would love to sit with you again.'

'Mebbe tomorrow, or you can tell me when you got da time. You just come down, little one.'

'I will, Binna. Thank you. I hear the lubras are looking after you well though.'

'Yeah, my people, dey come to help me alla time. Dat Ningali, she busy with dat Kev but she still bin lookin out for me.'

Lisa reached for her hand. 'I will maybe see you tomorrow, Binna.' As she got to her feet, three of the camp lubras were coming her way.

'We lookin' after Binna, no worry, treatem real good,' said the older of the women. Lisa thanked her, and then saw Alan talking to Jack so wandered towards them.

'Here she is now,' said Alan. 'We'll see you at six, mate.'

'Be there, Alan. I'll let Billy know,' said Jack.

'Right to go, Lisa?' asked Alan.

'Sure am.' Lisa hopped on the back of the bike.

Jack watched the bike speed off. 'Dinner at the big house. Looking forward to it. Have to find Billy. What a treat with Zena's cooking.'

◊

Lisa sat patiently at the table, watching her aunt prepare dinner, when she heard a car pull up.

'They're here,' said Lisa, her voice filled with excitement.

'Yes, sweetheart, I can hear,' said Zena as she basted the roast with its juices and put the pan back in the oven.

'Knock knock,' boomed Jack's big voice.

'Come in, Jack,' said Alan as he greeted the two of them at the door.

'Billy, good to see you back. All been very worried,' he admitted as he shook his hand.

'Yes, boss, all good now.' Billy took off his black hat. His eyes met Lisa's gaze and they smiled, a knowing glance full of their afternoon together.

'You wash yourself off, Grasshopper, all that pig shit?' laughed Billy.

'Ha ha, very funny, yes I did,' she laughed, her eyes expressing delight.

'Let's go out onto the verandah, got a few nibblies out there. I'll get us some beers. Lisa, can you make Zena a gin and tonic?' asked Alan.

'Sure thing.' Billy watched her intently. A slow smile spread over his face and spilled into his eyes. He was feeling her all over again.

When Lisa came back onto the verandah, her face flashed with a brilliant light as she met Billy's gaze. Zena picked up on their playfulness. Billy's eyes twinkled with humour but there was something else, and it wasn't the pig shit episode.

'Lisa, dear, can you help me serve, please. We won't be a moment. Alan, if you could shift to the dining room?'

'Sure, this way gentlemen. Zena has us at the fancy eating table.'

As Zena carved the roast, she turned to Lisa. 'You were speaking to each other across the room with your eyes. Is there something I should know about?'

'No, Aunty. I think he is still amused by the sight of me sitting in the pig pen.'

'Just take the potatoes out and the vegetables and I'll join you,' said Zena. *Not so sure that is all of it, Lisa. Your heart is telling a story, a story only you and Billy know.* But she let it go.

'Here we are, gentlemen . . . it's good to have you at our table, and Billy, it's wonderful you have come back. The loss and sadness we all felt with Burnu, and then with you, but I will speak no more of that. Please everyone, help yourselves.'

'Good tucker, Zena,' said Jack as he shovelled the potatoes onto his plate.

Zena watched Lisa and Billy, who sat opposite each other. *Yes, definitely more to it; they have that special look when two people are one.*

'We are heading into town this Saturday, Jack. We caught up with John the Publican of the RSL when we were in Walgett today, so we confirmed that we would be available to play. Just a local dance, really. You are welcome to come,' invited Zena.

'That sounds good, Zena. Been a while since I put my dancing shoes on. Billy can look after the joint, what about that?'

'Yes, boss, orright,' smiled Billy.

'Oh, but I thought Lisa and Billy would like to come too,' said Zena.

'We would love to, Aunty, but they won't let Billy in, and I am still too young,' reminded Lisa.

'True,' agreed Alan.

'Well, maybe, they have something good playing at the pictures?' added Zena.

'No, Aunty, I don't want to do that. They were really rude to Billy the last time, and he had to sit in a different section, the darky section as that horrible woman said, and it's so full of smoke. It smells awful and then it stays on your clothes and in your hair.'

'Just the three of us then it seems,' smiled Alan. 'Don't like me smoking, kid?'

Lisa laughed. 'Your smoking doesn't bother me, Alan. It's when I'm stuck in a room with no windows and there are 100 people smoking. I might as well be puffing up too.'

Billy smiled. His thoughts were running wild. Alone again on Saturday. He looked at Lisa across the table and knew she was thinking the same.

◊

Saturday arrived, and Alan loaded their equipment into the Zephyr. 'See you later Lisa, be good,' said Alan.

Zena came down the stairs. 'Yes, I second that, Lisa. Be good. We should be back around midnight. Don't forget to lock the Tack Room and the back door.'

'No problem, Aunty, have a great time. Hope Jack gets a few dances with the single ladies.'

'And the married ones too, you know, kid . . . they are not dead yet. Hope to wear old Jack out,' said Alan.

'Lisa...' Zena paused.

'Yes?'

'Oh . . . it doesn't matter. See you when we get home.' Zena got into the Zephyr. *Why tell her something or ask about something that may not even exist, but at the pit of her stomach she knew. Billy.*

◊

Billy waited until the Zephyr headed through the gate and then waited another hour. He set off for the homestead, his heart pounding like the sound of Jed's hooves on the road.

Lisa met him at the door, a thousand kisses covering his face, as he held her tightly. Billy kissed her eagerly, pressing her against the wall, moving against her slowly while intensifying his kiss. It was like lightning running through her body, and she breathed his scent as deeply as she could.

'Grasshopper, I couldn't wait to be with you again.' A slow, warm smile spread across his face.

Lisa took Billy's hand, and they walked to her bedroom. As she closed the door, he pressed her closer, his smooth, soft lips seeking her mouth. He wanted to take her every way he could imagine, giving her pleasure until they were exhausted.

He eased into her body at first, and they made love hungrily. Lisa cried out, her body convulsing with intense pleasure. It was if their bodies were created to be together, and as they lay naked and entwined, Billy whispered, 'I love you, Lisa. Always be my grasshopper.'

They lay watching the night, and the pale glow of the moon shone through the uncurtained window. Lisa sought his lips, and he traced her neck with kisses. She moaned. *No words can tell you the ecstasy of my bliss, Billy. I am so happy.*

Lisa dozed peacefully in his arms. He looked at her beautiful face in the moonlight and felt the pain of leaving her again. Another hour passed as he kissed her softly. He cocked his ear to the dogs barking madly outside. Maybe a fox. She did not stir when he left her bed. He pulled the sheet up over her body and disappeared into the night, back to his tent before someone noticed him missing.

◊

Billy rolled over in his tent when he saw the car headlights and heard Jack call out goodnight. Jack was coming across the paddock, heading for the men's sleeping quarters. The moon grew higher and Billy could still feel and taste his girl as he lay in the dark.

◊

As Zena came up the back stairs and put the key in the door, it sprang open. 'Alan, I didn't have to turn it. That's odd. I told Lisa to lock it before she went to sleep.'

'Probably forgot,' said Alan. 'Bloody dogs are barking though.'

'At us, silly. They are barking at us. I'll go look in on her,' said Zena, a pang of fear unsettling her. As she opened the door gently, her niece slept peacefully.

'All good?' asked Alan as Zena came into the bedroom.

'Yes, darling, seems to be. What a good night. I think we wore Jack out. The single ladies were impressed. I didn't think he would come home with us.'

'No, Jack is very mindful of his job and what has to be done, but I'm sure he took a few phone numbers. I'm beat, let's hit the sack,' yawned Alan.

When Zena switched the light out, she did not tell Alan about the two water glasses on the sink. Someone had joined her niece. *No guesses who, Lisa.* She smiled. Her niece deserved some pure happiness, and she had seemed to find this with Billy. Almost a grown woman now, Zena would never begrudge her this, especially not after everything Lisa had been through before.

◊

He sat quietly, well away from the bore and the dogs, but he had no doubts the wind carried his smell. *Bark, bark, stupid fucking dogs.* He had watched as Lisa in her bedroom, the big picture windows clearly showing the two figures embracing before she hit the lights. *Bastard Billy, he's getting some. Gunna get some of that too. I'll come for you, Lisa, take you away with me. Far away.*

THIRTY-SEVEN

PREJUDICE

Alan chatted about the previous night and 'Jack the lady killer'.

'I can't imagine him dancing,' giggled Lisa.

'Sure was, wore his damn boots out, Lisa. You missed a good night,' said Alan. 'Had all the single women after him.'

Lisa just shook her head. It would have been a sight to see, that's for sure. 'I want to head into Walgett today and go for my 'L' plates. I rang a few days ago and booked myself in for the test. Billy said he would drive me in, so we would have to leave here just after lunch. Can Jack spare him?'

'Sure, kid, and that's a big step. You've certainly had enough practice in that paddock basher. The ute's gear stick has never recovered. You can take the Land Rover to drive in if you like.'

Lisa beamed. 'We'll be careful, Alan, thank you.' She jumped up and hugged him as he headed out to work for the day.

A silence filled the kitchen momentarily, before Zena came and sat down next to Lisa.

'We have had this conversation before, darling girl. I have told you many times, never hesitate to tell me if anything is bothering you or you need an ear . . . well, just to discuss anything.'

'Yes I know, Aunty,' Lisa answered nervously.

'Last night, the door was not locked, and I noticed two glasses on the sink.'

Lisa hesitated. 'It was Billy. He was here, and we had a lovely night.'

'Is there anything you need to tell me or want to tell me about the night?'

'No, Aunty, it's all good. He makes me feel so many things, and I just want to stay with him, be with him.'

'What does he make you feel?' queried Zena.

'Safe, loved. His spirit touches my soul, and it surrounds me . . . us. I can't explain it, and that sounds weird, but I just can't get enough of him. I never feel any fear with him and I never feel he is overpowering me or wanting something I don't want to freely give. We just seem to fit . . . and I don't care about the colour of his skin.'

'I know those feelings, most women do, and especially those who find their soulmate. I had and still have those feelings for Alan. Do you think you are in love? Dare I ask that?' probed Zena gently.

Lisa paused. 'Aunty, I think I am in love. It feels deep, but it's also playful. We're friends, remember, we were friends first but now I want more of him.'

'I understand that, but you are still young, Lisa, and for that matter, so is he. Do you think you are ready for a relationship that includes intimacy after all you've been through? Are you really ready? The physical side of a relationship can be intense at the beginning, and I feel for you, in that your innocence in that regard was taken away. You suffered abuse and trauma before you could experience what comes naturally. That's why I'm worried. You may get into a situation that you cannot deal with emotionally.'

'I know, Aunty. I am aware of our age but I have experienced so much more than other girls at my age, and Billy is an old soul. I think I will always have those horrible images of the superintendent and Lenny, and I do wake in fear some nights. Yes, the nightmares also come, but I control my mind now, I control the things I think and want. I know I will never ever forget those awful experiences, and they are always present, but with Billy it's so different. I trust him and I trust my feelings for him. We know what we want.'

'Lisa, you know the road will be hard for both of you, a white girl and a black boy and yes, I know his skin is lighter because of his white mother, but it will still be very tough. You will have to contend with so much racism,' warned Zena.

'I would fight for him, and I know he would do the same for me. I want to be with Billy . . . always.' Lisa's voice trailed off.

Zena took her niece's hands and kissed her forehead. 'Alan and I want you to be happy. If Billy makes you this happy, then so be it. Now, no more words, you have to get going if you're to be out of here by noon.'

'Thank you, Aunty. Please know that your support, well from both of you, means the world to me.'

'Lisa, we are here, always. Never doubt that.'

◊

The day grew hotter as Lisa worked feverishly to finish her chores. Billy was meeting her at the compound gates at noon as her driving test was at 3.00 p.m. Time for a quick shower, read of the road rules on the way in to Walgett, grab a sandwich somewhere and hopefully she would get her 'L' plates.

When she came inside, the house was empty. The note said, *Riding Noir to Woodside, dropping off gift for Mitch. Z.*

Lisa raced for the shower. As she was drying herself, there was a loud banging on the back door.

'It's me. Billy.'

'Come in and sit down, just have to get some clothes on.'

Lisa threw on her lemon dress and pinned up her long black hair. When she came out, Billy sat waiting patiently. 'You look beautiful, Lisa, like yellow wildflowers.'

'You just say all the right things!' She kissed his lips. 'And you look gorgeous too. I have always loved that black hat on you, Billy.'

'Come on, we can't be late.' She grabbed his hand and they scrambled down the back stairs, climbed into the Land Rover and sped off.

'Feel good driving da Land Rover,' grinned Billy.

'Suits you. Hey, I thought we could grab a sandwich before the test, sort of have lunch together. What do you think?'

'Yep, Billy is hungry, sound good.'

'We should be in Walgett around 1.30 p.m., so it gives us a little time.'

Lisa read the driving questions all the way into Walgett. Billy opened the gates as he didn't want her to get red dust over the yellow dress. By the time they got there, they needed something cool to wash the dust away.

Billy parked the Land Rover not far from the motor registry, and they walked to a milk bar.

'Here, you sit and I'll go order,' said Lisa.

The waitress brought their lunch out to their table and glanced at Billy. Her face said it all.

'Anything wrong?' asked Lisa.

'Err . . . no dear, enjoy your lunch.' She hurried back inside.

Lisa could feel the waitress's eyes still staring at them from inside the café. She overheard their conversation, her blood boiling. *Here we go. Why don't they mind their own business!*

'Hey, Ernie, get a load of that. That white girl, sitting with that darky,' said Narelle, the waitress, pointing at them, without bothering to hide it.

'He's not that dark, Narelle. A creamy with a bit of the tar brush in him, that's for sure, but she is bloody gorgeous. Strange-looking pair. Probably off a property around here. Mind your business now, Narelle, and get back to work.'

'Don't look right if you ask me,' she scoffed. 'Darky mixing with a white girl.'

Billy grabbed the handbook and started to read to Lisa, but as he got to the third question, Lisa noticed Mitch walking towards them. She began to shift nervously in her seat.

'What's up?' asked Billy.

'Nothing really, but umm . . . Don't turn around. Mitch, our neighbour's son, is walking this way.'

'No worry, Lisa, it be orright.' He gently reached for her hand.

'Well, what do we have here?' drawled Mitch as he noticed Billy's hand holding Lisa's. 'You like the white stuff, hey Billy?' he almost hissed.

'Mitch, that is so not necessary, and Billy is my friend. Anyway, I heard your good news about getting married to Tess. Congratulations,' Lisa said cheerily, trying to change the subject.

'It easily could have been you, little lady, but you wouldn't open your legs,' Mitch snarled.

Lisa looked shocked, and Billy stood up to face him, a good inch taller. He could easily take him on.

'No more. You speak no more,' warned Billy.

'Fuck off, you stupid black bastard! I will say what I want to her.' His big hand swiped the silver milkshake containers off the table, rolling them into the gutter. His eyes glared with hatred.

Lisa could see Billy's fists clenching in and out. 'Gutless boong, won't even take a swipe, hiding behind that white pussy.'

Billy suddenly grabbed Mitch's shirt and flung him hard to the ground.

'Hey, you two, knock it off!' bellowed Ernie, racing out of the shop to confront them.

He glared at Mitch. 'Seen it all, mate, watching from inside, now get on your way before I call the cops. These two were do-ing nothing.' He stepped into the gutter, picking up the milkshake containers. 'Go on, get!'

Mitch rolled to his feet. 'Bitch,' he growled at Lisa. 'You,' he said pointing at Billy. 'Wait till I see you on your own, darky, no skirt to hide behind.'

Billy made a move towards Mitch, but Lisa pulled him back. 'No, Billy. Let's just find a quiet place to sit and read.' She turned to the shopkeeper. 'Thank you. I'm so sorry for the commotion.'

'Saw it all, don't have to apologise. I know that bloke. Mitchell Walker. Mr Big Shot. Should ring his bloody parents,' he muttered as he headed inside the café.

'Let's go, Billy. There's a park just around the corner. We can sit there for thirty minutes or so.'

Lisa took his hand, but Billy tried to pull away. Lisa held on to his hand, steadfast. 'No, you are not doing that. I am proud to walk with you and proud you are holding my hand.'

Billy smiled down at her. 'Beautiful Grasshopper.'

After going over the handbook, Lisa looked at her watch. 'It's a ten-minute walk from here, we best go now, Billy.' As they walked, they encountered numerous disapproving stares. It only served to make Lisa hold Billy's hand tighter.

'Are you nervous?' asked Billy.

'A little, but I've been driving for so long now that I feel fair-ly confident. Anyway, it's just the 'L' plate test. I told the lady on the phone that I had been driving for some time with my family on our property.'

'I'll wait here for you.' He watched Lisa go inside and sit the test. Billy smiled as he saw the look on her face. *My grasshopper is concentrating.*

He sat on a short brick wall, outside the registry, pulled his big hat over his eyes and waited. His thoughts were of Burnu, now with the Sky Gods.

'Hey you, sleeping on the job?' teased Lisa as she walked towards him, proudly holding up her 'L' plates. 'I passed with flying colours. I can now officially drive on the road with these 'L' plates!'

'Did you tell them you bin driving but no gear box left,' Billy laughed.

'Of course not. Come on, let's go home.' Lisa took his hand.

When they reached Woori, it was early evening. 'Come in, Billy,' Lisa invited as he parked the Land Rover. Billy was hesitant. 'Come on, silly, it's okay.' They walked up to the homestead, hand in hand.

'Hello, you two, no guesses by the smile on your face,' said Zena as she rose from the kitchen table.

'Here are my official "L" plates.' Lisa held them up proudly.

Zena hugged her niece. 'I am sure it was a shoe-in with all the driving you do around here, but I am delighted for you. You are an official driver. Next step, your real licence. Billy, can I get you anything? A cup of tea, water?'

'No, missus, all good. I be on my way to see if Jack needs anything.' Billy tipped his hat and was gone.

'Did you want me to ask him for dinner?' asked Zena.

'That would have been nice, Aunty,' said Lisa shyly.

'Next time, darling girl.'

'We ran into Mitch in town. Not good. In fact, it was awful.'

'Why, what happened? I rode Noir over to Woodside and dropped the wedding gift off to Kate. I just assumed Mitch was out working when I didn't see him. But Kate and I did have a lovely chat, and I feel so sorry for her. She is not happy about what has happened, and Tess Dunphy is certainly not her choice for a daughter-in-law.'

'Mitch was really rude to us, calling Billy a darky and a boong, but this lovely old man in the café came out and told Mitch to get lost. It was just before my 'L-plate' test, so it was a bit unnerving. The café owner said he knew Mitch and should call his parents.'

'Oh dear, this is not good, Lisa. Kate said he had been like a bear with a sore head and hoped fatherhood would make him settle. But from my experience, children do not help those in a loveless marriage to find love. It's either there or it isn't. Theirs is a forced situation, and Mitch being so headstrong would not like to lose power over any situation. Not using birth control is like playing with fire.'

Lisa swallowed hard. She had made love with Billy on two occasions now. It had crossed her mind about protection or telling Billy to withdraw, but she had wanted him so badly, she hadn't wanted to stop.

'Why don't you go wash up and help me with dinner. Alan won't be far behind, and I'm sure the news of what happened today with Mitch will certainly fire him up.'

'There he is now.' The sound of the motorbike came to a stop. 'Ladies,' Alan greeted them as he stepped into the kitchen.

'Did you pass, Lisa?' he asked as Zena handed him a beer. 'Here, pull up a chair and tell me all about it.'

'I had this lovely lady who gave me the eye test. I told her I'd been driving for over twelve months and wanted to sit for my official licence, not the 'L' plates, but she said no, this is mandatory. But I will certainly go back and get my official licence soon.'

'Well done, proud of you.' He took another gulp of the cold beer. 'Hardly touches the sides, Zena. Bloody hot out there today.'

'Tell Alan the other news,' prompted Zena.

'I wanted to forget that part,' sighed Lisa.

'No, Alan needs to know this. You understand that we keep no secrets.'

'Just someone tell me, please,' said Alan, rolling his eyes.

'We ran into Mitch, and he was really rude to Billy, wanted to start a fight. It was the shopkeeper of the milk bar who told Mitch to get lost.'

'What did Billy do?' asked Alan.

'He was ready for a fight but really restrained himself,' said Lisa.

'Lucky for Mitch. Billy is bigger and stronger, and from what the other blacks tell me, he can fight. Look what happened to Jimmy.' Alan looked at Zena. 'Do you want me to call Dave, sort of a man-to-man chat?'

'I think just let sleeping dogs lie. I dropped off that gift to Kate, and she is quite despondent about the wedding and the future daughter-in-law. Hearing this will only sadden my friend further. Nothing eventuated, Alan, and Billy kept his cool, so I think Mitch will have his hands full in the weeks to come. And anyway, he may think you will call Dave, which will keep him on his toes.'

'What do you think, Lisa?' queried Alan.

'Just angry words, and as you said, no harm done. But it was insulting for Billy.'

'I'll see how the boy feels in the morning. Only a few more days of shearing, and we are done, season over. By the way, Kev said Binna told Ningali she wants to head back to the river. Misses her old humpy and no doubt the old girl is thinking about the lubras moving on at the end of the season. Ningali will lose her bloke as well. Seem to get on like a house on fire, those two. Very chummy.'

Lisa's face crumpled. She had given it no thought, happy in her own world. Alan and Zena both saw the visible change in her face.

'Lisa, you know this happens every year. Billy will leave. Kev will leave, and they all find work someplace else . . . they all do,' reminded Alan.

She felt tears welling in her eyes. 'I know, Alan, but I just don't want him to go. I want him to stay, here at Woori.' Her head bowed.

Zena looked at Alan and shook her head. 'Let's get dinner organised. Tomorrow is another day. I'll go and see Binna tomorrow.'

Sleep was fitful, and Lisa tossed and turned. Her mind was filled to capacity thinking of ways to keep Billy at Woori. She would do everything in her power to have him stay or she would go with him. *I would leave Woori for him.*

THIRTY-EIGHT

TRAGEDY

The next morning, Lisa followed Alan down to the sheds. There were two people she wanted to see. Billy and Binna. As the shed came into view, Jack was talking to Kev and Billy, and they waved at the approaching ute.

'Morning,' Alan called out as they pulled up next to the men.

'Heard the little lady is nearly a qualified driver now,' smiled Jack. 'L plates?'

'Yep, that's right.' Lisa beamed as she looked at Billy. *Could he read her thoughts? That she wanted to just be near him?* Their eyes locked until Jack's voice boomed out, 'Attention, please.'

'Jack is so like a general from an army, Alan. No wonder everyone listens when he says attention. I'm off to see if Binna is awake,' chuckled Lisa as she got out of the ute, heading to the black's camp. As she came around the corner, Ningali was sitting with Binna in the dirt, swatting flies.

'Hey, here is da little one,' said Ningali, cackling and pointing.

'Hello, Ningali, hello Binna. Good morning to you both. I'm so happy to see you. May I sit down?'

'Yes, little one, you come next to Binna,' said Ningali, patting the ground.

'I heard you want to go home . . . or back down to the river. Aunty will come and see you today, probably early.'

'Yeah, season nearly finished, and we gotta get back to our place. These peoples, dey all move on, so we got to go too,' said Ningali.

'That makes me so sad. It's lovely having you both here, so close. You don't have to go,' said Lisa.

'Yeah, Binna, she feel more in her own spirit country out at da river. Me likem too,' added Ningali.

You got da sadness?' asked Binna.

'Yes, you are all going. I want to keep you all here,' admitted Lisa.

Ningali laughed. 'You connected to us, like we connected to da land. Da land is our mother. Da land is our food and our spirit.' She picked up the red dirt and let it run through her hand.

'Billy, da boy, he go too?' queried Binna.

'Yes, I am afraid so,' said Lisa, eyes downcast.

'Dis why da heart feel sad. Boy make you happy. He live in your mind, your body, dey all connected, mind, body, spirit, land. Spirit so strong, it stay, even after death. Dat spirit return to the Dreamtime. Billy, his spirit with you, always.'

'Thanks, Binna. Well, I'll be on my way, so the next time I see you it might be down at your usual spot, with your fires swirling into the sky. As I said, Aunty will be down sometime this morning.' Lisa hugged them goodbye.

◊

'She got da big sadness, Binna,' said Ningali.

Binna nodded. 'She need Billy to protect her. I feel da danger still here . . . in her circle.'

Zena arrived a short time later in the Land Rover. 'Hello, my friends. I have heard your news. When would you like to go?'

'We go now, no waiting, we ready to go back,' said Binna.

'Not much to pack then, I gather?' said Zena, a smile crossing her face.

'No, missus, just da new things you givem to us,' said Ningali as she clutched the different dresses under one arm.

'Well, let's get into the Land Rover. Here Binna, I'll help you up.' Zena and Ningali assisted the elderly lady to her feet and over to the Land Rover.

'Can you get up there, Binna, it's a little high,' added Zena, but Ningali came behind and pushed Binna from her rear end.

Zena started to laugh. 'Not the most grateful entrance, Ningali. Let's head up to the homestead. I have a hamper ready. It will give you a head start on the food side. I have a jerry can full of water, which I'll leave with you also.'

'Boss lady, always kind heart,' smiled Binna.

As she drove, a sadness came over Zena. Binna looked so frail and so vulnerable, and it worried Zena, especially since nothing had eventuated with finding the person who had caused the damage and the theft around the place. She felt it was safer for them to stay at Woori, but Binna wanted to get on her way. After picking up the hamper at home, they headed to the river. There was no talking them out of the decision.

When Alan and Lisa came in for lunch, it was later than usual.

'Saw you take the ladies out early this morning,' commented Alan.

'Yes, there was no changing Binna's mind. She wanted to get on her way, but I gave them a few things in terms of food and water. Ningali will get down to the river for their maugro and the other bush tucker she seems to find. But there was almost an inner peace with Binna. I mean, she always has that aura but there was . . . like this spirit around her, like she was in a different place. Maybe she was just concentrating on going back to a place she loves. She told Ningali it was good to be with her people, but it was too many people.'

'Probably the shearers and piccaninnies and all the dogs, I guess. Lots of noise for the old girl, so she would have missed the quietness of her own little camp. It's certainly not that quiet down here at times,' agreed Alan.

'I'm going to ride out tomorrow to see them, Lisa. Do you want to ride Topi?' asked Zena. 'Be good to get out together on the horses.'

'Oh, that would be wonderful. Great idea, Aunty. He needs the exercise and it would be good to see that they have settled back into their spot by the river. It's been ages since we rode together.'

'Very good, we can leave here around noon. Time enough for you to get your chores done.'

'When will you have time to sit with me and go over the final end of season do? It's a cat's whisker away. Two days to go,' reminded Alan. 'Time just flies, you wait all year, they come and then they go. Goodbye September.'

'Yes, I know, but I sort of have a mental list of what Cookie and I can knock up. It's all under control, Alan,' she smiled.

Lisa winced. She did not want to hear this discussion. 'If you'll excuse me,' she said and took off down the stairs, Dougy barking at her feet.

'Taking it hard?' Alan asked Zena.

'Yes, too hard. There is no doubt in my mind Alan, and she even admitted it. They are . . . in love.'

'Shit. When did she tell you this?'

'The other day, and I did go over the intimacy side of things, and whether she was ready,' added Zena.

'What will we do? They are both young,' Alan mused.

'Nothing we can do, the heart wants what the heart wants. Lisa wants him to stay, and she wants to continue their relationship . . . on all levels. Said she is ready,' confirmed Zena.

'Well, I have to admit, an extra hand or two would make a difference, not getting any younger, and I do like the boy. It would mean we could get away when we wanted to for a break and also concentrate on breeding good stock horses.'

'Could be an option, darling husband, and it would make her so very happy,' smiled Zena.

'Let me think about it. Right now, I just want to get the season over, just one more day. It's October next week and before you know it, it's Christmas. The other thing that keeps rolling around in my head is the fact that we have not caught whoever is loitering about here.'

'Yes, I have to agree on that score. I am very concerned about those two ladies out there,' stated Zena.

'I'm sure they'll be alright. They know the land, they are part of the land, and it's just two women who really have nothing to offer in terms of money, valuables, even youth. You know what I mean, and besides, they have been out there on their own for a long time, without any problems,' reassured Alan.

'Yes, I know, but we have never had the trouble we are having now. It's different, so I worry,' said Zena firmly. She felt in her bones that trouble was ahead.

◊

Dinner that night was a much quieter affair. Billy's imminent departure and the season coming to an end for another twelve months was playing on Lisa's mind. 'Tired?' asked Alan. 'Haven't said a great deal tonight.'

'I just want to be with my thoughts. I'm a little sad it's all ending,' replied Lisa. 'I think I'll turn in, Aunty.'

'Understand, kid, but you know it's the same as last year,' said Alan. 'Always seasonal. You have a good morning planned with the ride out to see your ladies. Now that's something to look forward to. I wouldn't mind doing it myself.'

Lisa brightened slightly. 'Yes, I am looking forward to that, Alan. I'll see you both in the morning.'

After showering, Lisa headed to her bed, slipped off the robe and stretched, standing naked before the large mirror. She touched her breasts and could feel Billy's body moving over her. She closed her eyes and thought of the pleasure he gave her.

◊

The face in the dark watched her intently. She was more beautiful naked than he could have ever imagined. He sat crouched on the other side of the fence, watching through the big picture windows. He began to masturbate as Lisa slowly moved around the room touching herself. As he ejaculated, he lost his balance and bounced against the electric fence, which gave him a jolt. *Fuck . . . fuck!* He started to run, the dogs barking incessantly.

◊

Lisa's head snapped around. The dogs were howling. She grabbed her robe. *What was that? It sounded like something moving about.* She came running out to Alan and Zena, but they were already on their feet.

'Dogs are going mad,' grimaced Alan as he grabbed his torch and a 22 rifle. 'I thought I heard something too,' said Lisa.

'Both of you stay here. I'll just do a wander around the perimeter. The fences are electrified at night, so if anyone is hanging about, they would not be in the compound. Just Dougy, but he is going nuts too,' said Alan.

'Are you sure it wasn't Dougy scratching or something, Lisa?' asked Zena.

'I don't know, I heard something . . . maybe it was Dougy, but there was something definitely out there,' said Lisa, shaking.

'Please draw your curtains before you go to bed, Lisa, and maybe it's a good idea to get into that practice. You can't see out when the light is on but anyone out there sure as hell can see you. I know you love them open to catch the first and last light of the day, but for now, let's not stand in open windows at night, particularly if you don't have much on,' advised Zena.

'Let's sit tight for the minute. Alan won't be long, he's just checking the perimeter of the house. Thank goodness for the dogs all going crazy. It alerts us as well but it's such a racket, it could wake the dead.'

They saw Alan's torch as he came up the back stairs. 'Nothing, and I shone it out over the bore and across the plains. Zilcho. Could have been a fox or a rabbit. Who knows? Let's go to bed. I'll put the dogs out for the scent tomorrow.'

The room seemed so dark with the curtains drawn. Lisa would miss the beautiful rays that shone through her room in the morning. She kicked the bed covers off. Two days to go, one for work and one for the end of season farewell. An ache and sense of acute loneliness started to penetrate her heart. The grief when Billy finally did go again would be unbearable.

◊

He travelled the road quickly. He knew he had to get back to the river before dawn, find food and recharge. Shearing season was about to end, and he had to make his move quickly and during the day. Things were not locked in the daytime, the fences were off, and people were coming and going and were largely down at the sheds. He would grab a horse behind the

Tack Room, take the girl and go. They would never find them once he got going. But for now, he needed food and water. He was starving as he moved under the cover of darkness down towards the river.

◇

Lisa threw her legs over the bed and pulled on her jeans and top, walking over to the curtains and drawing them apart. She wandered out into the kitchen and slumped down into a chair. Food was the last thing she wanted. Alan and Zena's voices were not too far away, obviously near the Tack Room saddling up the horses.

Her aunt and uncle both came up the back stairs together. 'Morning sweetheart, we were just looking at the mares. Pregnant and getting fat. Be exciting times when the foals start dropping. I have thrown the saddles and bridles over the yard rails, so all set to go. It's a glorious morning. Alan is going to do your chores so we can have an early start.'

'Yeah, kid, you owe me one,' he grinned as he sat facing his niece.

Lisa smiled. 'I certainly do, Alan. The pigs are all yours.'

'Now for brekkie and then I'll leave you girls to it. Come on, Lisa, no fiddling with your food,' admonished Zena as she put down fresh cut fruit and cereals.

'I'm not that hungry,' grumbled Lisa. 'I'd rather get on the road.'

'Come on, kid, the boy is still here and maybe, who knows, for a bit longer,' said Alan teasingly.

'What?' Lisa's eyes flew open. 'What do you mean, Alan?'

'Eat your breakfast, and I'll let Zena fill you in on the details.'

Lisa looked over at her aunt and met her eyes.

Zena nodded. 'It's good news, Lisa. I think you'll like what we've come up with.'

A thousand things went through Lisa's mind, and she felt her excitement growing. 'Can you tell me now?' Her curiosity was peaking.

'Nope!' Alan looked amused.

'On the way out, Lisa, so eat up and we can get going,' added her aunt.

With breakfast over, Lisa followed Zena out, and they grabbed their saddles for Noir and Topi. 'Tell me now, Aunty, please! I can't stand it.'

'Okay, because I know you're not going to give me a minute's peace,' said Zena. 'We thought we would offer Billy a permanent position here on the property and—'

Zena had not even finished her sentence when Lisa squealed and threw her arms around her neck.

'Steady, my girl, you're scaring the horses,' Zena laughed.

'Oh, Aunty, is this for real? Really truly?'

'Yes, really truly, but you are forgetting one thing.'

Lisa looked puzzled. 'What's that?'

'Billy has to say yes, and he may not want to. His kind are somewhat nomadic and like to move from station to station. It really is entirely his decision and whatever he decides, you are going to have to accept that, Lisa.'

'He won't say no, Aunty. I know he won't, he will want to stay here with us.' Lisa was adamant.

'Well, let's not be too sure. From my experience, always expect the unexpected. Now come on, give those mares a biscuit of hay. I will just duck in and get some water for us and then we can get going,' said Zena.

It was a wonderful feeling as they rode out to see the ladies. 'You can take that grin off your face,' Zena laughed. 'It may become a permanent fixture, looking like Gus the clown.'

'Can't help myself,' Lisa shouted. 'It's just so . . . so wonder-ful!'

'Settle now, we have an hour's ride in front of us before the ladies' camp comes into view. A nice steady canter now.'

They rode on until finally the camp came into view, and Lisa smiled when she saw the smoke curling into the air. A familiar and welcoming sight.

'No movement up there, probably sleeping,' observed Zena as they pulled near a tree. 'Just tether them, Lisa,' instructed Zena as she made her way up to the camp. Lisa quickly scamp-ered behind her.

As she got to the entrance of the humpy, Zena let out a blood-curdling scream. 'Dear God, what has happened here!' Binna lay on her side, her frail body smashed, the dry, caked blood evident from a deep gash to her forehead. Ningali was face down a bit further into the scrub. 'No, no, no!' Zena wailed.

Lisa shrieked and fell to her knees, shaking all over. 'Quick, get some water, Lisa. Use their jerry can, it's just over there.' It was laying on its side but there was still some water left. Zena ripped off the bandana that she wore under her hat and gave it to Lisa. 'Wet it . . . find one of their tin cups and pour the wa-ter into it.'

The tears were streaming down Lisa's face, and she trembled at the sight of her two best friends covered in blood and not moving. Zena gulped as she turned her old friend over. There was no sign of life as she felt for Binna's pulse. The gash on her forehead was very deep from a brutal blow, and there was blood under her fingernails. She cradled the frail old lady, holding her tightly, wishing breath back into her lifeless body. But it was not to be. Zena lay her down on the earth gently, brushing the fine white hair, now matted with blood, out of her eyes. Her heart heaved with pain. She grabbed one of the dresses she had made, closed Binna's eyes and placed the dress over her face, sobs racking her body.

Lisa sat there in shock, holding the tin cup, her heart breaking as the tears coursed down her face at the loss of her friend. As Zena walked towards Ningali, she heard a soft moan.

'Ningali, it's me, Zena. Ningali, I am going to turn you over slowly.' Zena squatted down and put both hands across Ningali's body, turning her slowly so she was face up. As she did so, Ningali cried out in pain.

'Boss lady, pain here, da bad pain,' she moaned, pointing to her ribs. One of her eyes was black and severely swollen, such that the eye had closed, and her lip was badly split open, the blood forming in bubbles as she tried to speak.

'Don't speak, Ningali. I would say you have broken ribs. Lisa, bring the water here please and dunk the bandana in cold water so I can place it on her forehead.'

Zena half lifted her and manoeuvred her body so that Ningali's head rested in her lap. 'Who did this, Ningali? Who did this?'

'We bin sitting here in da cool night air, we finish your good tucker and fall asleep. Me hear da noise, mebbe a possum, but then he come, he come out of da darkness. I say who dat, you go leave dis place, but he stood lookin. He bad man, lookem real bad. Me stand and say go from dis place but he laugh, so I pushed him and next thing I feel da punches and dat alla remember.'

Ningali suddenly looked at Binna and then began to wail. She realised with Binna's face covered that her mother had now joined the spirits.

The three of them sat for some time, Ningali wailing and chanting, even with her split lip. Lisa and Zena were sobbing over the loss of their beautiful and gentle friend, Binna. It was clear as Zena looked around, all of the food had been taken from the large hamper she had given the women. The basket had been thrown to one side. Whoever had been here was looking for food.

'Ningali, my dear friend, we have to move. Lisa, be strong now, we have to keep our heads. We cannot do anything for Binna now. Throw some more wood on the fire so nothing comes in here.'

Lisa stood up, wiped her eyes and gathered sticks and wood, throwing them on top of the smouldering fire. 'Now, give me a hand with Ningali, and we will get her onto Noir. Take the saddle off for me. We'll have to ride bare back to Woori. I can swing up behind her. It's going to be painful for her, but there is nothing I can do about it. I have to get her home.'

They managed to get Ningali up onto Noir as she cried out in pain. 'Steady now, Lisa, keep focused, we have a job to do and we will be moving slower,' her aunt cautioned as they headed for home.

When they got to the compound gates, Ningali had almost passed out from the pain. Alan's ute was parked at the gate, and Zena breathed a sigh of relief. 'Quick, Lisa, run inside. Alan should be there. He can help me lift her down. It's alright, Ningali, you are safe. We are here at Woori.'

Lisa sprinted up the back steps, screaming Alan's name. 'For God's sake, kid, what's the matter?' he yelled as he met her at the back door.

'Come quick, Alan, it's Ningali, we have to help her.' Lisa pleaded, her voice cracked from sobbing. She stood at the top of the stairs, paralysed.

Alan shot out, tearing down the back stairs and running for the compound gates. 'Fuck, what's happened?' he roared at Zena as he saw the limp Ningali, her back leaning into his wife.

'I'll explain when we get her into the house. Binna is dead, and I am sure Ningali has broken ribs,' said Zena, her voice choking on sobs. Alan lifted Ningali gently off Noir, but she cried out in pain.

'Lisa, get the door open,' Alan shouted as he carried her inside.

'Just lay her down in the spare bedroom, Alan. I'll get some clean cloths to wipe her face and give her something for her pain,' said Zena.

'What can I do?' asked Lisa, still in shock.

'Put the horses away, kid. Give them a feed and see what you can do to help your aunt,' advised Alan. 'I have to call Michael Raby and the Royal Flying Doctor.'

Zena returned to the bedroom and began to wipe Ningali's face. 'Here, take this, it will take the pain away.' Zena passed her the two white pills with some water. 'Take these, Ningali, it will help with the pain,' she repeated. 'Just rest. Alan is calling the Royal Flying Doctor. I know you have your bush medicine but we just want to make sure nothing else is broken. Rest, we have things under control.' *Anything but control; it's bloody chaos.* The vision of Binna clouded her mind.

Zena walked into the office once she had ensured that Ningali was comfortable and resting, and sat down opposite Alan, her tears falling freely. It felt like Woori was imploding.

When Alan got off the phone, he pulled his wife to her feet and held her tightly. 'My darling wife, breathe, there's nothing you can do but try to reassure and console Ningali and Lisa.' He kissed her forehead. She trembled in his arms, and Alan felt the anger rise in his body. *I am coming for you. I know you are close. You are dead when I find you,* his mind roared.

Zena wiped her eyes and pulled back. 'What did Michael say?'

'He's on his way. I'll go out with Kev in the ute to collect Binna's body and bring it back here. I can't bloody well believe it. Two funerals and both healers, respected elders . . . our wonderful friends,' choked Alan.

Zena nodded. 'Such a great loss, Alan. First Burnu and now Binna. What about the Royal Flying Doctor? Ningali's face looks terrible, and I'm worried she has concussion.'

'Let them sort it out when they get here, which should be late this afternoon. I'm going to make you both a cup of tea. Come on.' Alan took her hand.

Lisa sat staring out the window, the tears running down her face. Zena went to her and cradled her head. 'It's alright, Lisa. You just let it out. This is a terrible tragedy and our grief will be significant. Our beautiful friend was taken in such a terrible way.'

'What were her injuries?' asked Alan.

'She had a very deep gash to her forehead, but I doubt a hand would have caused that damage. It must have been some sort of a blunt object, maybe a stick, and there was blood under her fingernails,' revealed Zena.

'Yeah, if the gash was deep, it was obviously some sort of implement he bashed her with, but with the blood under her fingernails, she has tried to either defend herself or she has attacked the person, trying to scratch them,' said Alan, his voice full of anger. 'That would be a bloody joke anyway, as if that poor old girl could attack anyone with success or defend herself. The bastard must have laughed at that.'

'Whoever it was, they were looking for food. The big cane basket, the hamper I made up, was empty,' added Zena.

'So, someone is on the run, starving and desperate. Saw their fire and went there. When Michael arrives, we take the dogs, all of them, as we did before. I meant to do that this morning, run them around the fence line, but it just slipped my mind with all the talk of Billy in the kitchen this morning.'

'Lisa, why don't you go and lie down for a while. Alan and I will deal with this. It's a terrible shock to us all but you just rest for now.'

Lisa slowly rose from her chair. 'It's like this horrible nightmare, Aunty,' she sobbed as she left for her room.

Alan looked at his wife, whose face was filled with sadness. 'Not a bad idea if you did the same.'

'No, I'll stay here and just keep looking in on Ningali,' said Zena, blowing her nose.

'Okay . . . I'll head down to the sheds and let Kev and Billy know. Going to be a sombre affair tomorrow at the end-of-season do. It will now be a bloody wake. But you know, there is a positive in this.'

Zena shook her head and slumped her shoulders. 'What on earth could that be, Alan?' she said, staring at him in disbelief.

'Binna had a few days here with her people, and she took enjoyment from that, mixing with the lubras and piccaninnies, but also too, sitting with Burnu. They had a fair few talk talks. May be a good thing to bury them close together. Spiritual elders and good friends.'

Zena sighed. 'I never thought of it like that . . . and yes, that would be a lovely idea. But first things first. We have to get her body back here, and I have to speak to Ningali. But most of all, Alan, we have to catch the vile person who did this.'

Alan gritted his teeth. 'I am hoping for that very soon. He is still here, and I am still waiting. We'll get him. See you in a bit.' He pulled his wife to him in a tight embrace and raced out to the ute. It was time to get moving.

◊

Alan pulled the ute up and waved Kev over. He took the news badly and became visibly upset. Kev wanted to come up to the house to see Ningali immediately.

'She's resting, Kev, and needs it. I'll take you up there later this evening.'

'Me gunna kill dat bastard, me getta da gun, shoot him plenty orright.'

'Yes, Kev, but we have to catch him first. We're getting the dogs, all of them, and heading to the river. Just waiting for the Royal Flying Doctor and the coppers. Whoever did this was on his way to the river, maybe, but he had obviously seen their camp.'

Alan stayed with Kev until he saw the plane fly over. No sooner had he said that, he noticed the police vehicle pulling up at the last entrance gate.

Alan waved to Michael, gesturing with his finger to head to the homestead.

'I have to head off now, Kev, but I'll be back down to get you. Can you let Billy know when he gets back in from mustering.'

'Sure boss, me tellem Billy.'

No doubt Zena had heard the plane as Alan drove to the homestead. *Be there in a jiffy, my darling.*

◇

Zena rushed out to meet the pilot and smiled when she saw it was Derek, the same pilot who flew Old Harry out. 'Hello, Derek,' Zena greeted him warmly.

'Hi Zena, good to see you. What have you got for me?'

'It was an assault on the Aboriginal woman who is lying down inside. Her name is Ningali, and she has been a friend for many years. I think she maybe has a concussion and broken ribs, but you can figure that one out. We also have an elderly lady who is deceased, the mother of Ningali. Alan will head down in the ute shortly to bring her body back.'

'This is very bad news . . . shocking,' commiserated Derek. 'Do we know who did it or why?'

'My guess is they were looking for food and he or they came across the ladies' camp. The girls may have been defensive, and this is the end result. Ningali is lying down, but she may be able to give us some more information after resting.'

'I'll follow you then.' They headed inside. Lisa was up as Derek came inside.

'Oh, hello, I remember you. I'm Lisa,' she greeted as she extended her hand.

'Now, how can I forget such a lovely young lady,' Derek smiled warmly. 'Just going to take a look at Ningali.'

'Down this way, Derek, just follow me,' instructed Zena. 'I had best sit with you; she may not like a white man with her alone.'

'Sure thing, Zena,' agreed Derek.

Lisa felt the anger building in her. Another stinking person who violates and causes pain. Another stinking person who beats women. She looked up when she heard Alan's ute. They had better catch the monster who did this.

THIRTY-NINE

A SOMBRE AFFAIR

Alan waited for Police Chief Michael Raby at the compound gates. They shook hands and looked at each other gravely.

'More drama and problems, Alan?' asked Michael.

'Yeah, mate, much worse. As I said, the old girl, Binna, is dead, and Ningali is lucky she did not follow the same fate. Come inside. Derek the Royal Flying Doctor is here.' They both came up the stairs and sat down in the kitchen.

Lisa was sitting at the table, her face still white with shock. 'Hey, kid,' said Alan softly as the men came through the door.

'The good doctor underway already?'

'Yes, it's the same man who came for Harry,' said Lisa.

'Derek? That is good news. Top bloke. We just sit and wait then and see what he has to say.' Alan drummed his fingers in agitation on the table.

'When he's done, we'll head out to get Binna's body,' said Alan.

'Does Ningali remember anything? Did she give a description of the attacker?' enquired Michael.

'Did she say anything, Lisa?' Alan directed the question to her.

'No . . . nothing, but she was in a lot of pain. We were just focused on getting her here. She started wailing when she saw Binna.'

'Well, hopefully when she comes around, she may remember something. Often people can recall events when they get some consciousness back,' said Michael. 'Clarity can return after the incident but that is up to the mind.'

Zena came around the corner with Derek. 'Oh hello, Michael, lovely to see you, but not under these circumstances.' Her voice was filled with sadness. 'This is Derek, from the RFD.'

'Nice to meet you, Derek. Yes, tragic circumstances,' said Michael. 'Do you think it's the same person, Alan, that has been lurking about?'

'I would say so, Michael. I'd like to get my hands on him. This is not a woman's work.'

Michael nodded. 'Definitely male. Is Ningali up to talking?'

'Derek, what do you think?' asked Zena, expressing her concern.

'Look, yes, she's okay. She may have concussion. I'd say she took a couple of punches to the head and face from the assailant probably belting her around, and then a king hit, which knocked her out cold. My standard tests indicate possible fracture to the ribs. The eye and lips will heal. She just needs rest and ice packs for the ribs.'

'Too early to speak to her, Derek?' ventured Alan.

'No, I'd say not. You can have a go, Michael. I'll wait here with Alan,' said Derek.

'I had best go in with you, Michael,' said Zena. 'Just this way.'

Zena had fluffed up some cushions behind Ningali, who looked a sorry sight. She had taken a severe beating.

'Ningali, this is Michael Raby, the policeman from Walgett Station. He wants to ask a few questions. Are you up to it, my friend?'

'Hard to talk, boss lady, but me gonna try.' Her voice was barely a whisper.

'Maybe just nod your head, Ningali, as I ask the questions. That might make it easier,' advised Michael, taking out his note pad and pen.

'Was it a male?'

Ningali nodded and croaked, 'Black male.'

'Was he on foot?'

'Yes, no horse, boss.'

'Tall?'

'Yeah, he da tall one, mean, and he had da one eye. He want da food and me try to stop him.'

'Oh God!' Zena let out a gasp.

'Do you know who this is, Zena?'

'Yes, it's Jimmy! He's worked here for a few seasons. He has a foul temper but Jack, our manager, kept everything under control. He was working up north on a big station with Billy, who happens to be here working this season, but he pulled a knife on Billy when they were up there, so Billy thumped him. The punch must have connected heavily as we heard Jimmy lost his eye. It has to be him. Alan will just die when he hears this news, so will everyone else. How could he do such a thing!' Zena was shaking with rage.

'Rest up, Ningali. You did good. We are all just outside.' Zena closed the door, leaving her friend to rest in peace.

'How did you go?' asked Alan.

'One eye, tall, wanted food,' choked Zena.

'It's Jimmy! That little bastard!' thundered Alan.

'Oh no, why is he here? Has he been doing all these things around here?' cried Lisa, terror and fear striking at her heart.

'Why . . . why would he want to do all these awful things? You have always been good to him, Aunty.'

'Lost his fucking marbles, that's why, kid,' Alan fumed.

'Right then, as we have some sort of identification, we need to collect the body that is out there, and I need to make a report,' said Michael.

'You boys go, then. I'll talk to Ningali about the burial and suggest what you said, Alan. I really like that thought, laying Binna to rest next to Burnu,' said Zena, tearfully.

'I'll go collect Kev. The three of us will fit in the front bench seat, Michael. We'll pick you up in about ten minutes. Just need a quick chat to the crew. I'll get Billy to dig the grave with Jack,' said Alan.

'We'll see you when you get back then,' said Zena. 'Derek will check on Ningali periodically. There's no doubt that you have a bed here, Derek. Please stay and have some dinner, and you can get an early start in the morning, but it's up to you.'

'Thanks for the offer, Zena, but after I identify the body and provide a death certificate, I have to head back to base. You never know who needs us out here.'

'Yes, of course. I'll put the kettle on, and we can sit and wait. They will be about two hours, I guess,' acknowledged Zena.

◊

When Alan got back down to the sheds, the crew had gathered. Billy paced agitatedly while Alan addressed Jack. 'We need to prepare a grave, another bloody grave, Jack. Binna has been murdered, and we need to send her to the Big Sky to travel to her ancestors. Kev and I will head out to their camp with Michael, the copper from Walgett Station. He's up at the house waiting for us. We need to bring back Binna's body.'

'Dreadful news, Alan. I just can't believe it. Where's Ninga-li?' asked Jack 'We all took a shine to her.'

'Yeah, she's a cheeky bugger. Been badly beaten, and she's resting up at the house. Took a couple of clouts to the face and ribs. Probably thought he had killed her too. We've just had the flying doctor tend to her.'

'Who did this, Alan?' asked Jack.

He took a deep breath. 'Ningali gave a description, Tall, black and one eye.'

Billy's eyes distorted with fury. 'Jimmy! I get dat Jimmy. I get him dis time. Bastard!'

'Not before me, brudder. I killem that fella,' raged Kev.

'Settle down now, both of you. You will do no such thing. I would say Jimmy is down by that river somewhere, but right now, we have to bury another person who was dear to us, and in the most dignified way. She was a spiritual elder and never was there a better person who walked the earth. First things first.' Alan stared the men down.

Billy's eyes were downcast but inside he was seething with anger. He had known Binna and Ningali since he could re-member, and he would make Jimmy pay for what he'd done to them.

'Billy, I'll leave you and Jack to the grave. Get those lubras organised. You may need some ochre. It has to be a special cer-emony, one befitting a spiritual elder of the land.'

'Where's Lisa?' Billy's voice rising with concern. He knew how much she loved Binna.

'Safe, mate,' replied Jack. 'Up at the house with Zena and Ningali. Derek the Royal Flying Doctor is up there too.'

Alan interrupted. 'I know this is a terrible time for all of us, but please get on with your job here, and I will see you when I get back. Come on, Kev. We'll let the dogs off when we get back to the house and pick up Michael,' said Alan. 'But we have to go and collect Binna from their camp. I can't leave her out there any longer,' he choked.

They headed back to the homestead, and Kev crossed the bore, letting off the hunting dogs. Alan unleashed the ones around the compound. 'Kev,' Alan called out, 'Go around the perimeter and let Bear off, the Cross-Rottweiler. He's my best hunting dog. Let him sniff around. Someone was outside looking into the big windows last night.'

'Sure thing, boss,' said Kev. The big Rotty was powerful and could bring down a 100 kilogram boar with no effort. He also had an extraordinary sense of smell. Kev watched him race around the fence, and he stopped, directly opposite the big picture window. He did not move but kept scratching and sniffing, his tail wagging in recognition of finding something.

'Onto somethin, hey boy. You keepem dat smell, gunna find dat smell someplace soon,' said Kev.

Alan grabbed Michael Raby and as they drove off, the dogs raced with them, barking at each other and chasing the ute.

'Boss, dat Bear dog, he pickem up da smell. He scratchin' and diggin,' said Kev.

'Which part of the fence, Kev?'

'Dat big window, lookem over da bore and da plains.'

Alan cursed. 'Lisa's room. She said she heard something there last night, probably that bastard crouching in the dark. Thank Christ I had the fences on.'

As they reached the ladies' humpy, they could see smoke was still weaving up into the sky. They jumped out of the ute to walk over to the dead woman's body. The dogs were running and barking madly. Alan grabbed Bear by the collar. 'Come on up here, boy.'

Sadness filled the atmosphere. Alan looked at the elderly lady and saw Zena had covered her face with the bright dress she had made for her. His gut knotted.

'Kev, get the tarp,' he instructed softly as he let Bear off, who covered the area sniffing and wagging his tail. 'Pick it up, Bear, pick it up.' The big dog followed a trail down the gentle slope and then started to run towards the river, the other dogs following.

'Yeah, good boy, you are onto it,' Alan said as he whistled him back.

Kev pointed to the ground. 'I see da footprints, boss, and dat bloody dog, he gone and pick up da scent. Dat bad man, he heading dat way boss, same direction as dat Bear was running. Me go to find him. Shoot him proper.'

'No, you won't, or you'll end up in jail. No bloody good to me then, Kev. Stay put!' ordered Alan.

'Come on and give me a hand to wrap Binna up. Gently now, mate.' They laid her down on the tarp. Michael put gloves on as he started to inspect the area.

'Signs of a struggle, Alan, things scattered around, and it looks as if Binna had a go at him too. The blood under her fingernails indicates scratch marks, and the gash on her forehead is from something not human, to cause it to be so deep. Very brave for one so frail, for him it would have been like swatting a fly,' commiserated Michael as he looked around.

'This is where Ningali must have lay. Look at the old blood all over these gum leaves. But she put up a struggle as well by the scuff marks here in the dust,' observed Michael.

'Wait . . . over here.' Michael pointed as he bent down to pick up a thick broken limb of a tree. 'Blood all over the end of this, and I would say this is what he struck Binna with.' He placed the tree limb in a large plastic bag.

They wrapped up Binna's body in the tarp and carried her down to the ute, placing her in the back.

'We'll head back now, bury Binna tomorrow and have our end-of-season send-off, which is looking more like a wake. Then we'll get back out here with the dogs. I will hunt the bastard down,' growled Alan.

◊

Jimmy heard the dogs in the distance and sprang to his feet, cocking his ear. They were moving away. He would sleep now and take off for the homestead in the night to reach it by morning. He lay in the dark and felt the space where his eye had been. *You take my life away, Billy. Now I take her and then you. Come for her . . . I be waiting. Destroy you.*

◊

'Here they are now, Derek, that's the ute, and I can hear the dogs. Hard to miss with that many barking. Lisa, can you give Kev a hand to get them back under the leash.'

'Yes, Aunty.' She wandered out slowly. Her heart ached, knowing her dear friend's body lay cold in the back of the ute. Derek was already at the ute.

'Where do you want to do this, Derek?' asked Alan.

'I just need a flat bench or something like that,' replied Derek.

'Kev, just head to the Tack Room, that building you can see there with the horse yards attached to it. There's a small room off to the left from the main saddles and bridles area, and you'll find a work bench. I'll clear the stuff off, and we can place Binna on it.'

Derek nodded in agreement. 'I just need to identify her and make a note of the injuries for my report. Is Ningali up to identifying her? Does she want to see her mother?' queried Derek.

'Don't know, really, don't know what their custom is in that regard. But let's get your job done, and I'll ask Zena when I get inside. Michael, you will obviously take note of the injuries as well. I'll leave you both to it.'

After clearing the work bench and placing Binna's body on the bench with Kev, Alan headed into the house, where Zena sat solemnly.

'It's under way. Binna is in that small room just opposite the saddles, my work area. Just doing what they need to do. Derek asked if Ningali would like to identify her mother or see her before she is buried,' he said softly, placing his arms around his wife.

'I am not sure, Alan. You know they don't speak their relative's name after they die as they believe it will disturb the dead person's spirit, but I will ask her.'

Zena made her way up the hallway and knocked softly on the door. 'Ningali,' whispered Zena as her friend slowly opened her good eye. 'We are going to bury Binna tomorrow. Alan thought it might be a good idea to bury her close to where Burnu is buried, seeing as they were great friends and healers. The crew and the lubras have been told, but I also wanted to check to see if you wanted to see your mother one last time.'

Tears rolled down Ningali's cheeks. 'Binna she be gone already. She travel to the ancestors, be with da spirits. Speak no more of her name.'

'Okay, rest now, but Binna will be buried tomorrow. I'll let you know when.' She closed the door gently behind her.

'I will make the identification, Alan. I'll go across now,' said Zena.

'I'm coming with you.' He followed his wife down the stairs.

When she got to the Tack Room, she gave a rueful smile, 'Hi gentlemen, what a tough day. It's almost too sad to speak of.' Zena sat down amongst the saddles, the horror of the situation having exhausted her.

'I'm done here now, Zena. I've scraped the tissue from under her fingernails, which will be sent away. How about you, Michael?' asked Derek.

'Yep, all good. Tragic ending to a respected elder. Can you step forward, Zena please,' asked Michael. 'Do we have a last name?'

'No, they have only ever had the one name, and Binna was never quite sure how old she was either,' said Zena sadly.

Michael pulled the cover back. 'Do you confirm the identity of the deceased as an Aboriginal lady called Binna.'

'Yes, I can confirm this is the deceased.' Zena's voice cracked at the sight of her beloved friend. Michael placed the tarp back over her face.

'If you could also sign here too please, Zena,' said Michael, as he watched her shaking hand scrawl her name.

'What's next?' asked Alan. He watched the police officer fold the documentation away into his briefcase. 'I will make a report for the coroner. It's standard if someone dies from an accident or injury or the death was violent and unnatural. When do you think you'll ride to the river, Alan? I really should be there too,' added Michael.

'Day after tomorrow. The burial will take place tomorrow in the morning and then we have our usual wrap up party, end of season, but it will be very sombre this year, that's for sure. Jack, my manager, will clean up down at the sheds, and I'll head down to the river with the dogs on Thursday, maybe about nine if that suits you.'

'Very good, Alan,' said Michael. 'I will see you Thursday here at the front gates. My condolences to both of you and Lisa.'

Alan and Zena wrapped the tarpaulin tightly around Binna's body. 'Sleep well, old girl, we will miss you,' Alan said as he took off his hat.

Kev sat patiently on the small wooden stool on the landing of the Tack Room.

'I bin waiting to see if Ningali is orright,' said Kev.

'She is resting now, Kev. The doctor has given her a painkilling injection and sleeping medication, so Ningali is sleepy. Can it wait until tomorrow as I don't want to disturb her? Rest is most important,' said Zena.

Kev didn't reply and Zena sensed his sorrow. 'Come on then, just for a short moment, Kev.'

He followed Zena up the back stairs of the homestead and down the hallway to where Ningali was resting. He took off his hat and waited silently as Zena slowly opened the bedroom door.

Kev's eyes widened in shock at the damage to Ningali's face. 'Come in, Kev. Her eyes are fluttering, so she is not fully asleep as yet.'

'Ningali,' Zena said softly. 'I have someone who wants to see if you are okay.'

She opened her eye slightly and whispered, 'I see you, Kev, you proper good.'

The big black man felt his chest heave as he came to her side and gently took her hand. He knew some of his brothers were prone to violence, and women were frequently beaten, but he had no time for violence, especially brutality towards women or children.

'I see you tomorrow, Ningali. You rest now.' He kissed her cheek, put his hat back on and left, seething with rage.

Alan waited outside. 'You take the motorbike, Kev, it's just inside the compound gates. Keys are in it. Mate, just another thing, can you come up early tomorrow morning, say about 5.30 a.m. and help me take Binna's body down for the burial.'

'Sure, boss, see you tomorrow,' said Kev.

'Come on, let's sit on the verandah.' Alan locked the Tack Room door. 'I could do with a beer. Where's Lisa?' he asked as they started to walk towards the house.

'Probably with Ningali. I asked her to keep watch on her if I'm not around,' replied Zena.

'I can hear hooves Alan, and they are moving very fast.' Zena stopped and craned her head towards the gate. 'It's Billy. He's just arrived at the gates. No doubt worried about Lisa.'

Billy walked towards them, removing his hat. 'I have come to see if Lisa is orright.' The worry in his voice was evident.

Lisa had heard the hooves and then his voice. 'Billy!' she sobbed as she ran down the stairs, flinging herself into his arms, her head resting on his chest.

'Grasshopper,' he whispered as he stroked her hair.

'We'll leave you two to it. Come in when you're ready, Lisa,' said Zena, her voice close to exhaustion.

◊

Lisa looked up into Billy's beautiful brown eyes and sobbed gently. 'It's orright, Lisa. Billy here now.' He bent to kiss her lips softly.

'Come.' He took her hand. 'Jed is outside. Bareback today, Grasshopper.'

'Where are we going, Billy?'

'Nowhere really, just to get out and ride across da land. Always feel good.'

Billy opened the compound gates and loosened the bridle he had looped through the cyclone wire. He threw his leg over Jed and held out his arm for Lisa as she swung up. She shifted up against his back and her arms encircled his waist, resting her head on his shoulder. He made her feel better already. Jed danced and was eager to get going.

'Hang on.' Billy turned the big horse's head for the open road, which led to the far back paddocks. He cantered along, feeling the stallion beneath him and Lisa's arms tightly around him as the brilliant colours of the sunset covered the plains. They rode until they hit the boundary fence, turned, and then followed the fencing, the bore parallel to them. It was almost ethereal, the colours, the animals and the wind that raced through their hair as Jed carried them back to the homestead. Lisa soaked up the peaceful ambience, which was in stark contrast to all that she had witnessed today.

◊

Zena nodded in Lisa and Billy's direction as she sat with Alan on the verandah. 'Yes, I can see,' murmured Alan. 'He's obviously ridden up to that last paddock where the snake got Burnu. Going along the boundary fence line. Still got to get that bloody old ram out of there. Just can't bring myself to go into that paddock.'

'Don't blame yourself, Alan. It was just a tragedy. The snakes are everywhere and you know that.'

They sat and watched the two figures in the distance heading towards them. 'I know how they feel. I always feel better when I ride. It's something so simple but something that makes you feel free; it clears the head. I love that phrase: "And into the saddle I go". But this really has been one of our worst days, Alan.'

He nodded. 'I hope we catch that murdering bastard Jimmy tomorrow. I am sure he will still be down at the river, and then we can close the lid on all this shit.'

'Yes, I agree. We need to put this past year of awfulness behind us all. Especially Lisa. She has been through so much. But Billy is good for her, and I am so glad he's here. There is no doubt they have a deep spiritual connection, and he watches out for her. I'll ask him to stay for dinner. I know that will make Lisa happy. Just the four of us, and of course, one bed-ridden lady. Not too sure Ningali likes being cooped up in a house, but for now it will have to be that way while she mends,' said Zena.

'They are people of the bush and the land, and you are probably right. I would say she feels hemmed in. Anyway, the meds make her that dozy, such that I doubt she'd care right now where she is resting. She'll be right in a few days, start to come good. She's just lucky she is not dead. I am sure Jimmy meant to kill the pair of them. No witnesses then,' added Alan.

'I can't believe the damage he has caused, and what he has done. To murder people,' Zena said, aghast. 'But then revenge is a strange thing, Alan, it can consume you.'

'Yeah, that may be, but he is about to find out he cannot do whatever he wants to do. Bear is onto his scent. I will get him. Anyway, no more talk of this; let's try to keep it lighter. Today has been brutal. I'll go see Lisa and Billy at the gate.'

Alan got up and waited for them to get back. He stood staring down towards the river road. *Not long now, Jimmy. We are coming for you.*

◊

Billy saw Alan waiting and squeezed Lisa's hand. 'It's okay, Billy, please don't worry. He is probably just meeting us.'

'Just had a wonderful ride with Billy,' said Lisa as they pulled up at the gate. 'It's so lovely this time of day.' Lisa slipped off the horse. 'I feel a lot better.'

'So I can see. Billy, why don't you put Jed in the home yards and come in for dinner. Chicken casserole with rice. Pretty good tucker.'

Billy smiled. 'Okay, boss. Do I need to wash up?'

'Nope, come as you are, we want to talk to you about something.'

Lisa's face beamed as Billy led Jed to the yards. 'Come on, son, we want to get an early night. It's been an exhausting and emotional day. I just want to run something by you. Please help your aunt in the kitchen, kid.'

'Sure, Alan.' As Lisa raced up the back steps, her aunt walked in, bringing an empty tray back from Ningali's room.

'How is she, Aunty?' Lisa asked as she set the table.

'Doing well considering she has just lost her mother and was almost bashed to death. Only had a few mouthfuls, but at least I got something into her. Just take this glass of water into her and leave it on the bedside table. She is resting now. The sedative Derek gave her is making her sleepy. Fractured ribs are very painful but fortunately they mend. Are Billy and Alan talking about what we have suggested?'

'Yes, I believe so, they are out on the verandah,' said Lisa. She had seen them wander in there after securing Jed.

'Then let's get dinner ready so we can serve when they appear. We all need an early night.'

◊

When Billy sat down on the verandah, he had no idea what Alan would ask. He feared he would be questioned about his feelings for Lisa and their time together in her bedroom.

'Billy, I have come to respect you as a worker, and with age and experience, you will only get better. Jack may not always be around, and you know Woori well. Zena and I have discussed this matter, and we wanted to ask you if you'd like to stay on as my permanent station hand, and if Jack should ever leave, to become overseer.'

Billy's eyes widened, and Alan saw the surprise in his face. 'You don't have to answer now, son, I know your people like to move on, but if you want to stay, and I know Lisa would wish that, and, well, us too, we would all love to have you here.'

'Don't need to think, boss. Billy love to stay.'

Alan slapped Billy on the back. 'You just made me very happy, Billy. I could do with a hand. I'm not getting any younger either. Let's go tell the girls. This is the only good news we have had today.'

Zena turned as they walked into the kitchen together. 'Well, give me some good news, Alan.'

'The boy said yes. Welcome to Woori, Billy.'

Lisa squealed. 'Hooray. Oh Billy, I am so glad!' Her eyes filled with tears as she flung her arms around him.

'It's been an emotional day, Billy, for everyone,' said Zena, wiping her eyes.

'Grasshopper.' Billy gazed down into her eyes as he lifted her chin.

'I just had this feeling with Burnu gone, you would go too,' said Lisa, almost crying with relief.

'No,' he said softly. 'Never again. Not without you.'

'Let's sit. It's going to be a big day tomorrow with sadness and farewells, and of course, the job ahead of us the following day,' said Alan. He wanted to say something about Binna at the table, but knew better. It was important not to disturb her sleep with the spirits.

'Before I sit, I'll just check on Ningali and see if she needs anything. Please start, I won't be long.'

Zena ducked into Ningali's room, and she opened her eyes. 'Just dozin, boss lady,' she said sleepily.

'We're just having dinner, but I will pop back in after it and help you to the bathroom. Rest now.'

As Zena came back into the kitchen, the chatter was on a happier note. Despite the grief of the day, Alan tried to keep the mood light and talked about Billy's role and the broodmare program he and Zena had planned.

'Sleeping?' asked Alan as Zena sat down.

'Dozing more like it. The meds Derek gave her are doing their work. I will be so glad to see the end of this day. It's like a bad dream; it is so many things, and all of them horrible.'

'I know,' said Alan as he took her hand and kissed it. 'But we will get through it.'

Zena turned to Billy. 'Thank you for saying yes, it will really help things around here,' she smiled wearily.

'Boss lady . . . really lookin forward to it . . . Billy love Woori.' He beamed at her.

Alan interjected, 'And by the way, we do know there is a lot of affection between you two, so don't duck and weave. It's as clear as the nose on Lisa's face.'

Billy looked at Lisa. 'Yes, boss, Billy like Lisa, but always respectful.'

Alan looked pleased at this. He really did like the boy. There was never any pretence at trying to be someone he was not.

'We will say goodnight, Billy, and thank you for being here to support our girl. Lisa, please show Billy out and then lock the back door. Don't forget the electric fencing will come on shortly, so Billy needs to be out of the compound,' advised Alan.

'Will do.' Lisa followed Billy to the landing at the top of the stairs. She met his lips softly and wanted to bury herself in his warmth.

'Goodnight, Grasshopper, I see you tomorrow. I go see Kev now. He pretty upset about Ningali.'

'Oh gosh, I didn't even think. Could you please tell Kev we are bringing Ningali down for the burial tomorrow. I'll see you then, Billy.'

He gathered Lisa in his arms 'One more,' he murmured as he brushed her lips lightly with his own. Billy tipped his hat and disappeared into the night, the only sound now was of Jed's hooves on the road.

FORTY

SINISTER INTENTIONS

Alan had been up early with Kev to bring Binna's body down to the burial site. The sun had not yet woken and the stillness of the morning was almost befitting the return of her body to the earth. *Spiritual*, Alan thought as they loaded her tiny body into the back of the ute.

'Thanks, mate,' said Alan. 'Sad times, but we will be down later with Ningali. I'll take the motorbike now. Any problems, just let me know.'

Kev made no comment; it was almost as if he did not wish to disturb the spirits. He just tipped his hat and drove away.

By the time Alan and Zena arrived with Ningali and Lisa to the sheds, the crew and the lubras were waiting.

Billy and Jack had dug a hole about five metres away from Burnu. There was a big earth mound at the head of the grave. Rocks, sticks and artefacts were placed into the mound as well as strips of bark and branches of the eucalypt tree surrounding the grave site. Alan opened up the campfire chair and helped Ningali ease into it as Lisa and Zena flanked either side of her.

The black women had painted ochre on their arms and face, and as they held bunches of eucalypt, their clapsticks began in rhythm to the haunting sound of Billy's digeridoo. They began to chant in perfect unison, and the women who were dancing waved the branches high and then met the ground with them, the red dust swirling around their feet. Fires burned around them, the smell of burning eucalypt wafting into the air, the Spirits of the Land making their presence felt. They sang loudly, their dancing and foot stomping meaningful as they looked to the sky and then to the earth until one of the women made a guttural sound and with a flick of her arm, the dance finished.

Alan helped Ningali to her feet. She slowly walked towards the grave site and then stopped. Binna's body lay wrapped in the tarpaulin, which had been covered in eucalypt and painted with ochre.

Kev took off his hat, and the other men followed. *She da sorry sight* he thought to himself when he looked at Ningali. *She bin hurt bad. Me get you, Jimmy. Me and the Remington. We don't miss.*

Billy played the digeridoo and stopped when Ningali spoke in her own language. Her hand gestures were telling a story, no doubt about Binna, and the women began to wail. Ningali finished and then nodded, a silent command for Binna's body to go into the ground.

Billy and Kev stepped forward with Jack and Alan, and they tenderly lifted the old lady's body. Zena and Lisa supported Ningali as they watched Binna's body being lowered into the ground. The lubras threw the red dust over Binna, and more branches and bark followed into the grave.

'Goodbye, my beautiful friend. Thank you for all that you did for me and Lisa,' Zena said softly, barely able to say the words for the choking sobs that wracked her body. Lisa was too grief-stricken to speak, and Billy watched her under lowered eyes, wanting to go to her. He could feel her pain.

Alan had the final word. 'I speak for my wife and family and for those who have known this wonderful elder. Binna was a great healer, storyteller and spiritual leader, and one who would always lend her ear to anyone, black or white. She never discriminated because of skin colour and believed everything had a soul, from the plants to the rocks and animals, and that the land belonged to all things. Her spirit returns to the Dreamtime.'

'Thank you, everyone,' said Jack, 'Please be here at around two as Cookie will have the usual food prepared for our end-of-season send-off. I know this is a very sad time, but we pay our respects to the deceased, and we also thank everyone for a good season.'

Alan came over to Zena, and they helped Ningali back into the Land Rover. 'Are you coming, Lisa?' Zena called out. 'I'll need your help shortly.'

'Yes, Aunty, I will come up. I just wanted to sit and talk with Billy. I won't be long.'

Zena waved to her niece, and they headed to the homestead. Ningali did not speak on the short trip but when Alan looked in the rear vision mirror, he saw the tears coursing down her face.

'Here, let me help you, Ningali. You need to rest now,' said Zena.

They both helped her up the back stairs and then into the bedroom. 'I'll leave you to it,' said Alan as he went to his office.

Zena sat on the side of the bed, lost for words and feeling the heaviness of grief. 'Lovely service, Ningali. Binna would have loved it.'

Ningali nodded but uttered no words. She was almost catatonic. Perhaps she was processing everything in her mind. 'I'll let you rest now but I'll come in to see if you need anything, my friend. I'll just be outside, doing a few things for the end-of-season send-off.'

Ningali nodded and lay back on the pillows. It was almost as if her spirit had died.

Zena felt so helpless, but her anger over the murder of her friend Binna only served to make her seek revenge for the person who did this. She wanted to get the day over, if only so that the dogs could track Jimmy down tomorrow.

'Get busy, Zena,' she said to herself. 'There's work to be done.' She left Ningali to rest and headed to the kitchen.

'Hey,' said Lisa, coming through the back door. Her voice sounded so fragile. 'I just feel so sad, so devastated, Aunty. How can we ever replace Binna? Why do people have to kill or hurt others? It destroys lives, their actions . . . what they do.'

'People are all different but everyone feels the sadness and the loss, darling girl. Burnu and then Binna, two very respected elders . . . they can never be replaced. But we are lucky they were a part of our lives. And they always will be. You will find over time that you'll revisit their memory, so they will live on in your heart. Keep busy, Lisa. I find that helps, so let's get on with getting this food prep for Cookie. I want this day over. Tomorrow is the day we hopefully get our revenge and find Jimmy. He must pay for what he has done.'

They worked together for a good two hours until Zena looked at the clock. 'It's 1.30 p.m., Lisa. Time to get this food down there. Help me carry it to the Land Rover, will you. The lean-to is set up, just have to give all this to Cookie.'

'Alan,' Zena sang out. 'We're ready.'

He followed the girls down the stairs. 'Dougy, old boy.' Alan leaned down to pat his head.

'He's always so happy,' said Lisa. 'Can he come down with us?'

'Yeah, kid, why not. Up you get, Dougy.' The dog leaped into the back seat of the Land Rover. They took off towards the sheds and as they got closer, the sounds of Ned's harmonica could be heard.

Zena smiled. 'Ned and his harmonica . . . Oh look, there's Kev with his guitar. What a pair, and it seems to lighten the mood.'

'Yeah, he's not too bad,' said Alan.

Cookie came out of his kitchen. 'Aaah, my helpers! Thank you, lovely ladies, just plonk it down in the usual place. Got steak and sausages. No beast killed, so this will have to do.'

'Yes, Cookie, tragic events stopped the usual procedures,' commented Alan.

'This will be fine,' said Zena as she carried the food to the table.

The piccaninnies chased each other, and the lubras giggled and laughed. It would be almost the usual party had it not been for Binna's death.

Cookie rang his bell. 'Got an earlier start than usual, but it's been a long day, so dig in and make the most of it. Lisa and Zena will dish out the grub, so don't be shy in stepping up.'

Alan piped up, 'Thanks, Cookie. And everyone, thanks for a great season. As usual, you have all worked bloody hard. Good to have you here, Kev, hope you will be back, and that goes for the lot of you. Jack, thank you once again for keeping these buggers in line. Billy, great work. We now pay our respects to our two elders who travel to the Dreamtime to meet their ancestors.'

Ned started his harmonica, and Kev picked up the guitar again. A few of the lubras started with their clapping sticks. The noise was festive and bright, a contrast to the sombre mood this morning.

'Oh bugger, Lisa,' said Zena, looking for the plastic box that contained all the salad servers. 'I've left the box with the servers up at the house on the dresser in the kitchen. Cookie also wanted more matches. Can you race up and get it for me? Oh, can you also check quickly on Ningali, please?'

'Sure, Aunty.' Lisa walked to the Land Rover, Dougy following her. 'No, you stay here,' she said as he madly wagged his tail at the driver's door.

◊

Jimmy had sat quietly in the distance, watching them load things into the Land Rover. He snorted. *End of season, dey all be down at da sheds.* He had made his way up along the boundary fence, crouching low at any sign of movement. The peppercorn trees, pig shed and the dog kennels were good for coverage as he moved swiftly, jumping over the narrowest part of the bore and moving to the side of the house and in through the compound gate. Jimmy looked up as he saw the Land Rover in the distance heading towards the homestead. He crouched down around the side of the house out of view. *Who come back?*

Jimmy smiled. She was on her own. He quickly moved across to the Tack Room and opened the door, grabbing a bridle and some hay rope, which he threw on the floor. He then hid, listening to the sounds of her feet. The back door opened and slammed. *I get her first.* He looked up at the back door, ready to make his move.

◊

Lisa grabbed the plastic box and put it on the kitchen table as well as the box of Redhead matches for Cookie. The dogs were barking madly. 'It's just me, guys, settle down,' she called out.

'Now, I will just see my friend.' As she walked up the corridor, she could hear Ningali snoring. Lisa chuckled. Snoring and the dogs. *It's a wonder you can sleep, Ningali, with them barking like that.* She opened the door softly, but Ningali opened her eyes slightly.

'Da little one,' her voice said groggily.

'Yep, just me Ningali, with orders to check on you.' Lisa smiled.

'I bin orright, me just resting.'

'Well, I will leave you to it. Aunty will be back here shortly.' She closed the door gently.

Lisa froze when she came out to the kitchen. A tall, bedraggled figure, with a beastly appearance and a craggy black face stood staring at her with one eye. 'Jimmy.' Lisa's voice was barely a rasp, her heart was battering her chest. He smiled, his eyes alight with crazed desire as he studied her.

'What do you want?' Lisa started to back away slowly, her panic rising.

Jimmy regarded her with a sneer, and his very closeness terrified her. Lisa turned to run but tripped over the leg of the kitchen chair, knocking it over and landing on the floor. He was upon her swiftly as she screamed and tried to kick out at him.

'Get away from me, Jimmy. Get out of here,' she screamed as she felt his hands on her. 'Nooo,' she wailed, and her fists flailed at his face. He laughed in a frightening way as Lisa struggled against him.

'Jimmy gonna fuck you . . . you white trash. You likem blackfella, but I'm gunna take ma time in da bush. You come with me.'

◊

Ningali opened her eyes, the screams from Lisa piercing the silence. Through her drug haze, she heard the name Jimmy, then Lisa screaming, the sound of things smashing and then silence. He had brought his fists down heavily on Lisa's face, knocking her out.

Da little one in big trouble, dat bastard, he here! Ningali moved gingerly as she swung her legs over the bed, the pain hitting her in waves as she made her way to the bedroom door.

◊

Jimmy heard the shuffling feet and froze. *Who was here?* As Ningali came around the corner, he sneered.

'You black bitch, you still alive. Me gunna finish you off.' He rushed at Ningali and knocked her over, the pain from her ribs searing through her body as she collapsed in the hallway.

He grabbed the matches and the newspaper and went to the big room with the curtains, quickly rolling up balls of newspaper and lighting them under the curtains. He stood up and laughed. 'Jimmy burn Woori, destroy your life like you destroy mine. Fire – it clean and destroy everythin.'

Jimmy looked at Ningali curled up on the hallway floor and booted her in the ribs as he passed her. 'Black bitch.'

Lisa was unconscious. He picked her up and threw her over his shoulder, the blood oozing from her forehead. When Jimmy got to the bottom of the stairs, he ran to the Tack Room, grabbing the bridle and rope. She did not move as he tied her hands, and he smiled. *She out cold. Me gonna taste your flesh, real soon.* He took off to the home yards where he saw the coloured horse, slipping the bridle over its head.

Lisa began to stir and felt the restraint on her wrists as she sat up. She tasted the blood trickling into her mouth and screamed. 'Shut the fuck up, bitch.' Jimmy raced back to the Tack Room and slapped her mouth hard. He grabbed her and threw her over Topi, and then swung up on the horse, booting him hard in his ribs to move. Jimmy headed out of the gates and took off for the river.

◊

The fire in the sitting room leaped into life, the curtains igniting quickly, and the flames then tore through the room, spreading quickly. It was Ned who stopped playing and pointed. The smoke was curling into the air.

'Alan, fuck . . . look, that's fire, up there,' yelled Ned, pointing in the direction of the homestead.

They all turned and stared in disbelief.

'Oh, God no, Alan, it's Woori,' screamed Zena. 'Lisa . . . Ningali!' Hysteria and panic flooded into her voice.

'Come on, everybody. Anyone who can lend a hand, follow me,' cried out Alan.

Kev ran for the ute, and the crew followed, all piling in, along with Jack and Billy. 'I'll take the bike,' bellowed Alan. 'Get on, Zena.'

They all roared off in the direction of the homestead, which was well alight by the time they reached the compound gates. The Land Rover was parked at the compound gates with no sign of Lisa.

'Billy, grab the horses in the home yards and let them all out. I have had them there only to fatten them and watch their condition during the first trimester. Let them out now to run free and let the dogs off, all of them!'

Zena and the crew grabbed the hoses near the side of the house and began to spray water onto the homestead. Alan raced up the back stairs and could see the fire had started down the hallway from the large sitting room and was making its way towards him. He heard groaning and turned swiftly to his left where the hallway led to the bedrooms.

'Ningali!' he gasped as he quickly picked her up, the smoke choking their lungs. 'Where is Lisa?' Alan asked, his eyes wide with fear as he carried her down the stairs.

Zena screamed when she saw Ningali. 'Where's Lisa! Alan!' Her voice was hysterical as the thought of Lisa's unknown whereabouts exploded in her mind.

'This is useless now,' Alan thundered. 'The hoses aren't helping. We can't save the house, just get out all of you and get to safety, back to the sheds. I just hope to God the embers and flames don't reach the Tack Room.'

Once through the gates, Alan lay Ningali gently down. Zena and Kev squatted on the ground next to her.

'Ningali, please, please, can you tell me what has happened. Where's Lisa?' cried Zena.

'Dat Jimmy, he in da house, he takem Lisa, and she scream-in. Me try to help but can't do nuffin to help da baby girl.' She broke down, crying. 'He has da devil in his soul.'

'Oh, no. Alan.' Zena began sobbing, grief coming over her in waves at the sheer terror her niece must have felt. Billy came running back.

'Topi is gone,' said Billy. 'Where's Lisa?' he cried as he looked down at Ningali.

'It's Jimmy, he's taken her and is no doubt riding out on Topi. Ningali said he was in the house. Kev, can you pick up the tracks and see which way he is heading?' beseeched Alan.

'You bastard, Jimmy!' Billy roared as he looked to the skies, his eyes searching for the unseen. The anger and terror bubbled inside him at the thought of Jimmy anywhere near his love. He followed Kev, and they both looked at the hoof marks that led to the river.

Kev pointed to the ground. 'Dis ones, dis hooves, dey just new, boss,' said Kev. 'Dey fresh, heavier to da ground, so mean two fellas on da one horse.'

'Go and get your gun, Kev. Jack, what have you got down there in the way of a gun?' The panic was rising in Alan's voice.

'My 303, Alan. It'll blow his head clean off,' replied Jack.

'Get your guns, and be bloody fast, and get any crew that are left. We cannot lose any time.' He came to Zena's side. 'Go with them and take Ningali. She'll be okay down in the men's quarters. I'm sure there is a bunk she can lay on till we get back. Stay safe.'

He put a comforting arm around Zena and kissed her gently. 'We will get Lisa back. It will be alright,' soothed Alan, although he knew what Jimmy would do to her. He winced and felt the anger flare in him as they got Ningali to her feet.

Zena held Ningali, sorrow and rage choking her every thought. She would now completely rely on these men to return Lisa to her.

Jack turned as he was leaving. 'We'll get her back, Zena. Come on, Kev, we need to be moving. Cookie, look after the girls will you please, mate.'

'Sure, boss. I'll boil the billy.' He looked to the sky. *Please, nothing had better happen to that girl.*

◊

Alan was relieved as he saw the old ute speeding towards them, the crew huddled in the back. *It's a wonder the bloody thing can move with all those blokes in it.* As the ute pulled alongside them, Alan called out to Billy.

'Billy, head straight to the river. You blokes in the back, keep an eye out in all directions. You are looking for a coloured horse, brown and white swirls. Kev and Jack, you come with me.' They sped off, racing towards the river, the dogs, heads down, streaming behind. Alan had kept Bear separate in the Land Rover, knowing the dog would pick up the scent quickly when they got to the river.

'How much time do you think he has in front of us, Kev?' asked Alan.

'He bin on da road mebbe twenty minutes. He be ridin hard, dat bloke. We catch him, boss.'

'So, with the time for us to get going, he probably had thirty to forty minutes head start. That means we should be on top of him in just under the hour,' Alan said grimly.

Billy had to stay back further than he wanted as the dust was making the visibility hard. Alan hurtled at breakneck speed towards the river, and the old ute was groaning under the speed and the weight of the men.

When they finally reached the trail down to the river, Alan slammed on the brakes. 'Kev, get out and tell me what you can see.' Billy pulled up a few moments later, his eyes desperately searching for Lisa.

'Lookem boss, da tracks, on foot, dey go dis way, he headin up da river.'

'Where is the horse . . . why is he now on foot?' Alan spun around. 'Bastard! Come on.' They clambered down to the river track and followed the foot indentations. Bear was onto the scent and was well ahead of the men. The other dogs had caught up, and their barks were heard in the distance but moving towards them.

Billy was scrambling for any sign that would lead him to the man he wanted to kill and was distancing himself from the group.

Alan yelled out. 'Billy, stay with us. Kev has the gun. Come on, settle, we will find her, and I don't want you in any trouble now. Keep your cool, son.' Alan moved swiftly, following Kev and Jack with the rest of the crew.

◊

Jimmy could hear the dogs as he wrestled the struggling Lisa. She was slowing him down and when crossing the river, she had almost drowned the pair of them, kicking and struggling. 'Bloody dogs, dey coming, but by da time dey get here, you gonna taste some of Jimmy.'

Lisa started to scream, but his hand slapped her hard, stunning her momentarily. He threw her to the ground and drew her hands above her head with one hand, tearing at her shirt. She struggled violently as he bit into her breasts, her screams of pain punctuating the air. 'You gunna like this,' he yelled as he tugged at her jeans with his free hand, his madness and lust driving him on.

◇

'Did you hear that . . . that scream, it's Lisa,' bellowed Alan. 'Kev, this way, they are not too bloody far, probably just round that bend. Move!'

The men scampered along the bank and as they rounded the bend, they saw Jimmy and Lisa on the other side of the river. Jimmy was forcing himself on top of Lisa, while she struggled violently. His jeans were around his knees, and he was clearly attempting to rape her.

'Jimmy!' Alan yelled. 'Stop, you black bastard, let her go! Fire a warning shot, Kev, for Christ sake!'

At the sound of the shot, Jimmy turned and glared at the group who crowded the other side of the bank. He had chosen a section where the river was widest and deepest. His crossing this part of the river had taken time due to Lisa's struggling, which had given the group a chance to catch up. But it would also take longer to cross due to its width.

Jimmy started laughing. 'You boys, you gunna watch now.'

Billy glared at him, wanting to put his hands around Jimmy's throat and squeeze the life out of him. Lisa was whimpering, her half-naked body exposed, and the gut-wrenching pain he felt made him unable to process any other thought but to kill Jimmy.

'He not gunna stop, boss,' said Kev.

Jimmy turned his back on them, again forcing himself as the girl struggled, but her strength was fading. His lust was so strong he was oblivious to their yelling.

'I go, boss! I'm gunna kill Jimmy!' Billy started to make his way to the river to swim across. The dogs were now milling around on the bank. Alan wanted to send Bear across, but it was too dangerous with Kev about to shoot.

'Billy!' roared Alan. 'Stay put.' He could see the look on Billy's face. He felt as helpless as the rest of them.

'Kev, take the shot. Take the bloody shot, do it now!' Alan yelled.

'Lotta moving, boss. Don't wanna hit dat Lisa,' said Kev.

Jack grimaced. He knew how dangerous the shot would be with too much movement.

'Take the bloody shot, Kev, for Christ's sake. We can't wait, not one more bloody minute!' Alan felt the tension in his body as he ordered the command. *Please, let our girl be safe. Do it right, Kev.*

The black man raised his steady arm and had Jimmy well in his sights, but it was going to be a difficult shot. The girl was really struggling. If he hit the man's leg or any other body part that did not take him out, he knew he would be like a wounded beast. Dangerous. Very dangerous to Lisa. He thought of Ningali and Binna. *Dis for you.* Kev steadied his arm as never before and took aim at Jimmy's head as it bobbed up and down in the struggle, and fired. Jimmy's body seized and then fell limp, the full weight of his body crushing Lisa. The birds screeched and scattered and apart from the dogs moving, a silence fell across the river.

There was no movement. Alan stared intently, the fear rising in his body. He felt the tension in his jaw. *Please, dear God, please let her be alright.* Billy was already swimming across to her,

Bear and some of the dogs joining him as he rushed across to pull Jimmy off her. Lisa lay motionless.

As Billy reached her, only a whimpering sound could be heard as he grabbed Jimmy's lifeless body and rolled him over. He turned quickly to Alan and gave him the thumbs up.

'Thank Christ,' Alan groaned.

The bullet had entered the back of Jimmy's skull and exited through his forehead. He lay dead on the ground, part of his skull exposed, the blood seeping out from the bullet wound, his mouth ajar, the flies already swarming.

'Oh Lisa, my Lisa.' Billy kneeled on the ground, cradling his sobbing girl. 'Orright now.' He held her tightly, kissing her forehead softly, speaking in his native tongue.

'Leave them for a moment,' Alan instructed. 'The boy is good for her.'

'Think the bastard is dead, Kev, he sure ain't stirring. Bloody good shot, mate. He won't be hurting anyone anymore,' said Jack.

Billy helped Lisa get her jeans back on and then took off his shirt for her, covering her breasts. Her face was already showing the bruising where Jimmy had slapped her hard. He looked across at Jimmy, his murderous thoughts still present.

'My grasshopper, come, we go now.' His arm went around Lisa. 'We go dis way, Alan,' called out Billy. 'Da river will narrow and den we cross, near da track where we first stopped.'

Billy helped Lisa to her feet, and she was shivering, no doubt a combination of the sheer terror and wet clothing. He held her close to him, and Lisa closed her eyes as her head rested on his bare chest. 'Safe now,' he whispered as he guided her towards the track. Before they came out into the open, Billy momentarily stopped and put his arms gently around her.

'I keep you safe, always.' His hand glided through her tangled hair, picking out pieces of sticks. He knew how close he had come to losing her, either from Jimmy or the shot that Kev had placed into Jimmy's head. He never wanted to let go of her again.

Lisa finally spoke. 'I was so frightened, Billy, and . . . I so thought this was the face of death, that I would die out here and never see you or anyone again.' He bent and kissed her lips lightly. 'You here now and safe . . . safe with Billy' He spoke softly in his native tongue, soothing her. A gentle wind blew, and she looked up above her, surrounded by tall lemon-scented gums, and she saw the eagle. 'Spirit bird,' she whispered.

'Maybe Burnu. His spirit come back in da most powerful bird,' smiled Billy. By the time they reached the track, her body ached with fatigue and the soreness of the assault. The river bed at this end was narrow and only knee deep. Billy picked Lisa up and carried her to the Land Rover.

'Kev, take the ute with Jack, we'll head back now,' said Alan. He turned to look at the beautiful young girl whose life, once again, had nearly been shattered, and her look of soul-deep sorrow touched him. He came towards her. 'It's okay, Lisa, we got you.' He hugged her fiercely and felt her body shake with every breath.

Lisa was numb with shock, the anger and disbelief colliding within her. Her lips trembled as they tried to form words. Billy's arm around her pulled her even closer. 'Thank you . . . thank you, everyone,' her voice shaking as she lowered her head to Billy's chest and closed her eyes.

◊

Zena looked anxiously at her watch and hoped they had found Lisa by now. She sat in the men's shearing quarters with Ningali and held her hand, trying to comfort her. Cookie remained vigilant, watching for any movement towards the sheds. He suddenly jumped to his feet shouting. 'Look, Zena, look it's her horse, the coloured one!' He raced outside.

'Oh my God, Cookie, it is,' said Zena as she watched Topi galloping towards them. She quickly joined Cookie and moved her arms up in a stop motion to steady the horse. He seemed to be soothed by her voice, a voice he knew, and slowly his gait slowed down, trotting towards Zena, who quickly gathered the reins.

'Lather of sweat, old boy. I so wish you could talk. I'll just take him around the back of the sheds, Cookie, and give him a hose down. I'll be back, just keep a watch on the road for anything.'

◊

By the time the charred remains of Woori came into view, Dave and Kate Walker, as well as Mitch, were standing at the compound gates. Michael Raby was also there and pointed to the Land Rover, a cloud of dust filling the air as it approached where they stood.

Alan pulled up next to the police vehicle.

Kate was crying at the carnage, and Dave had his arm around her. 'What's happened, Alan?' cried Dave. 'We saw the smoke from our place, and Kate called but there was no answer, so she called Michael Raby at the police station, and he filled us in on what has been going on. We raced over here, thinking you would all be here but it was like a deserted ship.'

'Yeah, Dave, thanks so much, too much bloody trouble. We have all been down at the river, but Zena and a few others are up at the shearing shed. Think the trouble will stop now,' said Alan.

Mitch looked at Lisa sitting in the back seat with Billy, and he knew the trouble involved her. She looked distraught, and her face had clearly been punched, the bruising becoming darker. He wanted to say something but the words would not form. Lisa was still sitting next to her boong lover, but her vulnerability still managed to hook him.

'Jack, can you head back down there and make sure everything is okay. The crew and lubras will be packing up to move on. Need some organisation down there.'

'On my way, mate,' said Jack as he took off with the rest of the crew.

'Can we do anything, Alan?' asked Kate.

'Not really, Kate. Thanks for the offer, but we will all have to shack up down at the shearing shed for now. Won't do us any harm, it's comfortable, has showers, toilets, even a bloody kitchen with a chef. We'll be fine but it's going to be a task to sort through the mess.'

'Okay, but I'll come back tomorrow with a few things, Alan. The women have no clothing, so I'll see what I have and bring it across with me,' offered Kate.

'Thanks, Kate, appreciate that . . . never thought of that. Typical bloke, I guess.'

Alan stood and looked at the once-magnificent house that now smouldered. The fire had also burned the Tack Room to the ground, and he was grateful for the foresight to get the mares out of the yards and let them run free.

'Heavens,' said Kate as she turned around upon hearing the dogs.

'I let them all off, so they are just catching up,' said Alan as they came bounding towards him.

'We'll be off then,' said Dave. 'Come on, Mitch.'

Alan noted the boy stood quietly in the background and never said a word, but he was aware Mitch's eyes never left Lisa. When he saw her in the back of the Land Rover with Billy, Alan thought his facial expression echoed his inner thoughts. Resentment, anguish bordering on hate. But Alan had more than enough to deal with at the moment without worrying about that right now.

'Alan, if you're ready, I'll take a statement,' interrupted Michael Raby.

He wrote quickly as Alan spoke, shaking his head at the horrific statement he provided. At the end of it, he folded the documentation and placed it in the brief case, which sat on the front seat of the police car.

'There's no doubt in my mind, Alan, that Lisa is lucky to be alive. Jimmy was intent on doing harm, and you acted quickly, which was fortunate. The outcome had you not would have been gruesome. My guess . . . . probably rape and then murder. He seemed to have lost all control.'

Alan nodded. 'As per my statement, we yelled for him to let her go, and fired a warning shot, but to no avail.'

'Lucky you had Kev. That was a very dangerous shot to take,' said Michael.

Alan nodded. He knew the risk he had taken. The bullet could have easily hit Lisa and would have killed her outright.

'Jimmy made a mess of her face, Alan. She must have struggled so hard,' added Michael.

'Yeah, the kid put up a good fight, but at least she is in one piece.'

'Can I take Kev back down there, Alan? I need to collect Jimmy's body and take a few photos. Pigs and foxes will no doubt be alerted by the scent, so I want to collect the body before that. I can fold the back seats down in my car.'

'Sure, mate. You okay with that, Kev, giving Michael a hand?'

'Yes, boss. Me orright to help.'

Alan let out a big sigh, the tension of the day's events unfolding, but he knew there was a long road ahead in terms of rebuilding. Sadness filled his heart as he thought of the memories attached to the homestead. It had become a part of them. He watched Kev head out with Michael and then got into the Land Rover.'

'Okay back there, Billy?'

'Yes, boss,' he said softly, not wanting to disturb Lisa.

'Let's head to the sheds then. Zena will be pacing.'

Cookie sat outside on a wooden stool, facing the direction of the homestead. He had waved to Jack as he drove the ute up to where he was sitting, the crew quickly dispersing.

'Alan will fill you in, Cookie, got work to do here now. Good ending . . . for some.' The big bloke strode away.

'Here he is, Zena,' Cookie called out. She suddenly appeared at the doorway and ran towards the approaching Land Rover.

Alan stopped and then opened the door of the vehicle, Zena almost falling into his arms.

'Thank you.' She broke down, sobbing like a child until finally she calmed. 'My girl,' she whispered she looked inside the Land Rover. 'Safe, Billy?' she asked softly.

'Safe, missus. She bin sleeping.'

Zena looked up at Alan. 'The house?'

'Gone,' he admitted sadly. 'And the Tack Room . . . but the main thing, my darling wife, is you and Lisa are okay. We are all safe. But as you can see, the kid is battered and bruised,' Alan said worriedly.

Zena nodded and turned to Alan. 'I just hope this trauma will not bring the awful memories of the past flooding back, with everything coming again to the surface. I may need to call Helen Tyler, but for now, let's just be happy in that we are all here. We will face things as they come.'

Lisa opened her eyes and the sight of her aunt made her burst into tears. Zena extended her arms. 'Come, darling girl, let me hold you.'

Billy helped her out of the Land Rover, and they wept openly, holding onto each other. Zena pulled back and had her hands on both sides of Lisa's face as she examined the bruises. 'They will heal, Lisa. Let's walk this way. There's a lady who is wanting to see you.' Zena put an arm around her as they walked to the men's sleeping quarters.

Ningali cried out when she saw Lisa at the doorway. 'Da baby girl.' Lisa came and sat with her, the emotion flooding through them both.

'Cookie, please boil that billy. I think we could all use a good strong cuppa,' said Zena as she left Lisa and Ningali to find solace in each other's company.

She called out to the men. 'Ready whenever anyone can join us here at the table. Cookie has managed to rustle up a few items left from the season. Not much,' she said. 'Just a few cakes.'

They all sat at the small kitchen table the men had used for eating during the season. Although in discomfort, Ningali joined them as they watched the movement outside through the windows. The crew and their lubras were packing up and ready to move on.

'They have places to go, Alan. They have to get on the road,' said Jack.

Alan nodded. 'I hope they are back next year . . . what a mess this has been for them. Michael Raby has taken a statement and will no doubt come back to us. Plenty of witnesses, nearly the whole crew,' said Alan.

Lisa's face was quite swollen as she sat with Billy, her hands resting gently in his.

'I think you need to rest, Lisa . . . and you too, my friend,' said Zena, glancing at Ningali.

Alan got to his feet and came over to Lisa. 'How you doing, kid?'

Her eyes filled with tears. 'Thank you, Alan, thank you,' she whispered. He bent down to kiss her bruised face.

'I . . . I don't know where Topi is. Jimmy tried to drag him across the river, make him swim, but he reared and took off.'

'We have a surprise for you then,' Alan winked. 'That horse of yours headed home; he is out back . . . waiting for you to go see him.'

Lisa smiled and shook her head, the tears spilling down her face.

'Rest now, Billy will keep you safe,' reassured Alan.

He looked over at Ningali. 'You heard what the boss lady said . . . let me give you a hand, Ningali, you need to do the same.' Alan lifted her to her feet, helping her to a small bed. She lay down silently, but a smile crept across her face. *He da good person.*

Billy walked with Lisa to a small room at the end of the hallway in the men's sleeping quarters and covered her with a light sheet. 'I be right here, Lisa.'

Jack spoke quietly. 'Cookie and I will be the last to leave, Alan. We'll stay on a bit to help you, but I don't think Kev wants to go. Quite taken with Ningali.'

'Yeah, I've noticed that, Jack. Give it a couple of days to let things settle, if that's possible. What a bloody season. Got enough grub to last a few days and then I'll take Zena into town to shop for food and a few other things. I'll have to make some calls, insurance, bank accounts etcetera, but it's a relief to know . . . well, to know that Jimmy is not hanging around. Kate from the property next door will also bring a few things, so we will sort it.'

'Cookie and I will make a fire for tonight. Be good to feel the peace and sit under the stars,' said Jack.

'Good idea, mate. I'll leave it to you. I'll go and get the dog leads and kennels and bring them all back down here. Can't have them wandering around at night. When Kev comes back, you may help him catch those three pregnant mares and Noir. Bring them down to the yards here. I'll have to get some bridles and saddles in town as well, seeing as the Tack Room burned down. I'll stay up there until Michael gets back with Kev.'

Jack felt Alan's pain. He knew he was putting on a brave front, but the task ahead of him was enormous. He had lost everything.

As the evening fell, Jack started the fire and had placed a few bales of hay around it.

Kev had returned and caught the mares with Jack. All of the horses now had yards not far from the main shearing shed. Alan had chained the dogs around the perimeter of the sheds apart from Dougy, and Cookie busied himself preparing a meal. It would almost be normal except it wasn't.

'Let's go sit outside for a while, look at the moon and the stars, my darling wife. Kev, can you help Ningali up. There's a fold-up chair for her,' said Alan.

'Come, Grasshopper, we look at da Milky Way and da Southern Cross. Time to let da light in.' Lisa followed Billy, and he wrapped a blanket around her shoulders, sitting next to her.

'Food is ready, boss,' called out Cookie. 'Sausages and a bit of salad.'

'My appetite seems to have gone,' commented Alan. 'And as I look around, it looks like I'm not the only one. Anyway, let's not waste it. Cookie, you have done a fine job. Kev, when you've finished are you able to pick a tune for us sitting out here, mate?'

'Sure, boss. Me singem da good song, makem plenty good tunes.'

Alan had found some painkillers in the glove box of the Land Rover, which Zena gave to Ningali and Lisa.

Lisa remembered when Alan had first told her about the building of the shearing shed and the men's quarters. He had said everyone laughed for giving them individual rooms and a separate shower block to attract the best workers. It was certainly paying off now. They had their privacy in their own rooms.

Lisa shuddered at the thought of sleeping open-dormitory style. A haunting memory, so she squeezed her eyes shut.

As Kev started to play, there was some tranquillity in the air, but Lisa's hand stayed firmly in Billy's. He pointed out the stars to her and whispered stories only she could hear.

The night ended better than the day had started, but the despair and terror from the experience still lingered in everyone.

'I think it's time to hit the sack. We will have a better handle on things tomorrow,' said Alan.

'Goodnight, everyone,' said Zena, 'Thank you for all your help today.' She walked to one of the rooms.

'Going to stay here a bit with Cookie, mate, have a quiet beer,' said Jack.

'We go too, boss,' said Billy as he helped Lisa to her feet. Kev followed suit and helped Ningali.

'Just you two left, Jack. I be seeing you in da morning,' smiled Billy.

When they got to Lisa's room, Billy did not want to leave her, and he kissed her gently. 'I be right here, Lisa.'

'Where?' Lisa asked.

Billy pointed to the floor. 'Sleep now, I right next to my grasshopper. You see the light come in da door in da morning.' He pushed a small rock to keep the door ajar. The softness of his voice and his mere presence were the only things she wanted at that moment. Her eyes felt heavy as sleep took over, but sleep would be restless that night as Jimmy's face made many appearances.

The only sound was the crackling of the fire as the exhausting day closed in on them.

FORTY-ONE

FROM THE ASHES

The following morning, when Lisa looked in the mirror in her room, she gasped. Her left eye had closed, and the bruising was now a purplish black. Billy was gone but she heard her aunt's voice outside. She threw on her clothes and came outside, shielding her eyes from the bright sun, but a smile spread across her face. Billy stood with Topi.

'Oh, Billy, thank you.' She moved towards the young horse. 'There you are, my lovely boy,' her voice a soothing tone. 'I thought you had taken off,' she said as Topi nuzzled into her.

'Day or two, kid, you may like to ride with Billy,' said Alan.

'That would be great, but we don't have any gear, no bridles or saddles.'

'Zena and I will head into town tomorrow and pick up some new tack. We want to go up and see the house and do a few things here first. Jack will be on his way today.'

The big man came around the corner with Kev as his name was mentioned.

'Morning all,' his voice boomed. 'How is our girl this morning?'

'Yes, better, Jack . . . thank you, a bit sore.'

'All done up there, Alan, no need for anything else. Basically, all wrapped up now. Lucky we got all the wool out before the shit hit the fan.'

'Yeah, thanks, mate.' Alan rose to shake his hand.

'I've been up early, so I'm packed to go.' Jack walked towards Zena and gave her a huge hug. 'Take care, Zena. I'll be back next season. And to you, little lady, stay safe and well. Billy will be here to look after you.'

Lisa smiled. Woori was so lucky to have Jack as a manager, and she had grown to like him as much as Alan. He strode towards Cookie. 'See you, old son. You must have brushed up on your cooking. I could actually eat it this year.'

Cookie laughed and turned to Zena. 'I have left things in the fridge, and the big pantry has all the dry foods. You just need to do your own stocktake.' He kissed Zena on the cheek.

'I'll be off then. Take care everybody.' Cookie and Jack walked towards their vehicles.

Kev had joined Ningali, who sat silently watching everyone say their farewells.

'They all have places to go to, jobs awaiting, Alan,' said Zena, sadness filling her voice. She wondered if she would see them all next year.

'Kev . . . what are you up to, mate?' asked Alan.

'Me want to take Ningali wif me. Be on da road together, treat her real good. Proper true. You don't worry.'

Zena looked horrified. 'What, take Ningali?'

'Yep, me ask Ningali.' He smiled, confident she would say yes.

'What are your thoughts, my friend? asked Zena, directing her gaze towards Ningali. 'You haven't said much.' A slow smile spread across Ningali's face as she met Zena's eyes. Ningali loved this woman she had befriended long ago, but knew her life had changed. She wanted to roam. She was free.

'Me like to go with Kev. He da good fella.' The happiness was evident as Ningali spoke.

Zena felt her eyes brimming with tears. 'Ningali, we only want what makes you happy. I am sure Kev will look after you, but if that situation changes, you know where we are. You come back.'

Kev helped Ningali to her feet, and the two women stood looking at each other, silently communicating their friendship, their stories and how their lives had interacted on this land. 'Goodbye, my friend.' Zena held her closely.

Tears were running down Lisa's face as she hugged her friend goodbye. She was sad to see her go but happy for her at the same time. She knew in her heart that they would see each other again.

They all watched as Kev helped Ningali to the yellow ute he drove. Ningali started to giggle and turned to the watching eyes. 'Me lookem good in da flash yellow car.'

The childlike humour of Ningali broke the tension, and one by one, they all started to laugh.

Alan's arm came around Zena. 'She will be fine, darling wife. He's a good bloke.'

'I know, Alan, but I will miss her so much. I miss her already.' Her voice trembled.

'They have to do what they need to do. I'm sure they will both be back next year.'

'I hope so, Alan. I hope you are right. Who knows what next year will bring.' Her voice was heavy with sadness and loss. The thought of rebuilding was daunting. How could they ever replace Woori?

They waved as they watched Kev's yellow ute move through the last gate. Lisa was bereft as Billy tried to console her, and she thought of her aunt's words. *Everything changes, nothing ever stays the same.*

'I don't think I can face looking at the burned remains of our home, Alan,' said Zena sadly.

'I'll be there with you, Zena. We have to look at it sometime and let the insurance company know what is left, or for that matter, what is not left.'

'When did you want to go? asked Zena.

'Let's clean up here first. You can make a list of what we need in town tomorrow. Maybe we all go in, have some lunch somewhere and just enjoy some time out. There is certainly no great rush. The season is finished and no there's no housework, my love.'

'You always find humour, Alan, always a positive. But it all sounds okay to me,' said Zena as she wandered over to Lisa and Billy, who sat together comfortably, their eyes not leaving each other.

'Hello, over here . . . we're heading up to the house, to see what is left of it. Alan has made the suggestion of going into town tomorrow and getting what we need. Do you want to come, Lisa?'

'Yes, Aunty, it will do us good, I think,' replied Lisa.

'Yes, not much we can do here now. And we have to get clothes for us, so Mrs Dunphy will be pleased when I start ordering.'

'Let me help you with these dishes,' said Lisa as she started to clear plates from the table.

'Righto, Billy, the girls are okay here so let's duck over to the shearing sheds, do a quick stocktake and see what we need down here. Have to check the feed situation for the sheep, pigs and horses. Got to keep moving and organised, and hopefully, the horribleness of this situation begins to leave our heads. It's good to have you here.'

'Thanks, boss. It good to be here,' said Billy.

Alan made notes, and it was just after midday when they returned to the camp. Zena was sitting with Lisa when they reappeared. 'Might as well head up there,' said Alan. 'Everyone ready?'

'Yes, Alan, let's get it over with,' sighed Zena as they got into the Land Rover. As they drove towards the house, it was still smouldering. It was an ugly site, and the pain of loss seared through all of them. They picked their way through the remains, turning over things, but nothing was salvageable.

'Gone, all fucking gone,' groaned Alan.

Zena looked up as she saw a car in the distance. 'It's Kate.'

'Yeah, she said she would be up today, bringing a few things,' commented Alan.

The four stood silently as Kate pulled up in front of them. Her face was puzzled at the sight of Billy standing next to Lisa. *Odd. That young black fellow should have been on his way by now.*

There were three large boxes in the back of Dave's ute.

'Hello, Zena.' The two women hugged. 'Words cannot express how I feel for you,' Kate said solemnly.

'It's alright, Kate. We are kind of over the shock but thank you,' said Zena.

'I have a few things for you. One is food, dry and fresh, so you will need to refrigerate. Another box is women's clothing. You and I are about the same size, except for the top half.' A strained smile flickered across Kate's face. 'And the other box is men's clothing. So help yourself.'

'Billy, can you just grab those boxes out of the back for me?' asked Zena.

Kate's eyes followed the young boy, and she stared at him stonily. The penny dropped. This was who Mitch continually referred to as Lisa's boong lover.

'Kate, you are adorable. I am very grateful. We are actually on our way into town tomorrow. Going to pay Mrs Dunphy a visit.' Zena noticed at the mention of that name, Kate's face dropped.

'Dare I ask how are things going?'

'Up and down, Zena. Mitch . . . Well, I don't think he's coping, and he takes it out on Tess. They quarrel constantly. What they say to each other would turn the air blue, and I just know there is going to be heartbreak surrounding their marriage. I know where his heart lies. Dave and I just close our ears as it's very distressing, but not our business. I guess we all have our problems to sort, don't we?'

'Yes, Kate, some problems though are a lot bigger.' Zena looked at the crumbled, smoky mess in front of her.

Kate hugged her friend. 'Well, I'll be off then. If you need anything, please come over. It's hard not being able to just call you. But think of the pleasure you will have rebuilding.'

'Yes.' Zena nodded as they waved goodbye. *It is bloody hard, Kate, gut-wrenchingly hard . . . and pleasure rebuilding . . . not so sure. My strength seems to have deserted me.*

Alan's arm came around Zena. It was clear that seeing the remains of their house had caused her much grief.

They stood looking at the blackened ruins that once was their home. 'We will rebuild my darling. Bigger and better. The new Woori.'

A hollowness crept into her bones as Zena purveyed what was once their home.

'Rebuild, Alan?' Zena hesitated. 'I'm not sure I have the strength to start all over again.' Her voice quavered and her eyes grew moist.

'Why do you say that . . . what do you mean?' Alan knew the events of the past few months, particularly the loss of Binna, had made her despondent, but he was shocked at her response. A difference of opinion or conflict was rare between them. 'You are not being rational, Zena.' His voice was edged with surprise.

'Just everything, Alan. I guess everything has just worn me down, like the ocean that keeps battering the rocks, or the sand, with time, you just erode . . . fade into nothingness. I'm not sure I have the strength to get up. I need time.'

Zena dodged his eyes as Alan was clearly reeling from her words.

'Are you telling me you will leave Woori?' he stuttered.

Lisa spun around on hearing those words. 'Aunty, who is leaving? What is everyone talking about?'

Zena met Lisa's eyes and quietly spoke. 'It hasn't been the easiest time of late, and I feel as if my world has been smashed. Please . . . I am too weary to answer any more questions. I know I'm tired, maybe that's just it.'

'We can rebuild, Aunty . . . another Woori. You of all people are now not making any sense.'

Lisa began to panic and felt her world caving in. She could not understand her aunt's thinking.

Zena tried again. 'I have loved this place and I love my husband, but to rebuild? I have been a rock to everyone, but now I am just tired.'

'But you have Woori, Aunty, it is in your heart. You have Alan, you love each other.' Lisa was pleading.

Zena looked sadly at her young niece. 'Do I have Woori? Look at my Woori now.' Her voice sounded faint and far away.

Alan sighed. He didn't know what to do. Despair ripped through him.

He looked at Billy and Lisa, who understood what Zena had just said. Alan turned his wife's face towards him and kissed her lips gently. 'I know it will be hard, darling Zena, but just look at your support team. You have always been brave, my love, and you are stronger now, after all the crap that has happened. You and Lisa . . . both stronger. I know you do not feel that now, but deep down, you are.'

Zena shook her head and gazed across the vast plains. A faint smile crossed her lips as she took Alan's hand. In that moment, the love she felt for the land and for the man who stood before her was restored. Despite the utter destruction, everything was bathed in radiance. She called to her heart and her soul; like boats against a current, we must try, so the disaster of this horrible past will be no more.

My beloved Woori, you will rise again from the ashes, stronger and more beautiful than ever before.

EPILOGUE

Three years later

The new homestead stood proudly under a blazing sun. The insurance money had come through quickly, and the rebuild of Woori took just on two years. There were now three dwellings on the property, all carefully designed with much thought. The big house, Woori, was majestic and had the same big open windows to capture views from every room. The Tack Room was further away from the house with a self-contained one-bedroom cottage attached, and the last home was called Woo-ribilly, a beautiful three-bedroom stone cottage that sat neatly amongst the peppercorn trees. Alan said the fencers were the luckiest blokes as the compound surrounding the three buildings was massive.

Alan had moved quickly, and a team of builders had lived down in the shearing sheds until completion. They brought a lot of fun and laughter to what might have been an abysmal situation, especially as the two passing summers were very hot. The tradesmen kept Lisa and Zena busy cooking, and they had asked Cookie to come and help. Looking after the team of men

LINDA DOWLING

who beavered away, sun up until sun down seven days a week, was challenging, and there were always changing shifts where different men would arrive.

Dave Walker also sent some of his crew across to give a hand and would always sit and have a yarn with Alan. He was now a grandfather, and although he loved his grandchild, baby Tom, he had very little time for Tess. Nevertheless, he was always respectful to the girl who had produced his first grandson.

Mitch would often stay away for days, camping out with the Woodside crew. Dave said he would find any excuse not to come home. Often when he had a few too many beers at home, he would talk about Lisa, and the arguments with Tess that bellowed from the bedroom caused Kate much sorrow.

The year 1974 proved to be very special. Lisa and Zena were advised by Detective Collette that due to continual campaigns and the newly formed Women's Liberation Movement, reforms were being made to the welfare system. In 1973, ABC TV and the program *This Day Tonight* exposed the brutality of the Parramatta and Hay Institutions. He said that many protests occurred outside the Parramatta Girls Home in December that year, and after continual exposure of the horrors and abuse, it had closed in July 1974. It was pure joy and relief to hear that news, and a quiet drink was had by the fire at Woori.

When the builders, carpenters and plumbers finally left, it was early October 1974. They all bade Cookie a teary farewell and hoped to see him next year for the season.

Tomorrow would be a big day. Zena had already purchased anything and everything she could find in Sydney, and the six containers on the property were full of furniture, art and antiques. When not cooking for the tradesmen, she beavered away in the garden with Lisa and Billy, planting trees, eucalyptus of every type, her rose garden, and of course, the peppercorn trees for shade. It pleased Alan to no end to watch his wife rejuvenate, her soul restored.

Finally, it was just the four of them. A new chapter, a new beginning.

Billy had become like a son. He worked hard, and his love for Lisa and the land was evident. Alan pondered that when everything was lost and you enter a darkness, sometimes a new life emerges.

◊

Billy had lit a big fire and they sat under the open sky, the Milky Way spreading out before them.

Alan spoke. 'Feels good to have the place back to ourselves. You girls will have fun with the containers tomorrow,' he smiled.

'So looking forward to it, Alan,' said Zena excitedly. 'I just can't wait. Kate is coming tomorrow with Dave and their crew to assist, so it will be all hands on deck. Be good to catch up with her.'

'I can't wait either,' said Lisa enthusiastically. 'All those boxes.' Billy held her hand tightly. He knew their news would be a surprise.

'I think the design of the house is better in that we have separate wings, don't you think?' Alan asked.

'Yes, my darling husband, the architects have been very thoughtful with the plans. It looks amazing, and I do love the fact the Tack Room and horse yards are further away from the main house. But just wait until the furnishings and paintings are in. I cannot wait to see the finished product. As Lisa said, so many boxes to unpack!' laughed Zena, her face beaming.

'Shall I open up some bubbly for you girls and a couple of beers for me and Billy.'

'Sounds splendid. I have to tell you, Alan, I won't be sorry to leave these sheds,' jested Zena. 'I am so over single beds.'

'It has been tough on you girls,' winked Alan. They all laughed, but then suddenly Billy spoke. He was awkward initially but he quickly gathered himself, gazing at Lisa and then across to the people who had become his family.

'Me not dat good talking emotional stuff. But . . . I thank you for taking Billy into your home. I love Lisa and wanna be with her . . . for always. I always treat her proper good. Respectful . . . always.'

Lisa leaned into Billy and placed her head on his shoulder.

Alan quickly realised the seriousness of the moment as he moved to hold Zena's hand.

'Billy, we would also like to thank you. You have been amazing and wonderfully supportive of our family during this terrible time,' said Zena.

'Thank you, missus. But I . . . I love Lisa. I wanna make her mine.'

'Billy, we adore you and we understand your feelings for Lisa. We accept that . . . we actually accepted that a long time ago,' said Zena softly.

'Where do we go from here?' asked Alan.

Lisa spoke tentatively, 'Aunty, I would never want to hurt you . . . or Alan, and I have loved just being here and rebuilding, especially with Billy by my side. You know I never want to leave Woori, and Billy feels the same.'

'Yes, darling girl, I know that,' replied Zena. She knew there was more coming.

'I love Billy,' she repeated as she looked at the beautiful boy next to her. 'I am expecting his child.'

Zena's mouth dropped open. 'Oh, my darling girl, that is wonderful news,' cried Zena, leaping to her feet. Lisa stood up and felt the warm, enveloping arms of her aunt. Tears fell down her cheeks.

'Well, Billy . . . you are really my son-in-law now, I guess!' Alan slapped his back.

'Do you both know for sure?' asked Zena.

'Yes, Aunty. I have now missed two periods,' answered Lisa shyly.

'Goodness, you both kept that a secret then, but I . . . we are so happy,' gushed Zena.

'Over the bloody moon,' added Alan. 'The cottage Wooribilly was an afterthought, thinking it was just extra accommodation, but I guess we can give you the keys to the door.'

Love and hope filled the air. Their road would be tough but with love and support, they would manage. They would all manage.

◇

It was the 8th December 1974 when the wedding took place. Zena had arranged everything, and the house was filled with large bunches of bush flowers, the smell of eucalypt filling the air. Des and Mark had arrived two days prior and had busied themselves with the preparations.

Barbara, the florist from Dubbo, drove out to Woori with vases of white roses, gardenias and Cala lilies, which she placed around the home. Zena had ordered many flowers from her over the years, and the two had become good friends. Barbara would also perform the wedding ceremony, being a Justice of the Peace, and meet the guests as they arrived.

Alan, Des and Mark had erected a small bridal archway a few days prior, and Barbara had wrapped bunches of green foliage and an assortment of white flowers around the poles as well as white satin ribbon. Bales of hay were scattered around for the small number of guests and the caterers, and Julie, the photographer arrived just after Barbara. It was an elegant but very simple affair.

Lisa's gown was an A-line white chiffon dress with a white lace neckline and long lace sleeves. She wore the same diamond-drop earrings Zena had worn when she married Alan. Her bouquet was cream roses, stephanotis and white hydrangea with a touch of eucalyptus leaves. Her hair hung loosely, the sides pinned back and held with a simple gardenia.

Zena stepped back and felt the tears welling. She could remember the haunted face of the skinny young girl, her arms bruised and the dark circles under her eyes. 'My darling girl, we have come a long way. You are a vision.'

Lisa's lips trembled. 'Oh no, no no, my fault . . . no tears now.' Zena hugged her niece. 'I wonder how those two men are going down there in the cottage?' Zena looked at her watch. 'I will let the photographer know you are ready and just have a look at the table setting in the formal dining room. Gosh, I never thought when we designed that room your wedding would be the first formal occasion. What a christening for that room, just so very special.'

Lisa smiled as she watched her aunt leave. She looked in the large mirror across the room, her hands resting on her belly. She could still see the look on Billy's face when they had the first ultrasound, showing not one baby but two. 'My beautiful babies, rest well. I am marrying the man I love today, and how lucky am I that you will be present.'

◊

Zena looked around the dining room and let out a sigh. 'Barbara, you have done this so beautifully, thank you.' She watched her friend light the large white scented candles that scattered the table.

A small van approached the house. 'Oh, that would be the string musical trio. Nothing like a bit of background music. The guests won't be long, Barbara, so I'll leave it to you now.

Just show the musicians where to set up outside. Unfortunately, they will have to pack up there when the ceremony is finished and then set up again inside. Just too many flies to eat out there.' Barbara laughed. 'Never a truer word spoken, Zena.'

'I'll go and join the photographer. I have to find Lisa's father. See you in a bit.' Zena gave her an air kiss and rushed off in search of Des.

◊

'Well, Billy, old boy, we best make our way down to the altar,' said Alan. 'You look good. My Zena always knows what to pick.' Billy flashed a huge grin. He wore a simple white linen shirt with beautifully tailored navy pants. 'Best day of my life, boss.'

'Alan . . . not boss, Billy . . . not anymore.'

When they got to the small shady area under the trees, Alan nodded in satisfaction. Barbara had done a beautiful job. He could hear Zena's words, simple but elegant.

Billy stood nervously near the altar as Alan moved about the guests. Billy waved as one by one they wandered in.

Des, in a navy suit, sat with Mark. He had felt so proud to stand next to his beautiful daughter and have their photos taken. The lump in his throat would just not leave. Dave and Kate, Jack, Cookie and old Ned talked about next season. Ningali was as excited as a child, her face showing her emotions as she sat with Kev, who could not stop smiling. Michael Raby and Helen Tyler sat chatting with John the Publican.

The trio began playing 'The First Time Ever I Saw Your Face' as Des walked with Zena and Lisa, hooking her arm under his elbow. The three walked together towards Billy and stood under the little altar. When Lisa appeared, there was a small gasp from the guests. She looked radiant, almost ethereal. Ningali almost squealed, and Kev had to calm her. As Lisa came to Billy's side, he murmured the words 'My beautiful grasshopper.' He noticed that the little bush necklace he had made for her birthday many moons ago was wrapped around her small bouquet.

Zena joined Alan as she tearfully watched her brother give his only daughter away.

Barbara performed the ceremony beautifully. Her final words were 'They only knew they loved each other.'

The two caterers who stood in the background began to pour the champagne and handed the flutes around. It was Ningali who came to Lisa first, and they held each other tightly. It was a day for happiness and a day for tears.

'You look wonderful, my friend. Kev has been looking after you,' grinned Lisa.

'Yep, he orright, dat bloke, treat me proper good. Bin travelling around, we gets lotsa work. Happy now but I miss—' And then Ningali stopped. Lisa knew it was incorrect to mention their loved ones names when they had passed on.

'Me too, Ningali. I miss them both.'

'But little one, dey here,' said Ningali, her big brown eyes wide with happiness.

'Here? What do you mean?' asked Lisa, puzzled, her brow wrinkled in confusion.

'Dey spirits always about, always be with you. Live in da heart too. But your face, I know, it lookem . . . lookem different. Ningali know.'

Lisa smiled. Yes, her face was fuller. 'What do you know, Ningali?'

'Me know . . . you with da piccaninny.'

Billy came towards the pair. 'What you up to, Ningali?'

'Me tellem Lisa, I know dere's a piccaninny.'

Billy's eyes met Lisa's, a knowing and loving look as he took both her hands gently.

'Ningali, me lucky man of all da earth. Not one piccaninny but two.'

The surprised look on Ningali's face was priceless, and she let out a sound that shook the ground, clapping and singing something in her own tongue, taking the other guests by surprise.

The sun began to slowly set, and a magnificent orange filled the sky. As Lisa looked above her, a large eagle soared in the heavenly sky. 'Burnu . . . you are here.'

The darkness of yesterday faded with the evening light. Tomorrow and the future would bring new life and love to Woori, and that was all that was needed.

THE END

ACKNOWLEDGEMENTS

Thank you to Juliette Lachemeier (my wonderful editor) at The Erudite Pen, my brother Mark who supports me so unconditionally, Willo, (my gorgeous farmer), my Maianbar friends who are just so special, especially Shirley Anne, one of the bravest women I know. To my *Splintered Heart* readers who sent wonderful comments that truly inspired me. To Andrew Peat of Gunworld, Hillcrest, Queensland, who responded so quickly with his information on weaponry. To my Daintree Wildman who provided so much information without hesitation.

ABOUT THE AUTHOR

Linda Dowling grew up in the western suburbs of Sydney, Australia. During her childhood, she spent most of her time in rural areas and has continued to enjoy life in the bush or in areas with natural surrounds. Her aunt, a wonderful horsewoman, lived in Carinda, New South Wales and taught her a great deal about horses, riding and the outback. It was during her vacations with her aunt that Linda herself fell in love with the vast outback plains and the Aboriginal culture, their stories and their unique but simple way of living. Linda has a natural affinity with Indigenous peoples and was the only white girl selected to play for the Papua New Guinea softball teams at the Pan Pacific Masters.

In her professional life, Linda has established and managed four medico-legal firms, including her own. During the course of her career, she has been involved in reporting on coronial matters and inquests. She has also worked with the New South Wales Police State Crime Command Centre and in various Royal Commissions where she was exposed to the worst of human nature. Linda has drawn upon her professional and personal experiences while writing her Red Dust novel series, but the stories are a work of fiction and do not depict any person, living or dead. Her first novel in this series, *Splintered Heart*, was an award-winning finalist in the 2020 International Book Awards in the multicultural category.

Enjoyed the book? You can follow the author at:

Email: lsd777@bigpond.com

Facebook: facebook.com/authorreddustnovels

LinkedIn: linkedin.com/in/linda-dowling-10bb0635/

Praise for the award-winning *Splintered Heart* – Book one in the Red Dust Series

'Hooked! A book hard to keep down. Like the Aboriginal influence. Stories, healing, love and acceptance. Looking forward to the next book.' *Kindle review, Amshorty*

'Amazing author! Fabulous read! Congratulations.' *Dayle Ebsworth*

'Linda is an insightful and intelligent woman who has strong spiritual connections with our country and its people. Through her written words and also her art we are fortunate to be able to share her spirit and stories.' *Lynley Calnan*

'Fantastic read. Can't wait for the next book in the series.' *Kathleen*

'A compelling read. Prepare to laugh and cry This book will truly evoke a powerhouse of emotions. Steeped in culture perseverance and the unbreakable spirit of a young girl in 1960's Australia.' *Mary*

'I could not put my Kindle down. I read it while having breakfast, lunch & afternoon coffee time & then in bed at night...lol. Omgoodness...what Lisa went through. I cannot wait for the sequel Linda as you have left me with a story unfinished!! I need to know what is to follow! I hope you continue with your writing. Where on earth have you been hiding!! Love your work Linda.' *International Amazon Customer*